Nature-Inspired Optimization Algorithms

Nature-Inspired Optimization Algorithms

Xin-She Yang

School of Science and Technology
Middlesex University London, London

ELSEVIER

AMSTERDAM • BOSTON • HEIDELBERG • LONDON • NEW YORK OXFORD
PARIS • SAN DIEGO • SAN FRANCISCO • SINGAPORE • SYDNEY • TOKYO

Elsevier
32 Jamestown Road, London NW1 7BY
225 Wyman Street, Waltham, MA 02451, USA

First edition 2014

British Library Cataloguing-in-Publication Data
A catalogue record for this book is available from the British Library

Library of Congress Cataloging-in-Publication Data
A catalog record for this book is available from the Library of Congress

For information on all Elsevier publications
visit our Web site at store.elsevier.com

ISBN 978-0-12-810060-8

This book has been manufactured using Print On Demand technology. Each copy is produced to order and is limited to black ink. The online version of this book will show color figures where appropriate.

Contents

Preface

Nature-inspired optimization algorithms have become increasingly popular in recent years, and most of these metaheuristic algorithms, such as particle swarm optimization and firefly algorithms, are often based on swarm intelligence. Swarm-intelligence-based algorithms such as cuckoo search and firefly algorithms have been found to be very efficient.

The literature has expanded significantly in the last 10 years, intensifying the need to review and summarize these optimization algorithms. Therefore, this book strives to introduce the latest developments regarding all major nature-inspired algorithms, including ant and bee algorithms, bat algorithms, cuckoo search, firefly algorithms, flower algorithms, genetic algorithms, differential evolution, harmony search, simulated annealing, particle swarm optimization, and others. We also discuss hybrid methods, multiobjective optimization, and the ways of dealing with constraints.

Organization of the book's contents follows a logical order so that we can introduce these algorithms for optimization in a natural way. As a result, we do not follow the order of historical developments. We group algorithms and analyze them in terms of common criteria and similarities to help readers gain better insight into these algorithms.

This book's emphasis is on the introduction of basic algorithms, analysis of key components of these algorithms, and some key steps in implementation. However, we do not focus too much on the exact implementation using programming languages, though we do provide some demo codes in the Appendices.

The diversity and popularity of nature-inspired algorithms do not mean there is no problem that needs urgent attention. In fact, there are many important questions that remain open problems. For example, there are some significant gaps between theory and practice. On one hand, nature-inspired algorithms for optimization are very successful and can obtain optimal solutions in a reasonably practical time. On the other hand, mathematical analysis of key aspects of these algorithms, such as convergence, balance of solution accuracy and computational efforts, is lacking, as is the tuning and control of parameters.

Nature has evolved over billions of years, providing a rich source of inspiration. Researchers have drawn various inspirations to develop a diverse range of algorithms with different degrees of success. Such diversity and success do not mean that we should focus on developing more algorithms for the sake of algorithm developments, or even worse, for the sake of publication. We do not encourage readers to develop new algorithms such as grass, tree, tiger, penguin, snow, sky, ocean, or Hobbit algorithms.

These new algorithms may only provide distractions from the solution of really challenging and truly important problems in optimization. New algorithms may be developed only if they provide truly novel ideas and really efficient techniques to solve challenging problems that are not solved by existing algorithms and methods.

It is highly desirable that readers gain some insight into the nature of different nature-inspired algorithms and can thus take on the challenges to solve key problems that need to be solved. These challenges include the mathematical proof of convergence of some bio-inspired algorithms, the theoretical framework of parameter tuning and control; statistical measures of performance comparison; solution of large-scale, real-world applications; and real progress on tackling nondeterministic polynomial (NP)-hard problems. Solving these challenging problems is becoming more important than ever before.

It can be expected that highly efficient, truly intelligent, self-adaptive, and self-evolving algorithms may emerge in the not-so-distant future so that challenging problems of crucial importance (e.g., the traveling salesman problem and protein structure prediction) can be solved more efficiently.

Any insight gained or any efficient tools developed will no doubt have a huge impact on the ways that we solve tough problems in optimization, computational intelligence, and engineering design applications.

Xin-She Yang
London, 2013

1 Introduction to Algorithms

Optimization is paramount in many applications, such as engineering, business activities, and industrial designs. Obviously, the aims of optimization can be anything—to minimize the energy consumption and costs, to maximize the profit, output, performance, and efficiency. It is no exaggeration to say that optimization is needed everywhere, from engineering design to business planning and from Internet routing to holiday planning. Because resources, time, and money are always limited in real-world applications, we have to find solutions to optimally use these valuable resources under various constraints. Mathematical optimization or programming is the study of such planning and design problems using mathematical tools. Since most real-world applications are often highly nonlinear, they require sophisticated optimization tools to tackle. Nowadays, computer simulations become an indispensable tool for solving such optimization problems with various efficient search algorithms.

Behind any computer simulation and computational methods, there are always some algorithms at work. The basic components and the ways they interact determine how an algorithm works and the efficiency and performance of the algorithm.

This chapter introduces algorithms and analyzes the essence of the algorithm. Then we discuss the general formulation of an optimization problem and describe modern approaches in terms of swarm intelligence and bio-inspired computation. A brief history of nature-inspired algorithms is reviewed.

1.1 What is an Algorithm?

In essence, an *algorithm* is a step-by-step procedure of providing calculations or instructions. Many algorithms are iterative. The actual steps and procedures depend on the algorithm used and the context of interest. However, in this book, we mainly concern ourselves with the algorithms for optimization, and thus we place more emphasis on iterative procedures for constructing algorithms.

For example, a simple algorithm of finding the square root of any positive number $k > 0$ or x, can be written as

$$x_{t+1} = \frac{1}{2}\left(x_t + \frac{k}{x_t}\right), \tag{1.1}$$

starting from a guess solution $x_0 \neq 0$, say, $x_0 = 1$. Here, t is the iteration counter or index, also called the *pseudo-time* or *generation counter*.

Nature-Inspired Optimization Algorithms. http://dx.doi.org/10.1016/B978-0-12-416743-8.00001-4

This iterative equation comes from the rearrangement of $x^2 = k$ in the following form:

$$\frac{x}{2} = \frac{k}{2x}, \quad \Longrightarrow \quad x = \frac{1}{2}\left(x + \frac{k}{x}\right). \tag{1.2}$$

For example, for $k = 7$ with $x_0 = 1$, we have

$$x_1 = \frac{1}{2}\left(x_0 + \frac{7}{x_0}\right) = \frac{1}{2}\left(1 + \frac{7}{1}\right) = 4. \tag{1.3}$$

$$x_2 = \frac{1}{2}\left(x_1 + \frac{7}{x_1}\right) = 2.875, \quad x_3 \approx 2.654891304, \tag{1.4}$$

$$x_4 \approx 2.645767044, \quad x_5 \approx 2.6457513111. \tag{1.5}$$

We can see that x_5 after just five iterations (or generations) is very close to the true value of $\sqrt{7} = 2.64575131106459\ldots$, which shows that this iteration method is very efficient.

The reason that this iterative process works is that the series $x_1, x_2, \ldots, x_t$ converges to the true value $\sqrt{k}$ due to the fact that

$$\frac{x_{t+1}}{x_t} = \frac{1}{2}\left(1 + \frac{k}{x_t^2}\right) \to 1, \quad x_t \to \sqrt{k} \tag{1.6}$$

as $t \to \infty$. However, a good choice of the initial value x_0 will speed up the convergence. A wrong choice of x_0 could make the iteration fail; for example, we cannot use $x_0 = 0$ as the initial guess, and we cannot use $x_0 < 0$ either since $\sqrt{k} > 0$ (in this case, the iterations will approach another root: $\sqrt{k}$).

So a sensible choice should be an educated guess. At the initial step, if $x_0^2 < k$, x_0 is the lower bound and k/x_0 is upper bound. If $x_0^2 > k$, then x_0 is the upper bound and k/x_0 is the lower bound. For other iterations, the new bounds will be x_t and k/x_t. In fact, the value x_{t+1} is always between these two bounds x_t and k/x_t, and the new estimate x_{t+1} is thus the mean or average of the two bounds. This guarantees that the series converges to the true value of $\sqrt{k}$. This method is similar to the well-known bisection method.

It is worth pointing out that the final result, though converged beautifully here, may depend on the starting (initial) guess. This is a very common feature and disadvantage of deterministic procedures or algorithms. We will come back to this point many times in different contexts in this book.

Careful readers may have already wondered why $x^2 = k$ was converted to Eq. (1.1)? Why not write the iterative formula as simply the following:

$$x_t = \frac{k}{x_t}, \tag{1.7}$$

starting from $x_0 = 1$? With this and $k = 7$, we have

$$x_1 = \frac{7}{x_0} = 7, \quad x_2 = \frac{7}{x_1} = 1, \quad x_3 = 7, \quad x_4 = 1, \quad x_5 = 7, \quad \ldots, \tag{1.8}$$

which leads to an oscillating feature at two distinct stages, 1 and 7. You might wonder that it could be the problem of initial value x_0. In fact, for any initial value $x_0 \neq 0$, this formula will lead to the oscillations between two values: x_0 and k. This clearly demonstrates that the way to design a good iterative formula is very important.

From a mathematical point of view, an algorithm A tends to generate a new and better solution x_{t+1} to a given problem from the current solution x_t at iteration or time t. That is,

$$x_{t+1} = A(x_t), \tag{1.9}$$

where A is a mathematical function of x_t. In fact, A can be a set of mathematical equations in general. In some literature, especially those in numerical analysis, n is often used for the iteration index. In many textbooks, the upper index form $x^{(t+1)}$ or x^{t+1} is commonly used. Here, x^{t+1} does not mean x to the power of $t+1$. Such notations will become useful and no confusion will occur when used appropriately. We use such notations when appropriate in this book.

1.2 Newton's Method

Newton's method is a widely used classic method for finding the zeros of a nonlinear univariate function of $f(x)$ on the interval $[a, b]$. It was formulated by Newton in 1669, and later Raphson applied this idea to polynomials in 1690. This method is also referred to as the *Newton-Raphson method.*

At any given point x_t, we can approximate the function by a Taylor series for $\Delta x = x_{t+1} - x_t$ about x_t,

$$f(x_{t+1}) = f(x_t + \Delta x) \approx f(x_t) + f'(x_t)\Delta x, \tag{1.10}$$

which leads to

$$x_{t+1} - x_t = \Delta x \approx \frac{f(x_{t+1}) - f(x_t)}{f'(x_t)}, \tag{1.11}$$

or

$$x_{t+1} \approx x_t + \frac{f(x_{t+1}) - f(x_t)}{f'(x_t)}. \tag{1.12}$$

Since we try to find an approximation to $f(x) = 0$ with $f(x_{t+1})$, we can use the approximation $f(x_{t+1}) \approx 0$ in the preceding expression. Thus we have the standard Newton iterative formula

$$x_{t+1} = x_t - \frac{f(x_t)}{f'(x_t)}. \tag{1.13}$$

The iteration procedure starts from an initial guess x_0 and continues until a certain criterion is met.

A good initial guess will use fewer number of steps; however, if there is no obvious, good, initial starting point, any point on the interval $[a, b]$ can be used as the starting point. But if the initial value is too far away from the true zero, the iteration process may fail. So it is a good idea to limit the number of iterations.

Newton's method is very efficient and is thus widely used. For nonlinear equations, there are often multiple roots, and the choice of initial guess may affect the root into which the iterative procedure could converge. For some initial guess, the iteration simply does not work. This is better demonstrated by an example.

We know that the following nonlinear equation

$$x^x = e^x, \quad x \in [0, \infty),$$

has two roots $x_1^* = 0$ and $x_2^* = e = 2.718281828459$. Let us now try to solve it using Newton's method. First, we rewrite it as

$$f(x) = x^x - \exp(x) = 0.$$

If we start from $x_0 = 5$, we have $f'(x) = x^x(\ln x + 1) - e^x$, and

$$x_1 = 5 - \frac{5^5 - e^5}{5^5(\ln 5 + 1) - e^5} = 4.6282092.$$
$$x_2 = 5.2543539, \quad x_3 \approx 3.8841063, \ldots,$$
$$x_7 = 2.7819589, \ldots, \quad x_{10} = 2.7182818.$$

The solution x_{10} is very close to the true solution e. However, if we start from $x_0 = 10$ as the initial guess, it will take about 25 iterations to get $x_{25} \approx 2.7182819$. The convergence is very slow.

On the other hand, if we start from $x_0 = 1$ and the iterative formula

$$x_{t+1} = x_t - \frac{x_t^{x_t} - e^{x_t}}{x_t^{x_t}(\ln x_t + 1) - e^{x_t}}, \tag{1.14}$$

we get

$$x_1 = 1 - \frac{1^1 - e^1}{1^1(\ln 1 + 1) - e^1} = 0,$$

which is the exact solution for the other root $x^* = 0$, though the expression may become singular if we continue the iterations.

Furthermore, if we start from the initial guess $x_0 = 0$ or $x_0 < 0$, this formula does not work because of the singularity in logarithms. In fact, if we start from any value from 0.01 to 0.99, this will not work either; neither does the initial guess $x_0 = 2$. This highlights the importance of choosing the right initial starting point.

On the other hand, the Newton-Raphson method can be extended to find the maximum or minimum of $f(\boldsymbol{x})$, which is equivalent to finding the critical points or roots of $f'(\boldsymbol{x}) = 0$ in a d-dimensional space. That is,

$$\boldsymbol{x}^{t+1} = \boldsymbol{x}^t - \frac{f'(\boldsymbol{x}^t)}{f''(\boldsymbol{x}^t)} = A(\boldsymbol{x}^t). \tag{1.15}$$

Here $\boldsymbol{x} = (x_1, x_2, \ldots, x_d)^T$ is a vector of d variables, and the superscript T means the transpose to convert a row vector into a column vector. This current notation makes it easier to extend from univariate functions to multivariate functions since the form is identical and the only difference is to convert a scalar x into a vector $\boldsymbol{x}$ (in bold font now). It is worth pointing out that in some textbooks x can be interpreted as a vector form, too. However, to avoid any possible confusion, we will use $\boldsymbol{x}$ in bold font as our vector notation.

Obviously, the convergence rate may become very slow near the optimal point where $f'(\boldsymbol{x}) \to 0$. In general, this Newton-Raphson method has a quadratic convergence rate. Sometimes the true convergence rate may not be as quick as it should be; it may have nonquadratic convergence property.

A way to improve the convergence in this case is to modify the preceding formula slightly by introducing a parameter p so that

$$\boldsymbol{x}^{t+1} = \boldsymbol{x}^t - p\frac{f'(\boldsymbol{x}^t)}{f''(\boldsymbol{x}^t)}. \tag{1.16}$$

If the optimal solution, i.e., the fixed point of the iterations, is $\boldsymbol{x}_*$, then we can take p as

$$p = \frac{1}{1 - A'(\boldsymbol{x}_*)}. \tag{1.17}$$

The previous iterative equation can be written as

$$\boldsymbol{x}^{t+1} = A(\boldsymbol{x}^t, p). \tag{1.18}$$

It is worth pointing out that the optimal convergence of Newton-Raphson's method leads to an optimal parameter setting p, which depends on the iterative formula and the optimality $\boldsymbol{x}_*$ of the objective $f(\boldsymbol{x})$ to be optimized.

1.3 Optimization

Mathematically speaking, it is possible to write most optimization problems in the generic form

$$\underset{\boldsymbol{x}\in\Re^d}{\text{minimize}} \quad f_i(\boldsymbol{x}), \qquad (i = 1, 2, \ldots, M), \tag{1.19}$$

$$\text{subject to } h_j(\boldsymbol{x}) = 0, \quad (j = 1, 2, \ldots, J), \tag{1.20}$$

$$g_k(\boldsymbol{x}) \le 0, \quad (k = 1, 2, \ldots, K), \tag{1.21}$$

where $f_i(\boldsymbol{x})$, $h_j(\boldsymbol{x})$ and $g_k(\boldsymbol{x})$ are functions of the design vector

$$\boldsymbol{x} = (x_1, x_2, \ldots, x_d)^T. \tag{1.22}$$

Here the components x_i of $\boldsymbol{x}$ are called *design* or *decision variables*, and they can be real continuous, discrete, or a mix of these two.

The functions $f_i(\boldsymbol{x})$ where $i = 1, 2, \ldots, M$ are called the *objective functions* or simply *cost functions*, and in the case of $M = 1$, there is only a single objective. The space spanned by the decision variables is called the *design space* or *search space* $\Re^d$, whereas the space formed by the objective function values is called the *solution space* or *response space*. The equalities for h_j and inequalities for g_k are called *constraints*. It is worth pointing out that we can also write the inequalities in the other way, ≥ 0, and we can also formulate the objectives as a maximization problem.

In a rare but extreme case where there is no objective at all, there are only constraints. Such a problem is called a *feasibility problem* because any feasible solution is an optimal solution.

If we try to classify optimization problems according to the number of objectives, then there are two categories: single objective $M = 1$ and multiobjective $M > 1$. Multiobjective optimization is also referred to as *multicriteria* or even *multiattribute optimization* in the literature. In real-world problems, most optimization tasks are multiobjective. Though the algorithms we discuss in this book are equally applicable to multiobjective optimization with some modifications, we mainly place the emphasis on single-objective optimization problems.

Similarly, we can also classify optimization in terms of number of constraints $J + K$. If there is no constraint at all, $J = K = 0$, then it is called an *unconstrained optimization* problem. If $K = 0$ and $J \geq 1$, it is called an *equality-constrained* problem, whereas $J = 0$ and $K \geq 1$ become an *inequality-constrained* problem.

It is worth pointing out that in some formulations in the optimization literature, equalities are not explicitly included, and only inequalities are included. This is because an equality can be written as two inequalities. For example, $h(\boldsymbol{x}) = 0$ is equivalent to $h(\boldsymbol{x}) \leq 0$ and $h(\boldsymbol{x}) \geq 0$. However, equality constraints have special properties and require special care. One drawback is that the volume of satisfying an equality is essentially zero in the search space, thus it is very difficult to get sampling points that satisfy the equality exactly. Some tolerance or allowance is used in practice.

We can also use the actual function forms for classification. The objective functions can be either linear or nonlinear. If the constraints h_j and g_k are all linear, it becomes a linearly constrained problem. If both the constraints and the objective functions are all linear, it becomes a linear programming problem. Here "programming" has nothing to do with computing programming, it means planning and/or optimization. However, generally speaking, if all f_i, h_j, and g_k are nonlinear, we have to deal with a nonlinear optimization problem.

1.3.1 Gradient-Based Algorithms

Newton's method introduced earlier is for single-variable functions. Now let us extend it to multivariate functions.

For a continuously differentiable function $f(\boldsymbol{x})$ to be optimized, we have the Taylor expansion about a known point $\boldsymbol{x} = \boldsymbol{x}_t$ and $\Delta\boldsymbol{x} = \boldsymbol{x} - \boldsymbol{x}_t$:

$$f(\boldsymbol{x}) = f(\boldsymbol{x}_t) + (\nabla f(\boldsymbol{x}_t))^T \Delta\boldsymbol{x} + \frac{1}{2}\Delta\boldsymbol{x}^T \nabla^2 f(\boldsymbol{x}_t)\Delta\boldsymbol{x} + \ldots,$$

which is written as a quadratic form. $f(\boldsymbol{x})$ is minimized near a critical point when $\Delta\boldsymbol{x}$ is the solution to the following linear equation:

$$\nabla f(\boldsymbol{x}_t) + \nabla^2 f(\boldsymbol{x}_t)\Delta\boldsymbol{x} = 0. \tag{1.23}$$

This leads to

$$\boldsymbol{x} = \boldsymbol{x}_t - H^{-1}\nabla f(\boldsymbol{x}_t), \tag{1.24}$$

where $H = \nabla^2 f(\boldsymbol{x}_t)$ is the Hessian matrix, which is defined as

$$H(\boldsymbol{x}) \equiv \nabla^2 f(\boldsymbol{x}) \equiv \begin{pmatrix} \frac{\partial^2 f}{\partial x_1^2} & \cdots & \frac{\partial^2 f}{\partial x_1 \partial x_d} \\ \vdots & & \vdots \\ \frac{\partial^2 f}{\partial x_1 \partial x_d} & \cdots & \frac{\partial^2 f}{\partial x_d{}^2} \end{pmatrix}. \tag{1.25}$$

This matrix is symmetric due to the fact that

$$\frac{\partial^2 f}{\partial x_i \partial x_j} = \frac{\partial^2 f}{\partial x_j \partial x_i}. \tag{1.26}$$

If the iteration procedure starts from the initial vector $\boldsymbol{x}^{(0)}$, usually a guessed point in the feasible region of decision variables, Newton's formula for the tth iteration can be written as

$$\boldsymbol{x}^{(t+1)} = \boldsymbol{x}^{(t)} - H^{-1}(\boldsymbol{x}^{(t)}) f(\boldsymbol{x}^{(t)}), \tag{1.27}$$

where $H^{-1}(\boldsymbol{x}^{(t)})$ is the inverse of the Hessian matrix. It is worth pointing out that if $f(\boldsymbol{x})$ is quadratic, the solution can be found exactly in a single step. However, this method is not efficient for nonquadratic functions.

To speed up the convergence, we can use a smaller step size $\alpha \in (0, 1]$ and we have the modified Newton's method

$$\boldsymbol{x}^{(t+1)} = \boldsymbol{x}^{(t)} - \alpha H^{-1}(\boldsymbol{x}^{(t)}) f(\boldsymbol{x}^{(t)}). \tag{1.28}$$

Sometimes it might be time-consuming to calculate the Hessian matrix for second derivatives. A good alternative is to use an identity matrix $H = \boldsymbol{I}$ so that $H^{-1} = \boldsymbol{I}$, and we have the quasi-Newton method

$$\boldsymbol{x}^{(t+1)} = \boldsymbol{x}^{(t)} - \alpha \boldsymbol{I} \nabla f(\boldsymbol{x}^{(t)}), \tag{1.29}$$

which is essentially the steepest descent method.

The essence of the steepest descent method is to find the lowest possible objective function $f(\boldsymbol{x})$ from the current point $\boldsymbol{x}^{(t)}$. From the Taylor expansion of $f(\boldsymbol{x})$ about $\boldsymbol{x}^{(t)}$, we have

$$f(\boldsymbol{x}^{(t+1)}) = f(\boldsymbol{x}^{(t)} + \Delta\boldsymbol{s}) \approx f(\boldsymbol{x}^{(t)} + (\nabla f(\boldsymbol{x}^{(t)}))^T \Delta\boldsymbol{s}, \tag{1.30}$$

where $\Delta s = x^{(t+1)} - x^{(t)}$ is the increment vector. Since we are trying to find a better approximation to the objective function, it requires that the second term on the right side be negative. So,

$$f(x^{(t)} + \Delta s) - f(x^{(t)}) = (\nabla f)^T \Delta s < 0. \tag{1.31}$$

From vector analysis, we know that the inner product $u^T v$ of two vectors u and v is the largest when they are parallel but in opposite directions, so as to make their dot product negative. Therefore, we have

$$\Delta s = -\alpha \nabla f(x^{(t)}), \tag{1.32}$$

where $\alpha > 0$ is the step size. This the case when the direction Δs is along the steepest descent in the negative gradient direction. In the case of finding maxima, this method is often referred to as *hill climbing*.

The choice of the step size α is very important. A very small step size means slow movement toward the local minimum, whereas a large step may overshoot and subsequently makes it move far away from the local minimum. Therefore, the step size $\alpha = \alpha^{(t)}$ should be different at each iteration and should be chosen so that it minimizes the objective function $f(x^{(t+1)}) = f(x^{(t)}, \alpha^{(t)})$. Therefore, the steepest descent method can be written as

$$f(x^{(t+1)}) = f(x^{(t)}) - \alpha^{(t)} (\nabla f(x^{(t)}))^T \nabla f(x^{(t)}). \tag{1.33}$$

In each iteration, the gradient and step size will be calculated. Again, a good initial guess of both the starting point and the step size is useful.

Let us minimize the function

$$f(x_1, x_2) = 10x_1^2 + 5x_1x_2 + 10(x_2 - 3)^2,$$

where $(x_1, x_2) \in [-10, 10] \times [-15, 15]$. Using the steepest descent method, starting with a corner point as the initial guess, $x^{(0)} = (10, 15)^T$. We know that the gradient is

$$\nabla f = (20x_1 + 5x_2, 5x_1 + 20x_2 - 60)^T;$$

therefore, $\nabla f(x^{(0)}) = (275, 290)^T$. In the first iteration, we have

$$x^{(1)} = x^{(0)} - \alpha_0 \begin{pmatrix} 275 \\ 290 \end{pmatrix}.$$

The step size α_0 should be chosen such that $f(x^{(1)})$ is at the minimum, which means that

$$f(\alpha_0) = 10(10 - 275\alpha_0)^2$$
$$+5(10 - 275\alpha_0)(15 - 290\alpha_0) + 10(12 - 290\alpha_0)^2$$

should be minimized. This becomes an optimization problem for a single independent variable α_0. All the techniques for univariate optimization problems such as Newton's method can be used to find α_0. We can also obtain the solution by setting

$$\frac{df}{d\alpha_0} = -159725 + 3992000\alpha_0 = 0,$$

whose solution is $\alpha_0 \approx 0.04001$. At the second step, we have

$$\nabla f(\boldsymbol{x}^{(1)}) = (-3.078, 2.919)^T, \quad \boldsymbol{x}^{(2)} = \boldsymbol{x}^{(1)} - \alpha_1 \begin{pmatrix} -3.078 \\ 2.919 \end{pmatrix}.$$

The minimization of $f(\alpha_1)$ gives $\alpha_1 \approx 0.066$, and the new location is

$$\boldsymbol{x}^{(2)} \approx (-0.797, 3.202)^T.$$

At the third iteration, we have

$$\nabla f(\boldsymbol{x}^{(2)}) = (0.060, 0.064)^T, \quad \boldsymbol{x}^{(3)} = \boldsymbol{x}^{(2)} - \alpha_2 \begin{pmatrix} 0.060 \\ 0.064 \end{pmatrix}.$$

The minimization of $f(\alpha_2)$ leads to $\alpha_2 \approx 0.040$, and thus

$$\boldsymbol{x}^{(3)} \approx (-0.8000299, 3.20029)^T.$$

Then the iterations continue until a prescribed tolerance is met.

From the basic calculus, we know that first partial derivatives are equal to zero:

$$\frac{\partial f}{\partial x_1} = 20x_1 + 5x_2 = 0, \quad \frac{\partial f}{\partial x_2} = 5x_1 + 20x_2 - 60 = 0.$$

We know that the minimum occurs exactly at

$$\boldsymbol{x}_* = (-4/5, 16/5)^T = (-0.8, 3.2)^T.$$

We see that the steepest descent method gives almost the exact solution after only three iterations.

In finding the step size α_t in the preceding steepest descent method, we used $df(\alpha_t)/d\alpha_t = 0$. You may say that if we can use this stationary condition for $f(\alpha_0)$, why not use the same method to get the minimum point of $f(\boldsymbol{x})$ in the first place? There are two reasons here. The first is that this is a simple example for demonstrating how the steepest descent method works. The second reason is that even for complicated functions of multiple variables $f(x_1, \ldots, x_d)$ (say, $d = 500$), $f(\alpha_t)$ at any step t is still a univariate function, and the optimization of such $f(\alpha_t)$ is much simpler compared with the original multivariate problem. Furthermore, this optimal step size can be obtained by using a simple and efficient optimization algorithm.

It is worth pointing out that in our example, the convergence from the second iteration to the third iteration is slow. In fact, the steepest descent is typically slow once the local minimization is near. This is because near the local minimization the gradient is nearly zero, and thus the rate of descent is also slow. If high accuracy is needed near the local minimum, other local search methods should be used.

In some cases, the maximum or minimum may not exist at all; however, in this book we always assume they exist. Now the task becomes how to find the maximum or minimum in various optimization problems.

1.3.2 Hill Climbing with Random Restart

The problems discussed in the previous sections are relatively simple. Sometimes even seemingly simple problems may be difficult to solve.

For example, the following function,

$$f(x, y) = (x - y)^2 \exp(-x^2 - y^2), \tag{1.34}$$

has two global maxima at $(1/\sqrt{2}, -1/\sqrt{2})$ and $(-1/\sqrt{2}, 1/\sqrt{2})$ with $f_{\max} = 2/e \approx 0.735758882$.

If we use the gradient-based methods such as hill climbing, the final results may depend on the initial guess $\boldsymbol{x}_0 = (x_0, y_0)$. In fact, you can try many algorithms and software packages, and you will observe that the final results can largely depend on where you start. This maximization problem is equivalent to climbing onto two equal peaks, where you can reach only one peak at a time. In other words, the peak you reach will largely depend on where you start. There is some luck or randomness in the final results. To make reaching both peaks equally likely, the starting points must be distributed randomly in the search space. If we draw a biased sample as the starting point in one region, the other peak may never be reached.

A common strategy to ensure that all peaks are reachable is to carry out the hill climbing with multiple random restarts. This leads to a so-called *hill climbing with random restart*. It is a simple but very effective strategy.

A function with multiple peaks or valleys is a multimodal function, and its landscape is multimodal. With the hill climbing with random restart, it seems that the problem is solved. Suppose that, a function has k peaks, and if run the hill climbing with random restart n times. If $n \gg k$ and the samples are drawn from various search regions, it is likely to reach all the peaks of this multimodal function. However, in reality, things are not so simple. First, we may not know how many peaks and valleys a function has, and often there is no guarantee that all peaks are sampled. Second, most real-world problems do not have analytical or explicit forms of the function at all. Third, many problems may take continuous and discrete values, and their derivatives might not exist.

For example, even for continuous variables, the following function

$$g(x, y) = (|x| + |y|) \exp(-x^2 - y^2) \tag{1.35}$$

has a global minimum $f_{\min} = 0$ at $(0, 0)$. However, the derivative at $(0, 0)$ does not exist (due to the absolute functions). In this case, all the gradient-based methods will not work.

You may wonder what would happen if we smoothed a local region near $(0, 0)$. The approximation by a quadratic function can solve the problem. In fact, trust-region methods are based on the local smoothness and approximation in an appropriate region (trust region), and these methods work well in practice.

In reality, optimization problems are far more complicated, under various complex constraints, and the calculation of derivatives may be either impossible or too computationally expensive. Therefore, gradient-free methods are preferred. In fact, modern nature-inspire algorithms are almost all gradient-free optimization methods.

1.4 Search for Optimality

After an optimization problem is formulated correctly, the main task is to find the optimal solutions by some solution procedure using the right mathematical techniques.

Figuratively speaking, searching for the optimal solution is like treasure hunting. Imagine we are trying to hunt for a hidden treasure in a hilly landscape within a time limit. In one extreme, suppose we are blindfolded without any guidance. In this case, the search process is essentially a pure random search, which is usually not efficient. In another extreme, if we are told the treasure is placed at the highest peak of a known region, we will then directly climb up to the steepest cliff and try to reach the highest peak. This scenario corresponds to the classic hill-climbing techniques. In most cases, our search is between these extremes. We are not blindfolded, and we do not know where to look. It is a silly idea to search every single square inch of an extremely large hilly region so as to find the treasure.

The most likely scenario is that we will do a random walk while looking for some hints. We look someplace almost randomly, then move to another plausible place, then another, and so on. Such a random walk is a main characteristic of modern search algorithms. Obviously, we can either do the treasure hunting alone, so that the whole path is a trajectory-based search. I simulated annealing is such a kind of search. Alternatively, we can ask a group of people to do the hunting and share the information (and any treasure found). This scenario uses the so-called swarm intelligence and corresponds to the algorithms such as particle swarm optimization and a firefly algorithm, as we discuss later in detail. If the treasure is really important and if the area is extremely large, the search process will take a very long time. If there is no time limit and if any region is accessible (for example, no islands in a lake), it is theoretically possible to find the ultimate treasure (the global optimal solution).

Obviously, we can refine our search strategy a little bit further. Some hunters are better than others. We can only keep the better hunters and recruit new ones. This is something similar to the genetic algorithms or evolutionary algorithms where the search agents are improving. In fact, as we will see in almost all modern metaheuristic algorithms, we try to use the best solutions or agents, and we randomize (or replacc) the not-so-good ones, while evaluating each individual's competence (fitness) in combination with the system history (use of memory). With such a balance, we intend to design better and efficient optimization algorithms.

Classification of an optimization algorithm can be carried out in many ways. A simple way is to look at the nature of the algorithm, which divides the algorithms into two categories: deterministic algorithms and stochastic algorithms. *Deterministic algorithms* follow a rigorous procedure, and the path and values of both design variables and the functions are repeatable. For example, hill climbing is a deterministic algorithm, and for the same starting point, the algorithm will follow the same path whether you run the program today or tomorrow. On the other hand, *stochastic algorithms* always have some randomness. Genetic algorithms are a good example. The strings or solutions in the population will be different each time you run a program, since the algorithms use some pseudo-random numbers, though the final results may be no big difference, but the paths of each individual are not exactly repeatable.

There is a third type of algorithm that is a mixture or hybrid of deterministic and stochastic algorithms. Hill climbing with random restart is a good example. The basic idea is to use the deterministic algorithm but start with different initial points. This approach has certain advantages over a simple hill-climbing technique that may be stuck in a local peak. However, since there is a random component in this hybrid algorithm, we often classify it as a type of stochastic algorithm in the optimization literature.

1.5 No-Free-Lunch Theorems

A common question asked by many researchers, especially young researchers, is: There are so many algorithms for optimization, so what is the best one?

It is a simple question, but unfortunately there is no simple answer. There are many reasons that we cannot answer this question simply. One reason is that the complexity and diversity of real-world problems often mean that some problems are easier to solve, whereas others can be extremely difficult to solve. Therefore, it is unlikely to have a single method that can cope with all types of problems. Another reason is that there is a so-called *no-free-lunch* (NFL) theorem that states that there is no universal algorithm for all problems.

1.5.1 NFL Theorems

As for the NFL theorem, there are, in fact, a few such theorems, as proved by Wolpert and Macready in 1997 [23]. However, the main theorem states as follows: If any algorithm A outperforms another algorithm B in the search for an extremum of an objective function, then algorithm B will outperform A over other objective functions. In principle, NFL theorems apply to the scenario, either deterministic or stochastic, where a set of continuous (or discrete or mixed) parameters θ maps the objective or cost function into a finite set.

Let n_θ be the number of values of θ (either due to discrete values or the finite machine precisions) and n_f be the number of values of the objective function. Then the number of all the possible combinations of the objective functions is $N = n_f^{n_\theta}$, which is finite (but usually extremely large). The NFL theorem suggests that the *average* performance over *all* possible objective functions is the same for all search algorithms. Mathematically speaking, if $P(s_m^y|f, m, A)$ denotes the performance in the statistical sense of an algorithm A iterated m times on an objective function f over the sample set s_m, then we have the following statements about the averaged performance for two algorithms:

$$\sum_f P(s_m^y|f, m, A) = \sum_f P(s_m^y|f, m, B), \tag{1.36}$$

where $s_m = \{(s_m^x(1), s_m^y(2)), \ldots, (s_m^x(m), s_m^y(m))\}$ is a time-ordered set of m distinct visited points with a sample size of m.

The proof by induction can be sketched as follows: The search space is *finite* (though quite large). Thus the space of possible "objective" values is also finite. Objective function $f : \mathcal{X} \mapsto \mathcal{Y}$ gives $\mathcal{F} = \mathcal{Y}^{\mathcal{X}}$ the space of all possible problems. The main assumptions here are that the search domain is finite, there is no revisiting of visited points, and the finite set is closed under permutation (c.u.p).

For the case when $m = 1$, $s_1 = \{s_1^x, s_1^y\}$, so the only possible value of s_1^y is $f(s_1^x)$, and thus $\delta(s_1^y, f(s_1^x))$ where δ is the Dirac delta function. This means

$$\sum_f P(s_1^y | f, m = 1, A) = \sum_f \delta(s_1^y, f(s_1^x)) = |\mathcal{Y}|^{|\mathcal{X}|-1}, \tag{1.37}$$

which is independent of algorithm A. Here $|\mathcal{Y}|$ is the size or cardinality of $\mathcal{Y}$.

If it is true for m, or $\sum_f P(d_m^y | f, m, A)$ is independent of A, then for $m + 1$, we have $s_{m+1} = s_m \cup \{x, f(x)\}$ with $s_{m+1}^x(m + 1) = x$ and $s_{m+1}^y(m + 1) = f(x)$. Thus, we have (using the Bayesian approach)

$$\begin{aligned} P(s_{m+1}^y | f, m + 1, A) = {} & P(s_{m+1}^y(m + 1) | s_m, f, m + 1, A) \\ & \times P(s_m^y | f, m + 1, A). \end{aligned} \tag{1.38}$$

So we have

$$\begin{aligned} \sum_f P(s_{m+1}^y | f, m + 1, A) = {} & \sum_{f,x} \delta(s_{m+1}^m(m + 1), f(x)) \\ & \times P(x | d_m^y, f, m + 1, A) P(d_m^y | f, m + 1, A). \end{aligned} \tag{1.39}$$

Using $P(x | d_m, A) = \delta(x, A(s_m))$ and $P(s_m | f, m + 1, A) = P(s_m | f, m, A)$, the preceding expression leads to

$$\sum_f P(s_{m+1}^y | f, m + 1, A) = \frac{1}{|\mathcal{Y}|} \sum_f P(d_m^y | f, m, A), \tag{1.40}$$

which is also independent of A.

In other words, the performance is independent of algorithm A itself. That is to say, all algorithms for optimization will give the same average performance when averaged over *all possible* functions, which means that the universally best method does not exist for all optimization problems. In common language, it also means that any algorithm is as good (or bad) as a random search.

Well, you might say that there is no need to formulate new algorithms because all algorithms will perform equally. But this is not what the NFL theorem really means. The keywords here are *average performance* and *over all possible functions/problems*, measured in the statistical sense over a very large finite set. This does not mean that all algorithms perform equally well over some *specific* functions or over a *specific set* of problems. The reality is that no optimization problems require averaged performance over all possible functions.

Even though the NFL theorem is valid mathematically, its impact on optimization is limited. For any specific set of objective functions, some algorithms can perform much better than others. In fact, for a given *specific* problem set with specific objective functions, there usually exist some algorithms that are more efficient than others, if we do not need to measure their *average* performance. The main task is probably how to find these better algorithms for a given particular type of problem.

It is worth pointing out that the so-called NFL theorems have been proved for single objective optimization problems, and for multiobjective problems their extension is still under research.

Some recent studies suggest that the basic assumptions of the NFL theorems might not be valid for continuous domains. For example, Auger and Teytaud in 2010 suggested that continuous problems can be free [1]. In addition, Marshall and Hinton suggested that the assumption that time-ordered sets have m distinct points (a nonrevisiting condition) is not valid for realistic algorithms and thus violates the basic assumptions of nonrevisiting and close under permutation [15].

On the other hand, for coevolutionary systems such as a set of players coevolving to produce a champion, free lunches do exist, as proved by the original NFL researchers [24]. In this case, a single player (or both) tries to produce the next best move, and thus the fitness landscape depends on the moves by both players. Furthermore, for multiobjective optimization, Corne and Knowles proved that some algorithms are better than others [2].

1.5.2 Choice of Algorithms

Putting these theorems aside, how do we choose an algorithm, and what problems do we solve? Here, there are two choices and thus two relevant questions:

- For a given type of problem, what is the best algorithm to use?
- For a given algorithm, what kinds of problems can it solve?

The first question is harder than the second question, though it is not easy to answer either one. For a given type of problem, there may be a set of efficient algorithms to solve such problems. However, in many cases, we might not know how efficient an algorithm can be before we try it. In some cases, such algorithms may still need to be developed. Even for existing algorithms, the choice largely depends on the expertise of the decision maker, the available resources, and the type of problem. Ideally, the best available algorithms and tools should be used to solve a given problem; however, the proper use of these tools may still depend on the experience of the user. In addition, the resources such as computational costs, software availability, and time allowed to produce the solution will also be important factors in deciding what algorithms and methods to use.

On the other hand, for a given algorithm, the type of problem it can solve can be explored by using it to solve various kinds of problems and then comparing and ranking so as to find out how efficient it may be. In this way, the advantages and disadvantages can be identified, and such knowledge can be used to guide the choice of algorithm(s) and the type of problems to tackle. The good thing is that the majority of the literature (including hundreds of books) places tremendous emphasis on answering this question. Therefore, for traditional algorithms such as gradient-based algorithms and simplex methods, we know what types of problems they usually can solve. However, for new algorithms, as in the case of most nature-inspired algorithms, we have to carry out extensive studies to validate and test their performance. One of the objectives of this book is to introduce and review the recent algorithms and their diverse applications.

It is worth pointing out that any specific knowledge about a particular problem is always helpful for the appropriate choice of the best and most efficient methods for the optimization procedure. After all, subject knowledge and expertise have helped in many applications. For example, we try to use any tool to design an airplane from a table, even though it might not be feasible; however, if the design starts from the shape of a fish or a bird, the design will be more likely to be useful. From the algorithm development point of view, how to best incorporate problem-specific knowledge is still an ongoing and challenging question.

1.6 Nature-Inspired Metaheuristics

Most conventional or classic algorithms are deterministic. For example, the simplex method in linear programming is deterministic. Some deterministic optimization algorithms used the gradient information; they are called *gradient-based algorithms*. For example, the well-known Newton-Raphson algorithm is gradient-based, since it uses the function values and their derivatives, and it works extremely well for smooth unimodal problems. However, if there is some discontinuity in the objective function, it does not work well. In this case, a nongradient algorithm is preferred. Nongradient-based or gradient-free algorithms do not use any derivative, only the function values. Hooke-Jeeves pattern search and Nelder-Mead downhill simplex are examples of gradient-free algorithms.

For stochastic algorithms, in general we have two types: heuristic and metaheuristic, though their difference is small. Loosely speaking, *heuristic* means "to find" or "to discover by trial and error." Quality solutions to a tough optimization problem can be found in a reasonable amount of time, but there is no guarantee that optimal solutions will be reached. It can be expected that these algorithms work most but not all the time. This is good when we do not necessarily want the best solutions but rather good solutions that are easily reachable.

Further development of heuristic algorithms is the so-called metaheuristic algorithms. Here *meta* means "beyond" or "higher level," and these algorithms generally perform better than simple heuristics. In addition, all metaheuristic algorithms use certain tradeoffs of randomization and local search. It is worth pointing out that no agreed definitions of heuristics and metaheuristics exist in the literature; some use the terms heuristics and metaheuristics interchangeably. However, the recent trend tends to name all stochastic algorithms with randomization and local search as metaheuristic. Here we also use this convention. Randomization provides a good way to move away from local search to search on a global scale. Therefore, almost all metaheuristic algorithms tend to be suitable for global optimization.

Heuristics is a way, by trial and error, to produce acceptable solutions to a complex problem in a reasonably practical time. The complexity of the problem of interest makes it impossible to search every possible solution or combination. The aim is to find good, feasible solutions in an acceptable timescale. There is no guarantee that the best solutions can be found, and we even do not know whether an algorithm will work and why it works, if it does. The idea is to have an efficient but practical algorithm that will work most the time and that is able to produce good-quality solutions. Among the found quality solutions, we expect some to be nearly optimal, though there is no guarantee for such optimality.

Two major components of any metaheuristic algorithms are intensification and diversification, or exploitation and exploration. *Diversification* means to generate diverse solutions so as to explore the search space on a global scale. *Intensification* means to focus on the search in a local region by exploiting the information that a current good solution is found in this region. This is in combination with the selection of the best solutions. The selection of the best ensures that the solutions will converge to the optimality, whereas the diversification via randomization avoids the solutions being trapped at local optima and, at the same time, increases the diversity of the solutions. The good combination of these two major components will usually ensure that the global optimality is achievable.

Metaheuristic algorithms can be classified in many ways. One way is to classify them as population-based or trajectory-based. For example, genetic algorithms are *population-based* because they use a set of strings; so are particle swarm optimization (PSO), the firefly algorithm (FA), and cuckoo search, which all use multiple agents or particles.

On the other hand, simulated annealing uses a single agent or solution that moves through the design space or search space in a piecewise style. A better move or solution is always accepted, whereas a not-so-good move can be accepted with a certain probability. The steps or moves trace a *trajectory* in the search space, with a nonzero probability that this trajectory can reach the global optimum.

Before we introduce all popular metaheuristic algorithms in detail, let us look briefly at their history.

1.7 A Brief History of Metaheuristics

Throughout history, especially at the early periods of human history, we humans' approach to problem solving has always been heuristic or metaheuristic—by trial and error. Many important discoveries were made by "thinking outside the box," and often by accident; that is heuristics. Archimedes's "Eureka!" moment was a heuristic triumph. In fact, humans' daily learning experience (at least as children) is dominantly heuristic.

Despite its ubiquitous nature, *metaheuristics* as a scientific method to problem solving is indeed a modern phenomenon, though it is difficult to pinpoint when the metaheuristic method was first used. Mathematician Alan Turing was probably the first to use heuristic algorithms during the Second World War when he was breaking the Enigma ciphers at Bletchley Park. Turing called his search method *heuristic search*, since it could be expected it worked most of time, but there was no guarantee of finding the correct solution; however, his method was a tremendous success. In 1945, Turing was recruited to the National Physical Laboratory (NPL), UK, where he set out his design for the Automatic Computing Engine (ACE). In an NPL report on *Intelligent Machinery* in 1948, he outlined his innovative ideas of machine intelligence and learning, neural networks, and evolutionary algorithms.

The 1960s and 1970s were the two important decades for the development of evolutionary algorithms. First, scientist and engineer John Holland and his collaborators at the University of Michigan developed genetic algorithms in 1960s and 1970s. As early as 1962, Holland studied the adaptive system and was the first to use crossover and recombination manipulations for modeling such systems. His seminal book summarizing the development of genetic algorithms was published in 1975 [9]. In the same year, computer scientist Kenneth De Jong finished his important dissertation showing the potential and power of genetic algorithms for a wide range of objective functions, noisy, multimodal, or even discontinuous [4].

In essence, a *genetic algorithm* (GA) is a search method based on the abstraction of Darwinian evolution and natural selection of biological systems and representing them in the mathematical operators: crossover or recombination, mutation, fitness, and selection of the fittest. Genetic algorithms have become very successful in solving a wide range of optimization problems, and several thousand research articles and hundreds of books have been written on this subject. Some statistics shows that a vast majority of Fortune 500 companies are now using them routinely to solve tough combinatorial optimization problems such as planning, data mining, and scheduling.

During the same period, Ingo Rechenberg and Hans-Paul Schwefel, both then students at the Technical University of Berlin, developed a search technique for solving optimization problems in aerospace engineering, called *evolutionary strategy*, in 1963. Later, fellow student Peter Bienert joined them and began to construct an automatic experimenter using simple rules of mutation and selection. There was no crossover in this technique; only mutation was used to produce an offspring, and an improved solution was kept at each generation. This was essentially a simple trajectory-style hill-climbing algorithm with randomization. As early as 1960, aerospace engineer Lawrence J. Fogel intended to use simulated evolution as a learning process as a tool to study artificial intelligence. Then, in 1966, Fogel, together with A. J. Owen and M. J. Walsh, developed the evolutionary programming technique by representing solutions as finite-state machines and randomly mutating one of these machines [6]. These innovative ideas and methods have evolved into a much wider discipline, called *evolutionary algorithms* or *evolutionary computation*[10, 18].

Although our focus in this book is metaheuristic algorithms, other algorithms can be thought of as heuristic optimization techniques. These methods include artificial neural networks, support vector machines, and many other machine learning techniques. Indeed, they all intend to minimize their learning errors and prediction (capability) errors via iterative trial and error.

Artificial neural networks are now routinely used in many applications. In 1943, neurophysiologist and cybernetician Warren McCulloch and logician Walter Pitts proposed the artificial neurons as simple information-processing units. The concept of a neural network was probably first proposed by Alan Turing in his 1948 NPL report, *Intelligent Machinery* [3,21]. Significant developments were carried out in the neural network area from the 1940s and 1950s to the 1990s [19].

The support vector machine as a classification technique dates back to earlier work by Vladimir Vapnik in 1963 on linear classifiers; the nonlinear classification with kernel techniques were developed by Vapnik and his collaborators in the 1990s. A systematical summary in was published Vapnik's book, *The Nature of Statistical Learning Theory*, in 1995 [22].

The decades of the 1980s and 1990s were the most exciting time for metaheuristic algorithms. The next big step was the development of simulated annealing (SA) in 1983, an optimization technique pioneered by Scott Kirkpatrick, C. Daniel Gellat, and Mario P. Vecchi, inspired by the annealing process of metals [13]. It is a trajectory-based search algorithm starting with an initial guess solution at a high temperature and gradually cooling down the system. A move or new solution is accepted if it is better; otherwise, it is accepted with a probability, which makes it possible for the system to escape any local optima. It is then expected that if the system is cooled down slowly enough, the global optimal solution can be reached.

The actual first use of memory in modern metaheuristics is probably due to Fred Glover's Tabu search in 1986, though his seminal book on Tabu search was published later, in 1997 [8].

In 1992, Marco Dorigo finished his Ph.D. thesis on optimization and natural algorithms [5], in which he described his innovative work on ant colony optimization (ACO). This search technique was inspired by the swarm intelligence of social ants using pheromone as a chemical messenger. Then, in 1992, computer scientist John R. Koza of Stanford University published a treatise on genetic programming that laid the foundation of a whole new area of machine learning, revolutionizing computer programming [14]. As early as 1988, Koza applied his first patent on genetic programming. The basic idea is to use the genetic principle to breed computer programs so as to gradually produce the best programs for a given type of problem.

Slightly later in 1995, more significant progress came with the development of the *particle swarm optimization* (PSO) by American social psychologist James Kennedy, and engineer Russell C. Eberhart [12]. Loosely speaking, PSO is an optimization algorithm inspired by swarm intelligence of fish and birds and even by human behavior. The multiple agents, called *particles*, swarm around the search space, starting from some initial random guess. The swarm communicates the current best and shares the global best so as to focus on the quality solutions. Since its development, there have been about 20 different variants of particle swarm optimization techniques, which have been applied to almost all areas of tough optimization problems. There is some strong evidence that PSO is better than traditional search algorithms and even better than genetic algorithms for many types of problems, though this point is far from conclusive.

In around 1996 and later in 1997, Rainer Storn and Kenneth Price developed their vector-based evolutionary algorithm called differential evolution (DE) [20], which proves more efficient than genetic algorithms in many applications.

In 1997, the publication of No Free Lunch Theorems for Optimization," by David H. Wolpert and William G. Macready, sent out a shock wave to the optimization community [23,24]. Researchers had always been trying to find better algorithms, or even universally robust algorithms, for optimization, especially for tough NP-hard optimization problems. However, these theorems state that if algorithm A performs better than algorithm B for some optimization functions, then B will outperform A for other functions. That is to say, if averaged over all possible function space, both algorithms A and B will perform, on average, equally well. Alternatively, no universally better algorithms exist. That is disappointing, right? Then people realized that we do not need the average over all possible functions for a given optimization problem. What we want is to find the best solutions, which has nothing to do with average over all possible function space. In addition, we can accept the fact that there is no universal or magical tool, but we do know from our experience that some algorithms do indeed outperform others for given types of optimization problems. So the research may now focus on finding the best and most efficient algorithm(s) for a given set of problems. The objective is to design better algorithms for most types of problems, not for all problems. Therefore, the search is still on.

At the turn of the 21st century, things became even more exciting. First, in 2001 Zong Woo Geem et al. developed the *harmony search* (HS) algorithm [7], which has been widely applied in solving various optimization problems such as water distribution, transport modeling, and scheduling. In 2004, Sunil Nakrani and Craig Tovey proposed the honeybee algorithm and its application for optimizing Internet hosting centers [16], which was followed by the development of the virtual bee algorithm by Xin-She Yang in 2005. At the same time, the bees algorithm was developed by D. T. Pham et al. in 2005 [17], and the artificial bee colony (ABC) was developed by Dervis Karaboga in 2005 [11].

In late 2007 and early 2008, the *firefly algorithm* (FA) was developed by Xin-She Yang [25,26]; this algorithm has generated a wide range of interest, with more than 800 publications to date, as shown by a quick October 2013 search in Google Scholar. In 2009, Xin-She Yang at Cambridge University, UK, and Suash Deb at Raman College of Engineering, India, proposed an efficient *cuckoo search* (CS) algorithm [27,28]; it has been demonstrated that CS can be far more effective than most existing metaheuristic algorithms, including particle swarm optimization.[1] In 2010, the bat algorithm was developed by Xin-She Yang for continuous optimization, based on the echolocation behavior of microbats [29]. In 2012, the flower pollination algorithm was developed by Xin-She Yang, and its efficiency is very promising.

The literature is expanding rapidly, and the number of nature-inspired algorithms has increased dramatically. The brief survey by Iztok Fister Jr. et al. indicated that there are more than 40 nature-inspired algorithms.[2] As we can see, more and more metaheuristic algorithms are being developed. Such a diverse range of algorithms necessitates a systematic summary of various metaheuristic algorithms, and this book is such an attempt to introduce all the latest nature-inspired metaheuristics with diverse applications.

[1] Novel cuckoo search "beats" particle swarm optimization, *Science Daily*, news article (28 May 2010), www.sciencedaily.com.

[2] I. Fister Jr., X. S. Yang, I. Fister, J. Brest, D. Fister, A brief review of nature-inspire algorithms for optimization, http://arxiv.org/abs/1307.4186 (Accessed on 20 Aug 2013).

We discuss all major modern metaheuristic algorithms in the remainder of this book, including simulated annealing (SA), genetic algorithms (GA), ant colony optimization (ACO), bat algorithms (BA), bee algorithms, differential evolution (DE), particle swarm optimization (PSO), harmony search (HS), the firefly algorithm (FA), cuckoo search (CS), and the flower pollination algorithm (FPA), and others.

References

[1] Auger A, Teytaud O. Continuous lunches are free plus the design of optimal optimization algorithms. Algorithmica 2010;57(2):121–46.
[2] Corne D, Knowles J. Some multiobjective optimizers are better than others. Evol Comput 2003;4(2):2506–12.
[3] Copeland BJ. The essential turing. Oxford, UK: Oxford University Press; 2004.
[4] De Jong K. An analysis of the behavior of a class of genetic adaptive systems. Ph.D. thesis, University of Michigan, Ann Arbor, MI, USA; 1975.
[5] Dorigo M. Optimization, learning and natural algorithms. Ph.D. thesis, Politecnico di Milano, Italy; 1992.
[6] Fogel LJ, Owens AJ, Walsh MJ. Artificial intelligence through simulated evolution. New York, NY, USA: Wiley; 1966.
[7] Geem ZW, Kim JH, Loganathan GV. A new heuristic optimization: harmony search. Simulation 2001;76(2):60–8.
[8] Glover F, Laguna M. Tabu search. Boston, MA, USA: Kluwer Academic Publishers; 1997.
[9] Holland J. Adaptation in natural and artificial systems. Ann Arbor, MI, USA: University of Michigan Press; 1975.
[10] Judea P. Heuristics. New York, NY, USA: Addison-Wesley; 1984.
[11] Karaboga D. An idea based on honeybee swarm for numerical optimization. Technical Report, Erciyes University, Turkey; 2005.
[12] Kennedy J, Eberhart R. Particle swarm optimization. In: Proceedings of the IEEE International Conference on Neural Networks, Piscataway, NJ, USA; 1995. p. 1942–48.
[13] Kirkpatrick S, Gellat CD, Vecchi MP. Optimization by simulated annealing. Science 1983;220(4598):671–80.
[14] Koza JR. Genetic programming: on the programming of computers by means of natural selection. Cambridge, MA, USA: MIT Press; 1992.
[15] Marshall JA, Hinton TG. Beyond no free lunch: realistic algorithms for arbitrary problem classes. WCCI 2010 IEEE world congress on computational intelligence, Barcelona, Spain, July 18–23; 2010. pp. 1319–1324.
[16] Nakrani S, Tovey C. On honeybees and dynamic server allocation in Internet hosting centers. Adapt Behav 2004;12(3):223–40.
[17] Pham DT, Ghanbarzadeh A, Koc E, Otri S, Rahim S, Zaidi M. The bees algorithm. Technical Note, Manufacturing Engineering Center, Cardiff University, Cardiff, UK; 2005.
[18] Schrijver A. On the history of combinatorial optimization (till 1960). In: Aardal K, Nemhauser GL, Weismantel R, editors. Handbook of discrete optimization. Amsterdam, Netherlands: Elsevier; 2005. p. 1–68.
[19] Siegelmann HT, Sontag ED. Turing computability with neural nets. Appl Math Lett 1991;4(1):77–80.
[20] Storn R, Price K. Differential evolution: a simple and efficient heuristic for global optimization over continuous spaces. J Global Optim 1997;11(4):341–59.

[21] Turing AM. Intelligent machinery. National Physical Laboratory, UK, Technical Report; 1948.
[22] Vapnik V. The nature of statistical learning theory. New York, NY, USA: Springer-Verlag; 1995.
[23] Wolpert DH, Macready WG. No free lunch theorems for optimization. IEEE Trans Evol Comput 1997;1(1):67–82.
[24] Wolpert DH, Macready WG. Coevolutionary free lunches. IEEE Trans Evol Comput 2005;9(6):721–35.
[25] Yang XS. Nature-inspired metaheuristic algorithms. Bristol, UK: Luniver Press; 2008.
[26] Yang XS. Firefly algorithms for multimodal optimization. In: Watanabe O, Zeugmann T, editors. Proceedings of fifth symposium on stochastic algorithms, foundations and applications, SAGA 2009. Lecture Notes in Computer Science, vol. 5792; 2009. p. 169–78.
[27] Yang XS, Deb S. Cuckoo search via Lévy flights. In: Proceedings of world congress on nature & biologically inspired computing (NaBic 2009). USA: IEEE Publications; 2009. p. 210–14.
[28] Yang XS, Deb S. Engineering optimization by cuckoo search. Int J Math Modelling Num Optim 2010;1(4):330–43. (2010).
[29] Yang XS. A new metaheuristic bat-inspired algorithm. Nature-inspired cooperative strategies for optimization (NICSO 2010), vol. SCI 284. Springer; 2010. p. 65–74.

2 Analysis of Algorithms

Swarm intelligence (SI) and bio-inspired computation have received great interest and attention in the literature. In the communities of optimization, computational intelligence, and computer science, bio-inspired algorithms, especially those SI-based algorithms, have become very popular. In fact, these nature-inspired metaheuristic algorithms are now among the most widely used algorithms for optimization and computational intelligence. SI-based algorithms such as ant and bee algorithms, particle swarm optimization, cuckoo search, and firefly algorithms can possess many advantages over conventional algorithms.

In this chapter, we analyze the key components of these nature-inspired algorithms in terms of their evolutionary operators and functionalities. We do not intend to provide a detailed introduction to each algorithm, because these algorithms will be introduced one by one in later chapters. The main aim here is to provide an overview so that readers can critically analyze each algorithm while reading each chapter later.

2.1 Introduction

As we discussed in Chapter 1, an optimization algorithm is an iterative procedure, starting from an initial guess. After a certain (sufficiently large) number of iterations, it may converge toward to a stable solution, ideally the optimal solution to a problem of interest [19,30]. This is essentially a self-organizing system with solutions as states and the converged solutions as attractors. Such an iterative, self-organizing system can evolve according to a set of rules or mathematical equations. As a result, such a complex system can interact and self-organize into certain converged states, showing some emergent characteristics of self-organization. In this sense, the proper design of an efficient optimization algorithm is equivalent to finding efficient ways to mimic the evolution of a self-organizing system, especially evolving biological systems [1,16].

Alternatively, we can view an algorithm as Markov chains, and the behavior of an algorithm is controlled by its solution states and transition moves. Indeed, different views can help to analyze algorithms from different perspectives. We can also analyze an algorithm in terms of its key components, such as exploration and exploitation, or the ways that generate solutions using evolutionary operators. In this chapter, we review and discuss the majority of nature-inspired algorithms from different perspectives.

Nature-Inspired Optimization Algorithms. http://dx.doi.org/10.1016/B978-0-12-416743-8.00002-6

2.2 Analysis of Optimization Algorithms

An optimization algorithm can be analyzed from different perspectives. In this section, we analyze it as an iterative procedure, a self-organization system, two conflicting components, and three evolutionary operators.

2.2.1 Algorithm as an Iterative Process

Mathematically speaking, an algorithm A is an iterative process, that aims to generate a new and better solution $\boldsymbol{x}^{t+1}$ to a given problem from the current solution $\boldsymbol{x}^t$ at iteration or time t. For example, the Newton-Raphson method to find the optimal value of $f(\boldsymbol{x})$ is equivalent to finding the critical points or roots of $f'(\boldsymbol{x}) = 0$ in a d-dimensional space [28,25]. That is,

$$\boldsymbol{x}^{t+1} = \boldsymbol{x}^t - \frac{f'(\boldsymbol{x}^t)}{f''(\boldsymbol{x}^t)} = A(\boldsymbol{x}^t). \tag{2.1}$$

Obviously, the convergence rate may become very slow near the optimal point where $f'(\boldsymbol{x}^t) \to 0$. Sometimes the true convergence rate may not be as quick as it should be. A simple way to improve the convergence is to modify the previous formula slightly by introducing a parameter p, as follows:

$$\boldsymbol{x}^{t+1} = \boldsymbol{x}^t - p\frac{f'(\boldsymbol{x}^t)}{f''(\boldsymbol{x}^t)}, \quad p = \frac{1}{1 - A'(\boldsymbol{x}_*)}. \tag{2.2}$$

Here $\boldsymbol{x}_*$ is the optimal solution, or a fixed point of the iterative formula. It is worth pointing out that the optimal convergence of Newton-Raphson's method leads to an optimal parameter setting p, which depends on the iterative formula and the optimality $\boldsymbol{x}_*$ of the objective $f(\boldsymbol{x})$ to be optimized.

In general, we can write the preceding iterative equation as

$$\boldsymbol{x}^{t+1} = A(\boldsymbol{x}^t; p), \tag{2.3}$$

which is valid for a deterministic method; however, in modern metaheuristic algorithms, randomization is often used in an algorithm, and in many cases, randomization appears in the form of a set of m random variables $\boldsymbol{\varepsilon} = (\varepsilon_1, \ldots, \varepsilon_m)$ in an algorithm. For example, in simulated annealing, there is one random variable, while in particle swarm optimization [17], there are two random variables. In addition, there are often a set of k parameters in an algorithm. For example, in particle swarm optimization, there are four parameters (two learning parameters, one inertia weight, and the population size). In general, we can have a vector of parameters $\boldsymbol{p} = (p_1, \ldots, p_k)$. Mathematically speaking, we can write an algorithm with k parameters and m random variables as

$$\boldsymbol{x}^{t+1} = \boldsymbol{A}\Big(\boldsymbol{x}^t, \boldsymbol{p}(t), \boldsymbol{\varepsilon}(t)\Big), \tag{2.4}$$

where $\boldsymbol{A}$ is a nonlinear mapping from a given solution (a d-dimensional vector $\boldsymbol{x}^t$) to a new solution vector $\boldsymbol{x}^{t+1}$.

It is worth pointing out that the preceding formula (2.4) is for a trajectory-based, single-agent system. For population-based algorithms with a swarm of n solutions, we can extend the preceding iterative formula to the following:

$$\begin{pmatrix} x_1 \\ x_2 \\ \vdots \\ x_n \end{pmatrix}^{t+1} = A\Big(\big(x_1^t, x_2^t, \ldots, x_n^t\big); (p_1, p_2, \ldots, p_k); (\epsilon_1, \epsilon_2, \ldots, \epsilon_m)\Big) \begin{pmatrix} x_1 \\ x_2 \\ \vdots \\ x_n \end{pmatrix}^{t}, \tag{2.5}$$

where $p_1, \ldots, p_k$ are k algorithm-dependent parameters and $\epsilon_1, \ldots, \epsilon_m$ are m random variables.

This view of algorithm (2.4) is mainly dynamical or functional. It considers the functional (2.4) as a dynamical system, which will evolve toward equilibrium or attractor states. In principle, the behavior of the system can be described by the eigenvalues of A and its parameters in terms of linear and/or weakly nonlinear dynamical system theories. However, this does not provide sufficient insight into the diversity and complex characteristics. Self-organization may provide better insight, as we can see in a moment.

2.2.2 An Ideal Algorithm?

The number of iterations t needed to find an optimal solution for a given accuracy largely determines the overall computational efforts and the performance of an algorithm. A better algorithm should use less computation and fewer iterations.

In an extreme case for an iterative algorithm or formula (2.1), an ideal algorithm should only take one iteration $t = 1$. You may wonder if such an algorithm exists in practice. The answer is "Yes, it depends." In fact, for a quadratic function such as $f(x) = ax^2$ where $a > 0$, the well-known Newton-Raphson method

$$x_{t+1} = x_t - \frac{f'(x_t)}{f''(x_t)} \tag{2.6}$$

is the ideal algorithm. If we start the iteration from any random guess $x_0 = b$, we have

$$x_1 = x_0 - \frac{f'(x_0)}{f''(x_0)} = b - \frac{2ab}{2a} = 0, \tag{2.7}$$

which gives the global optimal solution $f_*(0) = 0$ at $x_* = 0$.

Obviously, we can extend this idea to the whole class of quadratic functions. It is even possible to extend to more generalized convex functions. However, many problems are not convex and certainly not quadratic. Therefore, the so-called ideal algorithm does not exist in general. As we mentioned earlier, there is no good algorithm for solving NP-hard problems.

There are many optimization algorithms in the literature, and no single algorithm is suitable for all problems. Even so, the search for efficient algorithms still forms a major effort among researchers. This search for the "Holy Grail" will continue unless some proves analytically otherwise.

Table 2.1 Similarity between self-organization and an optimization algorithm.

Self-Organization	Features	Algorithm	Characteristics
Noise, perturbations	Diversity	Randomization	Escape local optima
Selection mechanism	Structure	Selection	Convergence
Reorganization	State changes	Evolution	Solutions

2.2.3 A Self-Organization System

A complex system may be self-organizing under the right conditions: when the size of the system is sufficiently large with a sufficiently high number of degrees of freedom or possible states S. In addition, the system must be allowed to evolve over a long time away from noise and far from equilibrium states. Most important, a selection mechanism must be in place to ensure that self-organization is possible. That is, the main conditions for self-organization in a complex system are:

- The system size is large with a sufficient number of degrees of freedom or states.
- There is enough diversity in the system, such as perturbations, noise, or edge of chaos, or it is far from the equilibrium.
- The system is allowed to evolve over a long time.
- A selection mechanism or an unchanging law acts in the system.

In other words, a system with states S will evolve toward the self-organized state S_* driven by a mechanism $\alpha(t)$ with a set of parameters α. That is,

$$S \xrightarrow{\alpha(t)} S_*. \tag{2.8}$$

From the self-organization point of view, algorithm (2.4) is a self-organization system starting from many possible states $\boldsymbol{x}^t$ and tries to converge to the optimal solution/state $\boldsymbol{x}_*$, driven by the algorithm A in the following schematic representation:

$$f(\boldsymbol{x}^t) \xrightarrow{A} f_{\min}(\boldsymbol{x}_*). \tag{2.9}$$

By comparing the conditions for self-organization and characteristics of algorithms, we can carry out the comparison as shown in Table 2.1.

However, there are some significant differences between a self-organizing system and an algorithm. For self-organization, the avenues to the self-organized states may not be clear, and time is not an important factor. On the other hand, for an algorithm, the way that makes an algorithm converge is very important, and the speed of convergence is crucial so that the minimum computational cost is needed to reach truly global optimality.

2.2.4 Exploration and Exploitation

Nature-inspired optimization algorithms can also be analyzed from the ways they explore the search space. In essence, all algorithms should have two key components:

exploitation and *exploration*, which are also referred to as *intensification* and *diversification* [4].

Exploitation uses any information obtained from the problem of interest to help generate new solutions that are better than existing solutions. However, this process is typically local, and information (such as gradient) is also local. Therefore, it is for local search. For example, hill climbing is a method that uses derivative information to guide the search procedure. In fact, new steps always try to climb up the local gradient. The advantage of exploitation is that it usually leads to very high convergence rates, but its disadvantage is that it can get stuck in a local optimum because the final solution point largely depends on the starting point.

On the other hand, exploration makes it possible to explore the search space more efficiently, and it can generate solutions with enough diversity and far from the current solutions. Therefore, the search is typically on a global scale. The advantage of exploration is that it is less likely to get stuck in a local mode, and the global optimality can be more accessible. However, its disadvantages are slow convergence and the waste of some computational efforts because many new solutions can be far from the global optimality.

Therefore, final balance is required so that an algorithm can achieve good performance. Too much exploitation and too little exploration mean the system may converge more quickly, but the probability of finding the true global optimality may be low. On the other hand, too little exploitation and too much exploration can cause the search path to wander around with very slow convergence. The optimal balance should mean the right amount of exploration and exploitation, which may lead to the optimal performance of an algorithm. Therefore, balance is crucially important.

However, finding the way to achieve such balance is still an open problem. In fact, no algorithm can claim to have achieved such balance in the current literature. In essence, the balance itself is a hyperoptimization problem because it is the optimization of an optimization algorithm. In addition, such balance may depend on many factors, such as the working mechanism of an algorithm, its setting of parameters, tuning and control of these parameters, and even the problem to be considered. Furthermore, such balance may not universally exist, and it may vary from problem to problem.

These unresolved problems and mysteries can motivate more research in this area. We can expect that the amount of relevant literature will increase in the near future.

2.2.5 Evolutionary Operators

By directly looking at the operations of an algorithm, it is also helpful to see how it works. Let us take genetic algorithms as an example. *Genetic algorithms* (GA) are a class of algorithms based on the abstraction of Darwinian evolution of biological systems, pioneered by J. Holland and his collaborators in the 1960s and 1970s. Genetic algorithms use genetic operators such as crossover and recombination, mutation, and selection [14]. It has been shown that genetic algorithms have many advantages over traditional algorithms. Three advantages are distinct: gradient-free, highly explorative, and parallelism. No gradient/derivative information is needed in GA, and thus GA can deal with complex, discontinuous problems. The stochastic nature of crossover and mutation make GA explore the search space more effectively and the global optimality is more likely to be reached. In addition, genetic algorithms are population-based with multiple chromosomes, and thus it is possible to implement them in a parallel manner [29,30].

The three key evolutionary operators in genetic algorithms can be summarized as follows:

- *Crossover*. The recombination of two parent chromosomes (solutions) by exchanging part of one chromosome with a corresponding part of another so as to produce offsprings (new solutions).
- *Mutation*. The change of part of a chromosome (a bit or several bits) to generate new genetic characteristics. In binary encoding, mutation can be achieved simply by flipping between 0 and 1. Mutation can occur at a single site or multiple sites simultaneously.
- *Selection*. The survival of the fittest, which means the highest quality chromosomes and/characteristics will stay within the population. This often takes some form of elitism, and the simplest form is to let the best genes pass on to the next generations in the population.

Mathematically speaking, crossover is a mixing process with extensive local search in a subspace [2,3]. This can be seen by an example. For a problem with eight dimensions with a total search space $\Omega = \Re^8$, if the parent solutions are drawn from $\boldsymbol{x}_1 = [aaaaaabb], \boldsymbol{x}_2 = [aaaaaaaa]$ where a and b can be binary digits or a real value for the ith component/dimension of a solution to a problem. Whatever the crossover may be, the offsprings will be one of the four possible combinations: $[aaaaaaba]$, $[aaaaaaab]$, $[aaaaaaaa]$, or $[aaaaaabb]$. In any case, the first six variables are always $[aaaaaa]$. This means that the crossover or recombination will lead to a solution in a subspace where only the 7th and 8th variables are different. No solution will be in the subspace in which the first 6 variables will be different. In other words, the crossover operator will only create solutions within a subspace $S = [aaaaaa] \cup \Re^2 \subset \Omega$ in the present case. Therefore, crossover is a local search operator, though it can also become a global operator if the subspace is sufficiently large.

On the other hand, mutation provides a mechanism for global exploration. In the preceding example, if we mutate one of the solutions in the first dimension, it will generate a solution that may not be in the subspace. For example, for a solution $\boldsymbol{x}_1 = [aaaaaabb] \in S$, if its first a becomes b, then it generates a new solution $\boldsymbol{x}_q = [baaaaabb] \notin S$. In fact, $\boldsymbol{x}_q$ can be very difficult from the existing solutions and jump out of any previous subspace. For this reason, the mutation operator is a global operator. However, mutation can be local if the mutation rate is sufficiently low and the step sizes are very small. Therefore, the boundary between local or global can be vague and relative.

Both crossover and mutation will provide the diversity for new solutions. However, crossover provides good mixing, and its diversity is mainly limited in the subspace. Mutation can provide better diversity, though far-away solutions may drive the population away from converged/evolved characteristics.

It is worth pointing out that selection is a special operator that has a dual role: to choose the best solutions in a subspace and to provide a driving force for self-organization or convergence. Without selection, there is no driving force to choose what is best for the system, and therefore selection enables a system to evolve with a goal. With a proper selection mechanism, only the fitter solutions and desired stages may be allowed to gradually pass on, while unfit solutions in the population will gradually die out. Selection can be as simple as a high-degree elitism, and only the best is selected. Obviously, other forms of selection mechanisms, such as fitness-proportional crossover, can be used.

The role and main functions of three evolutionary operators can be categorized as follows:

- Crossover is mainly for mixing within a subspace. It will help make the system converge.
- Mutation provides a main mechanism for global search, and it can be generalized as a randomization technique.
- Selection provides a driving force for the system to evolve toward the desired states. It is essentially intensive exploitation.

Mutation can also take different forms, and one way is to simply use stochastic moves or randomization. For example, the traditional Hooke-Jeeves pattern search (PS) is also a gradient-free method, which has inspired many new algorithms. The key step in pattern search is the consecutive increment of one dimension followed by the increment along the other dimensions. The steps will be tried and shrunk when necessary [10].

Nowadays the pattern search idea can be generated by the following equation:

$$x_i = x_i + \delta x_i = x_i + (x_{\text{newmove}} - x_i), \quad i = 1, 2, \ldots, d. \tag{2.10}$$

This can be written as a vector equation

$$\boldsymbol{x} = \boldsymbol{x} + \delta \boldsymbol{x} = \boldsymbol{x} + (\boldsymbol{x}_{\text{newmove}} - \boldsymbol{x}). \tag{2.11}$$

In essence, $\delta \boldsymbol{x}$ acts as a mutation operator in $2d$ directions in a d-dimensional space. As we will see shortly, differential evolution uses this kind of mutation in higher dimensions.

In the rest of this chapter, we first briefly introduce the key steps of a few nature-inspired algorithms and then analyze them in terms of evolutionary operators and their ways for exploration and exploitation.

2.3 Nature-Inspired Algorithms

There are over a dozen popular, nature-inspired algorithms for optimization. In the rest of this chapter, we analyze each algorithm in terms of the previously mentioned evolutionary operators as well as exploration and exploitation.

2.3.1 Simulated Annealing

The simplest stochastic algorithm is probably the so-called *simulated annealing*, developed by Kirkpatrick et al. in 1983 [18] based on the characteristics of the metal annealing process. From the current solution or state x_i, a new solution x_j is accepted with a probability

$$p\big(x_i \to x_j | x(t) = x_i\big) = \frac{1}{Z} \exp\Big[- \frac{1}{T(t)} \max\{0, f(x_j) - f(x_i)\}\Big], \tag{2.12}$$

where f is the objective function to be minimized. Here, Z is a normalization factor.

The original article by Kirkpatrick et al. demonstrated how to solve very challenging problems. However, generating new solutions x_j from the current solution may depend on the implementation and problem of interest. Whatever the ways of generation might be, such generations of new solutions form a Markov chain, or more specifically, a random walk.

Therefore, the main operator is to generate new solutions by random walks, and consequently randomization acts as a mutation or explorative search mechanism. Selection is achieved by testing whether a solution is getting better (smaller for a minimization problem). Strictly speaking, simulated annealing is not an evolutionary algorithm, and thus there is no crossover operator in this algorithm. In addition, exploitation is relatively weak because the acceptance is carried out by a probability condition. That is why simulated annealing often converges very slowly in practice, though it is good at exploration and often has a good property of finding the global optimality at the expense of a large number of function evaluations.

2.3.2 Genetic Algorithms

Genetic algorithms (GA), developed by John Holland [14], essentially form the foundations of modern evolutionary computing. GA has three key genetic operators: crossover, mutation, and selection, as discussed earlier. Though there are no explicit mathematical equations in the original genetic algorithm, it did provide detailed procedures and steps on how to generate offspring from parent solutions/strings.

Crossover helps exploit and enhance the convergence. From empirical results and theoretical studies, all suggest a relatively higher probability p_c for crossover in the range of 0.6 to 0.95, whereas the mutation probability p_m is typically very low, around 0.001 to 0.05. These values correspond to a high degree of mixing and exploitation and a relatively lower degree of exploration. In practice, this means that genetic algorithms can often converge well and in many cases the global optimality can be achieved easily. The selection or survival of the fittest provides a good mechanism to select the best solution; elitism can guarantee that the best solution will remain in the population, which will enhance the convergence of the algorithm. However, the global optimality will be reachable under certain conditions, and mutation can be considered a double-edged sword; it can increase the probability of finding the global optimality while at the same time slowing down the convergence.

2.3.3 Differential Evolution

Differential evolution (DE) was developed by R. Storn and K. Price in 1996 and 1997 [23,24]. In fact, modern DE has strong similarity to the traditional mutation operator in the traditional pattern search. In fact, the mutation in DE can be viewed as the generalized pattern search in any random direction $(\boldsymbol{x}_p - \boldsymbol{x}_q)$ by

$$\boldsymbol{x}_i = \boldsymbol{x}_r + F(\boldsymbol{x}_p - \boldsymbol{x}_q), \tag{2.13}$$

where F is the differential weight in the range of $[0, 2]$. Here r, p, q, i are four different integers generated by random permutation.

In addition, DE also has a crossover operator that is controlled by a crossover probability $C_r \in [0, 1]$, and the actual crossover can be carried out in two ways: binomial and exponential. Selection is essentially the same as that used in genetic algorithms. It is to select the most fit, and, for the minimization problem, the minimum objective value. Therefore, we have

$$\boldsymbol{x}_i^{t+1} = \begin{cases} \boldsymbol{u}_i^{t+1} & \text{if } f(\boldsymbol{u}_i^{t+1}) \leq f(\boldsymbol{x}_i^t), \\ \boldsymbol{x}_i^t & \text{otherwise.} \end{cases} \tag{2.14}$$

Most studies have focused on the choice of F, C_r, and the population size n as well as the modification of the mutation scheme. In addition, it can be clearly seen that selection is also used when the condition in the preceding equation is checked. Almost all variants of DE use crossover, mutation, and selection, and the main differences are in the step of mutation and crossover. For example, DE/Rand/1/Bin use the three vectors for mutation and binomial crossover. There are more than 10 different variants [22].

2.3.4 Ant and Bee Algorithms

Ant algorithms, especially the ant colony optimization developed by M. Dorigo [5,6], mimic the foraging behavior of social ants. Primarily, all ant algorithms use pheromone as a chemical messenger and the pheromone concentration as the indicator of quality solutions to a problem of interest. From an implementation point of view, solutions are related to the pheromone concentration, leading to routes and paths marked by the higher pheromone concentrations as better solutions to questions such as discrete combinatorial problems.

Looking closely at ant colony optimization, we see that random route generation is primarily mutation, whereas pheromone-based selection provides a mechanism for selecting shorter routes. There is no explicit crossover in ant algorithms. However, mutation is not as simple an action as flipping digits in genetic algorithms; the new solutions are essentially generated by fitness-proportional mutation. For example, the probability of ants in a network problem at a particular node i to choose the route from node i to node j is given by

$$p_{ij} = \frac{\phi_{ij}^{\alpha} d_{ij}^{\beta}}{\sum_{i,j=1}^{n} \phi_{ij}^{\alpha} d_{ij}^{\beta}}, \tag{2.15}$$

where $\alpha > 0$ and $\beta > 0$ are the influence parameters, ϕ_{ij} is the pheromone concentration on the route between i and j, and d_{ij} is the desirability of the same route. The selection is subtly related to some *a priori* knowledge about the route, such as the distance s_{ij} is often used so that $d_{ij} \propto 1/s_{ij}$.

On the other hand, *bee algorithms* do not usually use pheromone [20]. For example, in the artificial bee colony (ABC) optimization algorithm [15], the bees in a colony are divided into three groups: employed bees (forager bees), onlooker bees (observer bees), and scouts. Randomization is carried out by scout bees and employed bees, and both are mainly mutation. Selection is related to honey or objective. Again, there is no explicit crossover.

Both ACO and ABC use only mutation and fitness-related selection, and they can have good global search ability. In general, they can explore the search space relatively effectively, but convergence may be slow because it lacks crossover, and thus the subspace exploitation ability is very limited. In fact, the lack of crossover is very common in many metaheuristic algorithms.

In terms of exploration and exploitation, both ant and bee algorithms have strong exploration ability, but their exploitation ability is comparatively low. This may explain why they can perform reasonably well for some tough optimization, but the computational efforts, such as the number of function evaluations, can be very high.

2.3.5 Particle Swarm Optimization

Particle swarm optimization (PSO) was developed by Kennedy and Eberhart in 1995 [17] based on swarm behavior, such as fish and bird schooling in nature. In essence, the position and velocity of a particle, $\boldsymbol{x}_i$ and $\boldsymbol{v}_i$, respectively, can be updated as follows:

$$\boldsymbol{v}_i^{t+1} = \boldsymbol{v}_i^t + \alpha \boldsymbol{\epsilon}_1 [\boldsymbol{g}^* - \boldsymbol{x}_i^t] + \beta \boldsymbol{\epsilon}_2 [\boldsymbol{x}_i^* - \boldsymbol{x}_i^t], \tag{2.16}$$

$$\boldsymbol{x}_i^{t+1} = \boldsymbol{x}_i^t + \boldsymbol{v}_i^{t+1}, \tag{2.17}$$

where $\boldsymbol{\epsilon}_1$ and $\boldsymbol{\epsilon}_2$ are two random vectors and with each entry taking the values between 0 and 1. The parameters α and β are the learning parameters or acceleration constants, which can typically be taken as, say, $\alpha \approx \beta \approx 2$.

By comparing the previous equations with the pattern search in Section 2.3, we can see that the new position is generated by a pattern-search-type mutation, whereas selection is implicitly done by using the current global best solution $\boldsymbol{g}^*$ found so far as well as through the individual best $\boldsymbol{x}_i^*$. However, the role of individual best is not quite clear, though the current global best seems very important for selection, as is shown in the accelerated particle swarm optimization [17,29,37].

Therefore, PSO consists of mainly mutation and selection. There is no crossover in PSO, which means that PSO can have high mobility in particles with a high degree of exploration. However, the use of $\boldsymbol{g}^*$ seems strongly selective, which may be like a double-edged sword. Its advantage is that it helps speed up the convergence by drawing toward the current best $\boldsymbol{g}^*$, while at the same time it may lead to premature convergence, even though this may not be the true optimal solution of the problem of interest.

2.3.6 The Firefly Algorithm

The *firefly algorithm* (FA) was developed by Xin-She Yang in 2008 [29,32,33] and is based on the flashing patterns and behaviour of tropical fireflies. FA is simple, flexible, and easy to implement.

The movement of a firefly i is attracted to another, more attractive (brighter) firefly j as determined by

$$\boldsymbol{x}_i^{t+1} = \boldsymbol{x}_i^t + \beta_0 e^{-\gamma r_{ij}^2} (\boldsymbol{x}_j^t - \boldsymbol{x}_i^t) + \alpha\, \boldsymbol{\epsilon}_i^t, \tag{2.18}$$

where the second term is due to the attraction, and β_0 is the attractiveness at zero distance $r = 0$. The third term is randomization, with α being the randomization parameter, and $\boldsymbol{\epsilon}_i^t$ is a vector of random numbers drawn from a Gaussian distribution at time t. Other studies also use the randomization in terms of $\boldsymbol{\epsilon}_i^t$ that can easily be extended to other distributions, such as Lévy flights [32,33]. A comprehensive review of the firefly algorithm and its variants has been carried out by Fister et al. [8].

From the preceding equation, we can see that mutation is used for both local and global search. When $\boldsymbol{\epsilon}_i^t$ is drawn from a Gaussian distribution and Lévy flights, it produces mutation on a larger scale. On the other hand, if α is chosen to be a very small value, then mutation can be very small and thus limited to a subspace. Interestingly, there is no explicit selection in the formula because $\boldsymbol{g}^*$ is not used in FA. However, during the update in the two loops in FA, ranking as well as selection is used.

One novel feature of FA is that attraction is used, the first of its kind in any SI-based algorithm. Since local attraction is stronger than long-distance attraction, the population in FA can automatically subdivide into multiple subgroups, and each group can potentially swarm around a local mode. Among all the local modes, there is always a global best solution that is the true optimality of the problem. FA can deal with multimodal problems naturally and efficiently.

From Eq. (2.18), we can see that FA degenerates into a variant of differential evolution when $\gamma = 0$ and $\alpha = 0$. In addition, when $\beta_0 = 0$, it degenerates into simulated annealing (SA). Further, when $\boldsymbol{x}_j^t$ is replaced by $\boldsymbol{g}^*$, FA also becomes the accelerated PSO. Therefore, DE, accelerated particle swarm optimization (APSO), and SA are special cases of the firefly algorithm, and thus FA can have the advantages of all these three algorithms. It is no surprise that FA can be versatile and efficient and can perform better than other algorithms such as GA and PSO.

2.3.7 Cuckoo Search

Cuckoo search (CS) is one of the latest nature-inspired metaheuristic algorithms, developed in 2009 by Xin-She Yang and Suash Deb [39]. CS is based on the brood parasitism of some cuckoo species. In addition, this algorithm is enhanced by the so-called Lévy flights [21] rather than by simple isotropic random walks. Recent studies show that CS is potentially far more efficient than PSO and genetic algorithms [11,12,40,41,26].

CS uses a balanced combination of a local random walk and the global explorative random walk, controlled by a switching parameter p_a. The local random walk can be written as

$$x_i^{t+1} = x_i^t + \alpha s \otimes H(p_a - \epsilon) \otimes (x_j^t - x_k^t), \tag{2.19}$$

where x_j^t and x_k^t are two different solutions selected randomly by random permutation, $H(u)$ is a Heaviside function, ϵ is a random number drawn from a uniform distribution, and s is the step size. Here, the $\otimes$ means the entry-wise product.

On the other hand, the global random walk is carried out by using Lévy flights [21]:

$$x_i^{t+1} = x_i^t + \alpha L(s, \lambda), \tag{2.20}$$

where

$$L(s, \lambda) = \frac{\lambda \Gamma(\lambda) \sin(\pi \lambda/2)}{\pi} \frac{1}{s^{1+\lambda}}, \quad (s \gg s_0 > 0). \tag{2.21}$$

Here $\alpha > 0$ is the step size scaling factor, which should be related to the scales of the problem of interest.

CS has two distinct advantages over other algorithms such as GA and SA: efficient random walks and balanced mixing. Since Lévy flights are usually far more efficient than any other random-walk-based randomization techniques, CS can be very efficient in global search. In fact, recent studies show that CS can have guaranteed global convergence [27]. In addition, the similarity between eggs can produce better new solutions, which is essentially fitness-proportional generation with a good mixing ability. In other words, CS has varying mutation realized by Lévy flights, and the fitness-proportional generation of new solutions based on similarity provides a subtle form of crossover. In addition, selection is carried out by using p_a where the good solutions are passed on to next generations, whereas not-so-good solutions are replaced by new solutions. Furthermore, simulations also show that CS can have autozooming ability in the sense that new solutions can automatically zoom into the region where the promising global optimality is located.

In addition, Eq. (2.20) is essentially the generalized simulated annealing in the framework of Markov chains. In Eq. (2.19), if $p_a = 1$ and $\alpha s \in [0, 1]$, CS can degenerate into a variant of differential evolution. Furthermore, if we replace x_j^t by the current best solution g^*, then (2.19) can further degenerate into accelerated particle swarm optimization (APSO) [37]. This means that SA, DE, and APSO are special cases of CS, and that is one of the reasons that CS is so efficient.

In essence, CS has strong mutation at both local and global scales, while good mixing is carried out by using solution similarity, which also plays the role of equivalent crossover. Selection is done by elitism, that is, a good fraction of solutions will be passed on to the next generation. Without the explicit use of g_*, we may also overcome the premature convergence drawback, as observed in particle swarm optimization.

2.3.8 The Bat Algorithm

The metaheuristic *bat algorithm* (BA) was developed by Xin-She Yang in 2010 [34]. It was inspired by the echolocation behavior of microbats. It is the first algorithm of its kind to use frequency tuning. Each bat is associated with a velocity $\boldsymbol{v}_i^t$ and a location $\boldsymbol{x}_i^t$, at iteration t, in a d-dimensional search or solution space. Among all the bats, there exists a current best solution $\boldsymbol{x}_*$. Therefore, the preceding three rules can be translated into the updating equations for $\boldsymbol{x}_i^t$ and velocities $\boldsymbol{v}_i^t$:

$$f_i = f_{\min} + (f_{\max} - f_{\min})\beta, \tag{2.22}$$

$$\boldsymbol{v}_i^t = \boldsymbol{v}_i^{t-1} + \left(\boldsymbol{x}_i^{t-1} - \boldsymbol{x}_*\right) f_i, \tag{2.23}$$

$$\boldsymbol{x}_i^t = \boldsymbol{x}_i^{t-1} + \boldsymbol{v}_i^t, \tag{2.24}$$

where $\beta \in [0, 1]$ is a random vector drawn from a uniform distribution.

The loudness and pulse emission rates are regulated by the following equations:

$$A_i^{t+1} = \alpha A_i^t, \tag{2.25}$$

and

$$r_i^{t+1} = r_i^0[1 - \exp(-\gamma t)], \tag{2.26}$$

where $0 < \alpha < 1$ and $\gamma > 0$ are constants. In essence, here α is similar to the cooling factor of a cooling schedule in simulated annealing.

BA has been extended to the multiobjective bat algorithm (MOBA) by Yang [36,38], and preliminary results suggest that it is very efficient.

In BA, frequency tuning essentially acts as mutation, whereas selection pressure is relatively constant via the use of the current best solution $\boldsymbol{x}_*$ found so far. There is no explicit crossover; however, mutation varies due to the variations of loudness and pulse emission. In addition, the variations of loudness and pulse emission rates also provide an autozooming ability so that exploitation becomes intensive as the search approaches the global optimality.

2.3.9 Harmony Search

Harmony search (HS) is a music-inspired algorithm developed by Zong Woo Geem et al. in 2001 [13]. It is not swarm-intelligence-based, but it is a metaheuristic algorithm [31]. In the standard HS, solutions are represented in terms of a population of harmonies, using the following three choices or rules (of a musician playing a piece of music): (1) play any famous piece of music from memory, (2) play something similar to a known piece (pitch adjustment), and (3) compose new or random notes. HS uses mainly mutation and selection, whereas crossover is not explicitly used. The first rule corresponds to selection or elitism, and the second and third rules are mutation.

Mutation can be local and global in HS. For example, pitch adjustment (the second rule) uses the following equation:

$$\boldsymbol{x}_{new} = \boldsymbol{x}_{old} + b_w \varepsilon, \tag{2.27}$$

where b_w is the bandwidth of the pitch adjustment, whereas ε is a random number drawn from $[-1, 1]$. This is a local random walk, and the distance of the random walk is controlled by the bandwidth. This part can be considered a local mutation action with an equivalent mutation rate of 0.1 to 0.3.

The third rule is essentially mutation on a larger scale, which is essentially equivalent to random walks. The selection is controlled by the probability of choosing a harmony from harmony memory. Similar to genetic algorithms, this choice of harmonies from the population is high, with a typical value of 0.9, which enables the system to converge in a subspace. However, this may be at the expense of reduced probability of finding the global optimality in some highly nonlinear problems.

2.3.10 The Flower Algorithm

The *flower pollination algorithm* (FPA) was developed by Xin-She Yang in 2012 [42], inspired by the flower pollination process of flowering plants. It has been extended to multiobjective optimization problems and found to be very efficient [43]. For simplicity, we use the following four rules:

1. Biotic and cross-pollination can be considered global pollination process, and pollen-carrying pollinators move in a way that obeys Lévy flights (Rule 1).
2. For local pollination, abiotic pollination and self-pollination are used (Rule 2).
3. Pollinators such as insects can develop flower constancy, which is equivalent to a reproduction probability that is proportional to the similarity of two flowers involved (Rule 3).
4. The interaction or switching of local pollination and global pollination can be controlled by a switch probability $p \in [0, 1]$, with a slight bias toward local pollination (Rule 4).

To formulate updating formulae, we must convert these rules into updating equations. For example, in the global pollination step, flower pollen gametes are carried by pollinators such as insects, and pollen can travel over a long distance because insects can often fly and move in a much longer range. Therefore, Rule 1 and flower constancy can be represented mathematically as

$$\boldsymbol{x}_i^{t+1} = \boldsymbol{x}_i^t + \gamma L(\lambda) \left(\boldsymbol{g}_* - \boldsymbol{x}_i^t \right), \tag{2.28}$$

where $\boldsymbol{x}_i^t$ is the pollen i or solution vector $\boldsymbol{x}_i$ at iteration t, and $\boldsymbol{g}_*$ is the current best solution found among all solutions at the current generation/iteration. Here γ is a scaling factor to control the step size.

Here $L(\lambda)$ is the parameter that corresponds to the strength of the pollination, which essentially is also a step size. Since insects may move over a long distance with various distance steps, we can use a Lévy flight to mimic this characteristic efficiently. That is, we draw $L > 0$ from a Lévy distribution

$$L \sim \frac{\lambda \Gamma(\lambda) \sin(\pi \lambda / 2)}{\pi} \frac{1}{s^{1+\lambda}}, \quad (s \gg s_0 > 0). \tag{2.29}$$

Here $\Gamma(\lambda)$ is the standard gamma function, and this distribution is valid for large steps $s > 0$. This step is essentially a global mutation step, which enables us to explore the search space more efficiently.

For the local pollination, both Rules 2 and 3 can be represented as

$$x_i^{t+1} = x_i^t + \epsilon \left(x_j^t - x_k^t \right), \tag{2.30}$$

where x_j^t and x_k^t are pollen from different flowers of the same plant species. This essentially mimics the flower constancy in a limited neighborhood. Mathematically, if x_j^t and x_k^t come from the same species or are selected from the same population, this equivalently becomes a local random walk if we draw ϵ from a uniform distribution in [0,1]. In essence, this is a local mutation and mixing step, which can help to converge in a subspace.

In principle, flower pollination activities can occur at all scales, both local and global. But in reality, adjacent flower patches or flowers in the not-so-far-away neighborhood are more likely to be pollinated by local flower pollen than by those far away. To mimic this feature, we can effectively use a switch probability (Rule 4) or a proximity probability p to switch between common global pollination to intensive local pollination. To start with, we can use a naïve value of $p = 0.5$ as an initial value. A preliminary parametric showed that $p = 0.8$ may work better for most applications.

Selection is achieved by choosing the best solutions and passing them on to the next generation. It also explicitly uses g_* to find the best solution as both selection and elitism. There is no explicit crossover, which is also true for many other algorithms such as particle swarm optimization and harmony search.

2.3.11 Other Algorithms

Many other algorithms have appeared in the literature. Fister Jr. et al. provided a brief survey [9], which may require more extensive analysis and comparisons. However, because this is not the main focus of this book, we will not go into more detail about these algorithms.

One thing we may notice by analyzing these algorithms is that mutation and selection are always used, whereas crossover is not used in most of these algorithms. This may raise the question and further need to analyze what exactly is the role of crossover. As we discussed earlier, crossover provides good mixing and convergence enhancement in a subspace, but if the crossover rate is too high, it may lead to premature convergence. On the other hand, too much exploration by mutation may slow down the convergence. The lack of explicit crossover in many algorithms may explain the observations or fact that many new algorithms can indeed provide better guarantee of the global optimality, but the number of iterations is not significantly reduced compared with those used in genetic algorithms and differential evolution. The only exception is the eagle strategy and coevolutionary algorithms.

Therefore, there is a strong need to further investigate how the two-stage eagle strategy and coevolutionary methods can work better. In addition, systematic tuning of parameters in algorithms and careful control of these algorithm-dependent parameters may be very useful in understanding how these algorithms behave and how to improve them in practice.

2.4 Parameter Tuning and Parameter Control

All nature-inspired algorithms have algorithm-dependent parameters. The setting of these parameters can largely influence the behavior and performance of an algorithm. How to best tune and control these algorithms is still a very challenging problem [7].

2.4.1 Parameter Tuning

In order to tune $A(\Phi, \boldsymbol{p})$ (for a given problem Φ and algorithm A with a set of parameters $\boldsymbol{p}$) so as to achieve its best performance, a parameter-tuning tool, i.e., a tuner, is needed. As with tuning a high-precision machinery, sophisticated tools are required. For tuning parameters in an algorithm, what tool can we use? One way is to use a better, existing tool (say, algorithm B) to tune an algorithm A. Now the question may become: How do you know B is better? Is B well tuned? If yes, how do you tune B in the first place? Naïvely, if we use another tool (say, algorithm C) to tune B. Now, again the question becomes, how has algorithm C been tuned? This can go on and on until the end of a long chain, say, algorithm Q. In the end, we need some tool/algorithm to tune this Q, which again comes back to the original question: How do we tune an algorithm A so that it can perform best?

It is worth pointing out that even if we have good tools to tune an algorithm, the best parameter setting and thus performance all depend on the performance measures used in the tuning. Ideally, the parameters should be robust enough to handle minor parameter changes, random seeds, and even problem instance [7]. However, in practice, they may not be achievable. According to Eiben [7], parameter tuning can be divided into iterative and noniterative tuners, single-stage and multistage tuners. The meanings of these terms are self-explanatory. In terms of the actual tuning methods, existing methods include sampling methods, screening methods, model-based methods, and metaheuristic methods. These methods' success and effectiveness can vary, and thus there are no well-established methods for universal parameter tuning.

2.4.2 Hyperoptimization

From our earlier observations and discussions, it is clear that parameter tuning is the process of optimizing the optimization algorithm; therefore, it is a hyperoptimization problem. In essence, a tuner is a meta-optimization tool for tuning algorithms.

For a standard unconstrained optimization problem, the aim is to find the global minimum f_* of a function $f(\boldsymbol{x})$ in a d-dimensional space. That is,

$$\text{Minimize } f(\boldsymbol{x}), \quad \boldsymbol{x} = (x_1, x_2, \ldots, x_d). \tag{2.31}$$

Once we choose an algorithm A to solve this optimization problem, the algorithm will find a minimum solution $f_{\min}$ that may be close to the true global minimum f_*. For a given tolerance δ, this may require t_δ iterations to achieve $|f_{\min} - f_*| \leq \delta$. Obviously, the actual t_δ will largely depend on both the problem objective $f(\boldsymbol{x})$ and the parameters $\boldsymbol{p}$ of the algorithm used.

The main aim of algorithm tuning is to find the best parameter setting $\boldsymbol{p}_*$ so that the computational cost or the number of iterations t_δ is the minimum. Thus, parameter tuning as a hyperoptimization problem can be written as

$$\text{Minimize } t_\delta = A(f(\boldsymbol{x}), \boldsymbol{p}), \tag{2.32}$$

whose optimality is $\boldsymbol{p}_*$.

Ideally, the parameter vector $\boldsymbol{p}_*$ should be sufficiently robust. For different types of problems, any slight variation in $\boldsymbol{p}_*$ should not much affect the performance of A, which means that $\boldsymbol{p}_*$ should lie in a flat range rather than at a sharp peak in the parameter landscape.

2.4.3 Multiobjective View

If we look at the algorithm-tuning process from a different perspective, it is possible to construct it as a multiobjective optimization problem with two objectives: one objective $f(\boldsymbol{x})$ for the problem Φ and one objective t_δ for the algorithm. That is,

$$\text{Minimize } f(\boldsymbol{x}) \text{ and Minimize } t_\delta = A(f(\boldsymbol{x}), \boldsymbol{p}), \tag{2.33}$$

where t_δ is the (average) number of iterations needed to achieve a given tolerance δ so that the found minimum $f_{\min}$ is close enough to the true global minimum f_*, satisfying $|f_{\min} - f_*| \leq \delta$.

This means that for a given tolerance δ, there will be a set of best parameter settings with a minimum t_δ. As a result, the bi-objectives will form a Pareto front. In principle, this bi-objective optimization problem (2.33) can be solved by any methods that are suitable for multiobjective optimization. But as δ is usually given, a natural way to solve this problem is to use the so-called ϵ-constraint or δ-constraint methods. The naming may be dependent on the notations; however, we will use δ-constraints here in this chapter.

For a given $\delta \geq 0$, we change one of the objectives (i.e.. $f(\boldsymbol{x})$) into a constraint, and thus the preceding problem (2.33) becomes a single-objective optimization problem with a constraint. That is,

$$\text{Minimize } t_\delta = A(f(\boldsymbol{x}), \boldsymbol{p}), \tag{2.34}$$

subject to

$$f(\boldsymbol{x}) \leq \delta. \tag{2.35}$$

Though the idea becomes clearer in this framework, we still need to choose a good tool to solve this multiobjective problem. Recently, Xin-She Yang et al. proposed a method for a self-tuning algorithm, which is outlined in detail in a later chapter in this book. Briefly speaking, this bi-objective optimization problem can be solved by using the algorithm A itself in an iterative manner, which essentially achieves parameter tuning and problem solving simultaneously.

2.4.4 Parameter Control

Related to parameter tuning, there is another issue of parameter control. Parameter values after parameter tuning are often fixed during iterations, whereas parameters should vary during iterations for the parameter control purpose. The idea of parameter control is to vary the parameters so that the algorithm of interest can provide the best convergence rate and thus may achieve the best performance. Again, parameter control is another tough optimization problem to be resolved. In the bat algorithm (BA), some basic form of parameter control has been attempted and found to be very efficient [34]. By controlling the loudness and pulse emission rate, BA can automatically switch from explorative moves to local exploitation that focuses on the promising regions when the global optimality may be nearby. Similarly, the cooling schedule in simulated annealing can be considered a form of basic parameter control.

On the other hand, eagle strategy (ES) is a two-stage iterative strategy with iterative switches [35]. ES starts with a population of agents in the explorative mode, then switches to the exploitation stage for local intensive search. Then it starts again with another set of explorative moves and subsequently turns into a new exploitation stage. This iterative, restart strategy has been found to be very efficient.

Both parameter tuning and parameter control are under active research. More efficient methods are strongly needed for this purpose.

2.5 Discussions

Many optimization algorithms are based on the so-called swarm intelligence and use population-based approaches. Most use some sort of three-key evolutionary operators: crossover, mutation, and selection. However, almost all algorithms use mutation and selection, whereas crossover may appear in some subtle way in some algorithms. Crossover is efficient in exploitation and can often provide good convergence in a local subspace. If this subspace is where the global optimality lies, then crossover with elitism can almost guarantee achievement of global optimality. However, if the subspace of crossover is not in the region where the global optimality lies, there is a danger of premature convergence.

The extensive use of mutation and selection can typically enable a stochastic algorithm to have a high ability of exploration. Since the exploitation is relatively low, the convergence rate is usually low compared with that of traditional methods such as Newton-Raphson. As a result, most metaheuristic algorithms can usually perform well for nonlinear problems, including relatively tough optimization. However, the number of function evaluations can be very high.

The role of crossover and mutation in exploration is rather subtle, whereas selection as an exploitation mechanism can be simple and yet effective. However, it is still not clear how the combination of crossover, mutation, and selection can directly link to the balance of exploration and exploitation. In fact, this is still an open question. For example, in genetic algorithms, the probability of crossover can be as high as 0.95, whereas the mutation can be typically low, in the range of 0.01 to 0.05. In comparison with other algorithms, exploration seems low, but genetic algorithms have been proven very effective. On the other hand, mutation-related Lévy flights in cuckoo search can have a high exploration ability, yet cuckoo search can converge very quickly. At the same time, it is not clear what percentage of the search is in exploration in the standard firefly algorithm, yet it has been shown that the firefly algorithm is very effective in dealing with multimodal, highly nonlinear problems.

Even in the standard particle swarm optimization, it is not clear what percentage of the search iterations is in the exploration. The use of the current global best can be advantageous and disadvantageous as well. The current global best may help speed up the convergence, but it may also lead to the wrong optimality if the current global best is obtained from a biased set of samples drawn from a subspace where a local optimum (not the global optimum) is located. All these points suggest that it is unknown how to achieve optimal balance of exploration and exploitation by tuning the combination of evolutionary operators.

In fact, fine balance cannot be achieved by putting together all evolutionary operators in a good way without tuning parameters. From experience, we know that the setting or values of any algorithm-dependent parameters can significantly affect the performance of an algorithm. To get good performance, we need to find the right values for parameters. In other words, parameters need to be fine-tuned so that the algorithm can perform to the best degree. Parameter tuning is still an active area of research [7].

Despite the importance of these problems, little progress has been made. On the contrary, there is some diversion in research efforts away from important problems in the current literature. Nature has evolved into millions of diverse species with a diverse range of characteristics, but this does not mean that researchers should develop millions of different algorithms, such as a grass algorithm, leaves algorithm, beatles algorithm, sky algorithm, universe algorithm, or hooligan algorithm. Emphasis should focus on solving important problems.

However, this does not mean that new algorithms should *not* be developed. The research community should encourage truly novel and efficient algorithms in terms of better evolutionary operators and better balance of exploration and exploitation.

2.6 Summary

Optimization algorithms based on swarm intelligence can have some distinct advantages over traditional methods. By using theories of dynamical systems and self-organization as well as the framework of Markov chains, we have provided a critical analysis of some recently nature-inspired algorithms. The analysis has focused on the way of achieving exploration and exploitation and the basic components of evolutionary operators such as crossover, mutation, and selection of the fittest.

Through analysis, it is found that most SI-based algorithms use mutation and selection to achieve exploration and exploitation. Some algorithms use crossover as well, but most do not. Mutation helps us explore on a global scale, whereas crossover explores in a subspace and thus is more likely to lead to convergence. Selection provides a driving mechanism to select the promising states or solutions.

The analysis also implies that there is room for improvement. Some algorithms such as PSO may lack mixing and crossover, and therefore hybridization may be useful to enhance their performance.

It is worth pointing out that the preceding analysis is based on the system behavior for continuous optimization problems, and it can be expected that these results are still valid for combinatorial optimization problems. However, care should be taken in combinatorial problems where neighborhood may have a different meaning, and therefore the subspace concept may also be different. Further analysis may help provide more elaborate insight.

References

[1] Ashby WR. Principles of the self-organizing system. In: Von Foerster H, Zopf GW Jr, editors. Principles of self-organization: transactions of the University of Illinois symposium. London, UK: Pergamon Press; 1962. p. 255–78.

[2] Belavkin RV. Optimal measures and Markov transition kernels. J Global Optim 2013;55(2):387–416.

[3] Belavkin RV. On evolution of an information dynamic system and its generating operator. Optim Lett 2012;6(5):827–40.

[4] Blum C, Roli A. Metaheuristics in combinatorial optimization: overview and conceptual comparison. ACM Comput Surv 2003;35(2):268–308.

[5] Dorigo M. Optimization, learning, and natural algorithms, Ph.D. thesis, Politecnico di Milano, Italy; 1992.

[6] Dorigo M, Di Caro G, Gambardella LM. Ant algorithms for discrete optimization. Artif Life 1999;5(2):137–72.

[7] Eiben AE, Smit SK. Parameter tuning for configuring and analyzing evolutionary algorithms. Swarm Evol Comput 2011;1(1):19–31.

[8] Fister I, Fister Jr I, Yang XS, Brest J. A comprehensive review of firefly algorithms, Swarm and evolutionary computation; 2013. http://dx.doi.org/10.1016/j.swevo.2013.06.001

[9] Fister Jr I, Yang XS, Fister I, Brest J, Fister D. A brief review of nature-inspired algorithms for optimization. <http://arxiv.org/abs/1307.4186>; 2013.

[10] Hooke R, Jeeves TA. "Direct search" solution of numerical and statistical problems. J Assoc Comput Machinery (ACM) 1961;8(2):212–29.

[11] Gandomi AH, Yang XS, Alavi AH. Cuckoo search algorithm: a metaheuristic approach to solve structural optimization problems. Eng Comput 2013;29(1):17–35.

[12] Gandomi AH, Yang XS, Talatahari S, Deb S. Coupled eagle strategy and differential evolution for unconstrained and constrained global optimization. Comput Math Appl 2012;63(1):191–200.

[13] Geem ZW, Kim JH, Loganathan GV. A new heuristic optimization algorithm: harmony search. Simulation 2001;76(1):60–8.

[14] Holland J. Adaptation in natural and artificial systems. Cambridge, MA, USA: MIT Press; 1975.

[15] Karaboga D. An idea based on honeybee swarm for numerical optimization. Technical report TR06. Turkey; Erciyes University, 2005.

[16] Keller EF. Organisms, machines, and thunderstorms: a history of self-organization, part two. Complexity, emergence, and stable attractors. Hist Stud Nat Sci 2009;39(1):1–31.

[17] Kennedy J, Eberhart RC. Particle swarm optimization. In: Proceedings of the IEEE international conference on neural networks, Piscataway, NJ, USA; 1995. p. 1942–48.
[18] Kirkpatrick S, Gellat CD, Vecchi MP. Optimization by simulated annealing. Science 1983;220(4598):671–80.
[19] Koziel S, Yang XS. Computational optimization, methods and algorithms. Germany: Springer; 2011.
[20] Nakrani S, Tovey C. On honey bees and dynamic server allocation in internet hosting centers. Adapt Behav 2004;12(3–4):223–40.
[21] Pavlyukevich I. Lévy flights, non-local search, and simulated annealing. J Comput Phys 2007;226(2):1830–44.
[22] Price K, Storn R, Lampinen J. Differential evolution: a practical approach to global optimization. Berlin, Germany: Springer-Verlag; 2005.
[23] Storn R. On the usage of differential evolution for function optimization. In: Biennial conference of the North American fuzzy information processing society (NAFIPS), Berkeley, CA, USA; 1996. p. 519–23.
[24] Storn R, Price K. Differential evolution: a simple and efficient heuristic for global optimization over continuous spaces. J Global Optim 1997;11(4):341–59.
[25] Süli E, Mayer D. An introduction to numerical analysis. Cambridge, UK: Cambridge University Press; 2003.
[26] Walton S, Hassan O, Morgan K, Brown MR. Modified cuckoo search: a new gradient free optimization algorithm. Chaos, Solitons & Fractals 2011;44(9):710–8.
[27] Wang F, He XS, Wang Y, Yang SM. Markov model and convergence analysis based on cuckoo search algorithm. Jisuanji Gongcheng/Comput Eng 2012;38(11):181–5.
[28] Yang XS. Introduction to computational mathematics. Singapore: World Scientific Publishing Ltd; 2008.
[29] Yang XS. Nature-inspired metaheuristic algorithms. 1st ed. Bristol, UK: Luniver Press; 2008.
[30] Yang XS. Engineering optimisation: an introduction with metaheuristic applications. Wiley; 2010.
[31] Yang XS. Harmony search as a metaheuristic algorithm. In: Geem ZW, editor. Music-inspired harmony search algorithm: theory and applications. Studies in computational intelligence, vol. 191. Berlin, Germany: Springer; 2009. p. 1–14.
[32] Yang XS. Firefly algorithms for multimodal optimization. In: Stochastic algorithms: foundations and applications, SAGA 2009. Lecture notes in computer sciences, vol. 5792, 2009. p. 169–78.
[33] Yang XS. Firefly algorithm, stochastic test functions and design optimisation. Int J Bio-Inspired Comput 2010;2(2):78–84.
[34] Yang XS. A new metaheuristic bat-inspired algorithm. In: Cruz C, González JR, Pelta DA, Terrazas G, editors. Nature inspired cooperative strategies for optimization (NISCO 2010). Studies in computational intelligence, vol. 284. Berlin, Germany: Springer; 2010. p. 65–74.
[35] Yang XS, Deb S. Eagle strategy using Lévy walk and firefly algorithms for stochastic optimization. In: Cruz C, González JR, Pelta DA, Terrazas G, editors. Nature inspired cooperative strategies for optimization (NISCO 2010). Studies in computational intelligence, vol. 284. Berlin: Springer; 2010. p. 101–11.
[36] Yang XS. Bat algorithm for multi-objective optimisation. Int J Bio-Inspired Comput 2011;3(5):267–74.
[37] Yang XS, Deb S, Fong S. Accelerated particle swarm optimization and support vector machine for business optimization and applications. In: Networked digital technologies 2011. Communications in computer and information science, vol. 136; 2011. p. 53–66.

[38] Yang XS, Gandomi AH. Bat algorithm: a novel approach for global engineering optimization. Eng Comput 2012;29(5):1–18.

[39] Yang XS, Deb S. Cuckoo search via Lévy flights. In: Proceedings of world congress on nature & biologically inspired computing (NaBIC 2009). USA: IEEE Publications; 2009. p. 210–14.

[40] Yang XS, Deb S. Engineering optimization by cuckoo search. Int J Math Model Num Optim 2010;1(4):330–43.

[41] Yang XS, Deb S. Multiobjective cuckoo search for design optimization. Comput Oper Res 2013;40(6):1616–24.

[42] Yang XS. Flower pollination algorithm for global optimization. In: Unconventional computation and natural computation. Lecture notes in computer science, vol. 7445; 2012. p. 240–49.

[43] Yang XS, Karamanoglu M, He XS. Multi-objective flower algorithm for optimization. Procedia Comput Sci 2013;18:861–8.

3 Random Walks and Optimization

By analyzing the main characteristics of metaheuristic algorithms, we know that randomization plays an important role in both exploration and exploitation, or diversification and intensification. In most cases, randomization is achieved by simple random numbers that are drawn from either a uniform distribution or a Gaussian normal distribution. In other cases, more sophisticated randomization techniques such as random walks and Lévy flights are used. This chapter provides a brief review of the basic ideas and theory of random walks, Lévy flights, and Markov chains. We also discuss initialization, step sizes, the efficiency of an algorithm, and eagle strategy. This helps us gain insight into the working mechanisms of nature-inspired metaheuristic algorithms.

3.1 Random Variables

Randomization is usually realized by using pseudorandom numbers, based on some common stochastic processes. The probability density distributions for random variables are commonly uniform distributions, Gaussian distributions, power-law distribution, and Lévy distributions.

A random variable can be considered an expression whose value is the realization or outcome of events associated with a random process such as noise level on a street. The values of random variables are real, though for some variables, such as the number of cars on a road, they can only take discrete values. Such random variables are called *discrete random variables*. If a random variable such as noise at a particular location can take any real values in an interval, it is called *continuous*. If a random variable can have both continuous and discrete values, it is called a *mixed type*. Mathematically speaking, a random variable is a function that maps events to real numbers. The domain of this mapping is called the *sample space*.

For each random variable, a probability density function can be used to express its probability distribution. For example, the number of phone calls per minute and the number of users of a Web server per day all obey the Poisson distribution

$$p(n; \lambda) = \frac{\lambda^n e^{-\lambda}}{n!}, \quad (n = 0, 1, 2, \ldots), \tag{3.1}$$

where $\lambda > 0$ is a parameter that is the mean or expectation of the occurrence of the event during a unit interval.

Nature-Inspired Optimization Algorithms. http://dx.doi.org/10.1016/B978-0-12-416743-8.00003-8

Various random variables have different distributions. Gaussian distribution or normal distribution is by far the most popular because many physical variables, including light intensity, errors/uncertainty in measurements, and many other processes, obey the normal distribution:

$$p(x; \mu, \sigma^2) = \frac{1}{\sigma\sqrt{2\pi}} \exp\left[-\frac{(x-\mu)^2}{2\sigma^2}\right], \quad -\infty < x < \infty, \tag{3.2}$$

where μ is the mean and $\sigma > 0$ is the standard deviation. This normal distribution is often denoted by $N(\mu, \sigma^2)$. In the special case when $\mu = 0$ and $\sigma = 1$, it is called a *standard normal distribution*, denoted by N(0, 1).

In the context of metaheuristics, another important distribution is the so-called Lévy distribution, which is a distribution of the sum of N identically and independently distribution random variables whose Fourier transform takes the following form:

$$F_N(k) = \exp[-N|k|^{\beta}]. \tag{3.3}$$

The inverse to get the actual distribution $L(s)$ is not straightforward, since the integral

$$L(s) = \frac{1}{\pi}\int_0^{\infty} \cos(\tau s) e^{-\alpha\, \tau^{\beta}} d\tau, \quad (0 < \beta \le 2), \tag{3.4}$$

does not have analytical forms, except for a few special cases. Here $L(s)$ is called the Lévy distribution with an index β. For most applications, we can set $\alpha = 1$ for simplicity. Two special cases are $\beta = 1$ and $\beta = 2$. When $\beta = 1$, the preceding integral becomes the Cauchy distribution. When $\beta = 2$, it becomes the normal distribution. In this case, Lévy flights become the standard Brownian motion.

Mathematically speaking, we can express the integral (3.4) as an asymptotic series, and its leading-order approximation for the flight length results in a power-law distribution

$$L(s) \sim |s|^{-1-\beta}, \tag{3.5}$$

which is heavy-tailed. The variance of such a power-law distribution is infinite for $0 < \beta < 2$. The moments diverge (or are infinite) for $0 < \beta < 2$, which is a stumbling block for mathematical analysis.

3.2 Isotropic Random Walks

A *random walk* is a random process that consists of taking a series of consecutive random steps. Mathematically speaking, let S_N denote the sum of each consecutive random step X_i; then S_N forms a random walk

$$S_N = \sum_{i=1}^{N} X_i = X_1 + \cdots + X_N, \tag{3.6}$$

where X_i is a random step drawn from a random distribution. This relationship can also be written as a recursive formula

$$S_N = \sum_{i=1}^{N-1} X_i + X_N = S_{N-1} + X_N, \tag{3.7}$$

which means the next state S_N will only depend on the current existing state S_{N-1} and the motion or transition X_N from the existing state to the next state. This is typically the main property of a Markov chain, introduced later.

Here the step size or length in a random walk can be fixed or varying. Random walks have many applications in physics, economics, statistics, computer sciences, environmental science, and engineering.

Consider a scenario: a drunkard walks on a street, and at each step he can randomly go forward or backward. This forms a random walk in one dimension. If this drunkard walks on a football pitch, he can walk in any direction randomly, which becomes a two-dimensional random walk. Mathematically speaking, a random walk is given by the following equation:

$$S_{t+1} = S_t + w_t, \tag{3.8}$$

where S_t is the current location or state at t, and w_t is a step or random variable with a known distribution.

If each step or jump is carried out in the d-dimensional space, the random walk discussed earlier,

$$S_N = \sum_{i=1}^{N} X_i, \tag{3.9}$$

becomes a random walk in higher dimensions. In addition, there is no reason why each step length should be fixed. In fact, the step size can also vary according to a known distribution. If the step length obeys the Gaussian distribution, the random walk becomes the Brownian motion (see Figure 3.1).

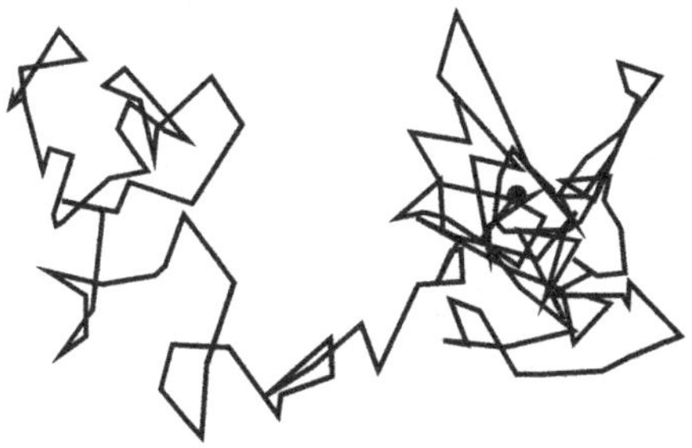

Figure 3.1 Brownian motion in 2D: A random walk with a Gaussian step-size distribution and the path of 50 steps starting at the origin (0, 0) (marked with •).

In theory, as the number of steps N increases, the central limit theorem implies that the random walk (3.9) should approach a Gaussian distribution. Because the mean of particle locations shown in Figure 3.1 is obviously zero, their variance will increase linearly with N, as shown later in this section.

Under the simplest assumptions, we know that a Gaussian distribution is stable. For a particle starting with an initial location $\boldsymbol{x}_0$, its final location $\boldsymbol{x}_N$ after N time steps is

$$\boldsymbol{x}_N = \boldsymbol{x}_0 + \sum_{i=1}^{N} \alpha_i s_i, \tag{3.10}$$

where $\alpha_i > 0$ is a parameter controlling the step sizes or scalings. If s_i is drawn from a normal distribution $N(\mu_i, \sigma_i^2)$, then the conditions of stable distributions lead to a combined Gaussian distribution

$$\boldsymbol{x}_N \sim N(\mu_*, \sigma_*^2), \tag{3.11}$$

where

$$\mu_* = \sum_{i=1}^{N} \alpha_i \mu_i, \quad \sigma_*^2 = \sum_{i=1}^{N} \alpha_i [\sigma_i^2 + (\mu_* - \mu_i)^2]. \tag{3.12}$$

We can see that the mean location changes with N and the variances increases as N increases, this makes it possible to reach any areas in the search space if N is large enough.

In the special case when $\mu_1 = \mu_2 = \cdots = \mu_N = 0$ (zero mean), $\sigma_1 = \cdots = \sigma_N = \sigma$, and $\alpha_1 = \cdots = \alpha_N = \alpha$, the above equations become

$$\mu_* = 0, \quad \sigma_*^2 = \alpha N \sigma^2. \tag{3.13}$$

A diffusion process can be viewed as a series of Brownian motions, and the motion obeys the Gaussian distribution. For this reason, standard diffusion is often referred to as the *Gaussian diffusion*. Since the mean of particle locations is obviously zero if $\mu_i = 0$, their variance will increase linearly with time $t = N$ or the number of steps. In general, in the d-dimensional space, the variance of Brownian random walks can be written as

$$\sigma^2(t) = |v_0|^2 t^2 + (2dD)t, \tag{3.14}$$

where v_0 is the drift velocity of the system. Here $D = s^2/(2\tau)$ is the effective diffusion coefficient, which is related to the step length s over a short time interval τ during each jump. If the motion at each step is not Gaussian, the diffusion is called *non-Gaussian diffusion*. If the step length obeys other distributions, we have to deal with more generalized random walks. A very special case is when the step length obeys the Lévy distribution. Such a random walk is called *Lévy flight* or *Lévy walk*.

3.3 Lévy Distribution and Lévy Flights

Loosely speaking, Lévy flights are random walks whose step length is drawn from the Lévy distribution, often in terms of a simple power-law formula $L(s) \sim |s|^{-1-\beta}$ where $0 < \beta \leq 2$ is an index. Mathematically speaking, a simple version of a Lévy distribution can be defined as

$$L(s, \gamma, \mu) = \begin{cases} \sqrt{\frac{\gamma}{2\pi}} \exp\left[-\frac{\gamma}{2(s-\mu)}\right] \frac{1}{(s-\mu)^{3/2}}, & 0 < \mu < s < \infty \\ 0 & \text{otherwise,} \end{cases} \tag{3.15}$$

where $\mu > 0$ is a minimum step and γ is a scale parameter. Clearly, as $s \to \infty$, we have

$$L(s, \gamma, \mu) \approx \sqrt{\frac{\gamma}{2\pi}} \frac{1}{s^{3/2}}. \tag{3.16}$$

This is a special case of the generalized Lévy distribution.

In general, Lévy distribution should be defined in terms of Fourier transform

$$F(k) = \exp[-\alpha|k|^{\beta}], \quad 0 < \beta \leq 2, \tag{3.17}$$

where α is a scale parameter. The inverse of this integral is not easy, since it does not have analytical form except for a few special cases.

For the case of $\beta = 2$, we have

$$F(k) = \exp[-\alpha k^2], \tag{3.18}$$

whose inverse Fourier transform corresponds to a Gaussian distribution. Another special case is $\beta = 1$, and we have

$$F(k) = \exp[-\alpha|k|], \tag{3.19}$$

which corresponds to a Cauchy distribution

$$p(x, \gamma, \mu) = \frac{1}{\pi} \frac{\gamma}{\gamma^2 + (x \quad \mu)^2}, \tag{3.20}$$

where μ is the location parameter while γ controls the scale of this distribution.

For the general case, the inverse integral

$$L(s) = \frac{1}{\pi} \int_0^{\infty} \cos(ks) \exp[-\alpha|k|^{\beta}] dk \tag{3.21}$$

can be estimated only when s is large. We have

$$L(s) \to \frac{\alpha\beta\Gamma(\beta)\sin(\pi\beta/2)}{\pi|s|^{1+\beta}}, \quad s \to \infty. \tag{3.22}$$

Here $\Gamma(z)$ is the Gamma function

$$\Gamma(z) = \int_0^{\infty} t^{z-1} e^{-t}\, dt. \tag{3.23}$$

In the case when $z = n$ is an integer, we have $\Gamma(n) = (n-1)!$.

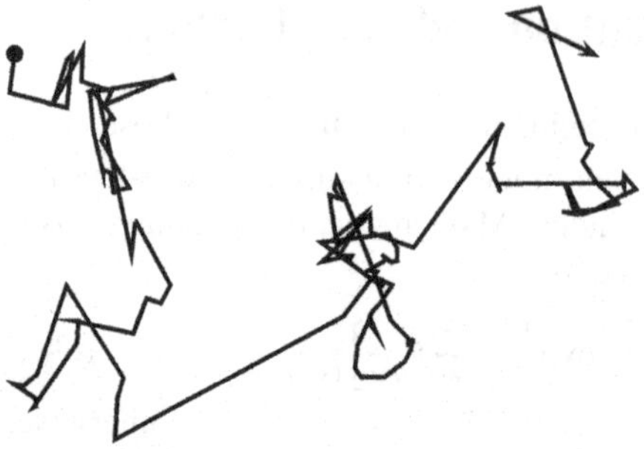

Figure 3.2 Lévy flights in 50 consecutive steps starting at the origin (0, 0) (marked with •).

Lévy flights are more efficient than Brownian random walks in exploring unknown, large-scale search spaces. There are many reasons to explain this efficiency, one of which is due to the fact that the variance of Lévy flights

$$\sigma^2(t) \sim t^{3-\beta}, \quad 1 \leq \beta \leq 2, \tag{3.24}$$

increases much faster than the linear relationship (i.e., $\sigma^2(t) \sim t$) of Brownian random walks [7].

Figure 3.2 shows the path of Lévy flights of 50 steps starting from (0, 0) with $\beta = 1$. It is worth pointing out that a power-law distribution is often linked to some scale-free characteristics, and Lévy flights can thus show self-similarity and fractal behavior in the flight patterns.

From the implementation point of view, the generation of random numbers with Lévy flights consists of two steps: the choice of a random direction and the generation of steps that obey the chosen Lévy distribution. The generation of a direction should be drawn from a uniform distribution, whereas the generation of steps is quite tricky. There are a few ways of achieving this, one of the most efficient and yet straightforward of which is to use the so-called Mantegna algorithm for a symmetric Lévy stable distribution. Here *symmetric* means that the steps can be positive and negative.

A random variable U and its probability distribution can be called stable if a linear combination of its two identical copies (or U_1 and U_2) obeys the same distribution. That is, $aU_1 + bU_2$ has the same distribution as $cU + d$, where $a, b > 0$ and $c, d \in \Re$. If $d = 0$, it is called strictly stable. Gaussian, Cauchy, and Lévy distributions are all stable distributions.

In Mantegna's algorithm, the step length s can be calculated by

$$s = \frac{u}{|v|^{1/\beta}}, \tag{3.25}$$

where u and v are drawn from normal distributions. That is,

$$u \sim N(0, \sigma_u^2), \quad v \sim N(0, \sigma_v^2), \tag{3.26}$$

where

$$\sigma_u = \left\{ \frac{\Gamma(1+\beta)\sin(\pi\beta/2)}{\Gamma[(1+\beta)/2]\beta 2^{(\beta-1)/2}} \right\}^{1/\beta}, \quad \sigma_v = 1. \tag{3.27}$$

This distribution (for s) obeys the expected Lévy distribution for $|s| \geq |s_0|$, where s_0 is the smallest step. In principle, $|s_0| \gg 0$, but in reality s_0 can be taken as a sensible value, such as $s_0 = 0.1$ to 1.

Studies show that Lévy flights can maximize the efficiency of resource searches in uncertain environments. In fact, Lévy flights have been observed among foraging patterns of albatrosses, fruit flies, and spider monkeys. Even humans such as the Ju/'hoansi hunter-gatherers can trace paths of Lévy-flight patterns. In addition, Lévy flights have many applications. Many physical phenomena, such as the diffusion of fluorescent molecules, cooling behavior, and noise, could show Lévy-flight characteristics under the right conditions [1,11–15,17].

3.4 Optimization as Markov Chains

In every aspect, a simple random walk we discussed earlier can be considered as a Markov chain.

3.4.1 Markov Chain

Briefly speaking, a random variable ζ is a Markov process if the transition probability, from state $\zeta_t = S_i$ at time t to another state $\zeta_{t+1} = S_j$, depends only on the current state ζ_i. That is,

$$\begin{aligned} P(i, j) &\equiv P(\zeta_{t+1} = S_j | \zeta_0 = S_p, \ldots, \zeta_t = S_i) \\ &= P(\zeta_{t+1} = S_j | \zeta_t = S_i), \end{aligned} \tag{3.28}$$

which is independent of the states before t. In addition, the sequence of random variables $(\zeta_0, \zeta_1, \ldots, \zeta_n)$ generated by a Markov process is subsequently called a *Markov chain*. The transition probability $P(i, j) \equiv P(i \to j) = P_{ij}$ is also referred to as the *transition kernel* of the Markov chain.

If we rewrite the random walk relationship (3.7) with a random move governed by w_t, which depends on the transition probability P, we have

$$S_{t+1} = S_t + w_t, \quad w_t \sim P, \tag{3.29}$$

which indeed has the properties of a Markov chain. Here $w_t \sim P$ means the random variable w_t obeys the probability distribution P, i.e., w_t is drawn from P. Therefore, a random walk is a Markov chain. In fact, simulated annealing is one of the well-known Markov chain algorithms [9].

We use $\pi_i(t)$ to denote the probability of the chain in the state i (or more accurately, S_i) at time t. This means that $\boldsymbol{\pi}(t) = (\pi_1, \ldots, \pi_m)^T$ is a vector of the state space. At time $t = 0$, $\boldsymbol{\pi}(0)$ is the initial vector.

The k-step transition probability $P_{ij}^{(k)}$ from state i to state j can be calculated by

$$P_{ij}^{(k)} = P(\zeta_{t+k} = S_j | \zeta_t = S_i), \tag{3.30}$$

where $k > 0$ is an integer. The matrix $\boldsymbol{P} = [P_{ij}^{(1)}] = [P_{ij}]$ is the transition matrix, which is a right stochastic matrix. A *right stochastic matrix* is defined as a probability (square) matrix whose entries are nonnegative, with each row summing to 1. That is,

$$P_{ij} > 0, \quad \sum_{j=1}^{m} P_{ij} = 1, \quad i = 1, 2, \ldots, m. \tag{3.31}$$

It is worth pointing out that the left transition matrix, though less widely used, is a stochastic matrix with each column summing to 1.

A Markov chain is regular if some power of the transition matrix $\boldsymbol{P}$ has only positive elements. That is, there exists a positive integer K such that $P_{ij}^{(K)} > 0$ for $\forall i, j$. This means that there is a nonzero probability to go from any state i to another state j. In other words, every state is accessible in a finite number of steps (not necessarily a few steps). If the number of steps K is not a multiple of some integer, the chain is called *aperiodic*. This means that there is no fixed-length cycle between certain states of the chain. In addition, a Markov chain is said to be *ergodic* or irreducible if it is possible to go from every state to every state [4,5].

In general, for a Markov chain starting with an initial $\boldsymbol{\pi}_0$ and a transition matrix $\boldsymbol{P}$, we have after k steps

$$\boldsymbol{\pi}_k = \boldsymbol{\pi}_0 \boldsymbol{P}^k, \quad \text{or} \quad \boldsymbol{\pi}_k = \boldsymbol{\pi}_{k-1} \boldsymbol{P}, \tag{3.32}$$

where $\boldsymbol{\pi}_k$ is a vector whose jth entry is the probability that the chain is in state S_j after k steps.

There is a fundamental theorem about a regular Markov chain. That is,

$$\lim_{k \to \infty} \boldsymbol{P}^k = \boldsymbol{W}, \tag{3.33}$$

where $\boldsymbol{W}$ is a matrix with all rows equal and all entries strictly positive.

As the number of steps k increases, it is possible for a Markov chain to reach a stationary distribution $\boldsymbol{\pi}^*$ defined by

$$\boldsymbol{\pi}^* = \boldsymbol{\pi}^* \boldsymbol{P}. \tag{3.34}$$

From the definition of eigenvalues of a matrix $\boldsymbol{A}$,

$$\boldsymbol{A}\boldsymbol{u} = \lambda \boldsymbol{u}, \tag{3.35}$$

we know that the previous equation implies that $\boldsymbol{\pi}^*$ is the eigenvector (of $\boldsymbol{P}$) associated with the eigenvalue $\lambda = 1$ that is also the largest eigenvalue. The unique stationary distribution requires the following detailed balance of transition probabilities:

$$P_{ij} \pi_i^* = P_{ji} \pi_j^*, \tag{3.36}$$

which is often referred to as the *reversibility condition*. A Markov chain that satisfies this reversibility condition is said to be reversible.

This discussion mainly relates to the case when the states are discrete. We can generalize the preceding results to a continuous-state Markov chain with a transition probability $P(u, v)$ and the corresponding stationary distribution

$$\pi^*(v) = \int_\Omega \pi^*(u)P(u, v)dv, \tag{3.37}$$

where Ω is the probability state space.

There are many ways to choose the transition probabilities, and different choices will result in different behavior of the Markov chain. In essence, the characteristics of the transition kernel largely determine how the Markov chain of interest behaves, which also determines the efficiency and convergence of Markov chain Monte Carlo (MCMC) sampling. There are several widely used sampling algorithms, including Metropolis algorithms, Metropolis-Hasting algorithms, independence sampling, random walk, and of course Gibbs sampler. Interested readers can refer to more advanced literature for details [5].

3.4.2 Optimization as a Markov Chain

To solve an optimization problem, we can search the solution by performing a random walk starting from a good initial but random-guess solution. However, simple or blind random walks are not efficient. To be computationally efficient and effective in searching for new solutions, we have to keep the best solutions found so far and increase the mobility of the random walk so as to explore the search space more effectively. Most important, we have to find a way to control the walk in such a way that it can move toward the optimal solutions more quickly rather than wander away from the potential best solutions. These are the challenges for most metaheuristic algorithms.

Further research along the route of Markov chains is the development of the *Markov chain Monte Carlo* (MCMC) method, which is a class of sample-generating methods. MCMC attempts to directly draw samples from some highly complex multidimensional distribution using a Markov chain with known transition probability. Since the 1990s, the MCMC method has become a powerful tool for Bayesian statistical analysis, Monte Carlo simulations, and potentially optimization with high nonlinearity.

An important link between MCMC and optimization is that some heuristic and metaheuristic search algorithms such as simulated annealing (introduced later) use a trajectory-based approach. They start with some initial (random) state and propose a new state (solution) randomly. Then, the move is accepted or not, depending on some probability. This is strongly similar to a Markov chain. In fact, the standard simulated annealing is a random walk [9].

Mathematically speaking, a great leap in understanding metaheuristic algorithms is to view MCMC as an optimization procedure. If we want to find the minimum of an objective function $f(\theta)$ at $\theta = \theta_*$ so that $f_* = f(\theta_*) \leq f(\theta)$, we can convert it to a target distribution for a Markov chain

$$\pi(\theta) = e^{-\gamma f(\theta)}, \tag{3.38}$$

where $\gamma > 0$ is a parameter that acts as a normalized factor. γ value should be chosen so that the probability is close to 1 when $\theta \to \theta_*$. At $\theta = \theta_*$, $\pi(\theta)$ should reach a

Markov Chain Algorithm for Optimization

Start with $\zeta_0 \in S$, at $t = 0$
while (criterion)
Propose a new solution Y_{t+1};
Generate a random number $0 \le P_t \le 1$;

$$\zeta_{t+1} = \begin{cases} Y_{t+1} & \text{with probability } P_t \\ \zeta_t & \text{with probability } 1 - P_t \end{cases} \tag{3.39}$$

end

Figure 3.3 Optimization as a Markov chain.

maximum $\pi_* = \pi(\theta_*) \ge \pi(\theta)$. This requires that the formulation of $L(\theta)$ should be nonnegative, which means that some objective functions can be shifted by a large constant $A > 0$ such as $f \leftarrow f + A$, if necessary.

By constructing a MCMC, we can formulate a generic framework as outlined by Ghate and Smith in 2008 [6], as shown in Figure 3.3. In this framework, simulated annealing and its many variants are simply a special case with

$$P_t = \begin{cases} \exp\left[-\frac{\Delta f}{T_t}\right] & \text{if } f_{t+1} > f_t \\ 1 & \text{if } f_{t+1} \le f_t \end{cases}.$$

In this case, only the difference Δf between the function values is important.

Algorithms such as simulated annealing discussed in this book use a single Markov chain, which may not be very efficient. In practice, it is usually advantageous to use multiple Markov chains in parallel to increase the overall efficiency. In fact, the algorithms such as particle swarm optimization and the firefly algorithm can be viewed as multiple interacting Markov chains, though such theoretical analysis remains very challenging. The theory of interacting Markov chains is complicated and yet still under development, and any progress in such areas will play a central role in understanding how population- and trajectory-based metaheuristic algorithms perform under various conditions. However, even though we do not fully understand why metaheuristic algorithms work, this does not hinder us from using these algorithms efficiently. On the contrary, such mysteries can drive and motivate us to pursue further research and development in metaheuristics.

3.5 Step Sizes and Search Efficiency

3.5.1 Step Sizes, Stopping Criteria, and Efficiency

As random walks are widely used for randomization and local search in metaheuristic algorithms [19,21], a proper step size is very important. Typically, we use the following generic equation:

$$\boldsymbol{x}^{t+1} = \boldsymbol{x}^t + s\epsilon_t, \tag{3.40}$$

where ϵ_t is drawn from a standard normal distribution with zero mean and unity standard deviation. Here, the step size s determines how far a random walker (e.g., an agent or a particle in metaheuristics) can go for a fixed number of iterations. Obviously, if s is too large, the new solution $\boldsymbol{x}^{t+1}$ that is generated will be too far away from the old solution (or more often the current best). Then such a move is unlikely to be accepted. If s is too small, the change is too small to be significant, and consequently such search is not efficient. So, a proper step size is important to maintain the search as efficiently as possible.

From the theory of simple isotropic random walks [7,10–12,14], we know that the average distance r (i.e., standard deviation) traveled in the d-dimension space is

$$r^2 = 2dDt, \tag{3.41}$$

where $D = s^2/2\tau$ is the effective diffusion coefficient. Here s is the step size or distance traveled at each jump, and τ is the time taken for each jump. The preceding equation implies that

$$s^2 = \frac{\tau r^2}{td}. \tag{3.42}$$

For a typical scale L of dimensions of interest, the local search is typically limited in a region of $L/10$. That is, $r = L/10$. Because the iterations are discrete, we can take $\tau = 1$. Typically in metaheuristics, we can expect that the number of generations is usually $t = 100$ to 1000, which means that

$$s \approx \frac{r}{\sqrt{td}} = \frac{L/10}{\sqrt{td}}. \tag{3.43}$$

For $d = 1$ and $t = 100$, we have $s = 0.01L$, whereas $s = 0.001L$ for $d = 10$ and $t = 1000$. Because step sizes could differ from variable to variable, a step size ratio s/L is more generic. Therefore, we can use $s/L = 0.001$ to 0.01 for most problems.

Let us suppose that we want to achieve an accuracy of $\delta = 10^{-5}$. Then we can estimate the number of steps or iterations $N_{\max}$ needed by pure random walks. This is essentially the upper bound for $N_{\max}$:

$$N_{\max} \approx \frac{L^2}{\delta^2 d}. \tag{3.44}$$

For example, for $L = 10$ and $d = 10$, we have

$$N_{\max} \approx \frac{10^2}{(10^{-5})^2 \times 10} \approx 10^{11}, \tag{3.45}$$

which is a huge number that is not easily achievable in practice. However, this number is still far smaller than that needed by a uniform or brute-force search method. It is worth pointing out that the previous estimate is the upper limit for the worst-case scenarios. In reality, most metaheuristic algorithms require far fewer numbers of iterations.

On the other hand, the preceding formula implies another interesting fact that the number of iterations will not affect much by dimensionality. In fact, higher-dimensional problems do not necessarily significantly increase the number of iterations. This may lead to a rather surprising possibility that random walks may be efficient in higher dimensions if the optimization is highly multimodal. This provides some hints for designing better algorithms by cleverly using random walks and other randomization techniques.

3.5.2 Why Lévy Flights are More Efficient

If we use Lévy flights instead of Gaussian random walks, we have an estimate

$$N_{\max} \approx \left(\frac{L^2}{\delta^2 d}\right)^{1/(3-\beta)}. \tag{3.46}$$

If we use $\beta = 1.5$, we have

$$N_{\max} \approx 2 \times 10^7. \tag{3.47}$$

We can see that Lévy flights can reduce the number of iterations by about 4 orders $[O(10^4)]$ from $O(10^{11})$ to $O(10^7)$. Obviously, if other values of β are used, reduction can be even more. As we will see later in this chapter, eagle strategy in combination with Lévy flights can reduce the number of iterations more significantly, from $O(10^{11})$ to $O(10^3)$.

However, before we further discuss search strategies, let us see how the modality of the objective landscape can affect the strategies used for finding the optimality in a vast search space.

3.6 Modality and Intermittent Search Strategy

Even if there is no guideline in practice, some preliminary work on the very limited cases exists in the literature and may provide some insight into the possible choice of parameters so as to balance these components. Ideally, the search strategy used for an optimization process should employ the knowledge of the modality of the objective landscape so that the optimality can be reached with the minimum computational effort. However, too much problem-specific knowledge may limit the usefulness of an algorithm. An algorithm that is flexible enough and able to cope with a diverse range of problems requires minimum input from the problem-specific settings and can almost treat the problems as the black-box type. This leads to various challenges, and there are no guidelines concerning them.

There have been various attempts in designing search strategies. One of these strategies is the so-called *intermittent search strategy*, which concerns the possibly optimal way to search for an unknown target in a vast search landscape. This strategy is iterative and consists of a slow detection phase and a fast search phase [2]. Here the slow phase is the detection phase via slowing down and intensive, static local search techniques.

The fast phase is the search without detection and can be considered an exploration technique. For example, the static target detection with a small region of radius a in a much larger domain of radius R, where $a \ll R$, can be modeled as a slow diffusive process in terms of random walks with a diffusion coefficient D.

It is worth pointing out that the following results assume that the targets are local optima or modes and the objective functions are multimodal. For unimodal functions, there is no need to balance exploration and exploitation because exploitation should be used mainly in the search process. For convex unimodal, any found local optimality is also the global optimal solution; therefore, intensive local search exploiting local information and update is preferred. Intermittent switch between exploration stage and exploitation stage can be optimal for multimodal functions where the areas/volumes of the local modes are small, compared with the area/volume of the search domain. Thus, we are dealing with target modes with sparsity.

Let τ_a and τ_R be the *mean* times spent in intensive detection stage and the time spent in the exploration stage, respectively, in the 2D case [2]. The diffusive search process is governed by the mean first-passage time, satisfying the following equations:

$$D\nabla_r^2 t_1 + \frac{1}{2\pi\tau_a}\int_0^{2\pi}[t_2(r) - t_1(r)]d\theta + 1 = 0, \tag{3.48}$$

$$\boldsymbol{u}\cdot\nabla_r t_2(r) - \frac{1}{\tau_R}[r_2(r) - t_1(r)] + 1 = 0, \tag{3.49}$$

where t_2 and t_1 are times spent during the search process at slow and fast stages, respectively, and $\boldsymbol{u}$ is the search speed [2].

After some lengthy mathematical analysis [2], the optimal balance of these two stages can be estimated as

$$r_{\text{optimal}} = \frac{\tau_a}{\tau_R^2} \approx \frac{D}{a^2}\frac{1}{\left[2 - \frac{1}{\ln(R/a)}\right]^2}. \tag{3.50}$$

Assuming that the search steps have a uniform velocity u at each step on average, the minimum times required for each phase can be estimated as

$$\tau_a^{\min} \approx \frac{D}{2u^2}\frac{\ln^2(R/a)}{[2\ln(R/a) - 1]} \tag{3.51}$$

and

$$\tau_R^{\min} \approx \frac{a}{u}\sqrt{\ln(R/a) - \frac{1}{2}}. \tag{3.52}$$

When $u \to \infty$, these relationships lead to the previous optimal ratio of two stages. An interesting observation is that the preceding results depend weakly on the domain size R, and thus balancing these two key components can lead to very efficient performance of the algorithm used [2]. In addition, increasing the global exploration velocity u can also reduce the overall search time and thus implicitly enhance the search efficiency of the algorithm. It should be emphasized that the previous result is only valid for 2D cases, and there is no general results for higher dimensions except in some special 3D cases. Now let us use this limited result to help choose the possible values of algorithm-dependent parameters in the eagle strategy [19] as an example.

Let us first use a multimodal test function to see how to find the fine balance between exploration and exploitation in an algorithm for a given task. Xin-She Yang's standing-wave test function can be a good example [18,8]:

$$f(\boldsymbol{x}) = 1 + \left\{ \exp\left[-\sum_{i=1}^{d} (\frac{x_i}{\sigma})^{10} \right] - 2\exp\left[-\sum_{i=1}^{d} x_i^2 \right] \right\} \cdot \prod_{i=1}^{d} \cos^2 x_i, \tag{3.53}$$

which is multimodal with many local peaks and valleys. It has a unique global minimum at $f_{\min} = 0$ at $(0, 0, \ldots, 0)$ in the domain $-20 \leq x_i \leq 20$, where $i = 1, 2, \ldots, d$ and $\sigma = 15$. In this case, we can estimate that $R = 20$ and $a \approx \pi/2$, which means that $R/a \approx 12.7$, and we have in the case of $d = 2$

$$p_e \approx \tau_{\text{optimal}} \approx \frac{1}{2[2 - 1/\ln(R/a)]^2} \approx 0.19. \tag{3.54}$$

This indicates that the algorithm should spend 80% of its computational effort on global explorative search and 20% of its effort on local intensive search.

However, it is worth pointing out that the optimal ratio between exploitation and exploration here is landscape-based or landscape-dependent. That is, the actual value will vary from problem to problem, and there is no universally optimal ratio. One special case is that when $R \gg a$ or $R/a \gg 1$, Eq. (3.54) gives

$$t_{\text{optimal}}(R \to \infty) \to 1/8. \tag{3.55}$$

This optimal ratio is valid only for multimodal problems in a vast region where the modal size is relatively small compared with the size of the search space. Furthermore, this is only for multimodal problems with unknown landscapes. Obviously, if we know a problem is unimodal, we should focus on exploitation without much exploration, and there are efficient algorithms such as Newton-Raphson methods that can converge very quickly.

On the other hand, there is another optimality that concerns the setting of parameters in an algorithm. Such optimality of algorithm-dependent parameters can be said to be algorithm-based or algorithm-dependent. Ideally, efficiency will become truly the highest when the landscape-based optimality matches the algorithm-based optimality. However, such a match itself is another higher-level optimization problem.

Even with the best possible setting of algorithm-dependent parameters with a known ratio between exploitation and exploration, the ways that sample the search space are also important, as we address in the next section.

3.7 Importance of Randomization

3.7.1 Ways to Carry Out Random Walks

Randomization is a way of enabling an algorithm to explore more in the search space, and it can be considered as a way of diversification as well as intensification, depending on the exact details of how the randomization is realized. There are many ways of carrying out intensification and diversification. In fact, each algorithm and its variants use different ways of achieving the balance between exploration and exploitation [3, 19,20].

By analyzing all the metaheuristic algorithms, we can categorically say that the way to achieve exploration or diversification is mainly by random walks in combination with a deterministic procedure. This ensures that the newly generated solutions distribute as diversely as possible in the feasible search space.

One of the simplest and yet most commonly used randomization techniques is to use a uniformly distributed random variable to sample the search space in terms of

$$x_{\text{new}} = \mathbf{L} + (\mathbf{U} - \mathbf{L}) * \epsilon_u, \tag{3.56}$$

where $\mathbf{L}$ and $\mathbf{U}$ are the lower-bound and upper-bound vectors, respectively. ϵ_u is a uniformly distributed random variable in $[0, 1]$. This is often used in many algorithms such as harmony search, particle swarm optimization, and bat algorithm. Obviously, the use of a uniform distribution is not the only way to achieve randomization. In fact, random walks such as Lévy flights on a global scale are more efficient.

A more elaborate way to obtain diversification is to use mutation and crossover. Mutation makes sure that new solutions are as far or different as possible from their parents or existing solutions, whereas crossover provides good mixing and yet limits the degree of overdiversification, since new solutions are generated by swapping parts of the existing solutions.

The generation of new solutions can be carried out around a promising or better solution locally and more intensively. This goal can be easily achieved by a local random walk

$$x_{\text{new}} = x_{\text{old}} + s\ \mathbf{w}, \tag{3.57}$$

where $\mathbf{w}$ is a random vector, typically drawn from a Gaussian distribution with zero mean. Here s is the scaling factor for the step size of the random walk. In general, the step size should be small enough so that only the local neighborhood is visited. If s is too large, the region visited can be too far away from the region of interest, which will increase diversification significantly but reduce intensification greatly. Therefore, a proper step size should be much smaller than (and be linked with) the scale of the problem. For example, the pitch adjustment in a harmony search and the move in simulated annealing are typically local random walks.

If we want to increase the efficiency of this random walk (and thus increase the efficiency of exploration as well), we can use other forms of random walks, such as

Lévy flights, where s is drawn from a Lévy distribution with large step sizes. In fact, any distribution with a long tail will help increase the step size and distance of such random walks.

On the other hand, the main way to achieve the exploitation is to generate new solutions around the most promising region, often around the current best solution, locally and more intensively. Even with the standard random walk, we can use a more selective or controlled walk around the current best $\boldsymbol{x}_{\text{best}}$ rather than any good solution. That is,

$$\boldsymbol{x}_{\text{new}} = \boldsymbol{x}_{\text{best}} + s\ \mathbf{w}. \tag{3.58}$$

Some intensification techniques are not easy to decode but may be equally effective. The crossover operator in evolutionary algorithms is a good example because as it uses the solutions or strings from parents to form offsprings or new solutions. In many algorithms, there is no clear distinction or explicit differentiation between intensification and diversification. These two steps are often intertwined and interactive, which may, in some cases, become an advantage. Good examples of such interaction are the genetic algorithms, harmony search, cuckoo search, and the bat algorithm. Readers can analyze any chosen algorithm to see how these components are implemented.

In addition, the selection of the best solutions is a crucial component for the success of an algorithm. Simple, blind exploration and exploitation may not be effective without the proper selection of the solutions of good quality. Simply choosing the best may be effective for optimization problems with a unique global optimum. Elitism and keeping the best solutions are efficient for multimodal and multi-objective problems. Elitism in genetic algorithms and selection of harmonics are good examples of the selection of the fittest.

In contrast with the selection of the best solutions, an efficient metaheuristic algorithm should have a way to discard the worse solutions so as to increase the overall quality of the populations during evolution. This is often achieved by some form of randomization and probabilistic selection criteria. For example, mutation in genetic algorithms acts as a way to do this. Similarly, in the cuckoo search, the castaway of a nest/solution is another good example.

Another important issue is the randomness reduction. Randomization is mainly used to explore the search space diversely on a global scale and to some extent, the exploitation on a local scale. As better solutions are found and as the system converges, the degree of randomness should be reduced; otherwise, it will slow down the convergence. For example, in particle swarm optimization, randomness is automatically reduced as the particles swarm together. This is because the distance between each particle and the current global best is getting smaller and smaller.

In other algorithms, randomness is not reduced but is controlled and selected. For example, the mutation rate is usually small so as to limit the randomness, whereas in simulated annealing, the randomness during iterations may remain the same, but the solutions or moves are selected and acceptance probability becomes smaller.

Finally, from the implementation point of view, the actual implementation does vary, even though the pseudo code should give a good guide and should not in principle lead to ambiguity. However, in practice, the actual way of implementing the algorithm does affect the performance to some degree. Therefore, validation and testing of any algorithm implementation are important.

3.7.2 Importance of Initialization

Ideally, the final results should be independent of the starting points for a good algorithm. However, the reality is that the results can largely depend on the initial start points for almost all stochastic algorithms. If the objective landscape is hilly and if the global optimality lies in an isolated small region, the initialization of the population is very important. If the random initialization does not produce any solution in the neighborhood of the global optimality the initial population, the chance that this population converges to the true optimality may be low. On the other hand, if the initial seeding produces a high number of solutions in the initial population that may lie in the neighborhood of the global optimum, the chance of the population that converges toward the true global optimality is very high. Therefore, the initialization of the population can be very important. Ideally, initialization should use importance sampling techniques, like those used in Monte Carlo methods, so that the solutions can be sampled according to the objective landscape. However, this requires sufficient knowledge of the problem and might not be suitable for any algorithm.

The ways to remedy these drawbacks are to run the algorithm many times with different initial configurations and population for each run, which can lead to some meaningful statistics, such as the mean and standard deviation. Alternatively, we should run the algorithm long enough so that it "forgets" the initial states and thus converge to the true global optimality, independent of the initial population. This is achievable from the Markov chain point of view. The main disadvantage is that the convergence rate may be slow and thus requires a very large number of iterations, thus leading to high computational costs.

In practice, most algorithms tend to use some sort of initialization to ensure that the newly generated solutions distribute as diversely as possible in the feasible search space, as we discussed earlier.

3.7.3 Importance Sampling

The techniques used in Monte Carlo methods, such as importance sampling, can be used to initialize the population in metaheuristic algorithms. For example, suppose the problem is to minimize an integral

$$\text{minimize} \int_a^b f(u)du \tag{3.59}$$

by choosing the right form of $f(u)$, which is essentially the optimization of a function. For this kind of problem, we can use the importance sampling technique.

For an integrand that varies rapidly in a narrow region, such as a sharp peak (e.g., $f(x) = e^{-(100x)^2}$), the only sampling points that are important are near the peaks; the sampling points far outside will contribute less. Thus, it seems that a lot of unnecessary sampling points are wasted. There are two main ways to use the sampling points more effectively: change of variables and importance sampling. The change of variables uses the integrand itself so that it can be transformed to a more uniform (flat) function. For example, the integral

$$I = \int_a^b f(u)du \tag{3.60}$$

can be transformed using a known function $u = g(v)$:

$$I = \int_{a_v}^{b_v} f[g(v)]\frac{dg}{dv}dv. \tag{3.61}$$

The idea is to make sure that the new integrand is (or is close to) a constant A:

$$\phi(v) = f[g(v)]\frac{dg(v)}{v} = A, \tag{3.62}$$

where $v = g^{-1}(u)$. This means that the uniform sampling can be used for ϕ. The new integration limits are $a_v = g^{-1}(a)$ and $b_v = g^{-1}(b)$.

3.7.4 Low-Discrepancy Sequences

In generating initial solutions in the initial population, there is no constraint on the type of randomness (at least in principle). Apart from the uniform and Gaussian distributions, we can use low-discrepancy sequences, Sobol sequences, Latin hypercubes, and others.

One of the interesting techniques is the so-called low-discrepancy sequence like those used in quasi-Monte Carlo methods. Quasi-random numbers are designed to have a high level of uniformity in multidimensional space; however, they are not statistically independent, which may counterintuitively lead to some advantages over standard Monte Carlo methods. There are many ways of generating quasi-random numbers using deterministic sequences, including radical inverse methods. Probably the most widely used is the van der Corput sequence, developed by the Dutch mathematician J. G. van der Corput in 1935. In this sequence, an arbitrary (decimal) integer n is expressed by a unique expansion in terms of a prime base b in the form

$$n = \sum_{j=0}^{m} a_j(n)b^j, \tag{3.63}$$

where the coefficients $a_j(n)$ can only take values $\{0, 1, 2, \ldots, b-1\}$. Here m is the smallest integer that leads to $a_j(n) = 0$ for all $j > m$. Then the expression in base b is reversed or reflected,

$$\phi_b(n) = \sum_{j=0}^{m} a_j(n)\frac{1}{b^{j+1}}, \tag{3.64}$$

and the reflected decimal number is a low-discrepancy number whose distribution is uniform in the interval $[0, 1)$.

For example, the integer $n = 6$ in base 2 can be expressed as 110 because $6 = 2 \times 2^2 + 1 \times 2^1 + 0 \times 2^0$, and $m = 2$. The expression 110 in base 2 is reversed or reflected as 011. When expressed in terms of a decimal number, it becomes the van der Corput number $\phi_2(6) = 0 \times 2^{-1} + 1 \times 2^{-2} + 1 \times 2^{-3} = 3/8$. This number is in the unit interval [0, 1]. For example, for the integers $0, 1, 2, \ldots, 15$, we have

$$0, \frac{1}{2}, \frac{1}{4}, \frac{3}{4}, \frac{1}{8}, \frac{5}{8}, \frac{3}{8}, \ldots, \frac{15}{16}. \tag{3.65}$$

If we plot these points in the unit interval, we can see that these points seem to "fill the gaps."

Similarly, if we use base 3, the integer 5 can be expressed as 12, since $5 = 1 \times 3^1 + 2 \times 3^0$. Now the reflection of the coefficients becomes 21. The number generated by the van der Corput sequence becomes $\phi_3(5) = 2 \times 3^{-1} + 1 \times 3^{-2} = \frac{7}{9}$.

Low-discrepancy sequences, including the Halton sequence, Sobol sequence, Faure sequence, and Niederreiter sequence, have been extended to higher dimensions. For example, Sobol's quasi-random sequence, developed in 1967, is among the most widely used in quasi-Monte Carlo simulations [16]. However, the applications of these sequences in nature-inspired algorithms still require more studies.

3.8 Eagle Strategy

3.8.1 Basic Ideas of Eagle Strategy

Eagle strategy (ES) is a recent metaheuristic strategy for optimization, developed in 2010 by Xin-She Yang and Suash Deb [19]. More extensive studies followed [20]. Eagle strategy uses a combination of crude global search and intensive local search, employing different algorithms to suit different purposes. In essence, the strategy first explores the search space globally using a Lévy flight random walk. If a promising solution is found, an intensive local search is employed using a more efficient local optimizer such as hill climbing, differential evolution, and/or cuckoo search. Then the two-stage process starts again with new global exploration, followed by a local search in a new region. The main steps are outlined in Figure 3.4.

The advantage of such a combination is to use a balanced tradeoff between global search (which is often slow) and a fast local search. Some tradeoff and balance are important. Another advantage of this method is that we can use any algorithms we like at different stages of the search or even at different stages of iterations. This makes it easy to combine the advantages of various algorithms so as to produce better results.

Here the only parameter is p_e, which controls the switch between local and global search. That is, it controls when to do exploitation and when to do exploration. It is worth pointing out that this is a methodology or strategy, not an algorithm. In fact, we can use different algorithms at different stages and at different times of the iterations. The algorithm used for the global exploration should have enough randomness to explore the search space diversely and effectively. This process is typically slow initially, and should speed up as the system converges (or when no better solutions can be found after

```
Eagle Strategy (ES)
Objective functions f1(x), ..., fN(x)
Initialize the population
while (stop criterion)
  Global exploration by randomization
  Evaluate the objectives and find promising solutions
  if pe <rand,
  Switch to an intensive, local search
  Local search around the promising solutions via an efficient optimizer
  if (better solution are found), update the current best; end
  end
end
Post-process the results and visualization.
```

Figure 3.4 Pseudo code of the eagle strategy.

a certain number of iterations). On the other hand, the algorithm used for the intensive local exploitation should be an efficient local optimizer. The idea is to reach the local optimality as quickly as possible, with the minimal number of function evaluations. This stage should be fast and efficient.

3.8.2 Why Eagle Strategy is So Efficient

In modern metaheuristic algorithms, the step sizes are controlled in such a way that they will do local search more efficiently. To illustrate this point, let us split the search process into two stages, like those in the efficient eagle strategy.

The first stage uses a crude/large step, say, $\delta_1 = 10^{-2}$, and then in the second stage we use the step size $\delta_2 = 10^{-5}$ so as to achieve the same final accuracy as discussed in the previous section. The first stage covers the whole region $L_1 = L$; the second stage covers local regions of size L_2. Typically, $L_2 = O(L_1/1000)$. Using the preceding values and $L_1 = 1$ and $L_2 = 0.01$, we have $N_{1,\max} \approx 10^5$ and $N_{2,\max} \approx 10^5$. In this case, the number of iterations can be reduced by about 5 orders (10^5) from $O(10^{10})$ to $O(10^5)$.

In addition, if we further use Lévy flights with the eagle strategy, these estimates can be reduced to

$$N_{1,\max} \approx N_{2,\max} \approx 2 \times 10^3, \tag{3.66}$$

which can be both practical and realistic. In fact, the good combination of Lévy flights with ES can reduce the number of iterations from $O(10^{10})$ to $O(10^3)$, which works almost like a magic.

Therefore, using a combination with good algorithms, ES can significantly reduce the computational efforts and may thus dramatically increase the search efficiency.

References

[1] Bell WJ. Searching behaviour: the behavioural ecology of finding resources. London, UK: Chapman & Hall; 1991.

[2] Bénichou O, Loverdo C, Moreau M, Voituriez R. Intermittent search strategies. Rev Mod Phys 2011;83(1):81–129.

[3] Blum C, Roli A. Metaheuristics in combinatorial optimization: overview and conceptual comparison. ACM Comput Surv 2003;35(3):268–308.

[4] Fishman GS. Monte Carlo: concepts, algorithms and applications. New York, NY, USA: Springer; 1995.

[5] Geyer CJ. Practical Markov chain Monte Carlo. Stat Sci 1992;7(6):473–511.

[6] Ghate A, Smith R. Adaptive search with stochastic acceptance probabilities for global optimization. Oper Res Lett 2008;36(3):285–90.

[7] Gutowski M. Lévy flights as an underlying mechanism for global optimization algorithms, ArXiv Mathematical Physics e-Prints; 2001 [accessed 28.06.13].

[8] Jamil M, Yang XS. A literature survey of benchmark functions for global optimisation problems. Int J Math Model Numer Optim 2013;4(2):150–94.

[9] Kirkpatrick S, Gellat CD, Vecchi MP. Optimization by simulated annealing. Science 1983;220(4598):670–80.

[10] Mantegna RN. Fast, accurate algorithm for numerical simulation of Lévy stable stochastic processes. Phys Rev E 1994;49:4677–83.

[11] Nolan J.P.. Stable distributions: models for heavy-tailed data. Berlin: Birkhauser; 2014.

[12] Pavlyukevich I. Lévy flights, non-local search and simulated annealing. J Comput Phys 2007;226(2):1830–44.

[13] Ramos-Fernandez G, Mateos JL, Miramontes O, Cocho G, Larralde H, Ayala-Orozco B. Lévy walk patterns in the foraging movements of spider monkeys (Ateles geoffroyi). Behav Ecol Sociobiol 2004;55:223–30.

[14] Reynolds AM, Frye MA. Free-flight odor tracking in Drosophila is consistent with an optimal intermittent scale-free search. PLoS One 2007;2:e354.

[15] Reynolds AM, Rhodes CJ. The Lévy flight paradigm: random search patterns and mechanisms. Ecology 2009;90:877–87.

[16] Sobol IM. A primer for the Monte Carlo method. CRC Press; 1994.

[17] Viswanathan GM, Buldyrev SV, Havlin S, da Luz MGE, Raposo EP, Stanley HE. Lévy flight search patterns of wandering albatrosses. Nature 1996;381:413–5.

[18] Yang XS. Firefly algorithm, stochastic test functions and design optimisation. Int J Bio Ins Comput 2010;2(2):78–84.

[19] Yang XS, Deb S. Eagle strategy using Lévy walk and firefly algorithm for stochastic optimization. In: Nature inspired cooperative strategies for optimization, NICSO 2010, 2010; 284:101–111.

[20] Yang XS, Deb S. Two-stage eagle strategy with differential evolution. Int J Bio Ins Comput 2012;4(1):1–5.

[21] Yang XS, Ting TO, Karamanoglu M. Random walks, Lévy flights, Markov chains and metaheuristic optimization. In: Future information communication technology and applications. Lecture notes in electrical engineering, 235; 2013. p. 1055–64.

4 Simulated Annealing

One of the earliest and yet most popular metaheuristic algorithms is *simulated annealing* (SA), which is a trajectory-based, random search technique for global optimization. It mimics the annealing process in materials processing when a metal cools and freezes into a crystalline state with the minimum energy and larger crystal sizes so as to reduce the defects in metallic structures. The annealing process involves the careful control of temperature and its cooling rate, often called the *annealing schedule*. SA has been successfully applied in many areas.

4.1 Annealing and Boltzmann Distribution

Since the first development of simulated annealing by Kirkpatrick et al. [7], SA has been applied in almost every area of optimization. The metaphor of SA came from the annealing characteristics in metal processing; however, SA has, in essence, strong similarity to the classic Metropolis algorithm by Metropolis et al. [8].

Unlike the gradient-based methods and other deterministic search methods that have the disadvantage of being trapped into local minima, SA's main advantage is its ability to avoid being trapped in local minima. In fact, it has been proved that simulated annealing will converge to its global optimality if enough randomness is used in combination with very slow cooling. Essentially, SA is a search algorithm as a Markov chain, which converges under appropriate conditions.

Metaphorically speaking, this is equivalent to dropping some bouncing balls over a landscape, and as the balls bounce and lose energy, they settle down to some local minima. If the balls are allowed to bounce enough times and lose energy slowly enough, some of the balls will eventually fall into the globally lowest locations; hence the global minimum can be reached.

The basic idea of the SA algorithm is to use random search in terms of a Markov chain, which not only accepts changes that improve the objective function but also keeps some changes that are not ideal. In a minimization problem, for example, any better moves or changes that decrease the value of the objective function f will be accepted; however, some changes that increase f will also be accepted with a probability p. This probability p, also called the *transition probability*, is determined by

$$p = \exp\left[-\frac{\Delta E}{k_B T}\right], \tag{4.1}$$

where k_B is the Boltzmann's constant, and for simplicity, we can set $k_B = 1$. T is the temperature for controlling the annealing process. ΔE is the change of the energy

Nature-Inspired Optimization Algorithms. http://dx.doi.org/10.1016/B978-0-12-416743-8.00004-X

level. This transition probability is based on the Boltzmann distribution in statistical mechanics.

The simplest way to link ΔE with the change of the objective function Δf is to use

$$\Delta E = \gamma \Delta f, \tag{4.2}$$

where γ is a real constant. For simplicity without losing generality, we can use $k_B = 1$ and $\gamma = 1$. Thus, the probability p simply becomes

$$p(\Delta f, T) = e^{-\Delta f/T}. \tag{4.3}$$

Whether or not a change is accepted, a random number r is usually used as a threshold. Thus, if $p > r$, or

$$p = \exp\left[-\frac{\Delta f}{T}\right] > r, \tag{4.4}$$

the move is accepted. In most cases, r can be drawn from a uniform distribution in [0,1].

4.2 Parameters

Here the choice of the right initial temperature is crucially important. For a given change Δf, if T is too high ($T \to \infty$), then $p \to 1$, which means almost all the changes will be accepted. If T is too low ($T \to 0$), then any $\Delta f > 0$ (worse solution) will rarely be accepted as $p \to 0$, and thus the diversity of the solution is limited, but any improvement Δf will almost always be accepted. In fact, the special case $T \to 0$ corresponds to the gradient-based method because only better solutions are accepted, and the system is essentially climbing up or descending along a hill. Therefore, if T is too high, the system is at a high energy state on the topological landscape, and the minima are not easily reached. If T is too low, the system may be trapped in a local minimum (not necessarily the global minimum), and there is not enough energy for the system to jump out the local minimum to explore other minima, including the global minimum. So, a proper initial temperature should be calculated.

Another important issue is how to control the annealing or cooling process so that the system cools down gradually from a higher temperature to ultimately freeze to a global minimum state. There are many ways of controlling the cooling rate or the decrease of the temperature.

Two commonly used annealing schedules (or cooling schedules) are linear and geometric. For a linear cooling schedule, we have

$$T = T_0 - \beta t, \tag{4.5}$$

or $T \to T - \delta T$, where T_0 is the initial temperature and t is the pseudo time for iterations. β is the cooling rate, and it should be chosen in such a way that $T \to 0$ when $t \to t_f$ (or the maximum number N of iterations), which usually gives $\beta = (T_0 - T_f)/t_f$.

On the other hand, a geometric cooling schedule essentially decreases the temperature by a cooling factor $0 < \alpha < 1$ so that T is replaced by αT or

$$T(t) = T_0 \alpha^t, \quad t = 1, 2, \ldots, t_f. \tag{4.6}$$

The advantage of the second method is that $T \to 0$ when $t \to \infty$, and thus there is no need to specify the maximum number of iterations. For this reason, we will use this geometric cooling schedule. The cooling process should be slow enough to allow the system to stabilize easily. In practice, $\alpha = 0.7 \sim 0.99$ is commonly used.

In addition, for a given temperature, multiple evaluations of the objective function are needed. If there are too few evaluations, there is a danger that the system will not stabilize and subsequently will not converge to its global optimality. If there are too many evaluations, it is time-consuming, and the system will usually converge too slowly, because the number of iterations to achieve stability might be exponential to the problem size.

Therefore, there is a fine balance between the number of evaluations and solution quality. We can either do many evaluations at a few temperature levels or do few evaluations at many temperature levels. There are two major ways to set the number of iterations: fixed or varied. The first uses a fixed number of iterations at each temperature; the second intends to increase the number of iterations at lower temperatures so that the local minima can be fully explored.

4.3 SA Algorithm

The simulated annealing algorithm can be summarized as the pseudo code shown in Figure 4.1.

To find a suitable starting temperature T_0, we can use any information about the objective function. If we know the maximum change max (Δf) of the objective function, we can use this to estimate an initial temperature T_0 for a given probability p_0. That is,

$$T_0 \approx -\frac{\max(\Delta f)}{\ln p_0}.$$

Simulated Annealing Algorithm

Objective function $f(\boldsymbol{x}), \quad \boldsymbol{x} = (x_1, ..., x_d)^T$
Initialize the initial temperature T_0 and initial guess $\boldsymbol{x}_{(0)}$
Set the final temperature T_f and the max number of iterations N
Define the cooling schedule $T \mapsto \alpha T$, $(0 < \alpha < 1)$
while ($T > T_f$ and $t < N$)
    Drawn $\boldsymbol{\epsilon}$ from a Gaussian distribution
    Move randomly to a new location: $\boldsymbol{x}_{t+1} = \boldsymbol{x}_t + \boldsymbol{\epsilon}$ (random walk)
    Calculate $\Delta f = f_{t+1}(\boldsymbol{x}_{t+1}) - f_t(\boldsymbol{x}_t)$
    Accept the new solution if better
    if not improved
        Generate a random number r
        Accept if $p = \exp[-\Delta f/T] > r$
    end if
    Update the best $\boldsymbol{x}_*$ and f_*
    $t = t + 1$
end while

Figure 4.1 Simulated annealing algorithm.

If we do not know the possible maximum change of the objective function, we can use a heuristic approach. We can start evaluations from a very high temperature (so that almost all changes are accepted) and reduce the temperature quickly until about 50% or 60% of the worse moves are accepted, and then use this temperature as the new initial temperature T_0 for proper and relatively slow cooling.

For the final temperature, it should be zero in theory so that no worse move can be accepted. However, if $T_f \to 0$, more unnecessary evaluations are needed. In practice, we simply choose a very small value, say, $T_f = 10^{-10} \sim 10^{-5}$, depending on the required quality of the solutions and time constraints.

4.4 Unconstrained Optimization

Based on the guidelines of choosing the important parameters such as the cooling rate, initial and final temperatures, and the balanced number of iterations, we can implement the simulated annealing using both Matlab and Octave.

For Rosenbrock's banana function

$$f(x, y) = (1 - x)^2 + 100(y - x^2)^2,$$

we know that its global minimum $f_* = 0$ occurs at (1,1) (see Figure 4.2). This is a standard test function and quite tough for most algorithms. However, by using our implemented SA, we can find this global minimum easily, and the last 500 evaluations during annealing are shown in Figure 4.3.

This banana function is still relatively simple because it has a curved narrow valley. We should validate SA against a wide range of test functions, especially those that are strongly multimodal and highly nonlinear.

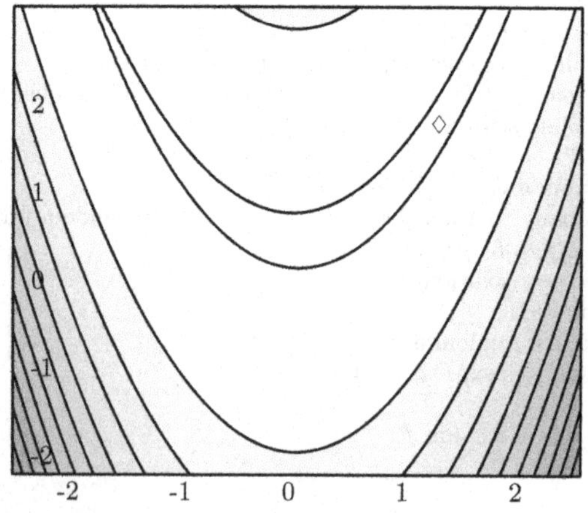

Figure 4.2 Rosenbrock's function with the global minimum $f_* = 0$ at (1,1).

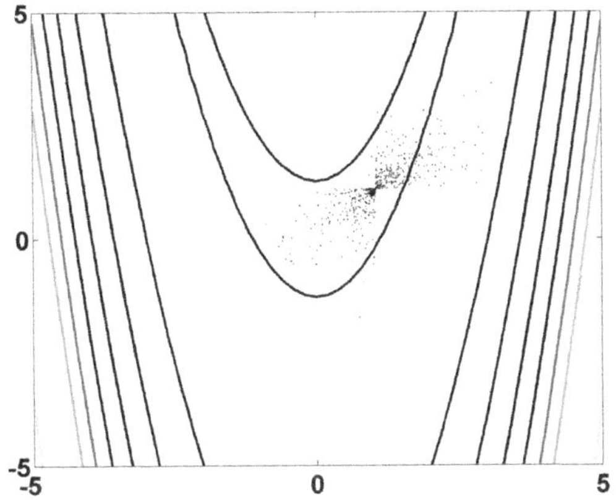

Figure 4.3 Five hundred evaluations during the annealing iterations. The final global best is marked with •.

4.5 Basic Convergence Properties

There are relatively extensive studies of the convergence properties of simulated annealing and its variants [1,2,4]. The description in this section is largely based on the analysis by Bertsimas and Tsitsiklis in 1993 [1].

We assume that the solutions in SA form a finite set S and that a real-valued objective function f is defined on this finite set S. We also assume that there is a proper subset S_* of S so that $S_* \subset S$ and f achieves the global minima on S_*. The iteration starts with an initial state $x_0 \in S$.

For each $i \in S$, we can define a set of neighbors of i as $S_i \subset S - \{i\}$. In addition, a cooling schedule $T(t)$ is defined as a nonincreasing function T so that the temperature $T(t)$ will approach zero when t is large. In this case, SA becomes a discrete-time inhomogeneous Markov chain $x(t)$. Starting from the current state i and randomly choosing a neighbor j of i, the probability of selecting any $j \in S_i$ can be defined as q_{ij}.

Furthermore, for every i, all the positive coefficients q_{ij} for $j \in S_i$ satisfy $\sum_{j \in S_i} q_{ij} = 1$. If we assume that the Markov chain $x(t)$ is aperiodic as well as irreducible (i.e., $q_{ij} = q_{ji}$ for all i, j), this Markov chain is also reversible. In this case, its corresponding invariant probability can be given by the so-called Gibbs distribution

$$\pi_T(i) = \frac{1}{Q_T} e^{-f(i)/T} \tag{4.7}$$

for $i \in S$. Here Q_T is a normalizing constant [1]. This relationship can be understood if we let $T(t)$ be held at a constant value T. It can be expected that this probability can be concentrated on S_* when $T \to 0$.

One of the fundamental questions is, will the iterations or the Markov chain formed by $x(t)$ converge to the optimal set S_*? If yes, how fast is the convergence rate? If not, what are the conditions needed to ensure the convergence takes place?

Based on the studies by Hajek (1988) and Hajek and Sasaki (1989) [4,5], the SA algorithm can converge in the statistical sense under the following conditions:

$$\lim_{t \to \infty} T(t) = 0, \quad \sum_{t=1}^{\infty} \exp[-\bar{h}/T(t)] \to \infty, \tag{4.8}$$

where $\bar{h} > 0$ is the smallest number such that every $i \in S$ communicates with S_* at a height $\bar{h}$. Here, the meaning of "state i communicates with S at height $\bar{h}$" is defined in the following sense: There exists a path in S in the consecutive neighbor of each preceding element that starts at state i and finishes at some state in S_*, and along this path, the largest value of f is $f + \bar{h}$. It is worth pointing out that this convergence is the convergence in probability P, not the almost sure convergence. That is,

$$\lim_{t \to \infty} P(x(t) \in S_*) \to 1, \tag{4.9}$$

which also requires implicitly that the Markov chain $x(t)$ is aperiodic and irreducible, as discussed previously.

To satisfy the two conditions, we can use one of the most widely used cooling schedules:

$$T(t) = \frac{h}{\log\, t}, \tag{4.10}$$

which gives

$$T(t) \to 0 \;\text{ as }\; t \to \infty, \tag{4.11}$$

and

$$\sum_{t=1}^{\infty} \exp[-\bar{h}/T(t)] = \sum_{t=1}^{\infty} \frac{1}{t^{\theta}}, \quad \theta = \frac{\bar{h}}{h}, \tag{4.12}$$

which approaches ∞ if $\theta = \bar{h}/h \le 1$. That is, SA will converge if and only if $h \ge \bar{h}$. In this case, the Markov chain becomes reversible and homogeneous. This also means that the approximate schedule $\tilde{T}(t)$ to $T(t) = h/\log\, t$ can be used:

$$\tilde{T}(t) = \frac{1}{k}, \quad \text{for} \quad t \in [t_k, t_{k+1}], \tag{4.13}$$

where

$$t_{k+1} = t_k + \exp(kh), \tag{4.14}$$

starting with $t_1 = 1$.

Now let us briefly analyze SA in terms of the eigenvalues of a Markov chain. The first eigenvalue λ_1 of a Markov chain is always $\lambda_1 = 1$. The convergence rate is usually governed by the second-largest eigenvalue λ_2. Chiang and Chow [3] showed that the eigenvalues of the transition probability matrix in SA are real, and its relaxation time is associated with λ_2 [3]. In fact, in the case when the objective function f has a unique global minimum, this relaxation time can be approximated by $\exp(k\bar{h})$. In other words, the convergence condition $h \ge \bar{h}$ means that the interval $[t_k, t_{k+1}]$ has a relaxation time $\exp[k(\bar{h} - h)]$ so that $\pi(i)|_{t_{k+1}}$ is very close to the invariant probability $\pi_{T=1/k}(i)$ as $k \to \infty$.

Another way of looking at why SA works is as follows: For a local minimum of depth h, the probability of escaping from this local minimum along any particular path is at most $\exp(-h/T)$. Therefore, if the number of candidate paths is sufficiently high, the overall escape probability can be significant. This is partly why the landscape of the objective function and structure of the state space are important in determining the search system behavior.

4.6 SA Behavior in Practice

Now we can discuss the real implications of such convergence results in practice. From a practical point of view, if we run the SA for N steps, the probability $P(x(N) \in S_*)$ may not give anything useful. In fact, we may be more concerned with the estimated probability that no state in S_* is visited during $t \geq N$. According to Bertsimas and Tsitsiklis [1], this probability for $T(t) = h/\log t$ can be approximated by

$$\max\ P\left[x(t) \notin S_* \middle| x(0)\right] \geq \frac{A}{t^a}, \tag{4.15}$$

where A and a are positive constants that depend on the objective f and the structures of the neighborhood. Obviously, this probability $A/t^a \to 0$ as $t = N \to \infty$. In other words, as the iterations proceed, the probability of not finding the global optimality approaches zero.

Even though these theoretical results can be rigorous, the true implications may not be so easy to interpret. In reality, it is not realistic to run an algorithm for a very long time, certainly not $t \to \infty$. In addition, the convergence rate also depends on the landscape of the objective function and the structure of the neighborhood. Therefore, when to stop the execution of an algorithm and how the algorithm actually behaves can be a very different matter.

Various studies and numerous applications show that the performance of SA is quite mixed. For some problems, SA can outperform the best known methods, whereas for other problems, specialized heuristics can perform better than SA [1]. This is true for applications such as graph partitioning problems, graph coloring problems, and traveling salesman problems.

In addition, the computation time is usually extensive because SA usually requires a high number of iterations. For some applications, such as image processing, the computation times can be quite excessive.

On the other hand, a common question asked by many researchers is, what effect do different cooling schedules have on performance? It was observed that about 10% of computation efforts may be typical when cooling schedules are changed [9]. Other studies show that about 40% of computational variations may be possible [11]. This has motivated nonmonotonic cooling schedules and many other studies such as parallel annealing and parallel tempering.

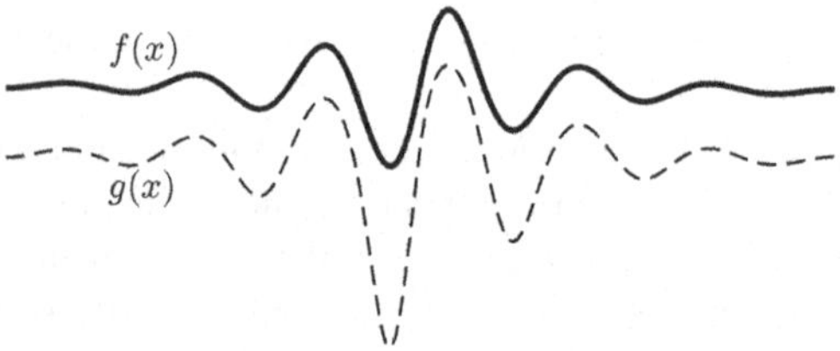

Figure 4.4 The basic idea of stochastic tunneling by transforming $f(x)$ to $g(x)$, suppressing some modes and preserving the locations of minima.

It is worth pointing out that SA's performance is also linked to the mixing ability of the Markov chain. At very high temperatures, rapid mixing in Markov chains can occur, leading to a random walk. However, for much lower temperatures, providing rapid mixing for SA Markov chains is still a very challenging task, despite the fact that the behavior at small temperatures is most relevant to the SA algorithm.

4.7 Stochastic Tunneling

To ensure the global convergence of simulated annealing, a proper cooling schedule must be used. When the functional landscape is complex, SA may become increasingly difficult to escape the local minima if the temperature is too low. Raising the temperature, as in so-called simulated tempering, may solve the problem, but the convergence is typically slow, and the computing time also increases.

Stochastic tunneling uses the tunneling idea to transform the objective function landscape into a different but more convenient one [6, 10]. The essence is to construct a nonlinear transformation so that some modes of $f(x)$ are suppressed and other modes are amplified while preserving the loci of minima of $f(x)$.

The standard form of such a tunneling transformation is

$$g(x) = 1 - \exp[-\gamma(f(x) - f_0)], \tag{4.16}$$

where f_0 is the current lowest value of $f(x)$ found so far. $\gamma > 0$ is a scaling parameter, and g is the transformed new landscape. From this simple transformation, we can see that $g \to 0$ when $f - f_0 \to 0$, that is, when f_0 is approaching the true global minimum. On the other hand, if $f \gg f_0$, then $g \to 1$, which means that all the modes well above the current minimum f_0 are suppressed. For a simple one-dimensional function, it is easy to see that such properties indeed preserve the loci of the function (see Figure 4.4).

As the loci of the minima are preserved, all the modes above the current lowest value f_0 are suppressed to some degree, while the modes below f_0 are expanded or amplified, which makes it easier for the system to escape local modes. Simulations and studies suggest that it can significantly improve the convergence for functions with complex landscape and modes.

The SA description is mainly for unconstrained problems. However, for constrained problems, we need to find a practical way to deal with constraints, since most real-world optimization problems are constrained. Common methods such as penalty methods can be used for constraint handling, and we discuss in detail the ways of incorporating nonlinear constraints in a later chapter.

References

[1] Bertsimas D, Tsitsiklis J. Simulated annealing. Stat Sci 1993;8(1):10–5.

[2] Cerny V. A thermodynamical approach to the travelling salesman problem: an efficient simulation algorithm. J Optim Theory Appl 1985;45(1):41–51.

[3] Chiang TS, Chow Y. On the eigenvalues and annealing rate. Math Oper Res 1988;13(3):508–11.

[4] Hajek B. Cooling schedules for optimal annealing. Math Oper Res 1988;13(2):311–29.

[5] Hajek B, Sasaki G. Simulated annealing—to cool or not. Syst Control Lett 1989; 12(4):443–7.

[6] Hamacher K, Wenzel W. The scaling behaviour of stochastic minimization algorithms in a perfect funnel landscape. Phys Rev E 1999;59(2):938–41.

[7] Kirkpatrick S, Gelatt CD, Vecchi MP. Optimization by simulated annealing. Science 1983;220(4598):671–80.

[8] Metropolis N, Rosenbluth AW, Rosenbluth MN, Teller AH, Teller E. Equations of state calculations by fast computing machines. J Chem Phys 1953;21(6):1087–92.

[9] van Laarhoven P, Aarts E. Simulated annealing: theory and applications. Dordrecht, Netherland: Kluwer Academic Publishers/D. Reidel; 1987.

[10] Wenzel W, Hamacher K. A stochastic tunneling approach for global optimization. Phys Rev Lett 1999;82(15):3003–7.

[11] Yang XS. Biology-derived algorithms in engineering optimization. In: Olariu S, Zomaya AY, editors. Handbook of bioinspired algorithms and applications. Boca Raton, FL, USA: Chapman & Hall/CRC; 2005. [chapter 32].

5 Genetic Algorithms

Genetic algorithms are among the most popular evolutionary algorithms in terms of the diversity of their applications. A vast majority of well-known optimization problems have been tried by genetic algorithms. In addition, genetic algorithms are population-based, and many modern evolutionary algorithms are directly based on genetic algorithms or have some strong similarities.

5.1 Introduction

The *genetic algorithm* (GA), developed by John Holland and his collaborators in the 1960s and 1970s [11,4], is a model or abstraction of biological evolution based on Charles Darwin's theory of natural selection. Holland was probably the first to use the crossover and recombination, mutation, and selection in the study of adaptive and artificial systems. These genetic operators form the essential part of the genetic algorithm as a problem-solving strategy. Since then, many variants of genetic algorithms have been developed and applied to a wide range of optimization problems, from graph coloring to pattern recognition, from discrete systems (such as the traveling salesman problem) to continuous systems (e.g., the efficient design of airfoil in aerospace engineering), and from financial markets to multiobjective engineering optimization.

There are many advantages of genetic algorithms over traditional optimization algorithms. Two of the most notable are. the ability to deal with complex problems and parallelism. Genetic algorithms can deal with various types of optimization, whether the objective (fitness) function is stationary or nonstationary (changes with time), linear or nonlinear, continuous or discontinuous, or with random noise. Because multiple offsprings in a population act like independent agents, the population (or any subgroup) can explore the search space in many directions simultaneously. This feature makes it ideal to parallelize the algorithms for implementation. Different parameters and even different groups of encoded strings can be manipulated at the same time.

However, genetic algorithms also have some disadvantages. The formulation of a fitness function, the use of population size, the choice of important parameters such as the rate of mutation and crossover, and the selection criteria of the new population should be carried out carefully. Any inappropriate choice will make it difficult for the algorithm to converge or it will simply produce meaningless results. Despite these drawbacks, genetic algorithms remain one of the most widely used optimization algorithms in modern nonlinear optimization.

Nature-Inspired Optimization Algorithms. http://dx.doi.org/10.1016/B978-0-12-416743-8.00005-1

5.2 Genetic Algorithms

The essence of GA involves the encoding of an optimization function as arrays of bits or character strings to represent chromosomes, the manipulation operations of strings by genetic operators, and the selection according to their fitness, with the aim to find a good (even optimal) solution to the problem concerned.

This is often done by the following procedure: (1) encoding the objectives or cost functions; (2) defining a fitness function or selection criterion; (3) creating a population of individuals; (4) carrying out the evolution cycle or iterations by evaluating the fitness of all the individuals in the population, creating a new population by performing crossover and mutation, fitness-proportionate reproduction, etc., and replacing the old population and iterating again using the new population; (5) decoding the results to obtain the solution to the problem. These steps can be represented schematically as the pseudo code of genetic algorithms shown in Figure 5.1.

One iteration of creating a new population is called a *generation*. The fixed-length character strings are used in most genetic algorithms during each generation, although there is substantial research on the variable-length strings and coding structures. The coding of the objective function is usually in the form of binary arrays or real-valued arrays in the adaptive genetic algorithms. For simplicity, we use binary strings for encoding and decoding in our discussion. The genetic operators include crossover, mutation, and selection from the population.

The crossover of two parent strings is the main operator with a higher probability p_c and is carried out by swapping one segment of one chromosome with the corresponding segment on another chromosome at a random position (see Figure 5.2). The crossover carried out in this way is a single-point crossover. Crossover can also occur at multiple sites, which essentially swap the multiple segments with those on their corresponding chromosome. Crossover at multiple points is used more often in genetic algorithms to increase the evolutionary efficiency of the algorithms.

The mutation operation is achieved by flopping the randomly selected bits (see Figure 5.3), and the mutation probability p_m is usually small. In addition, mutation can

```
Genetic Algorithm
------------------------------------------------------------
Objective function f(x),  x = (x_1, ..., x_d)^T
Encode the solutions into chromosomes (strings)
Define fitness F (eg, F ∝ f(x) for maximization)
Generate the initial population
Initialize the probabilities of crossover (p_c) and mutation (p_m)
   while ( t <Max number of generations )
       Generate new solution by crossover and mutation
       Crossover with a crossover probability p_c
       Mutate with a mutation probability p_m
       Accept the new solutions if their fitness increase
       Select the current best for the next generation (elitism)
       Update t = t + 1
   end while
Decode the results and visualization
------------------------------------------------------------
```

Figure 5.1 Pseudo code of genetic algorithms.

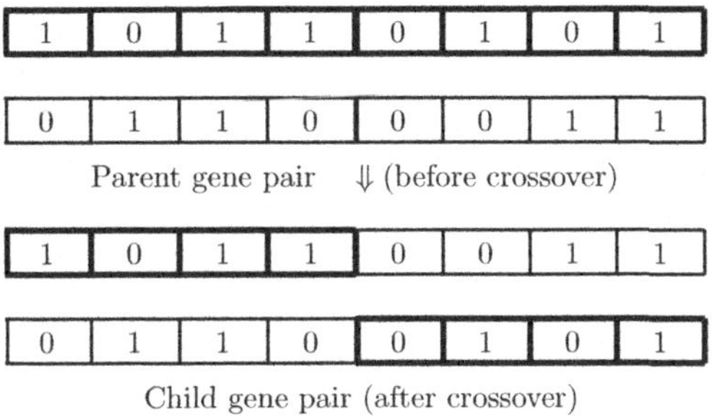

Figure 5.2 Diagram of crossover at a random crossover point (location) in genetic algorithms.

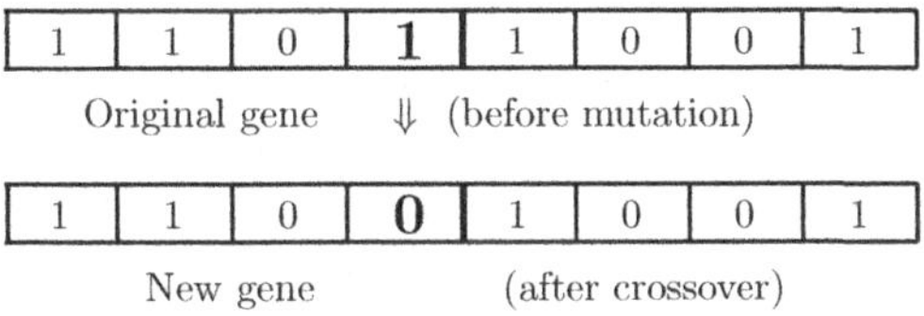

Figure 5.3 Schematic representation of mutation at a single site by flipping a randomly selected bit ($1 \rightarrow 0$).

also occur at multiple sites simultaneously, which can be advantages in practice and implementations.

The selection of an individual in a population is carried out by the evaluation of its fitness, and it can remain in the new generation if a certain threshold of the fitness is reached. In addition, selection can also be fitness-based so that the reproduction of a population is fitness-proportionate. That is to say, the individuals with higher fitness are more likely to reproduce.

5.3 Role of Genetic Operators

As introduced earlier, genetic algorithms have three main genetic operators: crossover, mutation, and selection. Their roles can be very different.

- *Crossover.* Swaping parts of the solution with another in chromosomes or solution representations. The main role is to provide mixing of the solutions and convergence in a subspace.
- *Mutation.* The change of parts of one solution randomly, which increases the diversity of the population and provides a mechanism for escaping from a local optimum.
- *Selection of the fittest, or elitism.* The use of the solutions with high fitness to pass on to next generations, which is often carried out in terms of some form of selection of the best solutions.

Obviously, in actual algorithms, the interactions between these genetic operators make behavior very complex. However, the role of the individual components remains the same.

Crossover is mainly an action with a subspace. This point becomes clear for a binary system where the strings consist of a and b. For example, for two strings $S_1 = [aabb]$ and $S_2 = [abaa]$, whatever the crossover actions will be, their offsprings will always be in the form $[a\ldots]$. That is, crossover can only result in solutions in a subspace where the first component is always a. Furthermore, two identical solutions will result in two identical offspring, no matter how the crossover has been applied. This means that crossover works in a subspace, and the converged solutions/states will remain converged.

On the other hand, mutation usually leads to a solution outside the subspace. For the previous example, if the mutation occurs on the first a and it flips to b, then the solution $S_3 = [babb]$ does not belong to the previous subspace. In fact, mutation typically generates solutions that may be further from current solutions, thus increasing the diversity of the population. This will enable the population to escape from a trapped local optimum.

One important issue is random selection among the population. For example, crossover requires two parents in the population. Do we choose them randomly or biased toward the solutions with better fitness? One way is to use a roulette wheel to do the selection; another is to use fitness-proportional selection. Obviously, there are other forms of selection in use, including linear ranking selection, tournament selections, and others.

Both crossover and mutation work without use of the knowledge of the objective or fitness landscape. Selection of the fittest, or elitism, on the other hand, does use the fitness landscape to guide what to choose and thus affects the search behavior of an algorithm. What is selected and how solutions are selected depend on the algorithm as well as the objective function values. This elitism ensures that the best solutions must survive in the population. However, very strong elitism may lead to premature convergence.

It is worth pointing out that these genetic operators are fundamental. Other operators may take different forms, and hybrid operators can also work. However, to understand the basic behavior of genetic algorithms, we will focus on these key operators.

5.4 Choice of Parameters

An important issue is the formulation or choice of an appropriate fitness function that determines the selection criterion in a particular problem. For the minimization of a function using genetic algorithms, one simple way of constructing a fitness function is to use the simplest form $F = A - y$, where A is a large constant (though $A = 0$ will do if the fitness is not required to be nonnegative) and $y = f(\mathbf{x})$. Thus, the objective is to maximize the fitness function and subsequently minimize the objective function $f(\mathbf{x})$. Alternatively, for a minimization problem, one can define a fitness function $F = 1/f(\boldsymbol{x})$, but it may have a singularity when $f \to 0$. However, there are many different ways of defining a fitness function. For example, we can use the individual fitness assignment relative to the whole population,

$$F(x_i) = \frac{f(\xi_i)}{\sum_{i=1}^{n} f(\xi_i)}, \tag{5.1}$$

where ξ_i is the phenotypic value of individual i, and n is the population size.

The appropriate form of the fitness function will make sure that the solutions with higher fitness should be selected efficiently. Poor fitness function may result in incorrect or meaningless solutions.

Another important issue is the choice of various parameters. The crossover probability p_c is usually very high, typically in the range of $0.7 \sim 1.0$. On the other hand, the mutation probability p_m is usually small (usually $0.001 \sim 0.05$). If p_c is too small, then the crossover occurs sparsely, which is not efficient for evolution. If the mutation probability is too high, the solutions could still "jump around," even if the optimal solution is approaching.

A proper criterion for selecting the best solutions is also important. How to select the current population so that the best individuals with higher fitness should be preserved and passed on to the next generation is a question that is still not fully answered. Selection is often carried out in association with certain elitism. The basic elitism is to select the fittest individual (in each generation) whose traits will be carried over to the new generation without being modified by genetic operators. This ensures that the best solution is achieved more quickly.

Other issues include the multiple sites for mutation and the use of various population sizes. Mutation at a single site is not very efficient; mutation at multiple sites will increase evolution efficiency. However, too many mutants will make it difficult for the system to converge or can even make the system go astray to the wrong solutions. In real ecological systems, if the mutation rate is too high under a high selection pressure, the whole population might go extinct.

In addition, the choice of the right population size n is also very important. If the population size is too small, there is not enough evolution going on, and there is a risk for the whole population to go extinct. In the real world, for a species with a small population, ecological theory suggests that there is a real danger of extinction for such species. Even if the system carries on, there is still a danger of premature convergence. In a small population, if a significantly more fit individual appears too early, it may reproduce enough offspring that they overwhelm the whole (small) population. This will eventually drive the system to a local optimum (not the global optimum). On the other hand, if the population is too large, more evaluations of the objective function are needed, which will require extensive computing time. Studies and empirical observations suggest that the population size $n = 40$ to 200 works for most problems.

Furthermore, for more complex problems, various GA variants can be used to suit specific tasks. Variants such as adaptive genetic algorithms and hybrid genetic algorithms can be found in the literature.

Using the basic procedure described, we can implement the genetic algorithms in any programming language. From the implementation point of view, there are two main ways to use encoded strings. We can either use a string (or multiple strings) for each individual in a population or use a long string for all the individuals or variables, as shown in Figure 5.4.

Figure 5.4 Encode all design variables into a single long string.

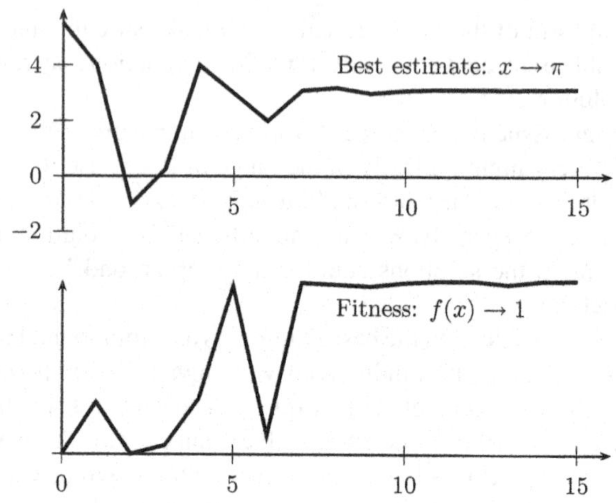

Figure 5.5 Typical outputs from a typical run. The best estimate will approach π; the fitness will approach $f_{\max} = 1$.

The well-known Easom function

$$f(x) = -\cos(x)e^{-(x-\pi)^2}, \quad x \in [-10, 10], \tag{5.2}$$

has the global maximum $f_{\max} = 1$ at $x_* = \pi$. The outputs from a typical run are shown in Figure 5.5, where the top figure shows the variations of the best estimates as they approach to $x_* \to \pi$, and the lower figure shows the variations of the fitness function.

Genetic algorithms are widely used, and there are many software packages in almost all programming languages. Efficient implementation can be found in both commercial and free codes. For this reason, we do not provide any implementation here.

5.5 GA Variants

There are several dozen GA variants which collectively can be called genetic algorithms. Numerous variants are based on the various modifications in basic genetic operators.

For the crossover operator, in addition to the multisite or N-site crossover and uniform cross, shuffled crossover uses the random permutations for two parents at N-points, and then shuffled offsprings are transformed back via an inverse permutation. Similarly, mutation can be achieved by flipping randomly chosen bits; by bitwise inversion, which inverts the whole string; or by random mutation, where the string is replaced by a new (random) one with a probability p_m. Again, elitism can also take many different forms. All these methods introduce slight variations in forms and behavior of genetic algorithms.

In all these variants, the length of the string/bits, the crossover and mutation probabilities, and the popular size n are all fixed. There is no strong reason for such fixture. On the other hand, if we allow the variations of these parameters, such as the population size and string length, we can have adaptive genetic algorithms. Mutation rate can also change based on the variations of the population. For example, if the solutions in the population do not improve for a certain number of iterations or generations, mutation rate can be increased temporarily. A relatively comprehensive review was carried out by Sharapov [15].

Genetic algorithms can be hybridized with other algorithms. For example, gradient-based methods can be used to enhance the performance of genetic algorithms. The global search capability of genetic algorithms is used to ensure a high probability of finding global optimality, whereas the derivatives or local information can be used to speed up local search. For this approach, genetic algorithms can be combined with various other algorithms to use the advantage of both algorithms.

The basic genetic operators can be used to evolve computer codes and other problems, which form the more general evolutionary computation [5,13].

As we pointed out in earlier chapters, algorithms are self-organization, and the parameters in the genetic algorithms can be tuned; some so-called self-organization genetic algorithms can also be developed. In fact, there are many variants of the genetic algorithms; interested readers can refer to more specialized literature.

5.6 Schema Theorem

One of the important theoretical results concerning genetic algorithms is probably Holland's schema theorem, derived from original work by John Holland [11].

Loosely speaking, a *schema* is a template string that consists of only 0, 1, or *. Here, the symbol * is a wildcard, which can take any allele value (0 or 1). Therefore, $H = 1{*}0{*}{*}1{*}$ is a schema representing a chromosome set of $2^4 = 16$ different gene sequences, all in the form [1*0**1*] where the four *s can be take 0 or 1 (thus 2^4 combinations). In this sense, a schema represents a subset of the space of all possible genes with the template H.

The order of a schema is the number of non * in the schema, usually noted as $o(H)$. In our example, $o(H) = 3$. In addition, the defining length $\delta(H)$ of a schema H is defined as the distance between the first and last non * gene in the schema. In our example, the first is 1 and the last is also 1, so $\delta(H) = 5$. It is worth pointing out that both $1 * *1$ and $10 * 1$ have the same defining length of 3, whereas $10 * *$ has a defining length of 1 and $*1 * *$ has a defining length of 0. For a given length m of a schema string, the defining length $\delta(H)$ is always less than or equal to the string length m. That is, $\delta(H) \leq m$.

Holland's fitness-proportional selection operator can be defined as the probability p that an individual h samples a schema H, and we have

$$p(h \in H) = \frac{k_{H,t} \bar{f}(H,t)}{n \bar{f}(t)}, \tag{5.3}$$

where n is the population size and $\bar{f}(t)$ is the average fitness at generation or time t,

$$\bar{f}(t) = \frac{1}{n} \sum_{i=1}^{n} f_i. \tag{5.4}$$

Here, $k_{H,t}$ is the number of individuals matching schema H at t, and $\bar{f}(H, t)$ is the mean fitness of individuals or instances matching schema H at t.

Therefore, the expectation or expected number of instances of H becomes

$$E[k_{H,t+1}] = n\ p(h \in H) = \frac{k_{H,t} \bar{f}(H, t)}{\bar{f}(t)}. \tag{5.5}$$

The well-known schema theorem can be stated as follows:

$$E[k_{H,t+1}] \geq k_{H,t} \frac{\bar{f}(H, t)}{\bar{f}(t)} \Big[1 - p_c \frac{\delta(H)}{m-1}\Big](1 - p_m)^{o(H)}, \tag{5.6}$$

where p_c and p_m are the crossover probability and mutation rate, respectively. This inequality always holds for any schema H under the condition of single-point crossover and gene-wise mutation.

If we assume $p_m \ll 1$, the preceding formula can be approximately written as

$$E[k_{H,t+1}] \geq k_{H,t} \frac{\bar{f}(H, t)}{\bar{f}(t)} \Big[1 - \frac{\delta(H)}{(m-1)} p_c - o(H) p_m\Big]. \tag{5.7}$$

This theorem implies that lower-order schemas with above-average fitness will be more likely to survive in the population. This is the so-called *Goldberg's building-block hypothesis* or conjecture [7]. Briefly speaking, the lower-order short schemas are often referred to as building blocks, and this hypothesis suggests that better solutions will be created in a stepwise manner by recombination or crossover, mutation of high fitness but short and low-order building blocks. Further mathematical analysis and practical implications still form an active research topic.

Despite the important results of this schema theorem, it has little information about the convergence rate of the genetic algorithms. Therefore, in the rest of this chapter we briefly outline some results concerning GA convergence.

5.7 Convergence Analysis

There are many studies of the convergence properties of genetic algorithms, and key results can be found in over a few dozen theoretical papers [3,10,12,14–16]. However, from an introductory point of view, we mainly introduce the results by Louis and Rawlins [12] in the rest of this chapter, and their results provide some good insight into the main characteristics of genetic algorithms.

Before we proceed, let us introduce the basic concept of *Hamming distance*, which is a distance measure between two strings of equal length. In essence, the Hamming distance is the number of symbols or positions of two strings at which their corresponding characters are different. In other words, if one starts with one string, it is the minimum number of replacements or substitutions needed to change into another string. For example, the Hamming distance between "theory" and "memory" is 3 because only the first 3 characters are different. The Hamming distance between "1234567" and "1122117" is 5.

The main results by Louis and Rawlins can be summarized as follows. For a population of n binary strings, each string has a fixed length of m, and there are $n(n-1)/2$ pairs of samples. The average Hamming distance can be estimated by a normal distribution with the mean H_0 and the standard deviation σ_0. That is,

$$H_0 = \frac{m}{2}, \quad \sigma_0 = \frac{\sqrt{m}}{2}. \tag{5.8}$$

The traditional single-point crossover by random pairing will not change the average Hamming distance.

In a population that contains a proportion p_j of a binary allele j, the probability of k copies of allele j that can be created in the next generation can be approximated by a binomial distribution

$$\binom{n}{k} p_j^k (1 - p_j)^{(n-k)}. \tag{5.9}$$

In principle, the probability of a particular frequency of allele occurrence can be estimated, but the mathematical analysis is complicated. For the current purpose, this probability $A(p,t)$ of the allele frequency taking value p at time t can be approximated by

$$A(p,t) = \frac{6p_0(1-p_0)}{n}\Big(1 - \frac{2}{n}\Big)^t, \tag{5.10}$$

whose detailed derivations can be found in Gale [6].

Therefore, in a flat objective landscape (without selection pressure), the probability that an allele remains fixed at time t is $P(t) = 1 - A(p,t)$. For a chromosome of length m, the probability that all alleles remain fixed can be estimated by

$$P(t,m) = \Big[1 - \frac{6p_0(1-p_0)}{n}\Big(1 - \frac{2}{n}\Big)^t\Big]^m, \tag{5.11}$$

which provides an upper bound for a flat function when the objective function is constant. For example, for a population of $n = 40$ with a 100-bit chromosome and after 100 generations, we have $t = 100$, $m = 100$, $n = 40$, and $p_0 = 0.5$ (binary). The initial Hamming average distance is $m/2$. Thus, the preceding probability becomes

$$P(t,m) = \Big[1 - \frac{6 \times 0.5(1-0.5)}{40}\Big(1 - \frac{2}{40}\Big)^{100}\Big]^{100} \approx 0.978. \tag{5.12}$$

This corresponds to an upper bound of 97.8% for the probability. However, if we increase the population size to $n = 100$ (keeping others constant), then the probability $P \approx 0.819$.

It is worth pointing out that this probability is essentially all alleles remaining fixed. In other words, it is the probability for premature convergence. As was shown briefly, increasing the population size can reduce this premature convergence probability, and large population sizes indeed occur in nature.

Other studies have provided more specific results that can be very useful in practice [1,2,8,9]. For example, the number of iterations $t(\zeta)$ in GA with a convergence probability of ζ can be estimated by

$$t(\zeta) \leq \left\lceil \frac{\ln(1-\zeta)}{\ln\left\{1-\min[(1-\mu)^{Ln}, \mu^{Ln}]\right\}} \right\rceil, \tag{5.13}$$

where μ = mutation rate, L = string length, and n = population size. This is valid for single objective optimization.

For multiobjective optimization, there are also some interesting results. For example, Villalobos-Arias et al. suggested that the transition matrix P of a metaheuristic algorithm has a stationary distribution π such that

$$|P_{ij}^k - \pi_j| \leq (1-\xi)^{k-1}, \quad \forall i, j, \quad (k = 1, 2, \ldots), \tag{5.14}$$

where ξ is a function of mutation probability μ, string length L, and population size. For example, $\xi = 2^{nL}\mu^{nL}$, so $\mu < 0.5$ [17]. It is worth pointing out that care must be taken in dealing with multiobjective optimization. Some algorithm variants may satisfy the preceding conditions, but they may not always converge in practice. This is due to the fact that some theoretical results have strict (almost unrealistic) assumptions. However, the previous conditions with certain elitism can usually lead to good convergence.

References

[1] Aytug H, Bhattacharrya S, Koehler GJ. A Markov chain analysis of genetic algorithms with power of 2 cardinality alphabets. Euro J Operational Res 1996;96(1):195–201.
[2] Aytug H, Koehler GJ. New stopping criterion for genetic algorithms. Euro J Operational Res 2000;126(2):662–74.
[3] Eiben AE, Aarts EHL, Van Hee KM. Global convergence of genetic algorithm: a Markov chain analysis. In: Schwefel H-P, Männer R, editors. Parallel problem solving from nature. Berlin, Germany: Springer; 1991. p. 4–12.
[4] De Jong K, Analysis of the behavior of a class of genetic adaptive systems, Ph.D. thesis, University of Michigan, Ann Arbor, MI, USA; 1975.
[5] Fogel DB. Evolutionary computation: toward a new philosophy of machine intelligence. 3rd ed. Piscataway, NJ.: IEEE Press; 2006.
[6] Gale JS. Theoretical population genetics. London, UK: Unwin Hyman Ltd; 1990.
[7] Goldberg DE. Genetic algorithms in search, optimisation and machine learning. Reading, MA, USA: Addison-Wesley; 1989.
[8] Greenhalgh D, Marshal S. Convergence criteria for genetic algorithms. SIAM J Comput 2000;30(1):269–82.
[9] Gutjahr WJ. Convergence analysis of metaheuristics. Anna Inf Sys 2010;10(1):159–87.
[10] He J, Kang LS. On the convergence rates of genetic algorithms. Theor Comput Sci 1999;229(1):23–9.
[11] Holland J. Adaptation in natural and artificial systems. Ann Arbor, MI, USA: University of Michigan Press; 1975.
[12] Louis SJ, Rawlins GJE. Predicting convergence time for genetic algorithms. In: Whitley LD, editor. Foundations of genetic algorithms, vol. 2. Los Altos, CA, USA: Morgan Kaufman; 1993. p. 141–61.

[13] Michalewicz Z. Genetic algorithms + data structures = evolution programs. Springer-Verlag; 1999.
[14] Rudolph G. Convergence analysis of canonical genetic algorithms. IEEE Trans Neural Netw 1994;5(1):96–101.
[15] Sharapov RR. Genetic algorithms: basic ideas, variants and analysis. In: Obinata G, Dutta A, editors. Vision systems: segmentation and pattern recognition. Vienna, Austria: I-Tech; June 2007.
[16] Suzuki J. A Markov chain analysis on simple genetic algorithms. IEEE Trans Sys Man Cybern 1995;25(4):655–9.
[17] Villalobos-Arias M, Coello CAC, Hernández-Lerma O. Asymptotic convergence of metaheuristics for multiobjective optimization problems. Soft Comput 2005;10(11):1001–5.

6 Differential Evolution

Differential evolution (DE) is a vector-based metaheuristic algorithm that has good convergence properties. There are many DE variants, and they have been applied in a wide range of disciplines. This chapter provides a brief introduction to the basic differential evolution and its main implementation details and variants. Fundamental convergence properties in terms of population variance are also discussed.

6.1 Introduction

Differential evolution, or DE, was developed in R. Storn and K. Price in their nominal papers in 1996 and 1997 [7,8]. DE is a vector-based metaheuristic algorithm, which has some similarity to pattern search and genetic algorithms due to its use of crossover and mutation. In fact, DE can be considered as a further development to genetic algorithms with explicit updating equations, which make it possible to do some theoretical analysis. DE is a stochastic search algorithm with self-organizing tendency and does not use the information of derivatives. Thus, it is a population-based, derivative-free method. In addition, DE uses real numbers as solution strings, so no encoding and decoding is needed.

As in genetic algorithms, design parameters in a d-dimensional search space are represented as vectors, and various genetic operators are operated over their bits of strings. However, unlike genetic algorithms, differential evolution carries out operations over each component (or each dimension of the solution). Almost everything is done in terms of vectors. For example, in genetic algorithms, mutation is carried out at one site or multiple sites of a chromosome, whereas in differential evolution, a difference vector of two randomly chosen population vectors is used to perturb an existing vector. Such vectorized mutation can be viewed as a more efficient approach from the implementation point of view. This kind of perturbation is carried out over each population vector and thus can be expected to be more efficient. Similarly, crossover is also a vector-based, component-wise exchange of chromosomes or vector segments.

Apart from using mutation and crossover as differential operators, DE has explicit updating equations. This also makes it straightforward to implement and to design new variants.

Nature-Inspired Optimization Algorithms. http://dx.doi.org/10.1016/B978-0-12-416743-8.00006-3

6.2 Differential Evolution

For a d-dimensional optimization problem with d parameters, a population of n solution vectors are initially generated. We have $\boldsymbol{x}_i$, where $i = 1, 2, \ldots, n$. For each solution $\boldsymbol{x}_i$ at any generation t, we use the conventional notation as

$$\boldsymbol{x}_i^t = (x_{1,i}^t, x_{2,i}^t, \ldots, x_{d,i}^t), \tag{6.1}$$

which consists of d-components in the d-dimensional space. This vector can be considered the chromosomes or genomes.

Differential evolution consists of three main steps: mutation, crossover, and selection.

Mutation is carried out by the mutation scheme. For each vector $\boldsymbol{x}_i$ at any time or generation t, we first randomly choose three distinct vectors $\boldsymbol{x}_p$, $\boldsymbol{x}_q$, and $\boldsymbol{x}_r$ at t (see Figure 6.1), and then we generate a so-called donor vector by the mutation scheme

$$\boldsymbol{v}_i^{t+1} = \boldsymbol{x}_p^t + F(\boldsymbol{x}_q^t - \boldsymbol{x}_r^t), \tag{6.2}$$

where $F \in [0, 2]$ is a parameter, often referred to as the *differential weight*. This requires that the minimum number of the population size is $n \geq 4$. In principle, $F \in [0, 2]$, but in practice, a scheme with $F \in [0, 1]$ is more efficient and stable. In fact, almost all the studies in the literature use $F \in (0, 1)$.

From Figure 6.1, we can see that the perturbation $\boldsymbol{\delta} = F(\boldsymbol{x}_q - \boldsymbol{x}_r)$ to the vector $\boldsymbol{x}_p$ is used to generate a donor vector $\boldsymbol{v}_i$, and such perturbation is directed.

The crossover is controlled by a crossover parameter $C_r \in [0, 1]$, controlling the rate or probability for crossover. The actual crossover can be carried out in two ways: binomial and exponential. The binomial scheme performs crossover on each of the d components or variables/parameters. By generating a uniformly distributed random number $r_i \in [0, 1]$, the jth component of $\boldsymbol{v}_i$ is manipulated as

$$\boldsymbol{u}_{j,i}^{t+1} = \begin{cases} \boldsymbol{v}_{j,i} & \text{if } r_i \leq C_r, \\ \boldsymbol{x}_{j,i}^t & \text{otherwise,} \end{cases} \qquad j = 1, 2, \ldots, d. \tag{6.3}$$

This way, it can be decided randomly whether to exchange each component with a donor vector or not.

In the exponential scheme, a segment of the donor vector is selected, and this segment starts with a random integer k with a random length L, which can include many

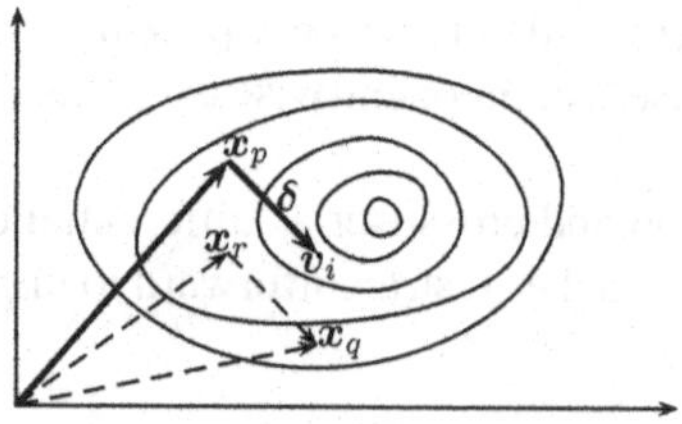

Figure 6.1 Schematic representation of mutation vectors in differential evolution with movement $\boldsymbol{\delta} = F(\boldsymbol{x}_q - \boldsymbol{x}_r)$.

Differential Evolution

Initialize the population $\boldsymbol{x}$ with randomly generated solutions
Set the weight $F \in [0,2]$ and crossover probability $C_r \in [0,1]$
while (stopping criterion)
  for $i = 1$ to n,
  For each $\boldsymbol{x}_i$, randomly choose 3 distinct vectors $\boldsymbol{x}_p$, $\boldsymbol{x}_r$ and $\boldsymbol{x}_r$
  Generate a new vector $\boldsymbol{v}$ by DE scheme (6.2)
  Generate a random index $J_r \in \{1, 2, ..., d\}$ by permutation
  Generate a randomly distributed number $r_i \in [0,1]$
  for $j = 1$ to d,
  For each parameter $\boldsymbol{v}_{j,i}$ (jth component of $\boldsymbol{v}_i$), update

$$\boldsymbol{u}_{j,i}^{t+1} = \begin{cases} \boldsymbol{v}_{j,i}^{t+1} & \text{if } r_i \leq C_r \text{ or } j = J_r \\ \boldsymbol{x}_{j,i}^{t} & \text{if } r_i > C_r \text{ and } j \neq J_r, \end{cases}$$

  end
  Select and update the solution by (6.5)
  end
end
Post-process and output the best solution found

Figure 6.2 Pseudo code of differential evolution.

components. Mathematically, this is to choose $k \in [0, d-1]$ and $L \in [1, d]$ randomly, and we have

$$\boldsymbol{u}_{j,i}^{t+1} = \begin{cases} \boldsymbol{v}_{j,i}^{t} & \text{for } j = k, \ldots, k - L + 1 \in [1, d], \\ \boldsymbol{x}_{j,i}^{t} & \text{otherwise.} \end{cases} \tag{6.4}$$

Because the binomial is simpler to implement, we will use the binomial crossover in our implementation.

Selection is essentially the same as that used in genetic algorithms. We select the fittest and, for the minimization problem, the minimum objective value. Therefore, we have

$$\boldsymbol{x}_i^{t+1} = \begin{cases} \boldsymbol{u}_i^{t+1} & \text{if } f(\boldsymbol{u}_i^{t+1}) \leq f(\boldsymbol{x}_i^t), \\ \boldsymbol{x}_i^t & \text{otherwise.} \end{cases} \tag{6.5}$$

All three components can be seen in the pseudo code shown in Figure 6.2. It is worth pointing out here that the use of J is to ensure that $\boldsymbol{v}_i^{t+1} \neq \boldsymbol{x}_i^t$, which may increase the evolutionary or exploratory efficiency. The overall search efficiency is controlled by two parameters: the differential weight F and the crossover probability C_r.

6.3 Variants

Most studies have focused on the choice of F, C_r and n as well as the modifications of (6.2). In fact, when generating mutation vectors, we can use many different ways of formulating (6.2), and this leads to various schemes with the naming convention: DE/x/y/z, where x is the mutation scheme (rand or best), y is the number of difference vectors, and z is the crossover scheme (binomial or exponential). So, DE/Rand/1/* means the basic DE scheme using random mutation and one difference vector with either a binomial or exponential crossover scheme.

The basic DE/Rand/1/Bin scheme is given in (6.2). That is,

$$v_i^{t+1} = x_p^t + F(x_q^t - x_r^t). \tag{6.6}$$

If we replace the x_p^t by the current best x_{best} found so far, we have the so-called DE/Best/1/Bin scheme,

$$v_i^{t+1} = x_{\text{best}}^t + F(x_q^t - x_r^t). \tag{6.7}$$

There is no reason that we should not use more than three distinct vectors. For example. if we use four different vectors plus the current best, we have the DE/Best/2/Bin scheme

$$v_i^{t+1} = x_{\text{best}}^t + F(x_{k_1}^t + x_{k_2}^t - x_{k_3}^t - x_{k_4}^t). \tag{6.8}$$

Furthermore, if we use five different vectors, we have the DE/Rand/2/Bin scheme

$$v_i^{t+1} = x_{k_1}^t + F_1(x_{k_2}^t - x_{k_3}^t) + F_2(x_{k_4}^t - x_{k_5}^t), \tag{6.9}$$

where F_1 and F_2 are differential weights in $[0, 1]$. Obviously, for simplicity, we can also take $F_1 = F_2 = F$.

Following the similar strategy, we can design various schemes. For example, these variants can be written in a generalized form

$$v_i^{t+1} = x_{k_1}^t + \sum_{s=1}^{m} F_s \cdot (x_{k_2(s)}^t - x_{k_3(s)}^t), \tag{6.10}$$

where $m = 1, 2, 3, \ldots$ and $F_s (s = 1, \ldots, m)$ are the scale factors. The number of vectors involved on the right-hand side is $2m + 1$. In the preceding variants, $m = 1$ and $m = 2$ are used [9, 14].

On the other hand, there is another type of variant that uses an additional influence parameter $\lambda \in (0, 1)$. For example the DE/rand-to-best/1/* variant can be written as

$$v_i^{t+1} = \lambda x_{\text{best}}^t + (1 - \lambda) x_{k_1}^t + F(x_{k_2}^t - x_{k_3}^t), \tag{6.11}$$

which introduces an extra parameter λ. Again, this type of variants can be written in a generalized form:

$$v_i^{t+1} = \lambda x_{\text{best}}^t + (1 - \lambda) x_{k_1}^t + F \sum_{s=1}^{m} (x_{k_2(s)}^t - x_{k_3(s)}^t). \tag{6.12}$$

In fact, more than 10 different schemes have been formulated; for details, refer to Price et al. [9]

There are other good variants of DE, including self-adapting control parameters in differential evolution (jDE) by Brest et al. [2], self-adaptive DE (SaDE) [6], and DE with the eagle strategy [11].

Multiobjective variants also exist. For a detailed review, refer to Das and Suganthan [4] or Chakraborty [3].

6.4 Choice of Parameters

The choice of parameters is important. Both empirical observations and parametric studies suggest that parameter values should be fine-tuned [4,5,9].

The scale factor F is the most sensitive one. Though $F \in [0, 2]$ is acceptable in theory, $F \in (0, 1)$ is more efficient in practice. In fact, $F \in [0.4, 0.95]$ is a good range, with a good first choice being $F = [0.7, 0.9]$.

The crossover parameter $C_r \in [0.1, 0.8]$ seems a good range, and the first choice can use $C_r = 0.5$.

It is suggested that the population size n should depend on the dimensionality d of the problem. That is, $n = 5d$ to $10d$. This may be a disadvantage for higher-dimensional problems because the population size can be large. However, there is no reason that a fixed value (say, $n = 40$ or 100) cannot be tried first.

6.5 Convergence Analysis

There are relatively extensive studies on the convergence properties and the parameter sensitivity of differential evolution in the literature [4,5,10,12–14]. For example, it has been observed that the performance of DE is more sensitive to the value of the scale factor F than to C_r. As another example, Xue et al. [10] analyzed the general variant in the form of Eq. (6.12), concluding that

$$2mF^2 + (1 - \lambda)^2 > 1, \quad \lambda \in (0, 1). \tag{6.13}$$

They also pointed out that λ should be reasonably large so as to give better convergence.

The main results in the rest of this section are primarily based on the studies by Zaharie [13,14]. One of the conditions to avoid premature convergence of any population-based algorithms is to maintain a good degree of diversity in the population [1]. Based on the flat objective landscape (thus without selection pressure), the variance of any DE variant can be computed using component-based expected variance $E(\text{var}(P))$ of the population $P = \{P_1, P_2, \ldots, P_n\}$. Because all the variants we mentioned earlier are linear, the expected variance of DE depends linearly on the variance of the current population $X = (\boldsymbol{x}_1, \ldots, \boldsymbol{x}_n)$. That is,

$$E(\text{var}(P)) = c \ \text{var}(X), \tag{6.14}$$

where c is a constant.

For the basic DE/rand/1/* schemes, Zaharie calculated the variance of the population without selection and obtained

$$E(\text{var}(P)) = \Big(1 + 2p_m F^2 - \frac{p_m(2 - p_m)}{n}\Big)\text{var}(X), \tag{6.15}$$

where p_m is the mutation probability that is related to the crossover parameter C_r as

$$p_m = \begin{cases} C_r(1 - \frac{1}{d}) + \frac{1}{d} & \text{(binomial crossover)}, \\ \frac{1-C_r^d}{d(1-C_r)} & \text{(exponential crossover)}. \end{cases} \tag{6.16}$$

If the initial population is $X^{(t=0)} = X(0)$, the variance of the population after t generations/iterations becomes

$$\mathrm{var}(P) = \left(1 + 2F^2 p_m - \frac{p_m(2 - p_m)}{n}\right)^t \mathrm{var}(X(0)). \tag{6.17}$$

This defines a critical value of F as

$$1 + 2F^2 p_m - \frac{p_m(2 - p_m)}{n} = 1, \tag{6.18}$$

which gives

$$F_c = \sqrt{\frac{(2 - p_m)}{n}}. \tag{6.19}$$

Therefore, the population variance decreases if $F < F_c$ and increases if $F > F_c$. Obviously, the population variance will remain constant when $F = F_c$.

For example, for $C_r = 0.5$ and $d = 10$ in the binomial crossover case, we have

$$p_m = C_r\left(1 - \frac{1}{d}\right) + \frac{1}{d} = 0.5 \times \left(1 - \frac{1}{10}\right) + \frac{1}{10} = 0.55. \tag{6.20}$$

Empirical observations suggest that $F \in [0.4, 0.95]$, with a good first choice of $F = 0.9$ [4,5,9]. Alternatively, for a given p_m, we can estimate the C_r value as

$$C_r = \frac{(p_m - 1/d)}{(1 - 1/d)}. \tag{6.21}$$

So, for a moderate $p_m = 0.5$ and $d = 10$, we have

$$C_r = \frac{(0.2 - 1/10)}{(1 - 1/10)} \approx 0.44. \tag{6.22}$$

Interestingly, when $d \to \infty$, $C_r \to p_m$.

Obviously, these results are valid for the basic DE/Rand/1/*. For other variants, the formulas are similar, with some modifications including the parameter λ.

These theoretical results mean that when $\mathrm{var}(P)$ is decreasing, the DE algorithm is converging. In other words, when $\mathrm{var}(P) \to 0$, the algorithm has converged. However, such convergence can be premature because the converged state may not be the true global optimality of the problem.

From the preceding formula (6.17), we can see that the variance or the population diversity also largely depends on the initial population, which is a significant drawback of DE. In addition, some difficulty may arise in dealing with nonsparable nonlinear functions. Furthermore, there is no sufficient evidence that DE can deal with combinatorial problems efficiently due to the potential difficulty in discretizing the differential operators and defining effective neighborhoods [4,3,9].

6.6 Implementation

The implementation of differential evolution is relatively straightforward, comparing with genetic algorithms. If a vector/matrix-based software package such as Matlab is used, the implementation becomes even more simple.

The simple version of the DE in Matlab/Octave given next is for unconstrained optimization, where Rosenbrock's function with three variables is solved by default. To solve constrained optimization problems, this program can easily be extended in combination with the penalty method discussed elsewhere in the book.

```
% Differential Evolution for global optimization
% Programmed by Xin-She Yang @Cambridge University 2008

% The basic version of scheme DE/Rand/1 is implemented
% Usage: de(para) or de;

function [best,fmin,N_iter]=de(para)
% Default parameters
if nargin<1,
   para=[10 0.7 0.9];
end

n=para(1);          % Population >=4, typically 10 to 25
F=para(2);          % DE parameter - scaling (0.5 to 0.9)
Cr=para(3);         % DE parameter - crossover probability

% Iteration parameters
tol=10^(-5);        % Stop tolerance
N_iter=0;           % Total number of function evaluations

% Simple bounds
Lb=[-1 -1 -1];
Ub=[2 2  2];

% Dimension of the search variables
d=length(Lb);

% Initialize the population/solutions
for i=1:n,
  Sol(i,:)=Lb+(Ub-Lb).*rand(size(Lb));
  Fitness(i)=Fun(Sol(i,:));
end

% Find the current best
[fmin,I]=min(Fitness);
best=Sol(I,:)
```

```
% Start the iterations by differential evolution
while (fmin>tol)
    % Obtain donor vectors by permutation
    k1=randperm(n);      k2=randperm(n);
    k1sol=Sol(k1,:);     k2sol=Sol(k2,:);
        % Random crossover index/matrix
        K=rand(n,d)<Cr;
        % DE/RAND/1 scheme
        V=Sol+F*(k1sol-k2sol);
        V=Sol.*(1-K)+V.*K;

        % Evaluate new solutions
        for i=1:n,
           Fnew=Fun(V(i,:));
           % If the solution improves
           if Fnew<=Fitness(i),
                Sol(i,:)=V(i,:);
                Fitness(i)=Fnew;
           end
          % Update the current best
          if Fnew<=fmin,
                best=V(i,:);
                fmin=Fnew;
          end
        end
        N_iter=N_iter+n;
end

% Output/display
disp(['Number of evaluations: ',num2str(N_iter)]);
disp(['Best=',num2str(best),' fmin=',num2str(fmin)]);


% Objective function -- Rosenbrock's 3D function
function z=Fun(u)
z=(1-u(1))^2+100*(u(2)-u(1)^2)^2+100*(u(3)-u(2)^2)^2;
```

References

[1] Beyer HG. On the dynamics of EAs without selection. In: Banzaf W, Reeves C, editors. Foundations of genetic algorithms. San Francisco, CA, USA: Morgan Kaufmann Publishers; 1999. p. 5–26.

[2] Brest J, Greiner S, Boskovic B, Mernik M, Zumer V. Self-adapting control parameters in differential evolution: a comparative study on numerical benchmark functions. IEEE Trans Evol Comput 2006;10(6):646–57.

[3] Chakraborty UK. Advances in differential evolution. Studies in computational intelligence, vol. 143. Heidelberg, Germany: Springer; 2008.

[4] Das S, Suganthan PN. Differential evolution: a survey of the state-of-the-art. IEEE Trans Evol Comput 2011;15(1):4–31.

[5] Jeyakumar G, Velayutham CS. Convergence analysis of differential evolution variants on unconstrained global optimization functions. Int J Art Intell Appl 2011;2(2):116–26.

[6] Qin AK, Huang VL, Suganthan PN. Differential evolution algorithm with strategy adaptation for global numerical optimization. IEEE Trans Evol Comput 2009;13(2):398–417.

[7] Storn R. On the usage of differential evolution for function optimization. In: Biennial conference of the North American fuzzy information processing society (NAFIPS); 1996. p. 519–23.

[8] Storn R, Price K. Differential evolution: a simple and efficient heuristic for global optimization over continuous spaces. J Global Optimization 1997;11:341–59.

[9] Price K, Storn R, Lampinen J. Differential evolution: a practical approach to global optimization. Germany: Springer; 2005.

[10] Xue F, Sanderson AC, Graves RJ. Multiobjective differential evolution: algorithm, convergence analysis and applications. In: Proceedings of congress on evolutionary computation (CEC 2005), Edinburgh, vol. 1. Edinburgh, Scotland: IEEE Publication; 2005. p. 743–50.

[11] Yang XS, Deb S. Two-stage eagle strategy with differential evolution. Int J Bio-Inspired Comput 2012;4(1):1–5.

[12] Zaharie D. A comparative analysis of crossover variants in differential evolution. In: Ganzha M, Paprzycki M, Pilichowski TP, editors. Proceedings of the international multiconferenceon computer science and information technology, October 15–17, 2007. Poland: Wisla; 2007. p. 171–81. (Polskie Towarzystwo Informatyczne, PIPS, Katowice).

[13] Zaharie D. Influence of crossover on the behavior of the differential evolution algorithm. Appl Soft Comput 2009;9(3):1126–38.

[14] Zaharie D. Differential evolution: from theoretical results to practical insights. In: Matousek R, editor. Proceedings of the 18th international conference on soft computing, June 27–29, Brno. Czech Republic: Brno University of Technology Press; 2012. p. 126–31.

7 Particle Swarm Optimization

Particle swarm optimization (PSO) was developed by Kennedy and Eberhart in 1995 based on swarm behavior in nature, such as fish and bird schooling. Since then, PSO has generated much wider interests and forms an exciting, ever-expanding research subject, called swarm intelligence. PSO has been applied to almost every area in optimization, computational intelligence, and design applications. There are at least two dozen PSO variants, and hybrid algorithms by combining PSO with other existing algorithms are also investigated extensively.

7.1 Swarm Intelligence

Many algorithms such as ant colony algorithms and firefly algorithm use the behavior of so-called *swarm intelligence* [7,3,14,15]. Particle swarm optimization, or PSO, was developed by Kennedy and Eberhart in 1995 [6] and has become one of the most widely used swarm-intelligence-based algorithms due to its simplicity and flexibility. Rather than use the mutation/crossover or pheromone, it uses real-number randomness and global communication among the swarm particles. Therefore, it is also easier to implement because there is no encoding or decoding of the parameters into binary strings as with those in genetic algorithms where real-number strings can also be used.

Many new algorithms that are based on swarm intelligence may have drawn inspiration from different sources, but they have some similarity to some of the components that are used in PSO. In this sense, PSO pioneered the basic ideas of swarm-intelligence-based computation.

7.2 PSO Algorithm

The PSO algorithm searches the space of an objective function by adjusting the trajectories of individual agents, called *particles*, as the piecewise paths formed by positional vectors in a quasi-stochastic manner [6,7,3]. The movement of a swarming particle consists of two major components: a stochastic component and a deterministic component. Each particle is attracted toward the position of the current global best $\boldsymbol{g}^*$ and its own best location $\boldsymbol{x}_i^*$ in history, while at the same time it has a tendency to move randomly.

When a particle finds a location that is better than any previously found locations, updates that location as the new current best for particle i. There is a current best for all n particles at any time t during iterations. The aim is to find the global best among all the

Nature-Inspired Optimization Algorithms. http://dx.doi.org/10.1016/B978-0-12-416743-8.00007-5

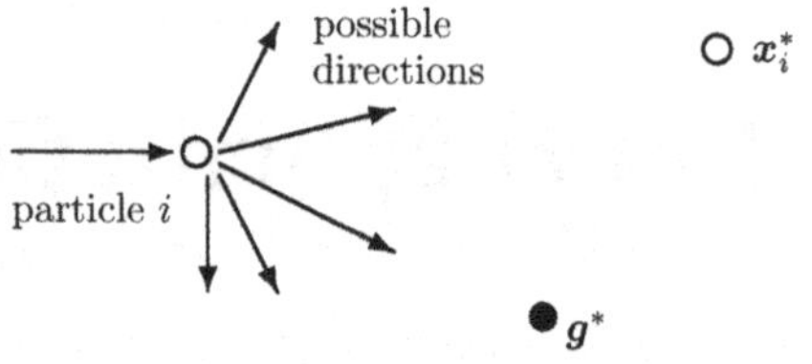

Figure 7.1 Schematic representation of the motion of a particle in PSO moving toward the global best g^* and the current best x_i^* for each particle i.

```
Particle Swarm Optimization
Objective function f(x), x = (x_1, ..., x_d)^T
Initialize locations x_i and velocity v_i of n particles.
Find g* from min{f(x_1), ..., f(x_n)} (at t = 0)
while ( criterion )
   for loop over all n particles and all d dimensions
   Generate new velocity v_i^{t+1} using equation (7.1)
   Calculate new locations x_i^{t+1} = x_i^t + v_i^{t+1}
   Evaluate objective functions at new locations x_i^{t+1}
   Find the current best for each particle x_i^*
   end for
   Find the current global best g*
   Update t = t + 1 (pseudo time or iteration counter)
end while
Output the final results x_i^* and g*
```

Figure 7.2 Pseudo code of particle swarm optimization.

current best solutions until the objective no longer improves or after a certain number of iterations. The movement of particles is schematically represented in Figure 7.1, where $x_i^{*(t)}$ is the current best for particle i, and $g^* \approx \min\{f(x_i)\}$ for $(i = 1, 2, \ldots, n)$ is the current global best at t.

The essential steps of the particle swarm optimization can be summarized as the pseudo code shown in Figure 7.2.

Let x_i and v_i be the position vector and velocity for particle i, respectively. The new velocity vector is determined by the following formula:

$$v_i^{t+1} = v_i^t + \alpha\epsilon_1[g^* - x_i^t] + \beta\epsilon_2[x_i^{*(t)} - x_i^t], \tag{7.1}$$

where ϵ_1 and ϵ_2 are two random vectors, and each entry takes the values between 0 and 1. The parameters α and β are the learning parameters or acceleration constants, which can typically be taken as, say, $\alpha \approx \beta \approx 2$.

The initial locations of all particles should distribute relatively uniformly so that they can sample over most regions, which is especially important for multimodal problems. The initial velocity of a particle can be taken as zero, that is, $v_i^{t=0} = 0$. The new position can then be updated by

$$x_i^{t+1} = x_i^t + v_i^{t+1}. \tag{7.2}$$

Although v_i can be any values, it is usually bounded in some range $[0, v_{\max}]$.

There are many variants that extend the standard PSO algorithm, and the most noticeable improvement is probably to use the inertia function $\theta(t)$ so that v_i^t is replaced by $\theta(t)v_i^t$

$$v_i^{t+1} = \theta v_i^t + \alpha\epsilon_1\big[g^* - x_i^t\big] + \beta\epsilon_2\big[x_i^{*(k)} - x_i^t\big], \tag{7.3}$$

where θ takes the values between 0 and 1 in theory [1,7]. In the simplest case, the inertia function can be taken as a constant, typically $\theta \approx 0.5 \sim 0.9$. This is equivalent to introducing a virtual mass to stabilize the motion of the particles, and thus the algorithm is expected to converge more quickly.

7.3 Accelerated PSO

The standard particle swarm optimization uses both the current global best g^* and the individual best $x_i^{*(t)}$. One of the reasons for using the individual best is probably to increase the diversity in the quality solutions; however, this diversity can be simulated using some randomness. Subsequently, there is no compelling reason for using the individual best unless the optimization problem of interest is highly nonlinear and multimodal.

A simplified version that could accelerate the convergence of the algorithm is to use only the global best. The so-called *accelerated particle swarm optimization* (APSO) was developed by Xin-She Yang in 2008 and then developed further in recent studies [13,4]. Thus, in APSO, the velocity vector is generated by a simpler formula

$$v_i^{t+1} = v_i^t + \alpha(\epsilon - 1/2) + \beta(g^* - x_i^t), \tag{7.4}$$

where ϵ is a random variable with values from 0 to 1. Here the shift 1/2 is purely out of convenience. We can also use a standard normal distribution $\alpha\epsilon_t$, where ϵ_t is drawn from $N(0, 1)$ to replace the second term. Now we have

$$v_i^{t+1} = v_i^t + \beta(g^* - x_i^t) + \alpha\epsilon_t, \tag{7.5}$$

where ϵ_t can be drawn from a Gaussian distribution or any other suitable distributions.

The update of the position is simply

$$x_i^{t+1} = x_i^t + v_i^{t+1}. \tag{7.6}$$

To simplify the formulation even further, we can also write the update of the location in a single step:

$$x_i^{t+1} = (1 - \beta)x_i^t + \beta g^* + \alpha\epsilon_t. \tag{7.7}$$

The typical values for this accelerated PSO are $\alpha \approx 0.1 \sim 0.4$ and $\beta \approx 0.1 \sim 0.7$, though $\alpha \approx 0.2$ and $\beta \approx 0.5$ can be taken as the initial values for most unimodal objective functions. It is worth pointing out that the parameters α and β should in general be related to the scales of the independent variables $\boldsymbol{x}_i$ and the search domain. Surprisingly, this simplified APSO can have global convergence [5].

A further improvement to the accelerated PSO is to reduce the randomness as iterations proceed. This means that we can use a monotonically decreasing function such as

$$\alpha = \alpha_0 e^{-\gamma t}, \tag{7.8}$$

or

$$\alpha = \alpha_0 \gamma^t, \quad (0 < \gamma < 1), \tag{7.9}$$

where $\alpha_0 \approx 0.5 \sim 1$ is the initial value of the randomness parameter. Here t is the number of iterations or time steps. $0 < \gamma < 1$ is a control parameter. For example, in our implementation, we can use $\gamma = 0.9$ to 0.97. Obviously, other non-increasing function forms $\alpha(t)$ can also be used as we can see in our demo implementation later. In addition, these parameters should be fine-tuned to suit your optimization problems of interest.

7.4 Implementation

The APSO has been implemented using both Matlab and Octave, and a simple program is provided here. This program can find the global optimal solution of most nonlinear functions in less than a minute on a desktop computer.

Now let us look at the 2D Michalewicz function

$$f(x, y) = -\left\{ \sin(x) \left[\sin\left(\frac{x^2}{\pi}\right) \right]^{2m} + \sin(y) \left[\sin\left(\frac{2y^2}{\pi}\right) \right]^{2m} \right\},$$

where $m = 10$. The stationary conditions $f_x = f_y = 0$ require that

$$-\frac{4m}{\pi} x \sin(x) \cos\left(\frac{x^2}{\pi}\right) - \cos(x) \sin\left(\frac{x^2}{\pi}\right) = 0,$$

and

$$-\frac{8m}{\pi} y \sin(x) \cos\left(\frac{2y^2}{\pi}\right) - \cos(y) \sin\left(\frac{2y^2}{\pi}\right) = 0.$$

The solution at (0,0) is trivial, and the minimum $f^* \approx -1.801$ occurs at about (2.20319, 1.57049) (see Figure 7.3).

```
% The Accelerated Particle Swarm Optimization
% (written by X S Yang, Cambridge University)
% Usage: pso(number_of_particles,Num_iterations)
% eg:   best=pso_demo(20,10);
% where best=[xbest ybest zbest]  %an n by 3 matrix
```

```
%   xbest(i)/ybest(i) are the best at ith iteration

function [best]=pso_simpledemo(n,Num_iterations)
% n=number of particles
% Num_iterations=total number of iterations
if nargin<2,   Num_iterations=10;  end
if nargin<1,   n=20;          end
% Michalewicz Function f*=-1.801 at [2.20319,1.57049]
% Splitting two parts to avoid long lines in printing
str1='-sin(x)*(sin(x^2/3.14159))^20';
str2='-sin(y)*(sin(2*y^2/3.14159))^20';
funstr=strcat(str1,str2);
% Converting to an inline function and vectorization
f=vectorize(inline(funstr));
% range=[xmin xmax ymin ymax];
range=[0 4 0 4];
% ----------------------------------------------------
% Setting the parameters: alpha, beta
% Random amplitude of roaming particles alpha=[0,1]
% alpha=gamma^t=0.7^t;
% Speed of convergence (0->1)=(slow->fast)
beta=0.5;
% ----------------------------------------------------
% Grid values of the objective function
% These values are used for visualization only
Ngrid=100;
dx=(range(2)-range(1))/Ngrid;
dy=(range(4)-range(3))/Ngrid;
xgrid=range(1):dx:range(2); ygrid=range(3):dy:range(4);
[x,y]=meshgrid(xgrid,ygrid);
z=f(x,y);
% Display the shape of the function to be optimized
figure(1);
surfc(x,y,z);
% ---------------------------------------------------
best=zeros(Num_iterations,3);   % initialize history
% ----- Start Particle Swarm Optimization -----------
% generating the initial locations of n particles
[xn,yn]=init_pso(n,range);
% Display the paths of particles in a figure
% with a contour of the objective function
 figure(2);
% Start iterations
for i=1:Num_iterations,
% Show the contour of the function
  contour(x,y,z,15); hold on;
% Find the current best location (xo,yo)
zn=f(xn,yn);
zn_min=min(zn);
```

```
xo=min(xn(zn==zn_min));
yo=min(yn(zn==zn_min));
zo=min(zn(zn==zn_min));
% Trace the paths of all roaming particles
% Display these roaming particles
plot(xn,yn,'.',xo,yo,'*'); axis(range);
% The accelerated PSO with alpha=gamma^t
  gamma=0.7; alpha=gamma.^i;
% Move all the particles to new locations
[xn,yn]=pso_move(xn,yn,xo,yo,alpha,beta,range);
drawnow;
% Use "hold on" to display paths of particles
hold off;
% History
best(i,1)=xo; best(i,2)=yo; best(i,3)=zo;
end   %%%%% end of iterations

% ----- All subfunctions are listed here -----
% Intial locations of n particles
function [xn,yn]=init_pso(n,range)
xrange=range(2)-range(1); yrange=range(4)-range(3);
xn=rand(1,n)*xrange+range(1);
yn=rand(1,n)*yrange+range(3);
% Move all the particles toward (xo,yo)
function [xn,yn]=pso_move(xn,yn,xo,yo,a,b,range)
nn=size(yn,2);  %a=alpha, b=beta
xn=xn.*(1-b)+xo.*b+a.*(rand(1,nn)-0.5);
yn=yn.*(1-b)+yo.*b+a.*(rand(1,nn)-0.5);
[xn,yn]=findrange(xn,yn,range);
% Make sure the particles are within the range
function [xn,yn]=findrange(xn,yn,range)
nn=length(yn);
for i=1:nn,
   if xn(i)<=range(1), xn(i)=range(1); end
   if xn(i)>=range(2), xn(i)=range(2); end
   if yn(i)<=range(3), yn(i)=range(3); end
   if yn(i)>=range(4), yn(i)=range(4); end
end
```

If we run the program, we get the global optimum after about 200 evaluations of the objective function (for 20 particles and 10 iterations), as shown in Figure 7.4. Obviously, this is a demo implementation, and a vectorized implementation for any higher dimensions can produce much better results, as we have done in various applications [13].

7.5 Convergence Analysis

From the statistical point of view, each particle in PSO forms a Markov chain, though this Markov chain is biased toward the current best, since the transition probability

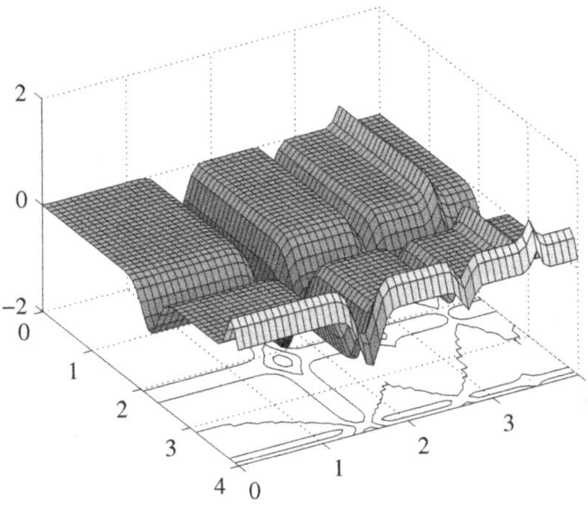

Figure 7.3 Michalewicz's function with the global optimality at (2.20319, 1.57049).

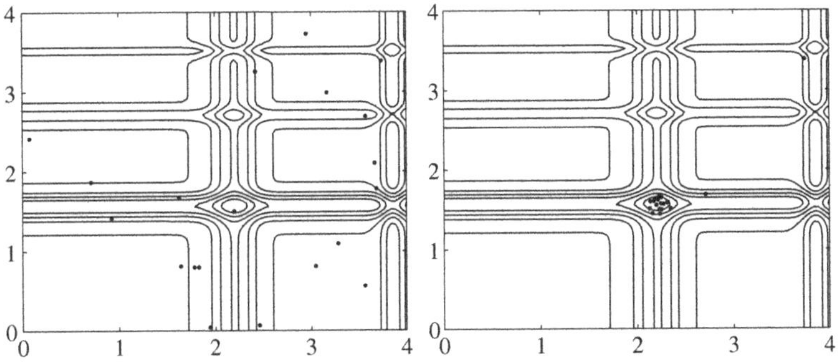

Figure 7.4 Initial and final locations of 20 particles after 10 iterations.

often leads to the acceptance of the move toward the current global best. In addition, the multiple Markov chains are interacting in terms of partially deterministic attraction movement. Therefore, any mathematical analysis concerning the rate of convergence of PSO may be difficult. However, there are some good results using both the dynamical system and Markov chain theories.

7.5.1 Dynamical System

The first convergence analysis in terms of dynamical system theories was carried out by Clerc and Kennedy in 2002 [2]. Mathematically, if we ignore the random factors, we can view the system formed by (7.1) and (7.2) as a dynamical system. If we focus on a single particle i and imagine there is only one particle in this system, then the global best $\boldsymbol{g}^*$ is the same as its current best $\boldsymbol{x}_i^*$. In this case, we have

$$\boldsymbol{v}_i^{t+1} = \boldsymbol{v}_i^t + \gamma(\boldsymbol{g}^* - \boldsymbol{x}_i^t), \quad \gamma = \alpha + \beta, \tag{7.10}$$

and

$$x_i^{t+1} = x_i^t + v_i^{t+1}. \tag{7.11}$$

Following the analysis of a 1D dynamical system for particle swarm optimization by Clerc and Kennedy [2], we can replace g^* with a parameter constant p so that we can see whether or not the particle of interest will converge toward p. Now we can write this system as a simple dynamical system

$$v(t+1) = v(t) + \gamma(p - x(t)), \quad x(t+1) = x(t) + v(t+1). \tag{7.12}$$

For simplicity, we focus on only a single particle. By setting $u_t = p - x(t+1)$ and using the notations for dynamical systems, we have

$$v_{t+1} = v_t + \gamma u_t, \tag{7.13}$$

$$u_{t+1} = -v_t + (1-\gamma)u_t, \tag{7.14}$$

or

$$Y_{t+1} = AY_t, \tag{7.15}$$

where

$$A = \begin{pmatrix} 1 & \gamma \\ -1 & 1-\gamma \end{pmatrix}, \quad Y_t = \begin{pmatrix} v_t \\ u_t \end{pmatrix}. \tag{7.16}$$

The general solution of this dynamical system can be written as

$$Y_t = Y_0 \exp[At]. \tag{7.17}$$

The main behavior of this system can be characterized by the eigenvalues λ of A

$$\lambda_{1,2} = 1 - \frac{\gamma}{2} \pm \frac{\sqrt{\gamma^2 - 4\gamma}}{2}. \tag{7.18}$$

It can be seen clearly that $\gamma = 4$ leads to a bifurcation.

Following a straightforward analysis of this dynamical system, we can have three cases. For $0 < \gamma < 4$, cyclic and/or quasi-cyclic trajectories exist. In this case, when randomness is gradually reduced, some convergence can be observed. For $\gamma > 4$, noncyclic behavior can be expected, and the distance from Y_t to the center (0, 0) is monotonically increasing with t. In a special case $\gamma = 4$, some convergence behavior can be observed. For detailed analysis, refer to [2]. Since p is linked with the global best, as the iterations continue it can be expected that all particles will aggregate toward the global best.

However, this global best is the best solution found by the algorithm during iterations, which may be different from the true global optimality of the problem of interest. This point will also become clearer in the framework of Markov chain theory.

7.5.2 Markov Chain Approach

Various studies on the convergence properties of the PSO algorithm have diverse results [2,9–12]. However, care should be taken in interpreting these results in practice, especially for the discussion of the implications from a practical perspective.

Many studies can prove the convergence of the PSO under appropriate conditions, but the converged states are often linked to the current global best solution $\boldsymbol{g}^*$ found so far. There is no guarantee that this $\boldsymbol{g}^*$ is the true global solution $\boldsymbol{g}_{\text{true}}$ to the problem. In fact, many simulations and empirical observations by many researchers suggest that in many cases, this $\boldsymbol{g}^*$ is often stuck in a local optimum, which is often referred to as the *premature convergence*. All these theories do not guarantee

$$\boldsymbol{g}^* \approx \boldsymbol{g}_{\text{true}}. \tag{7.19}$$

In fact, many statistically significant test cases suggest that

$$\boldsymbol{g}^* \neq \boldsymbol{g}_{\text{true}}. \tag{7.20}$$

According to a recent study by Pan et al. [9], the standard PSO does not guarantee that the global optimum is reachable, and the global optimality is searchable with a certain probability $p(\zeta_m^{(t)})$, where k is the kth iteration and m is the swarm size. Here ζ is the state sequences of the particles.

For a given swarm size m and iteration k, a Markov chain $\{\xi_i^{(k)}, k \geq 1\}$ formed by the ith particle at time k can be defined, and then the swarm state sequence $\zeta^{(k)} = (\xi_i^{(k)}, \ldots, \xi_m^{(k)})$ also forms a Markov chain for all $k \geq 1$. For the standard PSO with an inertia parameter θ shown in Eq. (7.3), the probability that $\zeta^{(k+1)}$ is in the optimal set Ω_* can be estimated by

$$p(\zeta^{(k+1} \in \Omega_* | k, m)$$
$$= 1 - p(\zeta^{(1)}) \cdot \prod_{j=1}^{k} \prod_{i=1}^{m} \left(1 - \frac{R_k}{\theta ||\boldsymbol{x}_i^k - \boldsymbol{x}_i^{k-1}||} \cdot \frac{R_k}{c||\boldsymbol{x}_i^{*(k)} - \boldsymbol{x}_i^k||} \cdot \frac{R_k}{c||\boldsymbol{g}_* - \boldsymbol{x}_i^k||}\right), \tag{7.21}$$

where $R_k > 0$ is a local radius and c is defined by $\epsilon_1, \epsilon_2 \sim U(0, c)$. Pan et al. showed that

$$0 \leq p\left(\zeta^{(k+1)} | k, m\right) \leq 1, \tag{7.22}$$

which means that the standard PSO will not guarantee to get to the global optimality nor guarantee to miss it. The equality $p = 1$ only holds for $m \to \infty$ and $k \to \infty$. Since the size is finite and the iteration is also finite, this probability is typically $0 < p < 1$.

However, that the standard PSO does not guarantee convergence does not mean that other variants cannot have global convergence. In fact, a recent study used the framework of Markov chain theory and proved that APSO can have global convergence [5].

7.6 Binary PSO

In the standard PSO, the positions and velocities take continuous values. However, many problems are combinatorial and their variables take only discrete values. In some cases, the variables can only be 0 and 1, and such binary problems require modifications of the PSO algorithm. Kennedy and Eberhart in 1997 presented a stochastic approach to discretize the standard PSO, and they interpreted the velocity in a stochastic sense [8].

First, the continuous velocity $\mathbf{v}_i = (v_{i1}, v_{i2}, \ldots, v_{ik}, \ldots, v_{id})$ is transformed using a sigmoid transformation

$$S(v_{ik}) = \frac{1}{1 + \exp(-v_{ik})}, \quad k = 1, 2, \ldots, d, \tag{7.23}$$

which applies to each component of the velocity vector $\mathbf{v}_i$ of particle i. Obviously, when $v_{ik} \to \infty$, we have $S(v_{ik}) \to 1$, while $S_{ik} \to 0$ when $v_{ik} \to -\infty$. However, because the variations at the two extremes are very slow, a stochastic approach is introduced.

Second, a uniformly distributed random number $r \in (0, 1)$ is drawn, then the velocity is converted to a binary variable by the following stochastic rule:

$$x_{ik} = \begin{cases} 1 & \text{if } r < S(v_{ik}), \\ 0 & \text{otherwise.} \end{cases} \tag{7.24}$$

In this case, the value of each velocity component v_{ik} is interpreted as a probability for x_{ik} taking the value 1. Even for a fixed value of v_{ik}, the actual value of x_{ik} is not certain before a random number r is drawn. In this sense, the *binary PSO* (BPSO) differs significantly from the standard continuous PSO.

In fact, since each component of each variable takes only 0 and 1, this BPSO can work for both discrete and continuous problems if the latter is coded in the binary system. Because the probability of each bit/component taking one is $S(v_{ik})$ and the probability of taking zero is $1 - S(v_{ik})$, the joint probability p of a bit change can be computed by

$$p = S(v_{ik})[1 - S(v_{ik})]. \tag{7.25}$$

Based on the runtime analysis of the BPSO by Sudholt and Witt [10], there are some interesting results on the convergence of BPSO. If the objective function has a unique global optimum in a d-dimensional space and the BPSO has a population size n with $\alpha + \beta = O(1)$, the expected number N of internations/generations of BPSO is

$$N = O\left(\frac{d}{\log d}\right), \tag{7.26}$$

and the expected freezing time is $O(d)$ for single bits and $O(d \log d)$ for nd bits.

One of the advantages of this binary coding and discritization is to enable binary representations of even continuous problems. For example, Kennedy and Eberhart provided an example of solving the second De Jong function and found that 110111101110110111101001 in a 24-bit string corresponds to the optimal solution 3905.929932 from this representation. However, a disadvantage is that the Hamming distance from other local optima is large; therefore, it is unlikely that the search will jump from one local optimum to another. This means that binary PSO can get stuck in a local optimum with premature convergence. New remedies are still under active research.

Various studies show that PSO algorithms can outperform genetic algorithms and other conventional algorithms for solving many optimization problems. This is partially due to that fact that the broadcasting ability of the current best estimates gives a better and quicker convergence toward the optimality. However, PSO algorithms do have some disadvantages, such as premature convergence. Further developments and improvements are still under active research.

Furthermore, as we can see from other chapters in this book, other methods such as the cuckoo search (CS) and firefly algorithms (FA) can perform even better than PSO in many applications. In many cases, DE, PSO, and SA can be considered special cases of CS and FA. Therefore, CS and FA have become an even more active area for further research.

References

[1] Chatterjee A, Siarry P. Nonlinear inertia variation for dynamic adaptation in particle swarm optimization. Comp Oper Res 2006;33(3):859–71.
[2] Clerc M, Kennedy J. The particle swarm. Explosion, stability, and convergence in a multidimensional complex space. IEEE Trans Evol Comput 2002;6(1):58–73.
[3] Engelbrecht AP. Fundamentals of computational Swarm intelligence. Hoboken, NJ, USA: Wiley; 2005.
[4] Gandomi AH, Yun GJ, Yang XS, Talatahari S. Chaos-enhanced accelerated particle swarm optimization. Commun Nonlinear Sci Numer Simul 2013;18(2):327–40.
[5] He XS, Xu L, Yang XS. Global convergence analysis of accelerated particle swarm optimization. Appl Math Comput [submitted, Sept 2013].
[6] Kennedy J, Eberhart RC. Particle swarm optimization. In: Proceedings of the IEEE international conference on neural networks, Piscataway, NJ, USA; 1995. p. 1942–48.
[7] Kennedy J, Eberhart RC, Shi Y. Swarm intelligence. London, UK: Academic Press; 2001.
[8] Kennedy J, Eberhart RC. A discrete binary version of the particle swarm algorithm. International conference on systems, man, and cybernetics, October 12–15, 1997, Orlando, FL, vol. 5. Piscataway, NJ, USA: IEEE Publications; 1997. p. 4104–9.
[9] Pan F, Li XT, Zhou Q, Li WX, Gao Q. Analysis of standard particle swarm optimization algorithm based on Markov chain. Acta Automatica Sinica 2013;39(4):381–9.
[10] Sudholt D, Witt C. Runtime analysis of a binary particle swarm optimizer. Theor Comput Sci 2010;411(21):2084–100.
[11] Trelea IC. The particle swarm optimization algorithm: convergence analysis and parameter selection. Inf Process Lett 2003;85(6):317–25.
[12] van den Bergh F, Engelbrecht AP. A study of particle swarm optimization particle trajectories. Inf Sci 2006;176(8):937–71.
[13] Yang XS, Deb S, Fong S. Accelerated particle swarm optimization and support vector machine for business optimization and applications. In: Networked digital technologies. Communications in computer and information science, vol. 136. Berlin, Germany: Springer; 2011. p. 53–66.

[14] Yang XS, Gandomi AH, Talatahari S, Alavi AH. Metaheuristics in water. In: Geotech Trans Eng. Waltham, MA, USA: Elsevier; 2013.
[15] Yang XS, Cui ZH, Xiao RB, Gandomi AH, Karamanoglu M. Swarm intelligence and bio-inspired computation: theory and applications. London, UK: Elsevier; 2013.

8 Firefly Algorithms

Nature-inspired metaheuristic algorithms, especially those based on swarm intelligence, have attracted much attention in the last 10 years. The firefly algorithm (FA) appeared about five years ago in 2008, and its literature has expanded dramatically with diverse applications. In this chapter, we first introduce the standard firefly algorithm and then briefly review the variants, together with a selection of recent publications. We also analyze the characteristics of FA and try to answer the question of why FA is so efficient.

8.1 The Firefly Algorithm

FA was first developed by Xin-She Yang in late 2007 and published in 2008 [48,49]. FA was based on the flashing patterns and behavior of fireflies. Therefore, let us start first with a description of the flashing behavior of tropical fireflies.

8.1.1 *Firefly Behavior*

The flashing light of fireflies is an amazing sight in the summer sky in the tropical and temperate regions. There are about 2000 firefly species, and most fireflies produce short, rhythmic flashes. The pattern of flashes is often unique for a particular species. The flashing light is produced by a process of bioluminescence; the true functions of such signaling systems are still being debated. However, two fundamental functions of such flashes are to attract mating partners (communication) and to attract potential prey [32]. In addition, flashing may also serve as a protective warning mechanism to remind potential predators of the bitter taste of fireflies.

The rhythmic flash, the rate of flashing, and the amount of time between flashes form part of the signal system that brings both sexes together [32]. Females respond to a male's unique pattern of flashing in the same species, whereas in some species such as *Photuris*, female fireflies can eavesdrop on the bioluminescent courtship signals and even mimic the mating flashing pattern of other species so as to lure and eat the male fireflies who may mistake the flashes as a potential suitable mate. Some tropical fireflies can even synchronize their flashes, thus forming emerging biological self-organized behavior.

We know that the light intensity at a particular distance r from the light source obeys the inverse-square law. That is to say, the light intensity I decreases as the distance r increases in terms of $I \propto 1/r^2$. Furthermore, the air absorbs light, which becomes weaker and weaker as the distance increases. These two combined factors make most

Nature-Inspired Optimization Algorithms. http://dx.doi.org/10.1016/B978-0-12-416743-8.00008-7

fireflies visable to a limit distance, usually several hundred meters at night, which is good enough for fireflies to communicate.

The flashing light can be formulated in such a way that it is associated with the objective function to be optimized, which makes it possible to formulate new optimization algorithms.

8.1.2 Standard Firefly Algorithm

Now we can idealize some of the flashing characteristics of fireflies so as to develop firefly-inspired algorithms. For simplicity in describing the standard FA, we now use the following three idealized rules:

- All fireflies are unisex, so one firefly will be attracted to other fireflies regardless of their sex.
- Attractiveness is proportional to a firefly's brightness. Thus for any two flashing fireflies, the less brighter one will move toward the brighter one. The attractiveness is proportional to the brightness, both of which decrease as their distance increases. If there is no brighter one than a particular firefly, it will move randomly.
- The brightness of a firefly is affected or determined by the landscape of the objective function.

For a maximization problem, the brightness can simply be proportional to the value of the objective function. Other forms of brightness can be defined in a similar way to the fitness function in genetic algorithms.

Based on these three rules, the basic steps of the FA can be summarized as the pseudo code shown in Figure 8.1.

```
Firefly Algorithm
Objective function f(x),    x = (x_1, ..., x_d)^T.
Generate an initial population of n fireflies x_i (i = 1, 2, ..., n).
Light intensity I_i at x_i is determined by f(x_i).
Define light absorption coefficient γ.
while (t <MaxGeneration),
for i = 1 : n (all n fireflies)
   for j = 1 : n (all n fireflies) (inner loop)
   if (I_i < I_j)
      Move firefly i towards j.
   end if
      Vary attractiveness with distance r via exp[−γr^2].
      Evaluate new solutions and update light intensity.
   end for j
end for i
Rank the fireflies and find the current global best g_*.
end while
Postprocess results and visualization.
```

Figure 8.1 Pseudo code of the firefly algorithm (FA).

8.1.3 Variations of Light Intensity and Attractiveness

In the firefly algorithm, there are two important issues: the variation of light intensity and formulation of the attractiveness. For simplicity, we can always assume that the attractiveness of a firefly is determined by its brightness, which in turn is associated with the encoded objective function.

In the simplest case for maximum optimization problems, the brightness I of a firefly at a particular location $\boldsymbol{x}$ can be chosen as $I(\boldsymbol{x}) \propto f(\boldsymbol{x})$. However, the attractiveness β is relative; it should be seen in the eyes of the beholder or judged by the other fireflies. Thus, it will vary with the distance r_{ij} between firefly i and firefly j. In addition, light intensity decreases with the distance from its source, and light is also absorbed in the media, so we should allow the attractiveness to vary with the degree of absorption.

In the simplest form, the light intensity $I(r)$ varies according to the inverse-square law,

$$I(r) = \frac{I_s}{r^2}, \tag{8.1}$$

where I_s is the intensity at the source. For a given medium with a fixed light absorption coefficient γ, the light intensity I varies with the distance r. That is,

$$I = I_0 e^{-\gamma r}, \tag{8.2}$$

where I_0 is the original light intensity at zero distance $r = 0$. To avoid the singularity at $r = 0$ in the expression I_s/r^2, the combined effect of both the inverse-square law and absorption can be approximated as the following Gaussian form:

$$I(r) = I_0 e^{-\gamma r^2}. \tag{8.3}$$

Because a firefly's attractiveness is proportional to the light intensity seen by adjacent fireflies, we can now define the attractiveness β of a firefly by

$$\beta = \beta_0 e^{-\gamma r^2}, \tag{8.4}$$

where β_0 is the attractiveness at $r = 0$. Since it is often faster to calculate $1/(1 + r^2)$ than an exponential function, this function, if necessary, can conveniently be approximated as

$$\beta = \frac{\beta_0}{1 + \gamma r^2}. \tag{8.5}$$

It may be advantageous to use this approximation in some applications. Both (8.4) and (8.5) define a characteristic distance $\Gamma = 1/\sqrt{\gamma}$ over which the attractiveness changes significantly from β_0 to $\beta_0 e^{-1}$ for Eq. (8.4) or $\beta_0/2$ for Eq. (8.5).

In the actual implementation, the attractiveness function $\beta(r)$ can be any monotonically decreasing functions such as the following generalized form:

$$\beta(r) = \beta_0 e^{-\gamma r^m}, \qquad (m \geq 1). \tag{8.6}$$

For a fixed γ, the characteristic length becomes

$$\Gamma = \gamma^{-1/m} \to 1, \qquad m \to \infty. \tag{8.7}$$

Conversely, for a given length scale Γ in an optimization problem, the parameter γ can be used as a typical initial value. That is,

$$\gamma = \frac{1}{\Gamma^m}. \tag{8.8}$$

The distance between any two fireflies i and j at $\boldsymbol{x}_i$ and $\boldsymbol{x}_j$, respectively, is the Cartesian distance

$$r_{ij} = \|\boldsymbol{x}_i - \boldsymbol{x}_j\| = \sqrt{\sum_{k=1}^{d} (x_{i,k} - x_{j,k})^2}, \tag{8.9}$$

where $x_{i,k}$ is the kth component of the spatial coordinate $\boldsymbol{x}_i$ of ith firefly. In a 2D case, we have

$$r_{ij} = \sqrt{(x_i - x_j)^2 + (y_i - y_j)^2}. \tag{8.10}$$

The movement of a firefly i attracted to another, more attractive (brighter) firefly j is determined by

$$\boldsymbol{x}_i^{t+1} = \boldsymbol{x}_i^t + \beta_0 e^{-\gamma r_{ij}^2} (\boldsymbol{x}_j^t - \boldsymbol{x}_i^t) + \alpha\, \boldsymbol{\epsilon}_i^t, \tag{8.11}$$

where the second term is due to the attraction. The third term is randomization, with α being the randomization parameter, and $\boldsymbol{\epsilon}_i$ is a vector of random numbers drawn from a Gaussian distribution or uniform distribution. For example, the simplest form is $\boldsymbol{\epsilon}_i$ can be replaced by `rand` $-\,1/2$, where `rand` is a random-number generator uniformly distributed in [0,1]. For most of our implementation, we can take $\beta_0 = 1$ and $\alpha \in [0, 1]$.

8.1.4 Controlling Randomization

A further improvement on the convergence of the algorithm is to vary the randomization parameter α so that it decreases gradually as the optima are approaching. For example, we can use

$$\alpha = \alpha_\infty + (\alpha_0 - \alpha_\infty)e^{-t}, \tag{8.12}$$

where $t \in [0, t_{\max}]$ is the pseudo time for simulations and $t_{\max}$ is the maximum number of generations. α_0 is the initial randomization parameter, whereas α_∞ is the final value. We can also use a similar function to the geometrical annealing schedule. That is,

$$\alpha = \alpha_0 \theta^t, \tag{8.13}$$

where $\theta \in (0, 1]$ is the randomness reduction constant. In most applications, we can use $\theta = 0.95 \sim 0.99$ and $\alpha_0 = 1$.

In addition, in the current version of the FA algorithm, we do not explicitly use the current global best $\boldsymbol{g}_*$, even though we only use it to decode the final best solutions. Our simulations indicated that the efficiency may improve if we add an extra term $\lambda \boldsymbol{\epsilon}_i (\boldsymbol{g}_* - \boldsymbol{x}_i)$ to the updating formula (8.11). Here λ is a parameter similar to α and β, and $\boldsymbol{\epsilon}_i$ is a vector of random numbers. These could form important topics for further research.

It is worth pointing out that (8.11) is a random walk, biased toward the brighter fireflies. If $\beta_0 = 0$, it becomes a simple random walk. Furthermore, the randomization term can easily be extended to other distributions such as Lévy flights.

The parameter γ now characterizes the variation of the attractiveness, and its value is crucially important in determining the speed of the convergence and how the FA algorithm behaves. In theory, $\gamma \in [0, \infty)$, but in practice, $\gamma = O(1)$ is determined by the characteristic length Γ of the system to be optimized. Thus, for most applications, it typically varies from 0.001 to 1000.

8.2 Algorithm Analysis

Now let us take a close look at the firefly algorithm and analyze its key characteristics.

8.2.1 *Scalings and Limiting Cases*

It is worth pointing out that the distance r defined in the previous section is *not* limited to the Euclidean distance. We can define other distance r in the d-dimensional hyperspace, depending on the type of problem we're interested in. For example, for job-scheduling problems, r can be defined as the time lag or time interval. For complicated networks such as the Internet and social networks, the distance r can be defined as the combination of the degrees of local clustering and the average proximity of vertices. In fact, any measure that can effectively characterize the quantities of interest in the optimization problem can be used as the "distance" r.

The typical scale Γ should be associated with the scale concerned in our optimization problem. If Γ is the typical scale for a given optimization problem for a very large number of fireflies, i.e., $n \gg k$, where k is the number of local optima, then the initial locations of these n fireflies should distribute relatively uniformly over the entire search space. As the iterations proceed, the fireflies would converge into all the local optima (including the global ones). By comparing the best solutions among all these optima, the global optima can easily be achieved. Our recent research suggests that it is possible to prove that the firefly algorithm will approach global optima when $n \to \infty$ and $t \gg 1$. In reality, it converges very quickly, as demonstrated later in this chapter.

There are two important limiting or asymptotic cases when $\gamma \to 0$ and $\gamma \to \infty$. For $\gamma \to 0$, the attractiveness is constant $\beta = \beta_0$ and $\Gamma \to \infty$. This is equivalent to saying that the light intensity does not decrease in an idealized sky. Thus, a flashing firefly can be seen anywhere in the domain. Therefore, a single (usually global) optima can easily be reached. If we remove the inner loop for j in Figure 8.1 and replace $\boldsymbol{x}_j$ with the current global best $\boldsymbol{g}_*$, then the FA degenerates into the special case of APSO, discussed earlier in this book. Subsequently, the efficiency of this special case is the same as that of PSO.

On the other hand, the limiting case $\gamma \to \infty$ leads to $\Gamma \to 0$ and $\beta(r) \to \delta(r)$, which is the Dirac delta function, meaning that the attractiveness is almost zero in the sight of other fireflies. This is equivalent to the case where the fireflies roam randomly in a very thick foggy region randomly. No other fireflies can be seen, and each firefly roams in a completely random way, which leads to simulated annealing (SA).

Because the firefly algorithm is usually a case between these two extremes, it is possible to adjust the parameter γ and α so that it can outperform both simulated annealing and PSO. In fact, FA can find the global optima as well as the local optima simultaneously and effectively. This advantage is demonstrated in detail later in the implementation.

A further advantage of FA is that different fireflies will work almost independently. It is thus particularly suitable for parallel implementation. It is even better than genetic algorithms and PSO because fireflies aggregate more closely around each optimum. We can expect that the interactions between different subregions are minimal in parallel implementation.

8.2.2 Attraction and Diffusion

The novel idea of attraction via light intensity as an exploitation mechanism was first used by Xin-She Yang in the firefly algorithm (FA) in 2007 and 2008. In FA, the attractiveness (and light intensity) is intrinsically linked with the inverse-square law of light intensity variations and the absorption coefficient. As a result, we have a novel term $\beta_0 \exp[-\gamma r^2]$, where β_0 is the attractiveness at the distance $r = 0$, and $\gamma > 0$ is the absorption coefficient [48].

The main function of such attraction is to enable an algorithm to converge quickly because these multi-agent systems evolve, interact, and attract, leading to some self-organized behavior and attractors. As the swarming agents evolve, it is possible that their attractor states will move toward the true global optimality.

This novel attraction mechanism is the first of its kind in the literature of nature-inspired computation and computational intelligence. This mechanism also motivated and inspired others to design similar or other kinds of attraction mechanisms. Other algorithms also used inverse-square laws, derived from nature. For example, the charged system search (CSS) used Coulomb's law; the gravitational search algorithm (GSA) used Newton's law of gravitation.

Whatever the attraction mechanism, from the metaheuristic point of view the fundamental principles are the same: that is, they allow the swarming agents to interact with one another and provide a forcing term to guide the convergence of the population.

Attraction mainly provides the mechanisms only for exploitation, but, with proper randomization, it is also possible to carry out some degree of exploration. However, the exploration is better analyzed in the framework of random walks and diffusive randomization. From the Markov chain point of view, random walks and diffusion are both Markov chains. In fact, Brownian diffusion such as the dispersion of an ink drop in water is a random walk. For example, the most fundamental random walks for an agent or solution $\boldsymbol{x}_i$ can be written as the following form:

$$\boldsymbol{x}_i^{(t+1)} = \boldsymbol{x}_i^{(t)} + \epsilon, \tag{8.14}$$

where t is a counter of steps. Here, ϵ is a random number drawn from a Gaussian normal distribution with a zero mean. This gives an average diffusion distance of a particle or agent that is a square root of the finite number of steps t. That is, the distance is the order of $\sqrt{Dt}$ where D is the diffusion coefficient. To be more specific, the variance of the random walks in a d-dimensional case can be written as

$$\sigma^2(t) = |v_0|^2 t^2 + (2dD)t, \tag{8.15}$$

where v_0 is the drift velocity that can be taken as zero here.

This means it is possible to cover the whole search domain if t is sufficiently large. Therefore, the steps in the Brownian motion B(t) essentially obey a Gaussian distribution with zero mean and time-dependent variance. A diffusion process can be viewed as a series of Brownian motion that obeys a Gaussian distribution. For this reason, standard diffusion is often referred to as *Gaussian diffusion*. If the motion at each step is not Gaussian, the diffusion is called *non-Gaussian diffusion*. On the other hand, random walks can take many forms. If the step lengths obey other distributions, we have to deal with more generalized random walks. A very special case is when step lengths obey the Lévy distribution. Such random walks are called *Lévy flights* or *Lévy walks*.

It is worth pointing out that the original firefly algorithm was developed to combine with Lévy flights, and good performance has been achieved [49].

8.2.3 Special Cases of FA

FA is indeed rich in many ways. First, it uses attraction to influence the behavior of a population. Because local attraction tends to be stronger than long-distance attraction, the population in FA can automatically subdivide into subgroups, depending on the modality of the problem, which enables FA to deal with multimodal, nonlinear optimization problems naturally.

Furthermore, if we look at the updating Eq. (8.11) more closely, this nonlinear equation provides much richer characteristics. First, if γ is very large, attractiveness or light intensity decreases too quickly. This means that the second term in (8.11) becomes negligible, leading to the standard SA. Second, if γ is very small (i.e., $\gamma \to 0$), the exponential factor $\exp[-\gamma r_{ij}^2] \to 1$. We have

$$\boldsymbol{x}_i^{t+1} = \boldsymbol{x}_i^t + \beta_0(\boldsymbol{x}_j^t - \boldsymbol{x}_i^t) + \alpha\epsilon_i^t. \tag{8.16}$$

Here, if we further set $\alpha = 0$, the Eq. (8.16) becomes a variant of differential evolution. On the other hand, if we replace $\boldsymbol{x}_j^t$ with the current global best solution $\boldsymbol{g}^*$, we have

$$\boldsymbol{x}_i^{t+1} = \boldsymbol{x}_i^t + \beta_0(\boldsymbol{g}^* - \boldsymbol{x}_i^t) + \alpha\epsilon_i^t, \tag{8.17}$$

which is essentially the APSO introduced by Xin-She Yang in 2008 [48].

Third, we set $\beta_0 = 0$ and let ϵ_i^t be related to $\boldsymbol{x}_i$; then (8.16) becomes a pitch adjustment variant in harmony search (HS).

Therefore, we can essentially say that DE, APSO, SA, and HS are special cases of FA. Conversely, FA can be considered a good combination of all four algorithms (DE, APSO, SA, and HS), to a certain extent. Furthermore, FA uses nonlinear updating equation, which can produce richer behavior and higher convergence than the linear updating equations used in standard PSO and DE. Consequently, it is again no surprise that FA can outperform other algorithms in many applications such as multimodal optimization, classifications, image processing, and feature selection, as we will see later in the applications.

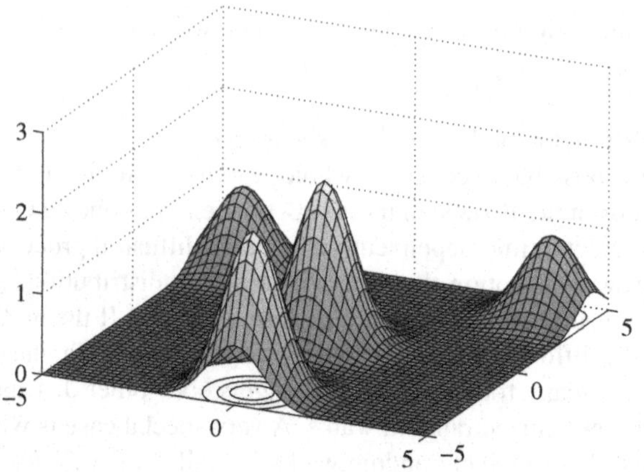

Figure 8.2 Landscape of a function with two equal global maxima.

8.3 Implementation

A demo version of FA implementation without Lévy flights can be found at the Mathworks file exchange Website.[1] In the implementation, the values of the parameters are $\alpha_0 = 0.5$, $\gamma = 1$ and $\beta_0 = 1$. Obviously, these parameters can be adjusted to suit solving various problems with different scales.

To demonstrate how the FA works, we use the simple example of the four-peak function

$$f(x, y) = e^{-(x-4)^2-(y-4)^2} + e^{-(x+4)^2-(y-4)^2} + 2\left[e^{-x^2-y^2} + e^{-x^2-(y+4)^2}\right],$$

where $(x, y) \in [-5, 5] \times [-5, 5]$. This function has four peaks, two local peaks with $f = 1$ at $(-4, 4)$ and (4,4) and two global peaks with $f_{\max} = 2$ at (0,0) and $(0, -4)$, as shown in Figure 8.2.

We can see that all four of these optima can be found using 25 fireflies in about 20 generations (see Figure. 8.3). So, the total number of function evaluations is about 500. This is much more efficient than most existing metaheuristic algorithms.

8.4 Variants of the Firefly Algorithm

8.4.1 FA Variants

The standard FA is very efficient, but there is still room for improvement. In the last five years, researchers have tried various ways to enhance the performance and speed up the convergence of the firefly algorithm. As a result, quite a few variants have been developed [19,42,37]. However, because the literature is expanding rapidly and more

[1] www.mathworks.com/matlabcentral/fileexchange/29693-firefly-algorithm.

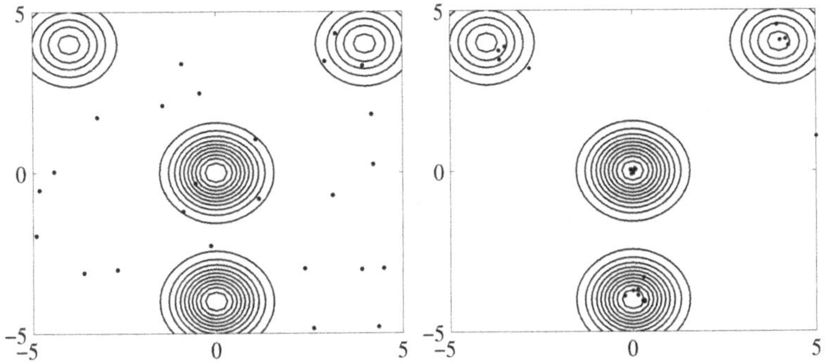

Figure 8.3 The initial locations of 25 fireflies (left) and their final locations after 20 iterations (right).

variations are appearing, it is not possible to list all these variants here. This section briefly summarizes some of these variants:

- *Discrete firefly algorithm (DFA).* Sayadi et al. [42] extended the firefly algorithm to deal with NP-hard scheduling problems and have developed a powerful version of discrete FA. Their results show that DFA can outperform existing algorithms such as ACO. Meanwhile, Durkota independently provided a good implementation of a DFA for QAP problems [14]. In addition, an FA-based method for image segmentation, developed by Hassanzadeh et al. [24], can be far more efficient than the Otsu's method and recursive Otsu method. On the other hand, Jati and Suyanto discretized the firefly algorithm and showed its effectiveness in solving the NP-hard traveling salesman problem [29]. Furthermore, Chandrasekaran and Simon proposed an efficient binary real-coded FA variant to study the network and reliability constrained unit commitment problem [9].
- *Chaotic firefly algorithm (CFA).* A chaotic FA was proposed by Coelho et al. in 2011, and this CFA outperformed other algorithms [11,12]. Yang studied the intrinsic chaotic characteristics of FA under different parameter ranges so that enhanced performance can be achieved by tuning β and γ [51]. At the same time, Gandomi et al. studied different chaotic maps and carried out extensive performance comparisons, concluding that some chaotic maps can indeed enhance the performance of FA by replacing some parameters in FA with these chaotic maps [21].
- *Lagrangian firefly algoirthm (LFA).* Another interesting variant is the Lagrangian firefly algorithm, which was proposed by Rampriya et al. to solve the unit commitment problem for a power system [41].
- *Memetic firefly algorithm (MFA).* Fister Jr. et al. developed a discrete variant of FA, called the memetic firefly algorithm, for solving combinatorial graph-coloring problems, with promising results [18].
- *Multiobjective discrete firefly algorithm (MDFA).* Apostolopoulos and Vlacho extended FA and developed a discrete version for multi-objective optimization of the economic emission load dispatch problem, and their comparison showed that this variant is very efficient [6]. Meanwhile, Arsuaga-Rios and Vega-Rodriguez

independently proposed another multi-objective FA (MOFA) for an optimal workload management tool for minimizing energy consumption in grid computing [4]. In addition, Li and Ye used FA to solve multi-objective production scheduling systems [33]. Furthermore, Marichelvam et al. presented a discrete FA variant for the multi-objective hybrid flowshop scheduling problem [35].

- *Mulitobjective firefly algorithm (MOFA).* Yang also extended FA for single-objective optimization to multi-objective optimization of continuous design problems [53].
- *Multi-objective enhanced firefly algorithm (MOEFA).* Amiri et al. presented a multi-objective enhanced FA for community detection in complex networks [3].
- *Hybrid firefly algorithms (HFA).* There are many hybrid algorithms achieved by hybridizing FA with other algorithms. For example, Giannakouris et al. combined FA with ant colony optimization and obtained good results [22]. Abdullah et al. combined FA with differential evolution to estimate nonlinear biological model parameters, and their study showed that this hybrid can be a powerful tool with less computation time for many applications [2]. An improved FA with adaptive strategies has been presented by Yan et al. [55].
- *Parallel firefly algorithm with predation (pFAP).* Luz et al. proposed a parallel implementation of FA with predation and applied it to the inverse heat conduction problem [34].

For discrete problems and combinatorial optimization, discrete versions of FA have been developed that have superior performance [42,29,18,14], which can be used for traveling-salesman problems, graph coloring, and other applications. In addition, the extension of FA to multi-objective optimization has also been investigated [6,53]. A few studies show that chaos can enhance FA's performance [11,51], whereas other studies have attempted to hybridize FA with other algorithms to enhance their performance [22,26,27,41].

Sometimes some improvements can be carried out by slightly modifying the standard FA, but it might not be proper to classify the improved algorithm as a new variant. For example, Farahani et al. used a Gaussian distribution to replace the uniform distribution for the scaling factor α, which indeed showed some improvement [17]. On the other hand, Wang et al. introduce a discovery rate to FA and presented a modified FA for UCAV path planning [47], and their results showed the modified FA indeed performed better.

8.4.2 How Can We Discretize FA?

The standard FA was initially developed for continuous, multimodal optimization problems. It can also be applied to solve combinatorial optimization problems; however, we have to find ways to convert continuous variables into discrete variables. There are different ways to achieve this task, and one of the widely used is the so-called sigmoidal logistic function

$$S(x) = \frac{1}{1+\exp(-x)}, \tag{8.18}$$

which converts a continuous variable into a binary variable S. This S-shaped function for x gives $S \to 1$ as $x \to +\infty$, and $S \to 0$ as $x \to -\infty$. However, in practice this is not so easy to achieve, because values might not vary in the right range. A common way is to combine with a random number r with a conditional switch. That is,

$$(u > r) \to 1, \quad (u \leq r) \to 0. \tag{8.19}$$

Obviously, once we have $S \in \{0, 1\}$, we can change it to $y = 2S - 1 \in \{+1, -1\}$ when necessary.

An interesting property of S is that its derivative can be calculated easily by

$$\frac{dS}{dx} = S(1 - S). \tag{8.20}$$

Other ways include signs and randomization. For example, we can use $y = \text{sign}(x)$ to generate $+1, 0, -1$. In addition, a simple (but not necessarily efficient) way is to use $y = \lfloor x \rfloor$, which is the largest integer not greater than x. Another way is to use the mod function. For example, we can use

$$x \leftarrow \lfloor x + k \rfloor \mod m, \tag{8.21}$$

where k and $m > 0$ are integers.

Another related issue is how new solutions can be generated. Once we have $S = +1$ or $S = -1$, we can use them as a step size and do local random walks at different time/iteration t. That is,

$$y^{t+1} = y^t + S. \tag{8.22}$$

However, if the design variables are binary only, we have to normalize the new variables. One way is to use mutation-like operations by swapping randomly between 0 and 1.

For randomization, one way is to use a random number associated with a discrete set. If the search space is discrete and a design variable z only takes values on a finite set, a random number u, often uniformly distributed, can be generated and map to the cardinality of the set. Once a random number is drawn, the corresponding value of the finite set can be used.

On the other hand, two key issues are how to define the distance and neighborhood in the discrete FA. For many combinatorial problems such as scheduling, the distance is not a physical distance. Therefore, care should be taken to define a distance measure properly. Any sensible metric, such as time delay, time difference, Hamming distance, edit distance, or Jaccard similarity, can be used as the distance.

For neighborhood, it is an even more challenging issue in combinatorial optimization. For example, to solve the traveling salesman problem, a neighborhood solution can be a local solution generated by swapping two links between four cities, the so-called 2-opt move [38].

It is worth pointing out that the ways of defining neighborhood solutions can significantly affect the overall performance of any implementation or variant of any nature-inspired algorithms. This is one of reasons that discrete metaheuristic algorithms form a significant part of current research activities.

8.5 Firefly Algorithms in Applications

FA has attracted much attention and has been applied to many applications [6,10,24, 42,50,25,26]. Since the first original publications by Yang in 2008, more than 810 publications about FA have been published. As we can see, the literature has expanded significantly, so it is not possible to review all 800 papers here. Therefore, we sample only a fraction of these publications. Our choices might be biased, though we intended to choose these representatives in an unbiased way.

Horng et al. demonstrated that the firefly-based algorithm used the least computation time for digital image compression [25,26], whereas Zhang and Wu used FA to study image registration [58]. Banati and Bajaj used FA for feature selection and showed that FA produced consistent and better performance in terms of time and optimality than other algorithms [7].

In engineering design problems, Gandomi et al. [20] and Azad and Azad [5] confirmed that FA can efficiently solve highly nonlinear, multimodal design problems. Basu and Mahanti [8] as well as Chatterjee et al. applied FA in antenna design optimization and showed that FA can outperform ABC [10]. In addition, Zaman and Matin also found that FA can outperform PSO and obtained global best results [57]. Furthermore, FA has been use to generate alternatives for decision makers with diverse options [28].

Sayadi et al. developed a discrete version of FA that can efficiently solve NP-hard scheduling problems [42], while a detailed analysis has demonstrated the efficiency of FA over a wide range of test problems, including multi-objective load dispatch problems [6,49,52]. For example, Yang et al. solved the non-convex economic dispatch problem with valve-loading effect using FA and achieved the best results over other methods [54]. Similarly, Swarnkar solved economic load dispatch problems with reduced power losses using FA [45].

Furthermore, FA can solve scheduling and traveling salesman problems in a promising way [39,29,56]. Jati and Suyanto solved the well-known traveling salesman problem by discrete FA, whereas Yousif et al. solved scheduling jobs on grid computing using FA [56]. Both studies showed that FA is very efficient.

For queueing systems, FA has been found very efficient, as demonstrated in the detailed study by Kwiecień and Filipowicz [31]. In addition, for mixed integer programming and load dispatch problems, FA has also been found very efficient as well [9,54].

Classifications and clustering are another important area of applications of FA with excellent performance [43,40]. For example, Senthilnath et al. provided an extensive performance study by comparing FA with 11 different algorithms and concluded that FA can be efficiently used for clustering [43]. In most cases, FA outperforms all other 11 algorithms. Tang et al. provided a comprehensive review of nature-inspired algorithms for clustering [46]. In addition, FA has been applied to training neural networks [36].

For optimization in dynamic environments, FA can also be very efficient, as shown by Farahani et al. [15,16] and Abshouri et al. [1].

On the other hand, Dutta et al. showed that FA can solve isospectral spring-mass systems effectively [13]. Kazem et al. presented support vector regression with the chaos-based FA for stock market price forecasting [30]. Grewal et al. presented a study of antenna failure correction using FA and showed that FA is very flexible and effective [23].

In the context of software testing, Srivastava et al. showed that FA can be modified to generate independent test sequences efficiently and achieves superior performance [44].

8.6 Why the Firefly Algorithm is Efficient

As the literature about FA expands and new variants emerge, all point out that the FA can outperform many other algorithms. Now we may ask naturally, "Why is it so efficient?" To answer this question, let us briefly analyze FA from a different angle.

FA is swarm-intelligence-based, so it has similar advantages as other swarm-intelligence-based algorithms. However, FA has two major advantages over other algorithms: automatical subdivision and the ability to deal with multimodality. First, FA is based on attraction and attractiveness. This leads to the fact that the whole population can automatically subdivide into subgroups, and each group can swarm around each mode or local optimum. Among all these modes, the best global solution can be found. Second, this subdivision allows the fireflies to be able to find all optima simultaneously if the population size is sufficiently higher than the number of modes. Mathematically, $1/\sqrt{\gamma}$ controls the average distance of a group of fireflies that can be seen by adjacent groups. Therefore, a whole population can subdivide into subgroups with a given average distance. In the extreme case when $\gamma = 0$, the whole population will not subdivide.

This automatic subdivision ability makes FA particularly suitable for highly nonlinear, multimodal optimisation problems. In addition, the parameters in FA can be tuned to control the randomness as iterations proceed, so convergence can also be sped up by tuning these parameters. These advantages make FA flexible to deal with continuous problems, clustering and classifications, and combinatorial optimization as well.

For example, let use two functions to demonstrate the computational cost saved by FA. For details, see the more extensive studies by Yang [49]. For De Jong's function with $d = 256$ dimensions,

$$f(\mathbf{x}) = \sum_{i=1}^{256} x_i^2. \tag{8.23}$$

Genetic algorithms required 25412 ± 1237 evaluations to get an accuracy of 10^{-5} of the optimal solution, whereas PSO needed 17040 ± 1123 evaluations. For FA, we achieved the same accuracy with 5657 ± 730 function evaluations. This saves computational costs of about 78% and 67% compared to GA and PSO, respectively.

For Yang's forest function

$$f(\mathbf{x}) = \left(\sum_{i=1}^{d} |x_i|\right) \exp\left[-\sum_{i=1}^{d} \sin(x_i^2)\right], \quad -2\pi \leq x_i \leq 2\pi, \tag{8.24}$$

GA required 37079 ± 8920 with a success rate of 88% for $d = 16$, and PSO required 19725 ± 3204 with a success rate of 98%. FA obtained a 100% success rate with just

5152±2493. Compared with GA and PSO, FA saved about 86% and 74%, respectively, of overall computational efforts.

In summary, FA has three distinct advantages:

- Automatic subdivision of the whole population into subgroups
- The natural capability of dealing with multimodal optimization
- High ergodicity and diversity in the solutions

All these advantages make FA unique and very efficient.

References

[1] Abshouri AA, Meybodi MR, Bakhtiary A. New firefly algorithm based on multiswarm and learning automata in dynamic environments. In: Third international conference on signal processing systems (ICSPS 2011), August 27–28, Yantai, China; 2011. p. 73–7.

[2] Abdullah A, Deris S, Anwar S, Arjunan SNV. An evolutionary firefly algorithm for the estimation of nonlinear biological model parameters. PLoS One 2013;8(3):e56310.

[3] Amiri B, Hossain L, Crawford JW, Wigand RT. Community detection in complex networks: Multi-objective enhanced firefly algorithm. Knowl Based Syst 2013;46(1):1–1.

[4] Arsuaga-Rios M, Vega-Rodriguez MA. Multi-objective firefly algorithm for energy optimization in grid environments. Swarm Intelligence. Lect Notes Comput Sci 2012;7461:350–1.

[5] Azad SK, Azad SK. Optimum design of structures using an improved firefly algorithm. Int J Optim Civil Eng 2011;1(2):327–40.

[6] Apostolopoulos T, Vlachos A. Application of the firefly algorithm for solving the economic emissions load dispatch problem. Int J Combin 2011[Article ID 523806].

[7] Banati H, Bajaj M. Firefly-based feature selection approach. Int J Comput Sci 2011;8(2):473–80.

[8] Basu B, Mahanti GK. Firefly and artificial bees colony algorithm for synthesis of scanned and broadside linear array antenna. Prog Electromagnet Res B 2011;32(1):169–90.

[9] Chandrasekaran K, Simon SP. Network and reliability constrained unit commitment problem using binary real coded firefly algorithm. Int J Electr Power Energy Syst 2012;42(1):921–32.

[10] Chatterjee A, Mahanti GK, Chatterjee A. Design of a fully digital controlled reconfigurable switched beam conconcentric ring array antenna using firefly and particle swarm optimization algorithm. Prog Elelectromagnet Res B 2012;36(1):113–31.

[11] Coelho LS, de Andrade Bernert DL, Mariani VC. A chaotic firefly algorithm applied to reliability-redundancy optimization. In: 2011 IEEE Congress on Evolutionary Computation (CEC'11); 2011. p. 517–21.

[12] Coelho LS, Mariani VC. Firefly algorithm approach based on chaotic Tinkerbell map applied to multivariable PID controller tuning. Comput Math Appl 2012;64(8):2371–82.

[13] Dutta R, Ganguli R, Mani V. Exploring isospectral spring-mass systems with firefly algorithm. Proc R Soc A 2011;467(2135):3222–40.

[14] Durkota K. Implementation of a discrete firefly algorithm for the QAP problem within the sage framework, B.Sc. Thesis. Czech Technical University; 2011. <http://cyber.felk.cvut.cz/research/theses/papers/189.pdf>; 2013 [accessed 23.05.13].

[15] Farahani SM, Abshouri AA, Nasiri B, Meybodi MR. Some hybrid models to improve firefly algorithm performance. Int J Artif Intell 2012;8(S12):97–117.

[16] Farahani SM, Nasiri B, Meybodi MR. A multiswarm based firefly algorithm in dynamic environments. In: Third international conference on signal processing systems (ICSPS 2011), August 27–28, Yantai, China; 2011. p. 68–72.
[17] Farahani SM, Abshouri AA, Basiri B, Meybodi MR. A Gaussian firefly algorithm. Int J Mach Learn Comput 2011;1(5):448–53.
[18] Fister I Jr, Fister I, Brest J, Yang XS. Memetic firefly algorithm for combinatorial optimization. In: Filipič B, Šilc J, editors. Bioinspired optimization methods and their applications (BIOMA2012), 24–25 May 2012, Bohinj, Slovenia; 2012. p. 75–86.
[19] Fister I, Fister I Jr., Yang XS, Brest J. A comprehensive review of firefly algorithms. Swarm Evol Comput 2013;13(1):34–46. www.sciencedirect.com/science/article/pii/S2210650213000461.
[20] Gandomi AH, Yang XS, Alavi AH. Mixed variable structural optimization using firefly algorithm. Comput Struct 2011;89(23–24):2325–36.
[21] Gandomi AH, Yang XS, Talatahari S, Alavi AH. Firefly algorithm with chaos. Commun Nonlinear Sci Numer Simulat 2013;18(1):89–98.
[22] Giannakouris G, Vassiliadis V, Dounias G. Experimental study on a hybrid nature-inspired algorithm for financial portfolio optimization. In: SETN 2010, Lecture notes in artificial intelligence (LNAI 6040); 2010. p. 101–111.
[23] Grewal NS, Rattan M, Patterh MS. A linear antenna array failure correction using firefly algorithm. Prog Electromagnet Res 2012;27:241–54.
[24] Hassanzadeh T, Vojodi H, Moghadam AME. An image segmentation approach based on maximum variance intra-cluster method and firefly algorithm. In: Proceedings of the seventh international conference on natural computation (ICNC 2011); 2011. p. 1817–21.
[25] Horng MH, Lee YX, Lee MC, Liou RJ. Firefly metaheuristic algorithm for training the radial basis function network for data classification and disease diagnosis. In: Parpinelli R, Lopes HS, editors. Theory and new applications of swarm intelligence; 2012. p. 115–32.
[26] Horng MH. Vector quantization using the firefly algorithm for image compression. Expert Syst Appl 2012;39(2):1078–91.
[27] Horng MH, Liou RJ. Multilevel minimum cross-entropy threshold selection based on the firefly algorithm. Expert Syst Appl 2011;38(9):14805–11.
[28] Imanirad R, Yang XS, Yeomans JS. Modeling-to-generate-alternatives via the firefly algorithm. J Appl Oper Res 2013;5(1):14–21.
[29] Jati GK, Suyanto S. Evolutionary discrete firefly algorithm for traveling salesman problem. ICAIS 2011, Lecture notes in artificial intelligence (LNAI 6943) 2011; 2011:393–403.
[30] Kazem A, Sharifi E, Hussain FK, Saberi M, Khadeer O. Support vector regression with chaos-based firefly algorithm for stock market price forecasting. Appl Soft Comput 2013;13(2):947–58.
[31] Kwiecień J, Filipowicz B. Firefly algorithm in optimization of queueing systems. Bull Pol Acad Sci Tech Sci 2012;60(2):363–8.
[32] Lewis SM, Cratsley CK. Flash signal evolution, mate choice and predation in fireflies. Ann Rev Entomol 2008;53(2):293–321.
[33] Li HM, Ye CM. Firefly algorithm on multi-objective optimization of production scheduling system. Adv Mech Eng Appl 2012;3(1):258–62.
[34] Luz EFP, Campos Velho HF, Becceneri JC. Firefly algorithm with predation: a parallel implementation applied to inverse heat conduction problem. In: Proceedings of 10th world congress on computational mechanics (WCCM 2012; conference presentation); 2012.
[35] Marichelvam MK, Prabaharan T, Yang XS. A discrete firefly algorithm for the multi-objective hybrid flowshop scheduling problems. IEEE Transl Evol Comput 2013. http://ieeexplore.ieee.org/xpl/articleDetails.jsp?arnumber=6412790.

[36] Nandy S, Sarkar PP, Das A. Analysis of nature-inspired firefly algorithm-based back-propagation neural network training. Int J Comput Appl 2012;43(22):8–16.
[37] Nasiri B, Meybodi MR. Speciation-based firefly algorithm for optimization in dynamic environments. Int J Artif Intell 2012;8(S12):118–32.
[38] Ouaarab A, Ahiod B, Yang XS. Discrete cuckoo search algorithm for the travelling salesman problem. Neural computing and applications 2013. http://link.springer.com/article/10.1007%2Fs00521-013-1402-2.
[39] Palit S, Sinha S, Molla M, Khanra A, Kule M. A cryptanalytic attack on the knapsack cryptosystem using binary firefly algorithm. In: Second international conference on computer and communication technology (ICCCT), 15–17 September 2011, India; 2011. p. 428–32.
[40] Rajini A, David VK. A hybrid metaheuristic algorithm for classification using micro array data. Int J Sci Eng Res 2012;3(2):1–9.
[41] Rampriya B, Mahadevan K, Kannan S. Unit commitment in deregulated power system using Lagrangian firefly algorithm. In: Proceedings of IEEE international conference on communication control and computing technologies (ICCCCT2010); 2010. p. 389–93.
[42] Sayadi MK, Ramezanian R, Ghaffari-Nasab N. A discrete firefly meta-heuristic with local search for makespan minimization in permutation flow shop scheduling problems. Int J Ind Eng Comput 2010;1(1):1–10.
[43] Senthilnath J, Omkar SN, Mani V. Clustering using firefly algorithm: performance study. Swarm Evol Comput 2011;1(3):164–71.
[44] Srivastava PR, Mallikarjun B, Yang XS. Optimal test sequence generation using firefly algorithm. Swarm Evol Comput 2013;8(1):44–53.
[45] Swarnkar KK. Economic load dispatch problem with reduce power losses using firefly algorithm. J Adv Comput Sci Technol 2012;1(2):42–56.
[46] Tang R, Fong S, Yang XS, Deb S. Integrating nature-inspired optimization algorithm to K-means clustering. In: The seventh international conference on digital information management (ICDIM2012), 22–24 August. Macau: IEEE Publications; 2012. p. 116–23.
[47] Wang GG, Guo LH, Duan H, Liu L, Wang HQ. A modified firefly algorithm for UCAV path planning. Int J Hybrid Inform Technol 2012;5(3):123–44.
[48] Yang XS. Nature-inspired metaheuristic algorithms. 1st ed. Frome, UK: Luniver Press; 2008.
[49] Yang XS. Firefly algorithms for multimodal optimisation. In: Watanabe O, Zeugmann T, editors. Proceedings fifth symposium on stochastic algorithms, foundations and applications. Lecture notes in computer science, vol. 5792; 2009. p. 169–78.
[50] Yang XS. Firefly algorithm, stochastic test functions and design optimisation. Int J Bio-Inspired Comput 2010;2(2):78–84.
[51] Yang XS. Chaos-enhanced firefly algorithm with automatic parameter tuning. Int J Swarm Intell Res 2012;2(4):125–36.
[52] Yang XS. Swarm-based metaheuristic algorithms and no-free-lunch theorems. In: Parpinelli R, Lopes HS, editors. Theory and new applications of swarm intelligence. Intech Open Science; 2012. p. 1–16.
[53] Yang XS. Multiobjective firefly algorithm for continuous optimization. Eng Comput 2013;29(2):175–84.
[54] Yang XS, Hosseini SSS, Gandomi AH. Firefly algorithm for solving non-convex economic dispatch problems with valve loading effect. Appl Soft Comput 2012;12(3):1180–6.
[55] Yan X, Zhu YL, Wu JW, Chen H. An improved firefly algorithm with adaptive strategies. Adv Sci Lett 2012;16(1):249–54.
[56] Yousif A, Abdullah AH, Nor SM, Abdelaziz A. Scheduling jobs on grid computing using firefly algorithm. J Theor Appl Inform Technol 2011;33(2):155–64.

[57] Zaman MA, Matin MA. Nonuniformly spaced linear antenna array design using firefly algorithm. Int J Microw Sci Technol 2012;vol. 2012 [Article ID: 256759].
[58] Zhang YD, Wu LN. A novel method for rigid image registration based on firefly algorithm. Int J Res Rev Soft Intell Comput 2012;2(2):141–6.

9 Cuckoo Search

Cuckoo search (CS) is one of the latest nature-inspired metaheuristic algorithms, developed in 2009 by Xin-She Yang of Cambridge University and Suash Deb of C.V. Raman College of Engineering. CS is based on the brood parasitism of some cuckoo species. In addition, this algorithm is enhanced by the so-called Lévy flights rather than by simple isotropic random walks. Recent studies show that CS is potentially far more efficient than PSO, genetic algorithms, and other algorithms.

9.1 Cuckoo Breeding Behavior

Cuckoos are fascinating birds, not only because of the beautiful sounds they make but also because of their aggressive reproduction strategy. Some species such as the *ani* and *Guira* cuckoos lay their eggs in communal nests, though they may remove otherbrids' eggs to increase the hatching probability of their own eggs. Quite a number of species engage in obligate brood parasitism by laying their eggs in the nests of other host birds (often other species) [19].

There are three basic types of brood parasitism: intraspecific brood parasitism, cooperative breeding, and nest takeover. Some host birds can engage in direct conflict with the intruding cuckoos. If a host bird discovers the eggs are not their own, they will either get rid of these alien eggs or simply abandon the nest and build a new nest elsewhere. Some cuckoo species, such as the New World brood-parasitic *Tapera*, have evolved in such a way that female parasitic cuckoos are often very specialized in mimicry in color and pattern of the eggs of a few chosen host species. This reduces the probability of their eggs being abandoned and thus increases their reproductivity.

In addition, the timing of egg laying of some species is also amazing. Parasitic cuckoos often choose a nest where the host bird just laid its own eggs. In general, the cuckoo eggs hatch slightly earlier than their host eggs. Once the first cuckoo chick is hatched, the first instinct action it will take is to evict the host eggs by blindly propelling the eggs out of the nest, which increases the cuckoo chick's share of food provided by its host bird. Studies also show that a cuckoo chick can also mimic the call of host chicks to gain access to more feeding opportunity.

9.2 Lévy Flights

On the other hand, various studies have shown that flight behavior of many animals and insects has demonstrated the typical characteristics of Lévy flights with power

Nature-Inspired Optimization Algorithms. http://dx.doi.org/10.1016/B978-0-12-416743-8.00009-9

law-like characteristics. A recent study by Reynolds and Frye shows that fruit flies, or *Drosophila melanogaster*, explore their landscape using a series of straight flight paths punctuated by sudden 90° turns, leading to a Lévy flight-style intermittent scale free search pattern [21]. Studies of human behavior, such as of the Ju/'hoansi hunter-gatherer foraging patterns, also show the typical feature of Lévy flights [4]. Even light can be related to Lévy flights [2]. Subsequently, such behavior has been applied to optimization and optimal search, and results show its promising capability [20].

9.3 Cuckoo Search

CS is one of the latest nature-inspired metaheuristic algorithms, developed in 2009 by Xin-She Yang and Suash Deb [30,32,33]. CS is based on the brood parasitism of some cuckoo species.

In addition, this algorithm is enhanced by the so-called Lévy flights [20] rather than by simple isotropic random walks. Recent studies show that CS is potentially far more efficient than PSO and genetic algorithms [30]. For simplicity in describing the standard CS, here we use the following three idealized rules:

- Each cuckoo lays one egg at a time and dumps it in a randomly chosen nest.
- The best nests with high-quality eggs will be carried over to the next generations.
- The number of available host nests is fixed, and the egg laid by a cuckoo is discovered by the host bird with a probability $p_a \in (0, 1)$. In this case, the host bird can either get rid of the egg or simply abandon the nest and build a completely new nest.

As a further approximation, this last assumption can be approximated by replacing a fraction p_a of the n host nests with new nests (with new random solutions). For a maximization problem, the quality or fitness of a solution can simply be proportional to the value of the objective function. Other forms of fitness can be defined in a similar way to the fitness function in genetic algorithms.

From the implementation point of view, we can use the following simple representations that each egg in a nest represents a solution, and each cuckoo can lay only one egg (thus representing one solution). The aim is to use the new and potentially better solutions (cuckoos) to replace a not-so-good solution in the nests. Obviously, this algorithm can be extended to the more complicated case where each nest has multiple eggs representing a set of solutions. Here we use the simplest approach, where each nest has only a single egg. In this case, there is no distinction between an egg, a nest, or a cuckoo, since each nest corresponds to one egg, which also represents one cuckoo.

This algorithm uses a balanced combination of a local random walk and the global explorative random walk, controlled by a switching parameter p_a. The local random walk can be written as

$$\boldsymbol{x}_i^{t+1} = \boldsymbol{x}_i^t + \alpha s \otimes H(p_a - \epsilon) \otimes (\boldsymbol{x}_j^t - \boldsymbol{x}_k^t), \tag{9.1}$$

where $\boldsymbol{x}_j^t$ and $\boldsymbol{x}_k^t$ are two different solutions selected randomly by random permutation, $H(u)$ is a Heaviside function, ϵ is a random number drawn from a uniform distribution, and s is the step size. Here, $\otimes$ means the entry-wise product of two vectors.

On the other hand, the global random walk is carried out using Lévy flights

$$x_i^{t+1} = x_i^t + \alpha L(s, \lambda), \tag{9.2}$$

where

$$L(s, \lambda) = \frac{\lambda \Gamma(\lambda) \sin(\pi \lambda/2)}{\pi} \frac{1}{s^{1+\lambda}}, \quad (s \gg s_0 > 0). \tag{9.3}$$

Here $\alpha > 0$ is the step size scaling factor, which should be related to the scales of the problem of interest. In most cases, we can use $\alpha = O(L/10)$, where L is the characteristic scale of the problem of interest, whereas in some cases $\alpha = O(L/100)$ can be more effective and avoid flying too far. Obviously, the α value in these two updating equations can be different, thus leading to two different parameters, α_1 and α_2. Here we use $\alpha_1 = \alpha_2 = \alpha$ for simplicity.

Based on these three rules, the basic steps of the CS can be summarized as the pseudo code shown in Figure 9.1.

The updating Eq. (9.2) is essentially a stochastic equation for a random walk. In general, a random walk is a Markov chain whose next state/location depends only on the current location (the first term in the preceding equation) and the transition probability (the second term). However, a substantial fraction of the new solutions should be generated by far field randomization, and their locations should be far enough from the current best solution; this will make sure that the system will not be trapped in a local optimum [30,32].

The literature on cuckoo search is expanding rapidly. It has received a lot of attention, and there are many recent studies using cuckoo search with a diverse range of applications [6,7,9–11,13,36]. For example, Walton et al. improved the algorithm

```
Cuckoo Search via Lévy Flights

Objective function f(x), x = (x_1, ..., x_d)^T
Generate initial population of n host nests x_i
while (t <MaxGeneration) or (stop criterion)
  Get a cuckoo randomly
  Generate a solution by Lévy flights [e.g., Eq.(9.2)]
  Evaluate its solution quality or objective value f_i
  Choose a nest among n (say, j) randomly
  if (f_i < f_j),
    Replace j by the new solution i
  end
  A fraction (p_a) of worse nests are abandoned
  New nests/solutions are built/generated by Eq.(9.1)
  Keep best solutions (or nests with quality solutions)
  Rank the solutions and find the current best
  Update t ← t + 1
end while
Postprocess results and visualization
```

Figure 9.1 Pseudo code of the cuckoo search for a minimization problem.

by formulating a modified CS algorithm [26]; Yang and Deb extended it to multi-objective optimization [33]. A comprehensive review can be found in the book edited by Yang [35].

9.3.1 Special Cases of Cuckoo Search

CS as a metaheuristic algorithm has surprisingly rich characteristics. If we look at the updating Eqs. (9.1) and (9.2) more closely, we can discover such subtle richness. From (9.1), we can group some factors together by setting $Q = \alpha s \otimes H(p_a - \epsilon)$; then we have $Q > 0$. As a result, Eq. (9.1) becomes the major updating equation of differential evolution (DE). Furthermore, we replace $\boldsymbol{x}_j^t$ with the current best solution $\boldsymbol{g}^*$ and set $k = i$, so we have

$$\boldsymbol{x}_i^{t+1} = \boldsymbol{x}_i^t + Q(\boldsymbol{g}^* - \boldsymbol{x}_i^t), \tag{9.4}$$

which is essentially a variant of the PSO without individual historical best. This case is very similar to the APSO developed by Yang et al. [29].

On the other hand, from (9.2), this random walk is in fact the simulated annealing (SA) with a Lévy-flight transition probability. In this case, we have an SA with a stochastic cooling scheduling controlled by p_a.

Therefore, differential evolution, PSO, and SA can be considered special cases of the cuckoo search algorithm. Conversely, we can say that CS is a good and efficient combination of DE, PSO, and SA in one algorithm. Therefore, it is no surprise that CS is very efficient.

9.3.2 How to Carry Out Lévy Flights

From the implementation point of view, the generation of random numbers with Lévy flights consists of two steps: the choice of a random direction and the generation of steps that obey the chosen Lévy distribution. The generation of a direction should be drawn from a uniform distribution, whereas the generation of steps is quite tricky. There are a few ways of achieving this, but one of the most efficient and yet straightforward ways is to use the so-called Mantegna algorithm for a symmetric Lévy stable distribution [15].

However, it is not trivial to generate pseudo-random step sizes that correctly obey this Lévy distribution. In Mantegna's algorithm, the step size s can be computed using two Gaussian distributions U and V via the following transformation:

$$s = \frac{U}{|V|^{1/\lambda}}, \tag{9.5}$$

where

$$U \sim N(0, \sigma^2), \quad V \sim N(0, 1). \tag{9.6}$$

Here $U \sim (0, \sigma^2)$ means that the samples are drawn from a Gaussian normal distribution with a zero mean and a variance of σ^2. The variance can be calculated by

$$\sigma^2 = \left[\frac{\Gamma(1+\lambda)}{\lambda\Gamma((1+\lambda)/2)} \cdot \frac{\sin(\pi\lambda/2)}{2^{(\lambda-1)/2}}\right]^{1/\lambda}. \tag{9.7}$$

This distribution (for s) obeys the expected Lévy distribution for $|s| \geq |s_0|$m where s_0 is the smallest step. In principle, $|s_0| \gg 0$, but in reality s_0 can be taken as a sensible value such as $s_0 = 0.1$ to 1.

These formulas look complicated, but the Γ function is just a constant for a given λ. For example, when $\lambda = 1$, we have $\Gamma(1 + \lambda) = 1, \Gamma((1 + \lambda)/2) = 1$ and

$$\sigma^2 = \left[\frac{1}{1 \times 1} \cdot \frac{\sin(\pi \times 1/2)}{2^0}\right]^{1/1} = 1. \tag{9.8}$$

It has been proved mathematically that the Mantegna algorithm can produce the random samples that obey the required distribution correctly [15].

9.3.3 Choice of Parameters

There are several parameters in CS. Apart from the population size n, there are switching probability p_a, step-size scaling factor α, and the Lévy exponent λ. However, the key parameters are p_a and n because we can take α and λ as constants. By varying their values, we found that we can set $\lambda = 1.5$ and $\alpha = 0.01$ for most problems.

For the key parameters, we have also tried to vary the number of host nests (or the population size n) and the probability p_a. We have used $n = 5, 10, 15, 20, 30, 40, 50, 100, 150, 250, 500$ and $p_a = 0, 0.01, 0.05, 0.1, 0.15, 0.2, 0.25, 0.3, 0.4, 0.5$. From our simulations, we found that $n = 15$ to 40 and $p_a = 0.25$ are sufficient for most optimization problems. Results and analysis also imply that the convergence rate, to some extent, is not sensitive to the parameters used. This means that the fine adjustment is not needed for any given problems.

Let us look at a simple example. One of the many test functions we have used is the bivariate Michalewicz function

$$f(x, y) = -\sin(x)\sin^{2m}\left(\frac{x^2}{\pi}\right) - \sin(y)\sin^{2m}\left(\frac{2y^2}{\pi}\right), \tag{9.9}$$

where $m = 10$ and $(x, y) \in [0, 5] \times [0, 5]$. This function has a global minimum $f_* \approx -1.8013$ at $(2.20319, 1.57049)$. This global optimum can easily be found using CS, and the results are shown in Figure 9.2, where the final locations of the nests are also marked with $\diamond$ in the figure. Here we have used $n = 15$ nests, $\alpha = 1$, and $p_a = 0.25$.

From the figure, we can see that as the optimum is approaching, most nests aggregate toward the global optimum. We also notice that the nests are also distributed at different (local) optima in the case of multimodal functions. This means that CS can find all the optima simultaneously if the number of nests are much higher than the number of local optima. This advantage may become more significant when we're dealing with multimodal and multi-objective optimization problems.

9.3.4 Variants of Cuckoo Search

Many variants of CS have been developed in the last few years. Despite the short history of this algorithm, CS has attracted great interest due to its simplicity, efficiency, and flexibility. As a result, the literature has expanded significantly. The standard CS

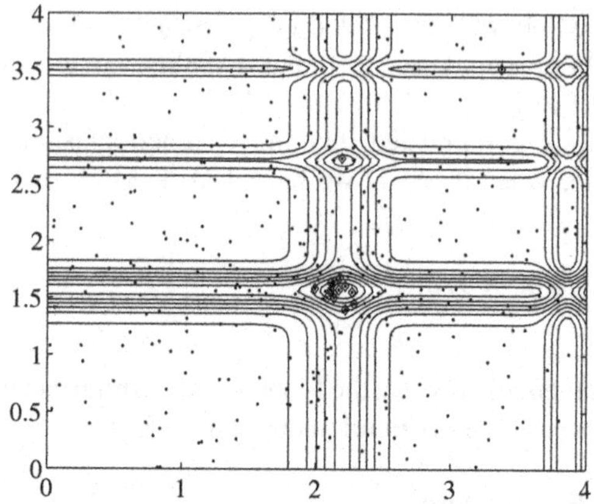

Figure 9.2 Search paths of nests using CS. The final locations of the nests are marked with ◇ in the figure.

is very powerful and efficient, but it was developed for continuous optimization. One useful extension is to produce a discrete version of CS so that it can solve scheduling problems and combinatorial optimization efficiently. There are many variants of CS in the literature; for a comprehensive review, refer to [34,12,35]. Here we outline only a few variants:

- *Modified cuckoo search (MCS).* One of the interesting and useful studies is the development of the modified cuckoo search by Walton et al. [26], which has been used to optimize mesh generation and other applications.
- *Improved cuckoo search (ICS).* Valian et al. [23] presented an improved cuckoo search for training feedforward neural networks in artificial intelligence applications [23,24]. At the same time, Vazquez [25] also used CS for training spiking neural models [25].
- *Quantum cuckoo search (QCS).* Layeb [14] presented a variant of CS by adding quantum behavior to the algorithm and so called it quantum cuckoo search. QCS has been applied to solve knapsack problems [14].
- *Discrete cuckoo search (DCS).* For discrete applications such as scheduling and combinatorial problems, there are a few variants in the literature. Ouaarab et al. [18] developed a discrete CS for solving traveling salesman problems (TSPs) [18]. Chandrasekaran and Simon [5] presented a multi-objective CS approach for multi-objective scheduling problems [5].
- *Multi-objective cuckoo search (MOCS).* Yang and Deb [33] developed a multi-objective CS approach for solving multi-objective engineering optimization problems [33].
- *Discrete multi-objective cuckoo search (DMOCS).* In the context of both multi-objective and scheduling problems, Chandrasekaran and Simon [5] developed a variant of CS for solving discrete multi-objective scheduling problems [5].

- *Hybrid cuckoo search (HCS).* There are variants that try to combine CS with other algorithms. For example, Wang et al. [28] combined CS with PSO and achieved good improvement [28]. Salimi et al. [22] combined modified CS with the conjugate gradient method [22].

There are many other variants; Fister et al. provided a brief review with detailed literature [12]. Yang and Deb provided a conceptual review [34]. The recent edited book has more extensive literature about cuckoo search and firefly algorithms [35].

9.4 Why Cuckoo Search is so Efficient

In addition to the analysis of the previous section showing that DE, PSO, and SA are special cases of the cuckoo search, recent theoretical studies also indicate that CS has global convergence [27], as outlined in the next subsection.

Theoretical studies of PSO have suggested that it can converge quickly to the current best solution but not necessarily the global best solutions. In fact, some analyses suggest that PSO updating equations do not satisfy the global convergence conditions, and thus there is no guarantee of global convergence. (See the chapter on particle swarm optimization in this book.) On the other hand, it has been proved that cuckoo search can satisfy the global convergence requirements and thus has guaranteed global convergence properties [27]. This implies that for multimodal optimization, PSO may converge prematurely to a local optimum, whereas CS can usually converge to the global optimality.

Furthermore, cuckoo search has two search capabilities: local search and global search, controlled by a switching/discovery probability. As mentioned in the previous section, the local search is very intensive, with about 1/4 of the search time (for $p_a = 0.25$), whereas global search takes about 3/4 of the total search time. This allows that the search space can be explored more efficiently on a global scale, and consequently the global optimality can be found with a higher probability.

A further advantage of CS is that its global search uses Lévy flights or process rather than standard random walks. Because Lévy flights have infinite mean and variance, CS can explore the search space more efficiently than algorithms using standard Gaussian processes. This advantage, combined with both local and search capabilities and guaranteed global convergence, makes CS very efficient. Indeed, various studies and applications have demonstrated that CS is very efficient [32,13,26,8].

9.5 Global Convergence: Brief Mathematical Analysis

Wang et al. provided a mathematical proof of global convergence for the standard CS; their approach is based on the Markov chain theory [27]. Their proof can be outlined as follows:

Because there are two branches in the updating formulas, the local search step only contributes mainly to local refinements, whereas the main mobility or exploration is carried out by the global search step. To simplify the analysis and to emphasize the global search capability, we now use a simplified version of cuckoo search. That is, we use only the global branch with a random number $r \in [0, 1]$, compared with a discovery/switching probability p_a. Now we have

$$\begin{cases} \boldsymbol{x}_i^{(t+1)} \leftarrow x_i^{(t)} & \text{if } r < p_a, \\ \boldsymbol{x}_i^{(t+1)} \leftarrow \boldsymbol{x}_i^{(t)} + \alpha \otimes L(\lambda) & \text{if } r > p_a. \end{cases} \tag{9.10}$$

Because our CS algorithm is a stochastic search algorithm, we can summarize it as the following key steps:

1. Randomly generate an initial population of n nests at the positions, $\boldsymbol{X} = \{\boldsymbol{x}_1^0, \boldsymbol{x}_2^0, \ldots, \boldsymbol{x}_n^0\}$, then evaluate their objective values so as to find the current global best $\boldsymbol{g}_t^0$.
2. Update the new solutions/positions by

$$\boldsymbol{x}_i^{(t+1)} = \boldsymbol{x}_i^{(t)} + \alpha \otimes L(\lambda). \tag{9.11}$$

3. Draw a random number r from a uniform distribution [0,1]. Update $\boldsymbol{x}_i^{(t+1)}$ if $r > p_a$. Then evaluate the new solutions to find the new, global best $\boldsymbol{g}_t^*$.
4. If the stopping criterion is met, then $\boldsymbol{g}_t^*$ is the best global solution found so far. Otherwise, return to step (2).

The global convergence of an algorithm. If f is measurable and the feasible solution space Ω is a measurable subset on $\Re^n$, algorithm A satisfies the preceding two conditions with the search sequence $\{x_k\}_{k=0}^{\infty}$, then

$$\lim_{k \to \infty} P(x_k \in R_{\epsilon,M}) = 1. \tag{9.12}$$

That is, algorithm A can converge globally with a probability of one. Here $P(x_k \in R_{\epsilon,M})$ is the probability measure of the kth solution on $R_{\epsilon,M}$ at the kth iteration.

The state and state space. The positions of a cuckoo/nest and its global best solution g in the search history form the states of cuckoos: $y = (x, g)$, where $x, g \in \Omega$ and $f(g) \le f(x)$. The set of all the possible states forms the state space, denoted by

$$Y = \{y = (x, g) | x, g \in \Omega, f(g) \le f(x)\}. \tag{9.13}$$

The states and state space of the cuckoo group/population. The states of all n cuckoos/nests form the states of the group, denoted by $q = (y_1, y_2, \ldots, y_n)$. All the states of all the cuckoos form a state space for the group, denoted by

$$Q = \{q = (y_1, y_2, \ldots, y_n), y_i \in Y, 1 \le i \le n\}. \tag{9.14}$$

Obviously, Q contains the historical global best solution g^* for the whole population and all individual best solutions $g_i (1 \le i \le n)$ in history. In addition, the global best solution of the whole population is the best among all g_i, so $f(g^*) = \min(f(g_i))$, $1 \le i \le n$.

The transition probability from state y_1 to y_2 in CS is

$$P(T_y(y_1) = y_2) = P(x_1 \to x_1')P(g_1 \to g_1')P(x_1' \to x_2)P(g_1' \to g_2), \tag{9.15}$$

where $P(x_1 \to x_1')$ is the transition probability at Step 2 in CS, and $P(g_1 \to g_1')$ is the transition probability for the historical global best at this step. $P(x_1' \to x_2)$ is the transition probability at Step 3, whereas $P(g_1' \to g_2)$ is the transition probability of the historical global best.

For globally optimal solution g_b for an optimization problem $< \Omega, f >$, the optimal state set is defined as $R = \{y = (x, g) | f(g) = f(g_b), y \in Y\}$.

For the globally optimal solution g_b to an optimization problem $< \Omega, f >$, the optimal group state set can be defined as

$$H = \{q = (y_1, y_2, \ldots, y_n) | \exists y_i \in R, 1 \leq i \leq n\}. \tag{9.16}$$

All these sets will ensure that the convergence conditions are met. Further detailed mathematical analysis proves that when the number of iteration approaches sufficiently large [27], the group state sequence will converge to the optimal state/solution set H. Therefore, the cuckoo search has guaranteed global convergence.

9.6 Applications

CS has been applied in many areas of optimization and computational intelligence with promising efficiency. For example, in engineering design applications, CS has superior performance over other algorithms for a range of continuous optimization problems, such as spring design and welded beam design [32, 13].

In addition, a modifed CS by Walton et al. [26] has been demonstrated to be very efficient for solving nonlinear problems such as mesh generation. Yildiz [36] has used CS to select optimal machine parameters in milling operation with enhanced results, and Zheng and Zhou [37] provided a variant of CS using Gaussian process.

In the context of data fusion and wireless sensor networks, CS has been shown to be very efficient [9, 10]. Furthermore, a variant of CS in combination with a quantum-based approach has been developed to solve knapsack problems efficiently [14]. From the algorithm analysis point of view, a conceptural comparison of CS with particle swarm optimization (PSO), differential evolution (DE), and artificial bee colony (ABC) by Civicioglu and Desdo [8] suggested that CS and differential evoluton algorithms provide more robust results than PSO and ABC. Gandomi et al. [13] provided a more extensive comparison study for solving various sets of structural optimization problems and concluded that CS obtained better results than other algorithms such as PSO and gentic algorithms (GA). Among the diverse applications, an interesting performance enhancement has been obtained by using CS to train neural networks as shown by Valian et al. [23] and reliability optimization problems [24].

For complex phase equilibrium applications, Bhargava et al. [1] have shown that CS offers a reliable method for solving thermodynamic calculations. At the same time, Bulatović et al. [3] solved a six-bar double dwell linkage problem using CS, and Moravej and Akhlaghi [16] solved the DG allocation problem in distribution networks with good convergence rate and performance.

As a further extension, Yang and Deb [33] produced the multi-objective cuckoo search (MOCS) for design engineering appplications. For multi-objective scheduling problems, much progress was made by Chandrasekaran and Simon [5] using CS algorithms, which demonstrated the superiority of their proposed methodology. Recent studies have demonstrated that cuckoo search can perform significantly better than other algorithms in many applications [13,17,37,36]. For a more detailed review, refer to Yang [35] and Yang et al. [31].

References

[1] Bhargava V, Fateen SEK, Bonilla-Petriciolet A. Cuckoo search: a new nature-inspired optimization method for phase equilibrium calculations. Fluid Phase Equilib 2013;337(1):191–200.
[2] Barthelemy P, Bertolotti J, Wiersma DS. A Lévy flight for light. Nature 2008;453(6948):495–8.
[3] Bulatović RR, Bordević SR, Dordević VS. Cuckoo search algorithm: a metaheuristic approach to solving the problem of optimum synthesis of a six-bar double dwell linkage. Mech Mach Theory 2013;61(1):1–3.
[4] Brown C, Liebovitch LS, Glendon R. Lévy flights in Dobe Ju/'hoansi foraging patterns. Human Ecol 2007;35(2):129–38.
[5] Chandrasekaran K, Simon SP. Multi-objective scheduling problem: hybrid appraoch using fuzzy assisted cuckoo search algorithm. Swarm Evol Comput 2012;5(1):1–6.
[6] Chifu VR, Pop CB, Salomie I, Suia DS, Niculici AN. Optimizing the semantic web service composition process using cuckoo search. In: Brazier FMT, Nieuwenhuis K, Palvin G, Warnier M, Badica C, editors. Intelligent distributed computing V. Studies in computational intelligence, vol. 382. Berlin, Germany: Springer; 2012. p. 93–102.
[7] Choudhary K, Purohit GN. A new testing approach using cuckoo search to achieve multi-objective genetic algorithm. J Comput 2011;3(4):117–9.
[8] Civicioglu P, Besdok E. A conception comparison of the cuckoo search, particle swarm optimization, differential evolution and artificial bee colony algorithms. Artif Intell Rev 2013;39(3):315–46.
[9] Dhivya M, Sundarambal M, Anand LN. Energy efficient computation of data fusion in wireless sensor networks using cuckoo-based particle approach (CBPA). Int J of Commun Netw Syst Sci 2011;4(4):249–55.
[10] Dhivya M, Sundarambal M. Cuckoo search for data gathering in wireless sensor networks. Int J Mobile Commun 2011;9(6):642–56.
[11] Durgun I, Yildiz AR. Structural design optimization of vehicle components using cuckoo search algorithm. Mater Test 2012;3(2):185–8.
[12] Fister Jr I, Yang XS, Fister I, Fister D. Cuckoo search: a brief literature review. In: Yang XS, editor. Cuckoo search and firefly algorithm: theory and applications. Heidelberg, Germany: Springer; 2013 [chapter 3].
[13] Gandomi AH, Yang XS, Alavi AH. Cuckoo search algorithm: a meteheuristic approach to solve structural optimization problems. Eng Comput 2013;29(1):17–35.
[14] Layeb A. A novel quantum-inspired cuckoo search for Knapsack problems. Int J Bio-inspired Comput 2011;3(5):297–305.
[15] Mantegna RN. Fast, accurate algorithm for numerical simulation of Lévy stable stochastic process. Phys Rev E 1994;49(5):4677–83.
[16] Moravej Z, Akhlaghi A. A novel approach based on cuckoo search for DG allocation in distribution network. Electr Power Energy Syst 2013;44(1):672–9.

[17] Noghrehabadi A, Ghalambaz M, Vosough A. A hybrid power series: cuckoo search optimization algorithm to electrostatic deflection of micro fixed-fixed actuators. Int J Multidisciplinary Sci Eng 2011;2(4):22–6.
[18] Ouaarab A, Ahiod B, Yang XS. Discrete cuckoo search algorithm for the travelling salesman problem, Neural Computing and Applications; in press. http://dx.doi.org/10.1007/s00521-013-1402-2.
[19] Payne RB, Sorenson MD, Klitz K. The cuckoos. Oxford, UK: Oxford University Press; 2005.
[20] Pavlyukevich I. Lévy flights, non-local search and simulated annealing. J Comput Phys 2007;226(2):1830–44.
[21] Reynolds AM, Frye MA. Free-flight odor tracking in Drosophila is consistent with an optimal intermittent scale-free search. PLoS One 2007;2(4):e354–63.
[22] Salimi H, Giveki D, Soltanshahi MA, Hatami J. Extended mixture of MLP experts by hybrid of conjugate gradient method and modified cuckoo search. Int J Artif Intell Appl 2012;3(1):1–3.
[23] Valian E, Mohanna S, Tavakoli S. Improved cuckoo search algorithm for feedforward neural network training. Int J Artif Intell Appl 2011;2(3):36–43.
[24] Valian E, Tavakoli S, Mohanna S, Haghi A. Improved cuckoo search for reliability optimization problems. Comput Ind Eng 2013;64(1):459–68.
[25] Vazquez RA. Training spiking neural models using cuckoo search algorithm. In: IEEE congress on evolutionary computation. New Orleans: IEEE publication; 2012.p. 679–86.
[26] Walton S, Hassan O, Morgan K, Brown MR. Modified cuckoo search: a new gradient free optimization algorithm. Chaos Solitons Fractals 2011;44(9):710–8.
[27] Wang F, He X-S, Wang Y, Yang SM. Markov model and convergence analysis based on cuckoo search algorithm. Comput Eng 2012;38(11):180–5.
[28] Wang F, Lou L, He X, Wang Y. Hybrid optimization algorithm of PSO and cuckoo search. In: Proceedings of the second international conference on artificial intelligence, management science and electronic commerce (AIMSEC'11). Zhengzhou: IEEE publication; 2011. p. 1172–5.
[29] Yang XS, Deb S, Fong S. Accelerated particle swarm optimization and support vector machine for business optimization and applications. In: Networked digital technologies 2011. Communications in computer and information science, vol. 136. Berlin, Germany: Springer; 2011. p. 53–66.
[30] Yang XS, Deb S. Cuckoo search via Lévy flights. In: Proceeings of world congress on nature & biologically inspired computing (NaBIC 2009). USA: IEEE Publications; 2009. p. 210–4.
[31] Yang XS, Cui ZH, Xiao RB, Gandomi AH, Karamanoglu M. Swarm intelligence and bio-inspired computation: theory and applications. Waltham, MA, USA: Elsevier; 2013.
[32] Yang XS, Deb S. Engineering optimization by cuckoo search. Int J Math Model Numer Optimisation 2010;1(4):330–43.
[33] Yang XS, Deb S. Multiobjective cuckoo search for design optimization. Comput Oper Res 2013;40(6):1616–24.
[34] Yang XS, Deb S. Cuckoo search: recent advances and applications, Neural Computing and Applications; in press. <http://link.springer.com/article/10.1007>.
[35] Yang XS. Cuckoo search and firefly algorithm: theory and applications. Studies in computational intelligence, vol. 516. Heidelberg, Germany: Springer; 2013.
[36] Yildiz AR. Cuckoo search algorithm for the selection of optimal machine parameters in milling operations. Int J Adv Manuf Technol. 2013;64(1–4):55–61.
[37] Zheng HQ, Zhou Y. A novel cuckoo search optimization algorithm based on Gauss distribution. J Comput Inform Syst 2012;8(10):4193–200.

10 Bat Algorithms

The *bat algorithm* (BA) is a bio-inspired algorithm developed by Xin-She Yang in 2010 that has been found very efficient. As a result, the literature has expanded significantly since then. This chapter provides a detailed introduction to BA and its new variants. A wide range of diverse applications and case studies are also reviewed and summarized briefly here.

10.1 Echolocation of Bats

10.1.1 Behavior of Microbats

Bats are fascinating animals. They are the only mammals with wings, and they also have advanced capability of echolocation. It is estimated that there are about 1000 different bat species, which accounts for up to 20% of all mammal species. Their size ranges from the tiny bumblebee bats (of about 1.5 to 2 g) to giant bats with a wingspan of about 2 m and weight of up to about 1 kg. Microbats typically have a forearm length of about 2.2 to 11 cm. Most bats use echolocation to a certain degree; among all the species, microbats are a famous example because they use echolocation extensively, whereas megabats do not [2,4,27].

Most microbats are insectivores. Microbats use a type of sonar, called *echolocation*, to detect prey, avoid obstacles, and locate their roosting crevices in the dark. These bats emit a very loud sound pulse and listen for the echo that bounces back from the surrounding objects. Their pulses vary in properties and can be correlated with their hunting strategies, depending on the species. Most bats use short, frequency-modulated signals to sweep through about an octave; others more often use constant-frequency signals for echolocation. Their signal bandwidth varies with species and often increases by using more harmonics.

Studies show that microbats use the time delay from the emission and detection of the echo, the time difference between their two ears, and the loudness variations of the echoes to build up a three-dimensional scenario of the surrounding. They can detect the distance and orientation of the target, the type of prey, and even the moving speed of the prey, such as small insects. Indeed, studies suggest that bats seem to be able to discriminate targets by the variations of the Doppler effect induced by the wing-flutter rates of the target insects [2].

Nature-Inspired Optimization Algorithms. http://dx.doi.org/10.1016/B978-0-12-416743-8.00010-5

10.1.2 Acoustics of Echolocation

Though each pulse lasts only a few thousandths of a second (up to about 8 to 10 ms), it has a constant frequency that is usually in the region of 25 kHz to 150 kHz. The typical range of frequencies for most bat species is in the region between 25 kHz and 100 kHz, though some species can emit higher frequencies up to 150 kHz. Each ultrasonic burst may last typically 5 to 20 ms, and microbats emit about 10 to 20 such sound bursts every second. When they are hunting for prey, the rate of pulse emission can be sped up to about 200 pulses per second when they fly near their prey. Such short sound bursts imply the fantastic ability of the signal processing power of bats. In fact, studies show that the equivalent integration time of the bat ear is typically about 300 to 400 μs.

As the speed of sound in air is typically $v = 340$ m/s at room temperature, the wavelength λ of the ultrasonic sound bursts with a constant frequency f is given by $\lambda = v/f$, which is in the range of 2 mm to 14 mm for the typical frequency range from 25 kHz to 150 kHz. Such wavelengths are obviously on the same order of their prey sizes [2,27].

Amazingly, the emitted pulse could be as loud as 110 dB, and, fortunately, they are in the ultrasonic region. The loudness also varies from the loudest when searching for prey to a quieter base when homing toward the prey. The traveling range of such short pulses is typically a few meters, depending on the actual frequencies. Microbats can manage to avoid obstacles as small as a thin human hair.

Obviously, some bats have good eyesight, and most bats also have very sensitive smell sense. In reality, they use all the senses in combination to maximize the efficient detection of prey and smooth navigation. However, here we are only interested in the echolocation and the associated behavior.

The echolocation behavior of microbats can be formulated in such a way that it can be associated with the objective function to be optimized, and this makes it possible to formulate new optimization algorithms. Here we first outline the basic formulation of BA and then discuss its implementation.

10.2 Bat Algorithms

If we idealize some of the echolocation characteristics of microbats, we can develop various bat-inspired or bat algorithms [32]. For simplicity, we now use the following approximate or idealized rules:

1. All bats use echolocation to sense distance, and they also "know" the difference between food/prey and background barriers.
2. Bats fly randomly with velocity $\boldsymbol{v}_i$ at position $\boldsymbol{x}_i$. They can automatically adjust the frequency (or wavelength) of their emitted pulses and adjust the rate of pulse emission $r \in [0, 1]$, depending on the proximity of their target.
3. Although the loudness can vary in many ways, we assume that the loudness varies from a large (positive) A_0 to a minimum value $A_{\min}$.

Another obvious simplification is that no ray tracing is used in estimating the time delay and three-dimensional topography. Though this might be a good feature for the

Bat Algorithm

Initialize the bat population $\boldsymbol{x}_i$ and $\boldsymbol{v}_i$ $(i = 1, 2, ..., n)$
Initialize frequencies f_i, pulse rates r_i and the loudness A_i
while (t <Max number of iterations)
  Generate new solutions by adjusting frequency,
  Update velocities and locations/solutions [(10.1) to (10.3)]
  if (rand $> r_i$)
    Select a solution among the best solutions
    Generate a local solution around the selected best solution
  end if
  Generate a new solution by flying randomly
  if (rand $< A_i$ & $f(\boldsymbol{x}_i) < f(\boldsymbol{x}_*)$)
    Accept the new solutions
    Increase r_i and reduce A_i
  end if
  Rank the bats and find the current best $\boldsymbol{x}_*$
end while

Figure 10.1 Pseudo code of the bat algorithm (BA).

application in computational geometry, we will not use this simplification here, since it is more computationally extensive in multidimensional cases.

In addition to these simplified assumptions, we also use the following approximations for simplicity. In general, the frequency f in a range $[f_{\min}, f_{\max}]$ corresponds to a range of wavelengths $[\lambda_{\min}, \lambda_{\max}]$. For example, a frequency range of [20 kHz, 500 kHz] corresponds to a range of wavelengths from 0.7 mm to 17 mm.

For a given problem, we can also use any wavelength for the ease of implementation. In the actual implementation, we can adjust the range by adjusting the frequencies (or wavelengths). The detectable range (or the largest wavelength) should be chosen such that it is comparable to the size of the domain of interest, then toned down to smaller ranges. Furthermore, we do not necessarily have to use the wavelengths themselves at all. Instead, we can also vary the frequency while fixing the wavelength λ. This is because λ and f are related, since λf is constant. We use this latter approach in our implementation.

For simplicity, we can assume $f \in [0, f_{\max}]$. We know that higher frequencies have short wavelengths and travel a shorter distance. For bats, the typical ranges are a few meters. The rate of pulse can simply be in the range of [0,1], where 0 means no pulses at all and 1 means the maximum rate of pulse emission.

Based on these approximations and idealized rules, the basic steps of BA can be summarized as the schematic pseudo code shown in Figure 10.1.

10.2.1 Movement of Virtual Bats

In simulations, we have to use virtual bats. We have to define the rules of how their positions $\boldsymbol{x}_i$ and velocities $\boldsymbol{v}_i$ in a d-dimensional search space are updated. The new solutions $\boldsymbol{x}_i^t$ and velocities $\boldsymbol{v}_i^t$ at time step t are given by

$$f_i = f_{\min} + (f_{\max} - f_{\min})\beta, \tag{10.1}$$

$$v_i^{t+1} = v_i^t + (x_i^t - x_*) f_i, \tag{10.2}$$

$$x_i^{t+1} = x_i^t + v_i^{t+1}, \tag{10.3}$$

where $\beta \in [0, 1]$ is a random vector drawn from a uniform distribution. Here x_* is the current global best location (solution), which is located after comparing all the solutions among all the n bats. Because the product $\lambda_i f_i$ is a constant, we can use f_i (or λ_i) to adjust the velocity change while fixing the other factor λ_i (or f_i), depending on the type of the problem of interest. In our implementation, we use $f_{\min} = 0$ and $f_{\max} = O(1)$, depending on the domain size of the problem of interest. Initially, each bat is randomly assigned a frequency that is drawn uniformly from $[f_{\min}, f_{\max}]$.

For the local search part, once a solution is selected among the current best solutions, a new solution for each bat is generated locally using random walk

$$x_{\text{new}} = x_{\text{old}} + \epsilon\, A^{(t)}, \tag{10.4}$$

where $\epsilon \in [-1, 1]$ is a random number, while $A^{(t)} = \langle A_i^t \rangle$ is the average loudness of all the bats at this time step. From the implementation point of view, it is better to provide a scaling parameter to control the step size. Therefore, we can rewrite this equation as

$$x_{\text{new}} = x_{\text{old}} + \sigma\, \epsilon_t A^{(t)}, \tag{10.5}$$

where ϵ_t is now drawn from a Gaussian normal distribution $N(0, 1)$, and σ is a scaling factor. In our demo implementation, we set $\sigma = 0.01$. Obviously, σ should be linked to the scalings of the design variables of an optimization problem under consideration.

The update of the velocities and positions of bats may have some similarity to the procedure in the standard particle swarm optimization, since f_i essentially controls the pace and range of the movement of the swarming particles. However, BA can be more effective because it uses frequency tuning and parameter control to influence exploration and exploitation.

10.2.2 Loudness and Pulse Emission

Furthermore, the loudness A_i and the rate r_i of pulse emission have to be updated accordingly as the iterations proceed. Because the loudness usually decreases once a bat has found its prey, whereas the rate of pulse emission increases, the loudness can be chosen as any value of convenience. For simplicity, we can also use $A_0 = 1$ and $A_{\min} = 0$, assuming $A_{\min} = 0$ means that a bat has just found the prey and temporarily stops emitting any sound. Now we have

$$A_i^{t+1} = \alpha A_i^t, \quad r_i^{t+1} = r_i^0 [1 - \exp(-\gamma t)], \tag{10.6}$$

where α and γ are constants. In fact, α is similar to the cooling factor of a cooling schedule in the simulated annealing discussed earlier in this book. For any $0 < \alpha < 1$ and $\gamma > 0$, we have

$$A_i^t \to 0, \quad r_i^t \to r_i^0, \quad \text{as } t \to \infty. \tag{10.7}$$

In the simplest case, we can use $\alpha = \gamma$, and we used $\alpha = \gamma = 0.9$ in our simulations. However, it is worth pointing out that the demo code does not include the variations of A and r, which is mainly to show the essence of frequency tuning in the bat algorithm.

The choice of parameters requires some experimentation. Initially, each bat should have different values of loudness and pulse emission rate; this can be achieved by randomization. For example, the initial loudness A_i^0 can typically be taken as 1, whereas the initial emission rate r_i^0 can be around zero or any value $r_i^0 \in (0, 1]$ if using (10.6). Their loudness and emission rates will be updated only if the new solutions are improved, which means that these bats are moving toward the optimal solution.

By analyzing BA closely, we can see that it can capture many charactersitics of other algorithms. If we replace the variations of the frequency f_i by a random parameter and setting $A_i = 0$ and $r_i = 1$, BA essentially becomes the standard PSO. Similarly, if we do not use the velocities, we use fixed loudness and rate: A_i and r_i. For example, for $A_i = r_i = 0.7$, this algorithm is virtually reduced to a simple harmony search (HS), as the frequency/wavelength change is essentially the pitch adjustment while the rate of pulse emission is similar to the harmonic acceptance rate (here with a twist) in the HS algorithm. In other words, HS and PSO can be considered the special cases of BA. Therefore, it is no surprise that BA is efficient.

The current studies imply that the proposed new algorithm is potentially more powerful and thus should be investigated further in many applications of engineering and in solving industrial optimization problems.

10.3 Implementation

From the pseudo code, it is relatively straightforward to implement BA in any programming language. For ease of visualization, we have implemented it using Matlab for various test functions.

There are many standard test functions for validating new algorithms. As a simple benchmark, let us look at the eggcrate function

$$f = x^2 + y^2 + 25(\sin^2 x + \sin^2 y), \quad (x, y) \in [-2\pi, 2\pi] \times [-2\pi, 2\pi].$$

We know that f has a global minimum $f_{\min} = 0$ at (0,0). In our implementation, we use $n = 25$ to 50 virtual bats, and $\alpha = 0.9$. For the multimodal eggcrate function, a snapshot of the last 10 iterations is shown in Figure 10.2, where all bats move toward the global best (0, 0).

For demonstration purposes, we simplify the bat algorithm by setting A and r as constants. The following Matlab code should work well for function optimization.

```
% ------------------------------------------------------%
% Bat-inspired algorithm for continuous optimization    %
% Programmed by Xin-She Yang @2010                      %
% ------------------------------------------------------%
function [best,fmin,N_iter]=bat_algorithm(para)
% Default parameters
if nargin<1,  para=[10 0.25 0.5];  end
n=para(1);      % Population size, typically 10 to 25
A=para(2);      % Loudness  (constant or decreasing)
r=para(3);      % Pulse rate (constant or decreasing)
```

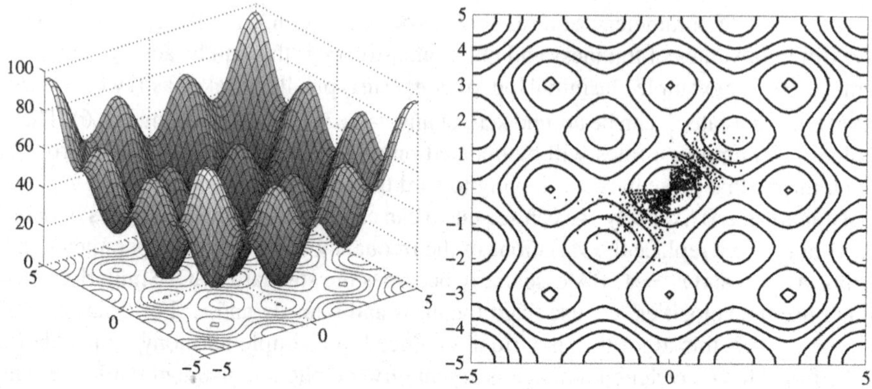

Figure 10.2 The eggcrate function (left) and the locations of 40 bats in the last 10 iterations (right).

```
% This frequency range determines the scalings
Qmin=0;           % Frequency minimum
Qmax=2;           % Frequency maximum
% Iteration parameters
tol=10^(-5);      % Stop tolerance
N_iter=0;         % Total number of function evaluations
% Dimension of the search variables
d=3;
% Initial arrays
Q=zeros(n,1);     % Frequency
v=zeros(n,d);     % Velocities
% Initialize the population/solutions
for i=1:n,
  Sol(i,:)=randn(1,d);
  Fitness(i)=Fun(Sol(i,:));
end
% Find the current best
[fmin,I]=min(Fitness);
best=Sol(I,:);
% Start the iterations -- Bat Algorithm
while (fmin>tol)
        % Loop over all bats/solutions
        for i=1:n,
          Q(i)=Qmin+(Qmin-Qmax)*rand;
          v(i,:)=v(i,:)+(Sol(i,:)-best)*Q(i);
          S(i,:)=Sol(i,:)+v(i,:);
          % Pulse rate
          if rand>r
              S(i,:)=best+0.01*randn(1,d);
          end
```

```
    % Evaluate new solutions
          Fnew=Fun(S(i,:));
    % If the solution improves or not too loudness
          if (Fnew<=Fitness(i)) & (rand<A) ,
               Sol(i,:)=S(i,:);
               Fitness(i)=Fnew;
          end

         % Update the current best
         if Fnew<=fmin,
               best=S(i,:);
               fmin=Fnew;
         end
       end
       N_iter=N_iter+n;
end
% Output/display
disp(['Number of evaluations: ',num2str(N_iter)]);
disp(['Best =',num2str(best),' fmin=',num2str(fmin)]);
% Objective function -- Rosenbrock's 3D function
function z=Fun(u)
z=(1-u(1))^2+100*(u(2)-u(1)^2)^2+(1-u(3))^2;
```

BA is much superior to other algorithms in terms of accuracy and efficiency for many test functions because it usually provides a fast convergence rate.

10.4 Binary Bat Algorithms

The basic bat algorithm works well for continuous problems. But to deal with discrete and combinatorial problems, some modifications are needed to discretize the bat algorithm. Nakamura et al. developed the so-called *binary bat algorithm* (BBA) for feature selection and image processing [21]. For feature selection, they proposed that the search space is modeled as a d-dimensional Boolean lattice in which bats move across the corners and nodes of a hypercube. For binary feature selection, a feature is represented by a bat's position as a binary vector.

In BBA, a sigmoid function is used to restrict a bat's position. That is,

$$x_i^j = \begin{cases} 1 & \text{if } S(v_i^j) > \rho, \\ 0 & \text{otherwise} \end{cases}, \tag{10.8}$$

and

$$S(v_i^j) = \frac{1}{1 + \exp[-v_i^j]}, \tag{10.9}$$

where the velocity component v_i^j corresponds to the jth dimension of bat i, and $\rho \sim U(0, 1)$ is a random number drawn from a uniform distribution. This means that the positions or coordinates of bats are in the Boolean lattice.

Obviously, it can be expected that this BBA variant can be extended to deal with other discrete and combinatorial problems. In addition, there are other ways to discretize the bat algorithm. In fact, any efficient ways to discrete swarm-based algorithms such as PSO can also be used to discretize BA and produce new variants of it. In fact, this has become an active research topic.

10.5 Variants of the Bat Algorithm

The standard BA has many advantages, a key one being that it can provide very quick convergence at an early stage of iteration by switching from exploration to exploitation if necessary. This makes BA an efficient algorithm for applications such as classifications and others when a fast solution is needed. However, if we allow the algorithm to switch to exploitation stage too fast by varying A and r too quickly, it may lead to stagnation after some initial stage. To improve performance, many methods and strategies have been attempted to increase the diversity of the solution and thus to enhance performance, which produced a few good BA variants.

From a quick but incomplete literature survey [38], we found the following BA variants:

- *Fuzzy logic bat algorithm (FLBA).* Khan and Sahai [14] presented a variant by introducing fuzzy logic into BA. They called their variant FLBA [14].
- *Multi-objective bat algorithm (MOBA).* Yang [33] extended BA to deal with multi-objective optimization, which has demonstrated its effectiveness for solving a few design benchmarks in engineering [33].
- *K-means bat algorithm (KMBA).* Komarasamy and Wahi [16] presented a combination of K-means and bat algorithm (KMBA) for efficient clustering [16].
- *Chaotic bat algorithm (CBA).* Lin et al. [17] presented a chaotic BA using Lévy flights and chaotic maps to carry out parameter estimation in dynamic biological systems [17]. Gandomi and Yang [10] proposed another CBA using various iterative maps [10].
- *Binary bat algorithm (BBA).* Nakamura et al. [21] developed a discrete version of BA to solve classifications and feature selection problems [21].
- *Improved bat algorithm (IBA).* Jamil et al. [13] extended BA with a good combination of Lévy flights and subtle variations of loudness and pulse emission rates. They tested the IBA versus more than 70 different test functions, and IBA proved to be very efficient [13].
- *Modified bat algorithm (MBA).* Huang et al. [11] developed this invariant by using orthogonal Latin square sampling as the initial population and incorporating autonomous danger-averting behavior. The researchers proved that MBA has guaranteed global convergence [11].

There are other improvements and variants of BA. For example, Wang and Guo [31] hybridized BA with harmony search and produced a hybrid BA for numerical optimization of function benchmarks [30]. They also applied BA to vehicle routing problems [31].

On the other hand, Fister, Jr., et al. [8] developed a hybrid BA using differential evolution as a local search part of BA [8]. We can expect that more variants are still under active research.

10.6 Convergence Analysis

Huang et al. carried out a detailed convergence analysis for BA using the finite Markov process theory [11].

In theory, an algorithm with an order-m reducible stochastic matrix P can be rewritten as

$$P = \begin{pmatrix} S & \cdots & 0 \\ R & \cdots & T \end{pmatrix}, \tag{10.10}$$

where $R \neq 0, T \neq 0$ and S is an order-q stochastic matrix (with $q < m$). Then we have

$$P^{\infty} = \lim_{k\to\infty} P^k$$

$$= \lim_{k\to\infty} \begin{pmatrix} S^k & \cdots & 0 \\ \sum_{i=1}^{k-1} T^i R S^{k-i} & \cdots & T^k \end{pmatrix} = \begin{pmatrix} S^{\infty} & \cdots & 0 \\ R^{\infty} & \cdots & T \end{pmatrix}, \tag{10.11}$$

which is a stable stochastic matrix and independent of the initial distribution [12]. In addition, we also have

$$P^{\infty} = [p_{ij}]_{m\times m}, \quad \begin{cases} p_{ij} > 0, & (1 \le i \le m, 1 \le j \le q), \\ p_{ij} = 0, & (1 \le i \le m, q < j \le m). \end{cases} \tag{10.12}$$

The search algorithm will converge with almost probability one to the global optimality, starting from any initial random states, if the transition probability p to a better solution or state is $p > 0$. Conversely, if the transition probability p to a worse state is greater, the algorithm will not converge.

With this main result, it has been proved that PSO will not converge to the global optimality [26], whereas BA will converge to the true global optimality [11].

Huang et al. concluded that for unconstrained function optimization, BA satisfies all the conditions for guaranteed global convergence. For nonlinear constrained problems, BA will converge with additional initialization of orthogonal Latin squares and has guaranteed global convergence to the true global optimality. They further concluded that

$$S^{\infty} = (1), \quad R^{\infty} = (1, 1, \ldots, 1)^T \tag{10.13}$$

and

$$P^{\infty} = \begin{pmatrix} 1 & 0 & \cdots & 0 \\ 1 & 0 & \cdots & 0 \\ \vdots & \vdots & & \vdots \\ 1 & 0 & \cdots & 0 \end{pmatrix}, \tag{10.14}$$

which leads to

$$\lim_{t \to \infty} p\{f(\boldsymbol{x}) \to f(\boldsymbol{x}_*)\} = 1. \tag{10.15}$$

That is, the global convergence is guaranteed.

They also proposed a BA variant, called a *modified bat algorithm* (MBA), can further improve the convergence rate with guaranteed global optimality. They also showed that this variant is suitable for large-scale, global optimization.

10.7 Why the Bat Algorithm is Efficient

Like many metaheuristic algorithms, BA has the advantage of simplicity and flexibility. BA is easy to implement, and such a simple algorithm can be very flexible to solve a wide range of problems, as we have seen in our review.

A natural question is: Why is the bat algorithm so efficient? There are many reasons for the success of bat-based algorithms. By analyzing the key features and updating equations, we can summarize the following three key points and features:

- *Frequency tuning*. BA uses echolocation and frequency tuning to solve problems. Though echolocation is not directly used to mimic the true function in reality, frequency variations are used. This capability can provide some functionality that may be similar to the key feature used in PSO, SA, and HS. Therefore, BA possesses the advantages of other swarm-intelligence-based algorithms.
- *Automatic zooming*. BA has a distinct advantage over other metaheuristic algorithms. That is, BA has a capability of automatically zooming into a region where promising solutions have been found. This zooming is accompanied by the automatic switch from explorative moves to local intensive exploitation. As a result, BA has a quick convergence rate, at least at early stages of the iterations, compared with other algorithms.
- *Parameter control*. Many metaheuristic algorithms used fixed parameters by using some pre-tuned algorithm-dependent parameters. In contrast, BA uses parameter control, which can vary the values of parameters (A and r) as the iterations proceed. This provides a way to automatically switch from exploration to exploitation when the optimal solution is approaching. This gives another advantage of BA over other metaheuristic algorithms.

In addition, preliminary theoretical analysis by Huang et al., discussed in an earlier section, suggested that BA has guaranteed global convergence properties under the right conditions, and BA can also solve large-scale problems effectively.

10.8 Applications

The standard BA and its many variants mean that the applications are also very diverse. In fact, since the original BA was developed [32], bat algorithms have been applied in almost every area of optimization, classifications, image processing, feature selection, scheduling, data mining, and other problems. In the rest of the chapter, we briefly highlight some of the applications [9,23,32,33,36,37]. This review is based on detailed review articles in the literature [34,35,38].

10.8.1 Continuous Optimization

Among the first set of applications of BA, continuous optimization in the context of engineering design optimization has been extensively studied and demonstrated that BA can deal with highly nonlinear problems efficiently and can find the optimal solutions accurately [32,36]. Case studies include pressure vessel design, car side design, spring and beam design, truss systems, tower and tall building design, and others. Tsai et al. [29] solved numerical optimization problems using BA [29].

In addition, Bora et al. [3] optimized the brushless DC wheel motors using BA with superior results [3]. BA can also handle multi-objective problems effectively [33].

10.8.2 Combinatorial Optimization and Scheduling

From the computational complexity point of view, continuous optimization problems can be considered easy to solve, though they may still be very challenging. However, combinatorial problems can be really hard, often nondeterministic polynomial time hard (NP-hard). Ramesh et al. [24] presented a detailed study of combined economic load and emission dispatch problems using BA [24]. They compared BA with ant colony algorithms (ABC), hybrid genetic algorithms, and other methods and concluded that BA is easy to implement and much superior to the other algorithms in terms of accuracy and efficiency.

Musikapun and Pongcharoen (2012) solved multistage, multimachine, multiproduct scheduling problems using BA, and they solved a class of NP-hard problems with a detailed parametric study. They also implied that the performance can be further improved by about 8.4% using an optimal set of parameters [20].

10.8.3 Inverse Problems and Parameter Estimation

Yang et al. use BA to study topological shape optimization in microelectronic applications so that materials of different thermal properties can be placed in such a way that the heat transfer is most efficient under stringent constraints [37]. It can also be applied to carry out parameter estimation as an inverse problem. If an inverse problem can be properly formulated, BA can provide better results than least-squares methods and regularization methods.

Lin et al. [17] presented a chaotic Lévy flight BA to estimate parameters in nonlinear dynamic biological systems, which proved the effectiveness of the proposed algorithm [17].

10.8.4 Classifications, Clustering, and Data Mining

Komarasamy and Wahi [16] studied K-means clustering using BA and concluded that the combination of both K-means and BA can achieve higher efficiency and thus perform better than other algorithms tested in their work [16].

Khan and Sahari presented a comparison study of BA with PSO, GA, and other algorithms in the context of e-learning and thus suggested that BA clearly has some advantages over other algorithms [14]. They also presented a study of clustering problems using BA and its extension as a bisonar optimization variant, with good results [15].

On the other hand, Mishra et al. [19] used BA to classify microarray data [19], whereas Natarajan et al. [22] presented a comparison study of cuckoo search and BA for Bloom filter optimization [22]. Damodaram and Valarmathi [5] studied phishing Website detection using modified BA and achieved very good results [5].

Marichelvam and Prabaharan [18] used BA to study hybrid flowshop scheduling problems so as to minimize the makespan and mean flow time [18]. Their results suggested that BA is an efficient approach for solving hybrid flowshop scheduling problems. Faritha Banu and Chandrasekar [7] used a modified BA to record deduplication as an optimization approach and data compression technique. Their results suggested that the modified BA can perform better than genetic programming [7].

10.8.5 Image Processing

Akhtar et al. [1] presented a study for full-body human-pose estimation using BA [1], and they concluded that BA performs better than PSO, particle filter (PF), and annealed particle filter (APF).

Du and Liu [6] presented a variant of BA with mutation for image matching, and they indicated that their bat-based model is more effective and feasible in imagine matching than other models, such as differential evolution and genetic algorithms [6].

10.8.6 Fuzzy Logic and Other Applications

Reddy and Manoj [25] presented a study of optimal capacitor placement for loss reduction in distribution systems using BA. It combines with fuzzy logic to find optimal capacitor sizes so as to minimize the total losses. Their results suggested that the real power loss can be reduced significantly [25]. Furthermore, Tamiru and Hashim [28] applied an approach based on BA to study fuzzy systems and to model exergy changes in a gas turbine [28].

At the time of writing, when we searched Google Scholar and other databases, we found other papers on BA that either had just been accepted or were conference presentations. However, they do not contain enough detail to be included in this review. In fact, as the literature is expanding, more and more papers on BA are emerging, so a further timely review will be needed within the next few years.

An interesting extension will be to use different schemes of wavelengths or frequency variations instead of the current linear implementation. In addition, the rates of pulse emission and loudness can also be varied in a more sophisticated manner. Another extension for discrete problems is to use the time delay between pulse emission and the echo bounced back. For example, in the traveling salesman problem, the distance between two adjacent nodes or cities can easily be coded as the time delay. Because microbats use time difference between their two ears to obtain three-dimensional information, they can identify the type of prey and the velocity of a flying insect. Therefore, a further natural extension to the current BA would be to use the directional echolocation and Doppler effect, which may lead to even more interesting variants and new algorithms.

References

[1] Akhtar S, Ahmad AR, Abdel-Rahman EM. A metaheuristic bat-inspired algorithm for full body human pose estimation. In: Ninth conference on computer and robot vision (CRV2012) 28–30 May 2012, Toronto, ON. Toronto, ON, Canada: Conference Publishing Service; 2012. p. 369–75.

[2] Altringham JD. Bats: biology and behaviour. Oxford, UK: Oxford University Press; 1996.

[3] Bora TC, Coelho LS, Lebensztajn L. Bat-inspired optimization approach for the brushless DC wheel motor problem. IEEE Trans Magn 2012;48(2):947–50.

[4] Colin T. The varienty of life. Oxford, UK: Oxford University Press; 2000.

[5] Damodaram R, Valarmathi ML. Phishing website detection and optimization using modified bat algorithm. Int J Eng Res Appl 2012;2(1):870–6.

[6] Du ZY, Liu B. Image matching using a bat algorithm with mutation. Appl Mech Mater 2012;203(1):88–93.

[7] Faritha Banu A, Chandrasekar C. An optimized appraoch of modified bat algorithm to record deduplication. Int J Comput Appl 2012;62(1):10–5.

[8] Fister Jr I, Fister D, Yang XS. A hybrid bat algorithm. Elekrotehnivški Vestn 2013;80(1–2):1–7.

[9] Gandomi AH, Yang XS, Alavi AH, Talatahari S. Bat algorithm for constrained optimization tasks. Neural Comput Appl 2013;22(6):1239–55.

[10] Gandomi AH, Yang XS. Chaotici bat algorithm. J Comput Sci 2013. <http://www.sciencedirect.com/science/article/pii/S1877750313001099>.

[11] Huang GQ, Zhao WJ, Lu QQ. Bat algorithm with global convergence for solving large-scale optimization problem. Appl Res Comput 2013;30(5):1323–8. [in Chinese].

[12] Iisufescu M. Finite Markov processes and their applications. Chichester, UK: John Wiley; 1980.

[13] Jamil M, Zepernic H-J, Yang XS. Improved bat algorithm for global optimization. Appl Soft Comput [submitted, Sept 2013].

[14] Khan K, Sahai A. A comparison of BA, GA, PSO, BP and LM for training feed forward neural networks in e-learning context. Int J Intell Sys Appl 2012;4(7):23–9.

[15] Khan K, Sahai A. A fuzzy c-means bi-sonar-based metaheuristic optimization algorithm. Int J Interact Multimedia Art Intell 2012;1(7):26–32.

[16] Komarasamy G, Wahi A. An optimized K-means clustering technique using bat algorithm. Euro J Sci Res 2012;84(2):263–73.

[17] Lin JH, Chou CW, Yang CH, Tsai HL. A chaotic Lévy flight bat algorithm for parameter estimation in nonlinear dynamic biological systems. J Comput Inf Tech 2012;2(2):56–63.

[18] Marichelvam MK, Prabaharam T. A bat algorithm for realistic hybrid flowshop scheduling problems to minimize makespan and mean flow time. ICTACT J Soft Comput 2012;3(1):428–33.

[19] Mishra S, Shaw K, Mishra D. A new meta-heuristic bat inspired classification approach for microarray data. Procedia Tech 2012;4(1):802–6.

[20] Musikapun P, Pongcharoen P. Solving multi-stage multi-machine multi-product scheduling problem using bat aglorithm. Second international conference on management and artificial intelligence (IPEDR), vol. 35. Singapore: IACSIT Press; 2012. p. 98–102.

[21] Nakamura RYM, Pereira LAM, Costa KA, Rodrigues D, Papa JP, Yang XS. BBA: a binary bat algorithm for feature selection. In: 25th SIBGRAPI conference on graphics, patterns and images (SIBGRAPI), August 22–25, 2012. IEEE Publication; 2012. p. 291–7.

[22] Natarajan A, Subramanian S, Premalatha K. A comparative study of cuckoo search and bat algorithm for Bloom filter optimisation in spam filtering. Int J Bio-Inspired Comput 2012;4(2):89–99.

[23] Parpinelli RS, Lopes HS. New inspirations in swarm intelligence: a survey. Int J Bio-Inspired Comput 2011;3(1):1–16.

[24] Ramesh B, Mohan VCJ, Reddy VCV. Application of bat algorithm for combined economic load and emission dispatch. Int J Electr Eng Telecommun 2013;2(1):1–9.

[25] Reddy VU, Manoj A. Optimal capacitor placement for loss reduction in distribution systems using bat algorithm. IOSR J Eng 2012;2(10):23–7.

[26] Ren ZH, Wang J, Gao YL. The global convergence of particle swarm optimization based on Markov chain. Control Theory Appl 2011;28(4):462–6.

[27] Richardson P. Bats. London: Natural History Museum; 2008.

[28] Tamiru AL, Hashim FM. Application of bat algorithm and fuzzy systems to model exergy changes in a gas turbine. In: Yang XS, editor. Artificial intelligence, evolutionary computing and metaheuristics. Studies in computational intelligence, vol. 427. Heidelberg, Germany: Springer; 2013. p. 685–719.

[29] Tsai PW, Pan JS, Liao BY, Tsai MJ, Istanda V. Bat algorithm inspired algorithm for solving numerical optimization problems. Appl Mech Mater 2011;148–149(1):134–7.

[30] Wang GG, Guo LH, Duan H, Liu L, Wang HQ. A bat algorithm with mutation for UCAV path planning. Sci World J 2012. Available from: <www.hindawi.com/journals/tswj/2012/418946/>.

[31] Wang GG, Guo LH. A novel hybrid bat algorithm with harmony search for global numerical optimization. J Appl Math 2013. Available from: <http://dx.doi.org/10.1155/2013/696491>.

[32] Yang XS. A new metaheuristic bat-inspired algorithm. In: Cruz C, González JR, Pelta DA, Terrazas G, editors. Nature inspired cooperative strategies for optimization (NISCO 2010). Studies in computational intelligence. Berlin, Germany: Springer; 2010. p. 65–74.

[33] Yang XS. Bat algorithm for multi-objective optimisation. Int J Bio-Inspired Comput 2011;3(5):267–74.

[34] Yang XS. Bat algorithm and cuckoo search: a tutorial. In: Yang XS, editor. Artificial intelligence, evolutionary computing and metaheuristics. Studies in computational intelligence, vol. 427; 2013. p. 421–34.

[35] Yang XS, Cui ZH, Xiao RB, Gandomi AH, Karamanoglu M. Swarm intelligence and bio-inpsired computation: theory and applications. London: Elsevier; 2013.

[36] Yang XS, Gandomi AH. Bat algorithm: a novel approach for global engineering optimization. Eng Comput 2012;29(5):464–83.

[37] Yang XS, Karamanoglu M, Fong S. Bat aglorithm for topology optimization in microelectronic applications. In: IEEE international conference on future generation communication technology (FGCT2012). London, UK: British Computer Society; 2012. p. 150–5. December 12–14.

[38] Yang XS. Bat algorithm: literature review and applications. Int J Bio-Inspired Comput 2013;5(3):141–9.

11 Flower Pollination Algorithms

The *flower pollination algorithm* (FPA) was developed by Xin-She Yang in 2012, inspired by the pollination process of flowering plants. FPA has been extended to multi-objective optimization with promising results. This chapter provides an introduction to FPA and its basic implementation.

11.1 Introduction

Real-world design problems in engineering and industry are usually multi-objective or multicriteria. These multiple objectives often conflict with one another, which makes it impossible to use any single design option without compromise. Common approaches are to provide good approximations to the true Pareto fronts of the problem of interest so that decision makers can rank different options, depending on their preferences or their utilities [1,5,15]. Compared with single-objective optimization, multi-objective optimization has its additional challenging issues such as time complexity, inhomogeneity, and dimensionality. It is usually more time consuming to obtain the true Pareto fronts because it typically requires us to produce many points on the Pareto front for good approximations.

In addition, even if accurate solutions on a Pareto front can be obtained, there is still no guarantee that these solution points will distribute uniformly on the front. In fact, it is often difficult to obtain the whole front without any part missing. For single-objective optimization, the optimal solution can often be a single point in the solution space, whereas for bi-objective optimization, the Pareto front forms a curve, and for tri-objective cases it becomes a surface. In fact, a higher-dimensional problem can have an extremely complex hypersurface as its Pareto front [11,20]. Consequently, it is typically more challenging to solve such high-dimensional problems.

In the current literature of engineering optimization, a class of nature-inspired algorithms have shown their promising performance and have thus become popular and widely used. These algorithms are mostly swarm intelligence based [5,7,9,15,14], as we have seen in this book.

The main aim of this chapter is to first introduce the basic flower pollination algorithm (FPA), developed by Xin-She Yang in 2012 [19], and then extend it to solve multi-objective optimization. We then discuss the results for solving function optimization benchmarks and design benchmarks in engineering.

Nature-Inspired Optimization Algorithms. http://dx.doi.org/10.1016/B978-0-12-416743-8.00011-7

11.2 Flower Pollination Algorithm

11.2.1 Characteristics of Flower Pollination

It is estimated that there are over a quarter of a million types of flowering plants in nature and that about 80% of all plant species are flowering species. It still remains a mystery how flowering plants came to dominate the landscape from the Cretaceous period [17]. Flowering plants have been evolving for at least 125 million years, and flowers have become so influential in evolution that, it is unimaginable what the plant world would look like without them. The main purpose of a flower is ultimately reproduction via pollination. Flower pollination is typically associated with the transfer of pollen, and such transfer is often linked with pollinators such as insects, birds, bats, and other animals. In fact, some flowers and insects have co-evolved into a very specialized flower-pollinator partnership. For example, some flowers can only attract and can only depend on a specific species of insect or bird for successful pollination.

Pollination can take two major forms: abiotic and biotic. About 90% of flowering plants belong to the biotic pollination group. That is, pollen is transferred by pollinators such as insects and animals. About 10% of pollination takes abiotic form, which does not require any pollinators. Wind and diffusion help with pollination of such flowering plants. Grass is a good example of abiotic pollination [5,17]. Pollinators, sometimes called pollen vectors, can be very diverse. It is estimated that there are at least 200,000 varieties of pollinators such as insects, bats, and birds. Honeybees are a good example of pollinators, and they have also developed the so-called flower constancy. That is, these pollinators tend to visit certain flower species exclusively, bypassing other flower species. Such flower constancy may have evolutionary advantages because it maximizes the transfer of flower pollen to the same or conspecific plants, thus maximizing the reproduction of the same flower species. Such flower constancy may be advantageous for pollinators as well because they can be sure that nectar supply is available with their limited memory and minimum cost of learning, switching, or exploring. Rather than focusing on some unpredictable but potentially more rewarding new flower species, pollinators might find that flower constancy requires minimum investment costs and more likely guaranteed intake of nectar [18].

Pollination can be achieved by self-pollination or cross-pollination. Cross-pollination, or allogamy, means that pollination can occur from the pollen of a flower of a different plant; self-pollination is the fertilization of one flower, such as peach flowers, from pollen of the same flower or different flowers of the same plant, which often occurs when no reliable pollinator is available. Biotic cross-pollination may occur at a long distance; pollinators such as bees, bats, birds, and flies can fly a long distance, so they can be considered global pollination. In addition, bees and birds may exhibit Lévy flight behavior with jump or fly distance steps obeying a Lévy distribution. Furthermore, flower constancy can be considered an incremental step using the similarity or difference of two flowers.

From the biological evolution point of view, the objective of flower pollination is the survival of the fittest and the optimal reproduction of plants in terms of numbers as well as the most fittest. This can be considered an optimization process of plant species. All of these factors and processes of flower pollination interact to achieve optimal reproduction of the flowering plants. This natural behavior may motivate us to design new optimization algorithms.

11.2.2 Flower Pollination Algorithm

FPA was developed by Xin-She Yang in 2012 [19], inspired by the flow pollination process of flowering plants. FPA has been extended to multi-objective optimization [20]. For simplicity, the following four rules are used:

1. Biotic and cross-pollination can be considered processes of global pollination, and pollen-carrying pollinators move in a way that obeys Lévy flights (Rule 1).
2. For local pollination, abiotic pollination and self-pollination are used (Rule 2).
3. Pollinators such as insects can develop flower constancy, which is equivalent to a reproduction probability that is proportional to the similarity of two flowers involved (Rule 3).
4. The interaction or switching of local pollination and global pollination can be controlled by a switch probability $p \in [0, 1]$, slightly biased toward local pollination (Rule 4).

To formulate the updating formulas, these rules have to be converted into proper updating equations. For example, in the global pollination step, flower pollen gametes are carried by pollinators such as insects, and pollen can travel over a long distance because insects can often fly and move in a much longer range. Therefore, Rule 1 and flower constancy (Rule 3) can be represented mathematically as

$$\boldsymbol{x}_i^{t+1} = \boldsymbol{x}_i^t + \gamma L(\lambda)(\boldsymbol{g}_* - \boldsymbol{x}_i^t), \tag{11.1}$$

where $\boldsymbol{x}_i^t$ is the pollen i or solution vector $\boldsymbol{x}_i$ at iteration t, and $\boldsymbol{g}_*$ is the current best solution found among all solutions at the current generation/iteration. Here γ is a scaling factor to control the step size.

In essence, $L(\lambda)$ is a step-size parameter, more specifically the Lévy-flights-based step size, that corresponds to the strength of the pollination. Since insects may travel over a long distance with various distance steps, a Lévy flight can be used to mimic this characteristic efficiently. That is, $L > 0$ is drawn from a Lévy distribution

$$L \sim \frac{\lambda \Gamma(\lambda) \sin(\pi\lambda/2)}{\pi} \frac{1}{s^{1+\lambda}}, \quad (s \gg s_0 > 0). \tag{11.2}$$

Here $\Gamma(\lambda)$ is the standard gamma function, and this distribution is valid for large steps $s > 0$. In theory, it is required that $|s_0| \gg 0$, but in practice s_0 can be as small as 0.1.

However, it is not trivial to generate pseudo-random step sizes that correctly obey this Lévy distribution (11.2). There are a few methods for drawing such random numbers; the most efficient one from our studies is the so-called Mantegna algorithm for drawing step size s by using two Gaussian distributions U and V by the following transformation [10]

$$s = \frac{U}{|V|^{1/\lambda}}, \tag{11.3}$$

Flower Pollination Algorithm (or simply Flower Algorithm)

```
Objective min or max f(x), x = (x_1, x_2, ..., x_d)
Initialize a population of n flowers/pollen gametes with random solutions
Find the best solution g_* in the initial population
Define a switch probability p ∈ [0, 1]
while (t <MaxGeneration)
    for i = 1 : n (all n flowers in the population)
      if rand < p,
        Draw a (d-dimensional) step vector L from a Lévy distribution
        Global pollination via x_i^{t+1} = x_i^t + γL(g_* − x_i^t)
      else
        Draw ε from a uniform distribution in [0,1]
        Do local pollination via x_i^{t+1} = x_i^t + ε(x_j^t − x_k^t)
      end if
      Evaluate new solutions
      If new solutions are better, update them in the population
    end for
      Find the current best solution g_*
end while
Output the best solution found
```

Figure 11.1 Pseudo code of the proposed flower pollination algorithm (FPA).

and

$$U \sim N(0, \sigma^2), \quad V \sim N(0, 1). \tag{11.4}$$

Here $U \sim (0, \sigma^2)$ means that the samples are drawn from a Gaussian normal distribution with a zero mean and a variance of σ^2. The variance can be calculated by

$$\sigma^2 = \left[\frac{\Gamma(1+\lambda)}{\lambda\Gamma((1+\lambda)/2)} \cdot \frac{\sin(\pi\lambda/2)}{2^{(\lambda-1)/2}}\right]^{1/\lambda}. \tag{11.5}$$

For the local pollination, both Rule 2 and Rule 3 can be represented as

$$\boldsymbol{x}_i^{t+1} = \boldsymbol{x}_i^t + \epsilon(\boldsymbol{x}_j^t - \boldsymbol{x}_k^t), \tag{11.6}$$

where $\boldsymbol{x}_j^t$ and $\boldsymbol{x}_k^t$ are pollen from different flowers of the same plant species. This essentially mimics the flower constancy in a limited neighborhood. Mathematically, if $\boldsymbol{x}_j^t$ and $\boldsymbol{x}_k^t$ come from the same species or are selected from the same population, this equivalently becomes a local random walk if ϵ is drawn from a uniform distribution in [0,1].

The main steps of FPA, or simply the flower algorithm, are summarized in Figure 11.1.

In principle, flower pollination activities can occur at all scales, both local and global. But in reality, adjacent flower patches or flowers in the not-so-far-away neighborhood are more likely to be pollinated by local flower pollen than those far away. To mimic this feature, a switch probability (Rule 4) or proximity probability p can be effectively used to switch between common global pollination to intensive local pollination. To start with, a naïve value of $p = 0.5$ may be used as an initial value. A preliminary parametric study indicated that $p = 0.8$ may work better for most applications.

11.3 Multi-Objective Flower Pollination Algorithms

A multi-objective optimization problem with m objectives can be written in general as

$$\text{Minimize} \quad f_1(\boldsymbol{x}), f_2(\boldsymbol{x}), \ldots, f_m(\boldsymbol{x}), \tag{11.7}$$

subject to the nonlinear equality and inequality constraints

$$h_j(\boldsymbol{x}) = 0, \quad (j = 1, 2, \ldots, J), \tag{11.8}$$

$$g_k(\boldsymbol{x}) \leq 0, \quad (k = 1, 2, \ldots, K). \tag{11.9}$$

To use the techniques for single-objective optimization or to extend the existing methods for solving multi-objective problems, there are different approaches to achieve this task. One of the simplest ways is to use a weighted sum to combine multiple objectives into a composite single objective

$$f = \sum_{i=1}^{m} w_i f_i \tag{11.10}$$

with

$$\sum_{i=1}^{m} w_i = 1, \quad w_i > 0, \tag{11.11}$$

where $w_i (i = 1, \ldots, m)$ are nonnegative weights.

The fundamental idea of this weighted sum approach is that these weighting coefficients act as the preferences for these multi-objectives. For a given set of $(w_1, w_2, \ldots, w_m)$, the optimization process will produce a single point of the Pareto front of the problem. For a different set of w_i, another point on the Pareto front can be generated. With a sufficiently large number of combinations of weights, a good approximation to the true Pareto front can be obtained. It has been proved that the solutions to the problem with the combined objective (11.10) are Pareto-optimal if the weights are positive for all the objectives, and these are also Pareto-optimal to the original problem (11.7). In practice, a set of random numbers u_i are first drawn for a uniform distribution $U(0, 1)$. Then, the weights w_i can be calculated by normalization. That is,

$$w_i = \frac{u_i}{\sum_{i=1}^{m} u_i}, \tag{11.12}$$

so that $\sum_i w_i = 1$ can be satisfied. For example, for three objectives f_1, f_2, and f_3, three random numbers or weights can be drawn from a uniform distribution [0, 1], and they may be $u_1 = 0.2915$, $u_2 = 0.9147$ and $u_3 = 0.6821$ in one instance of sampling runs. Then we have $\sum_i = 1.8883$, and $w_1 = 0.1544$, $w_2 = 0.4844$, $w_3 = 0.3612$. Indeed, $\sum_i w_i = 1.000$ is satisfied.

To obtain the Pareto front accurately with solutions relatively uniformly distributed on the front, random weights w_i should be used and should be as different as possible [12]. From the benchmarks that have been tested, the weighted sum with random weights usually works well, as can be seen in the following discussion.

11.4 Validation and Numerical Experiments

There are many different test functions for single-objective and multi-objective optimization [8,21–23], but a subset of some widely used functions can provide a wide range of diverse properties in terms of Pareto fronts and Pareto optimal sets. To validate the proposed MOFPA, a subset of these functions with convex, nonconvex, and discontinuous Pareto fronts has been selected, including seven single-objective test functions, four multi-objective test functions, four mono-objective design benchmarks, and a bi-objective design problem.

11.4.1 Single-Objective Test Functions

Before proceeding to solve multi-objective optimization problems, we should first validate the algorithm by solving some well-known single-objective test functions. There are at least 100 well-known test functions. However, there is no agreed set of test functions for validating new algorithms, though some reviews and literature do exist [8]. A subset of seven test functions with diverse properties is used here.

The Ackley function can be written as

$$f_1(\boldsymbol{x}) = -20\exp\left[-\frac{1}{5}\sqrt{\frac{1}{d}\sum_{i=1}^{d} x_i^2}\right] - \exp\left[\frac{1}{d}\sum_{i=1}^{d}\cos(2\pi x_i)\right] + 20 + e, \quad (11.13)$$

which has a global minimum $f_* = 0$ at $(0, 0, \ldots, 0)$.

The simplest of De Jong's functions is the so-called sphere function

$$f_2(\boldsymbol{x}) = \sum_{i=1}^{n} x_i^2, \quad -5.12 \leq x_i \leq 5.12, \quad (11.14)$$

whose global minimum is obviously $f_* = 0$ at $(0, 0, \ldots, 0)$. This function is unimodal and convex.

Easom's function is

$$f_3(\boldsymbol{x}) = (-1)^{d+1}\prod_{i=1}^{d}\cos(x_i)\exp\left[-\sum_{i=1}^{d}(x_i-\pi)^2\right], \quad (11.15)$$

whose global minimum is $f_* = -1$ at $\boldsymbol{x}_* = (\pi, \ldots, \pi)$ within $-100 \leq x_i \leq 100$. It has many local minima.

Griewank's function is

$$f_4(\boldsymbol{x}) = \frac{1}{4000}\sum_{i=1}^{d} x_i^2 - \prod_{i=1}^{d} \cos\left(\frac{x_i}{\sqrt{i}}\right) + 1, \quad -600 \le x_i \le 600, \tag{11.16}$$

whose global minimum is $f_* = 0$ at $\boldsymbol{x}_* = (0, 0, \ldots, 0)$. This function is highly multimodal.

Rastrigin's function,

$$f_5(\boldsymbol{x}) = 10d + \sum_{i=1}^{d}\Big[x_i^2 - 10\cos(2\pi x_i)\Big], \quad -5.12 \le x_i \le 5.12, \tag{11.17}$$

has a global minimum of $f_* = 0$ at $(0, 0, \ldots, 0)$. This function is highly multimodal.

Rosenbrock's function is

$$f_6(\boldsymbol{x}) = \sum_{i=1}^{d-1}\Big[(x_i - 1)^2 + 100(x_{i+1} - x_i^2)^2\Big], \tag{11.18}$$

whose global minimum $f_* = 0$ occurs at $\boldsymbol{x}_* = (1, 1, \ldots, 1)$ in the domain $-5 \le x_i \le 5$ where $i = 1, 2, \ldots, d$.

Zakharov's function,

$$f_7(\boldsymbol{x}) = \sum_{i=1}^{d} x_i^2 + \left(\frac{1}{2}\sum_{i=1}^{d} i x_i\right)^2 + \left(\frac{1}{2}\sum_{i=1}^{d} i x_i\right)^4, \tag{11.19}$$

has its global minimum $f_* = 0$ at $(0, 0, \ldots, 0)$.

To compare the performance of FPA with other existing algorithms, we first test each algorithm using the most widely used implementation and parameter settings. For genetic algorithms (GA), a crossover rate of $p_{\text{crossover}} = 0.95$ and a mutation rate of $p_{\text{mutation}} = 0.05$ are used. For PSO, a version with an inertia weight $\theta = 0.7$ is used, and its two learning parameters $\alpha = \beta$ are set as 1.5. Furthermore, to ensure a fair comparison, the same population size should be used whenever possible. So here $n = 25$ has been used for all three algorithms.

To get some insight into the parameter settings of FPA, a detailed parametric study has been carried out by varying p from 0.05 to 0.95 with a step increase of 0.05, $\lambda = 1, 1.25, 1.5, 1.75, 1.9$ and $n = 5, 10, 15, \ldots, 50$. It has been found that $n = 25$, $p = 0.8$, $\gamma = 0.1$, and $\lambda = 1.5$ work for most cases. The parameter values used for all three algorithms are summarized in Table 11.1.

The convergence behavior of genetic algorithms and PSO during iterations have been well studied in the literature. For FPA, various statistical measures can be obtained from a set of runs.

For a fixed population size $n = 25$, this is equal to the total number of function evaluations of 25,000. The best results obtained in terms of the means of the minimum values found in the 40 independent runs are summarized in Table 11.2.

Table 11.1 Parameter values for each algorithm.

PSO	$n = 25, \theta = 0.7, \alpha = \beta = 1.5$
GA	$n = 25, p_{\text{crossover}} = 0.95, p_{\text{mutation}} = 0.05$
FPA	$n = 25, \lambda = 1.5, \gamma = 0.1, p = 0.8$

Table 11.2 Comparison of algorithm performance: Mean values.

Functions	**GA**	**PSO**	**FPA**
f_1	8.29e-9	7.12e-12	5.09e-12
f_2	6.61e-15	1.18e-24	2.47e-26
f_3	−0.9989	−0.9998	−1.0000
f_4	5.72e-9	4.69e-9	1.37e-11
f_5	2.93e-6	3.44e-6	4.52e-7
f_6	8.97e-6	8.21e-8	6.19e-8
f_7	8.77e-4	1.58e-4	9.53e-5

11.4.2 Multi-Objective Test Functions

In the rest of this chapter, the parameters in MOFPA are fixed based on a preliminary parametric study, and $p = 0.8$, $\lambda = 1.5$, and a scaling factor $\gamma = 0.1$ are used. The population size $n = 50$ and the dimensionality $d = 10$ are used. The number of iterations is set to $t = 1000$. The following four functions are tested:

- ZDT1 function with a convex front [21,23]:

$$f_1(x) = x_1, \quad f_2(x) = g(1 - \sqrt{f_1/g}),$$

$$g = 1 + \frac{9\sum_{i=2}^{d} x_i}{d-1}, \quad x_1 \in [0, 1], \ i = 2, \ldots, 30, \tag{11.20}$$

  where d is the number of dimensions. The Pareto optimality is reached when $g = 1$.
- ZDT2 function with a nonconvex front:

$$f_1(x) = x_1, \quad f_2(x) = g\left(1 - \frac{f_1}{g}\right)^2,$$

  where g is the same as given in ZDT1.
- ZDT3 function with a discontinuous front:

$$f_1(x) = x_1, \quad f_2(x) = g\left[1 - \sqrt{\frac{f_1}{g}} - \frac{f_1}{g}\sin(10\pi f_1)\right],$$

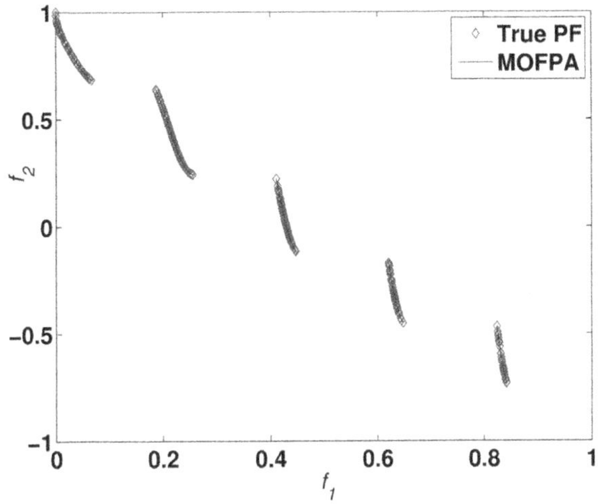

Figure 11.2 Pareto front of test function ZDT3.

where g in functions ZDT2 and ZDT3 is the same as in function ZDT1. In the ZDT3 function, f_1 is discontinuous and varies from 0 to 0.852 and f_2 from −0.773 to 1.

- LZ function (Li and Zhang, 2009; Zhang and Li, 2007):

$$f_1 = x_1 + \frac{2}{|J_1|} \sum_{j \in J_1} \left[x_j - \sin\left(6\pi x_1 + \frac{j\pi}{d}\right)\right]^2,$$

$$f_2 = 1 - \sqrt{x_1} + \frac{2}{|J_2|} \sum_{j \in J_2} \left[x_j - \sin\left(6\pi x_1 + \frac{j\pi}{d}\right)\right]^2, \tag{11.21}$$

where $J_1 = \{j|j \text{ is odd }\}$ and $J_2 = \{j|j \text{ is even }\}$ where $2 \le j \le d$. This function has a Pareto front $f_2 = 1 - \sqrt{f_1}$ with a Pareto set

$$x_j = \sin\left(6\pi x_1 + \frac{j\pi}{d}\right), \quad j = 2, 3, \ldots, d, \quad x_1 \in [0, 1]. \tag{11.22}$$

After generating 100 Pareto points by MOFPA, the Pareto front generated by MOFPA is compared with the true front of ZDT3 (see Figure 11.2).

Let us define the distance or error between the estimate Pareto front PF^e to its corresponding true front PF^t as

$$E_f = ||PF^e - PF^t||^2 = \sum_{j=1}^{N} (PF_j^e - PF_j^t)^2, \tag{11.23}$$

where N is the number of points.

The variation of convergence rates or the convergence property can be viewed by plotting out the errors during iterations. This is an absolute measure that depends on the number of points. Sometimes it is easier to use a relative measure in terms of the generalized distance

$$D_g = \frac{1}{N}\sqrt{\sum_{j=1}^{N}(PF_j - PF_j^t)^2}. \tag{11.24}$$

The results for all the functions are summarized in Table 11.3.

11.4.3 Analysis of Results and Comparison

To compare the performance of the proposed MOFPA with that of other established multi-objective algorithms, we have selected a few algorithms with available results from the literature. Where the results are not available, the algorithms have been implemented using well-documented studies and then new results using these algorithms were generated. In particular, other methods are also used for comparison, including vector evaluated genetic algorithms (VEGA), NSGA-II [4], multi-objective differential evolution (MODE), differential evolution for multi-objective optimization (DEMO) [16], multi-objective bees algorithms (Bees), and strength Pareto evolutionary algorithm (SPEA) [3,4]. The performance measures in terms of generalized distance D_g are summarized in Table 11.4 for all these major methods.

Table 11.3 Summary of results.

Functions	Errors (1000 Iterations)	Errors (2500 Iterations)
ZDT1	1.1E-6	3.1E-19
ZDT2	2.7E-6	4.4E-10
ZDT3	1.4E-5	7.2E-12
LZ	1.2E-6	2.9E-12

Table 11.4 Comparison of D_g for $n = 50$ and $t = 500$ iterations.

Methods	ZDT1	ZDT2	ZDT3	LZ
VEGA	3.79E-02	2.37E-03	3.29E-01	1.47E-03
NSGA-II	3.33E-02	7.24E-02	1.14E-01	2.77E-02
MODE	5.80E-03	5.50E-03	2.15E-02	3.19E-03
DEMO	1.08E-03	7.55E-04	1.18E-03	1.40E-03
Bees	2.40E-02	1.69E-02	1.91E-01	1.88E-02
SPEA	1.78E-03	1.34E-03	4.75E-02	1.92E-03
MOFPA	7.11E-05	1.24E-05	5.49E-04	7.92E-05

Table 11.5 Comparison of FPA with GA and PSO for benchmarks [2,20].

Cases	GA	PSO	FPA
Spring	2.6681	2.659	2.6586
Beam	2.4331	2.3810	1.72485
Reducer	2985.2[a]	2996.348	2993.7496
Vessel	5850.383	5850.383	5850.383

[a] This solution is not valid because the solution violates constraint g_{11}.

It is clearly seen from Table 11.4 that the proposed MOFPA obtained better results for almost all four cases (See Table 11.5).

11.5 Applications

Design optimization, especially design of structures, has many applications in engineering and industry. As a result, there are many different benchmarks with detailed studies in the literature [13,14]. For multi-objective optimization, MOFPA will be used to solve a disc brake design problem [6,14].

11.5.1 *Single-Objective Design Benchmarks*

11.5.1.1 *Spring Design Optimization*

Tensional and/or compressional springs are used widely in engineering. A standard spring design problem has three design variables: the wire diameter d, the mean coil diameter D, and the length (or number of coils) L (integer). The objective is to minimize the weight of the spring subject to various constraints, such as maximum shear stress, minimum deflection, and geometrical limits. For detailed descriptions, refer to earlier studies. This problem can be written compactly as

$$\text{Minimize } f(\boldsymbol{x}) = \frac{\pi(L+2)d^2 D}{4}, \tag{11.25}$$

subject to

$$g_1(\boldsymbol{x}) = \frac{8C_f P_{\max} D}{3.14156 d^3} - S \leq 0$$
$$g_2(\boldsymbol{x}) = \frac{8K P_{\max} L D}{C_f d^4} + 1.05(L+2)d - L_{free} \leq 0$$
$$g_3(\boldsymbol{x}) = d_{\min} - d \leq 0$$
$$g_4(\boldsymbol{x}) = (d+D) - D_{\max} \leq 0$$

$$g_5(\boldsymbol{x}) = 3 - \frac{D-d}{d} \leq 0$$
$$g_6(\boldsymbol{x}) = \delta - \delta_{pm} \leq 0$$
$$g_7(\boldsymbol{x}) = \frac{8KP_{\max}D^3L}{C_f d^4} + \frac{P_{\max} - P_{load}}{K} + 1.05(L+2)d - L_{free} \leq 0$$
$$g_8(\boldsymbol{x}) = \delta_w - \frac{P_{\max} - P_{load}}{K} \leq 0, \tag{11.26}$$

where

$$C_f = \frac{4S_i - 1}{4S_i - 4} + \frac{0.615}{S_i}, \quad S_d = \frac{D}{d}, \quad K = \frac{Gd^4}{8nD^3}, \tag{11.27}$$

$$D_{\max} = 3.0(\text{in}), \quad P_{\max} = 300.0(\text{lb}), \quad \delta_w = 1.25(\text{in}). \tag{11.28}$$

Here the maximum work load is 1000 lb, the maximum shear stress is $S = 189,000$ psi, and the shear modulus is 11.5×10^6 psi. In addition, the maximum coil free length is $L_{free} = 14$ in, the minimum wire diameter is $d_{\min} = 0.2$ in, and the maximum allowable defection under preload is $\delta_{pm} = 6.0$ in.

To make this benchmark more complicated, d takes only the following discrete values: 0.009, 0.0095, 0.0104, 0.0118, 0.0128, 0.0132, 0.014, 0.015, 0.0162, 0.0173, 0.018, 0.020, 0.023, 0.025, 0.028, 0.032, 0.035, 0.041, 01047, 0.054, 0.063, 0.072, 0.080, 0.092, 0.105, 0.120, 0.135, 0.148, 0.162, 0.177, 0.192, 0.207, 0.225, 0.244, 0.263, 0.283, 0.307, 0.331, 0.362, 0.394, 0.4375, 0.4999. Further, L can only be integers; thus this problem becomes a mixed-variable optimization problem.

Using FPA, we have obtained a better solution than Wu and Chow (1995) and Guo et al. (2004):

$$f_* = 2.6586 \text{ at } d = 0.283, \ D = 1.223049, \ L = 9. \tag{11.29}$$

The comparisons with the results obtained by GA and PSO are summarized in Table 11.2.

11.5.1.2 Welded Beam Design

The so-called welded beam design is a standard test problem for constrained design optimization [2]. The problem has four design variables: the width w and length L of the welded area, the depth h, and the thickness h of the main beam. The objective is to minimize the overall fabrication cost under the appropriate constraints of shear stress τ, bending stress σ, buckling load P, and maximum end deflection δ. The problem can be written as

$$\text{Minimize } f(\boldsymbol{x}) = 1.10471w^2L + 0.04811dh(14.0 + L), \tag{11.30}$$

subject to

$$
\begin{aligned}
g_1(\boldsymbol{x}) &= w - h \leq 0, \\
g_2(\boldsymbol{x}) &= \delta(\boldsymbol{x}) - 0.25 \leq 0, \\
g_3(\boldsymbol{x}) &= \tau(\boldsymbol{x}) - 13,600 \leq 0, \\
g_4(\boldsymbol{x}) &= \sigma(\boldsymbol{x}) - 30,000 \leq 0, \\
g_5(\boldsymbol{x}) &= 0.10471 w^2 + 0.04811 hd(14 + L) - 5.0 \leq 0, \\
g_6(\boldsymbol{x}) &= 0.125 - w \leq 0, \\
g_7(\boldsymbol{x}) &= 6000 - P(\boldsymbol{x}) \leq 0,
\end{aligned}
\tag{11.31}
$$

where

$$
\begin{aligned}
\sigma(\boldsymbol{x}) &= \frac{504,000}{hd^2}, & Q &= 6000\Big(14 + \frac{L}{2}\Big), \\
D &= \frac{1}{2}\sqrt{L^2 + (w+d)^2}, & J &= \sqrt{2}\, wL \left[\frac{L^2}{6} + \frac{(w+d)^2}{2}\right], \\
\delta &= \frac{65,856}{30,000 hd^3}, & \beta &= \frac{QD}{J}, \\
\alpha &= \frac{6000}{\sqrt{2} wL}, & \tau(\boldsymbol{x}) &= \sqrt{\alpha^2 + \frac{\alpha\beta L}{D} + \beta^2}, \\
P &= 0.61423 \times 10^6 \, \frac{dh^3}{6}\left(1 - \frac{d\sqrt{30/48}}{28}\right).
\end{aligned}
\tag{11.32}
$$

The simple limits or bounds are $0.1 \leq L, d \leq 10$ and $0.1 \leq w, h \leq 2.0$. Using FPA, we have the following optimal solution:

$$
\begin{aligned}
\boldsymbol{x}_* &= (w, L, d, h) \\
&= (0.2057296397, 3.4704886656, 9.0366239104, 0.2057296398),
\end{aligned}
\tag{11.33}
$$

with

$$
f(\boldsymbol{x}*)_{\min} = 1.7248523086. \tag{11.34}
$$

This solution is essentially the same as the solution obtained by Cagnina et al. [2].

$$
f_* = 1.724852 \text{ at } (0.205730, 3.470489, 9.036624, 0.205729). \tag{11.35}
$$

We have seen that FPA has found the optimal solutions that are either better than or the same as the solutions found so far in literature.

11.5.1.3 *Speed Reducer Design*

The optimal design of a speed reducer or a gearbox is another benchmark design problem with seven design variables [2]: the face width (b), module of the teeth (h), the number of teeth on pinion (z), the length (L_1) of the first shaft between bearing, the length (L_2) of the second shaft between bearings, the diameter (d_1) of the first shaft, and the diameter (d_2) of the second shaft. The main objective is to minimize the total weight of the speed reducer, subject to 11 constraints such as bending stress, deflection, and various limits on stresses in shafts.

This optimization problem can be written as [20]

$$f(b,h,z,L_1,L_2,d_1,d_2) = 0.7854bh^2(3.3333z^2 + 14.9334z - 43.0934) \\ -1.508b\left(d_1^2 + d_2^2\right) + 7.4777\left(d_1^3 + d_2^3\right) + 0.7854\left(L_1 d_1^2 + L_2 d_2^2\right), \quad (11.36)$$

subject to

$$\begin{aligned}
g_1 &= \frac{27}{bh^2 z} - 1 \le 0, \\
g_2 &= \frac{397.5}{bh^2 z^2} - 1 \le 0, \\
g_3 &= \frac{1.93L_1^3}{hzd_1^4} - 1 \le 0, \\
g_4 &= \frac{1.93L_2^3}{hzd_2^4} - 1 \le 0, \\
g_5 &= \frac{1}{110d_1^3}\sqrt{\left(\frac{745L_1}{hz}\right)^2 + 16.9 \times 10^6} - 1 \le 0, \\
g_6 &= \frac{1}{85d_2^3}\sqrt{\left(\frac{745L_2}{hz}\right)^2 + 157.5 \times 10^6} - 1 \le 0, \\
g_7 &= \frac{hz}{40} - 1 \le 0, \\
g_8 &= \frac{5h}{b} - 1 \le 0, \\
g_9 &= \frac{b}{12h} - 1 \le 0, \\
g_{10} &= \frac{1.5d_1 + 1.9}{L_1} - 1 \le 0, \\
g_{11} &= \frac{1.1d_2 + 1.9}{L_2} - 1 \le 0.
\end{aligned} \quad (11.37)$$

In addition, the simple bounds are $2.6 \le b \le 3.6, 0.7 \le h \le 0.8, 17 \le z \le 28, 7.3 \le L_1 \le 8.3, 7.8 \le L_2 \le 8.3, 2.9 \le d_1 \le 3.9$, and $5.0 \le d_2 \le 5.5$. z must be integers. The best solutions used by the flower algorithm with $n = 25$ after 1000 iterations are

$$b = 3.5,\ h = 0.7,\ z = 17,\ L_1 = 7.3,\ L_2 = 7.8, \\ d_1 = 3.34336445,\ d_2 = 5.285350625, \quad (11.38)$$

with

$$f\min = 2993.7495888, \tag{11.39}$$

which is better than $f_* = 2996.348165$ by others.

11.5.1.4 Pressure Vessel Design

Pressure vessels are literally everywhere, from champagne bottles to gas tanks. For a given volume and working pressure, the basic aim of designing a cylindrical vessel is to minimize the total materials cost. Typically, the design variables are the thickness d_1 of the head, the thickness d_2 of the body, the inner radius r, and the length L of the cylindrical section [2]. This is a well-known test problem for optimization algorithms and can be written as

$$\text{minimize } f(\boldsymbol{x}) = 0.6224 d_1 r L + 1.7781 d_2 r^2 + 3.1661 d_1^2 L + 19.84 d_1^2 r, \tag{11.40}$$

subject to the following constraints:

$$\begin{aligned} g_1(\boldsymbol{x}) &= -d_1 + 0.0193 r \leq 0 \\ g_2(\boldsymbol{x}) &= -d_2 + 0.00954 r \leq 0 \\ g_3(\boldsymbol{x}) &= -\pi r^2 L - \frac{4\pi}{3} r^3 + 1296000 \leq 0 \\ g_4(\boldsymbol{x}) &= L - 240 \leq 0. \end{aligned} \tag{11.41}$$

The simple bounds are

$$0.0625 \leq d_1, d_2 \leq 99 \times 0.0625 \tag{11.42}$$

and

$$10.0 \leq r \leq 200.0, \quad 10.0 \leq L \leq 240.0. \tag{11.43}$$

It is worth pointing out that the first two design variables can only take integer multiples of 0.0625; thus this essentially leads to a mixed-variable optimization problem. We can use a branch-and-bound method to incorporate the integer variables.

Using the proposed flower algorithm, we found that the best solution is $f_{\min} = 6059.714$ at

$$\boldsymbol{x}_* = (0.8125,\ 0.4375,\ 42.0984455958549,\ 176.6365958424394, \tag{11.44}$$

which is the true globally minimal solution.

The current best solution can be stored during iterations. Then we can calculate the errors D in terms of the difference between the current solution to the best mean solution after 40 independent runs. In our simulations, we have observed that the proposed algorithm approaches the optimal solution exponentially.

Among the three methods, the proposed FPA obtained the best result and converged most quickly.

11.5.2 Multi-Objective Design Benchmarks

The objectives are to minimize the overall mass and the braking time by choosing optimal design variables: the inner radius r, outer radius R of the discs, the engaging force F, and the number of the friction surface s. This is under the design constraints, such as the torque, pressure, temperature, and length of the brake [14].

This bi-objective design problem can be written as

$$\text{Minimize } f_1(\boldsymbol{x}) = 4.9 \times 10^{-5}(R^2 - r^2)(s - 1), \tag{11.45}$$

$$\text{Minimize } f_2(\boldsymbol{x}) = \frac{9.82 \times 10^6(R^2 - r^2)}{Fs(R^3 - r^3)}, \tag{11.46}$$

subject to

$$\begin{aligned}
g_1(\boldsymbol{x}) &= 20 - (R - r) \leq 0, \\
g_2(\boldsymbol{x}) &= 2.5(s + 1) - 30 \leq 0, \\
g_3(\boldsymbol{x}) &= \frac{F}{3.14(R^2 - r^2)} - 0.4 \leq 0, \\
g_4(\boldsymbol{x}) &= \frac{2.22 \times 10^{-3} F(R^3 - r^3)}{(R^2 - r^2)^2} - 1 \leq 0, \\
g_5(\boldsymbol{x}) &= 900 - \frac{0.0266Fs(R^3 - r^3)}{(R^2 - r^2)} \leq 0.
\end{aligned} \tag{11.47}$$

The simple limits are

$$55 \leq r \leq 80, \ 75 \leq R \leq 110, \ 1000 \leq F \leq 3000, \ 2 \leq s \leq 20. \tag{11.48}$$

It is worth pointing out that s is discrete. In general, MOFPA has to be extended in combination with constraint-handling techniques so as to deal with mixed integer problems efficiently. However, since there is only one discrete variable, the simplest branch-and-bound method is used here.

To see how the proposed MOFPA performs for real-world design problems, we have solved the same problem using other available multi-objective algorithms. Fifty solution points are generated using MOFPA to form an approximate to the true Pareto front after 1000 iterations, as shown in Figure 11.3.

The comparison of the convergence rates is plotted in the logarithmic scales in Figure 11.4. We can see clearly that the convergence rate of MOFPA is the highest in an exponentially decreasing manner. This suggests that MOFPA provides better solutions in a more efficient way.

These results for all test functions and design examples suggest that MOFPA is a very efficient algorithm for both single-objective and multi-objective optimization. The proposed algorithm can deal with highly nonlinear, multi-objective optimization problems with complex constraints and diverse Pareto optimal sets.

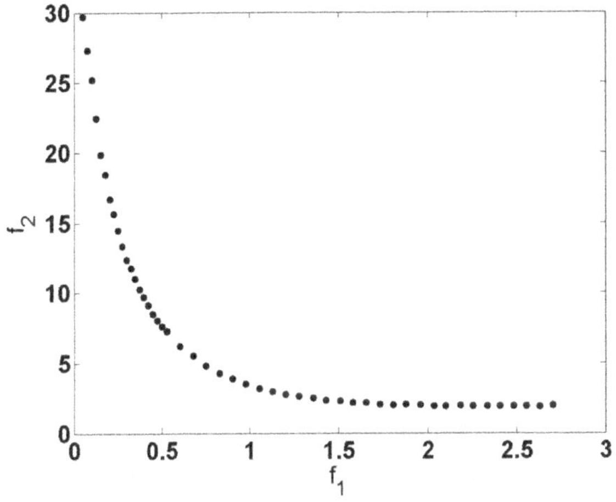

Figure 11.3 Pareto front of the disc brake design.

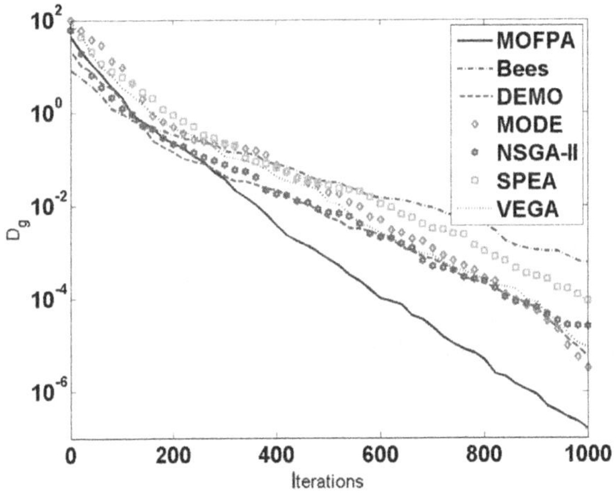

Figure 11.4 Convergence comparison for the disc brake design.

11.6 Further Research Topics

Multi-objective optimization in engineering and industry is often very challenging to solve, necessitating sophisticated techniques to tackle. Metaheuristic approaches have shown promise and popularity in recent years.

Here we have formulated a new algorithm, called the flower pollination algorithm, for solving multi-objective optimization by mimicking the pollination process of flowering plants. Numerical experiments and design benchmarks have shown that the proposed algorithm is very efficient with an almost exponential convergence rate based on the comparison of FPA with other algorithms for solving multi-objective optimization problems.

It is worth pointing out that mathematical analysis is highly needed so as to gain insight into the true working mechanisms of metaheuristic algorithms. FPA has advantages such as simplicity and flexibility, and in many ways it has some similarity to that of cuckoo search and other algorithms with Lévy flights. However, it is still not clear why FPA works well. In terms of number of parameters, FPA has only two key ones: p and a scaling factor γ, which makes the algorithm easier to implement. However, the nonlinearity in Lévy flights make it difficult to analyze mathematically. It can be expected that this nonlinearity in the algorithm formulations may be advantageous to enhance the performance of an algorithm. More research may reveal the subtlety of this feature.

For multi-objective optimization, an important issue is how to ensure that the solution points can distribute relatively uniformly on the Pareto front for test functions. However, for real-world design problems such as the design of a disc brake and a welded beam, the solutions are not quite uniform on the Pareto fronts, and there is still room for improvement. However, simply generating more solution points may not solve the Pareto uniformity problem easily. In fact, it is still a challenging problem of how to maintain a uniform spread on the Pareto front, which requires more study. It may be useful as a further research topic to study the combination of the flower algorithm with other approaches for multi-objective optimization, such as the ϵ-constraint method, weighted metric methods, Benson's method, utility methods, and evolutionary methods [12,15,3].

On the other hand, further studies can focus on more detailed parametric analysis and gain insight into how algorithm-dependent parameters can affect the performance of an algorithm. Furthermore, the linearity in the main updating formulas makes it possible to do some theoretical analysis in terms of dynamic systems or Markov chain theories, whereas the nonlinearity in terms of Lévy flights can be difficult to analyze exactly. All these subjects can form useful topics for further research.

References

[1] Abbass HA, Sarker R. The Pareto differential evolution algorithm. Int J Artif Intell Tool 2002;11(4):531–52.

[2] Cagnina LC, Esquivel SC, Coello CAC. Solving engineering optimization problems with the simple constrained particle swarm optimizer. Informatica 2008;32(2):319–26.

[3] Deb K. Multi-objective optimization using evolutionary algorithms. New York, NY, USA: Wiley; 2001.

[4] Deb K, Pratap A, Agarwal S, Mayarivan T. A fast and elitist multiobjective algorithm: NSGA-II. IEEE Trans Evol Comput 2002;6(2):182–97.

[5] Glover BJ. Understanding flowers and flowering: an integrated approach. Oxford, UK: Oxford University Press; 2007.

[6] Gong WY, Cai ZH, Zhu L. An effective multiobjective differential evolution algorithm for engineering design. Struct Multidisc Optim 2009;38(2):137–57.

[7] He S, Prempain E, Wu QH. An improved particle swarm optimizer for mechanical design optimization problems. Eng Optim 2004;36(5):585–605.
[8] Jamil M, Yang XS. A literature survey of benchmark functions for global optimization problems. Int J Math Model Numer Optim 2013;4(2):150–94.
[9] Li H, Zhang QF. Multiobjective optimization problems with complicated Pareto sets, MOEA/D and NSGA-II. IEEE Trans Evol Comput 2009;13:284–302.
[10] Mantegna RN. Fast, accurate algorithm for numerical simulation of Lévy stable stochastic process. Phys Rev E 1994;49(5):4677–83.
[11] Marler RT, Arora JS. Survey of multi-objective optimization methods for engineering. Struct Multidisc Optim 2004;26:369–95.
[12] Miettinen K. Nonlinear multiobjective optimization (international series in operations research & management science). Norwell, MA, USA: Kluwer Academic Publishers; 1999.
[13] Rangaiah G. Multi-objective optimization: techniques and applications in chemical engineering. Singapore: World Scientific Publishing; 2008.
[14] Ray L, Liew KM. A swarm metaphor for multiobjective design optimization. Eng Optim 2002;34(2):141–53.
[15] Reyes-Sierra M, Coello CAC. Multi-objective particle swarm optimizers: a survey of the state-of-the-art. Int J Comput Intell Res 2006;2(3):287–308.
[16] Robič T, Filipič B. DEMO: differential evolution for multiobjective optimization. In: Coello CA, editor. EMO. LNCS, vol. 3410. Berlin, Germany: Springer; 2005. p. 520–33.
[17] Walker M. How flowers conquered the world. BBC Earth News, <http://news.bbc.co.uk/earth/hi/earth_news/newsid_8143000/8143095.stm>; 2009 [accessed 16.10.13]
[18] Waser NM. Flower constancy: definition, cause and measurement. Am Nat 1986;127(5):596–603.
[19] Yang XS. Flower pollination algorithm for global optimization. In: Unconventional computation and natural computation. Lecture notes in computer science, vol. 7445. 2012; p. 240–49.
[20] Yang XS, Karamanoglu M, He XS. Multi-objective flower algorithm for optimization. Procedia Comput Sci 2013;18(1):861–8.
[21] Zhang QF, Zhou AM, Zhao SZ, Suganthan PN, Liu W, Tiwari S. Multiobjective optimization test instances for the CEC 2009 special session and competition. Technical report CES-487. UK: University of Essex; 2009.
[22] Zhang QF, Li H. MOEA/D: a multi-objective evolutionary algorithm based on decomposition. IEEE Trans Evol Comput 2007;11(6):712–31.
[23] Zitzler E, Deb K, Thiele L. Comparison of multiobjective evolutionary algorithms: empirical results. Evol Comput 2000;8(2):173–95.

12 A Framework for Self-Tuning Algorithms

The performance of any algorithm will largely depend on the setting of its algorithm-dependent parameters. The optimal setting should allow the algorithm to achieve the best performance for solving a range of optimization problems. However, such parameter tuning is itself a tough optimization problem. In this chapter, we present a framework for self-tuning algorithms so that an algorithm to be tuned can be used to tune the algorithm itself.

12.1 Introduction

Since all algorithms have algorithm-dependent parameters, the performance of an algorithm largely depends on the values or setting of these parameters. Ideally, there should be a good way to tune these parameters so that the performance of the algorithm can be optimal in the sense that the algorithm can find the optimal solution of a problem using the minimal number of iterations and with the highest accuracy. However, such tuning of algorithm-dependent parameters is itself a very tough optimization problem. In essence, it is a hyperoptimization problem, that is, the optimization of optimization. In fact, finding the best parameter setting of an algorithm is still an open problem.

There are studies on parameter tuning. For example, Eiben provided a comprehensive summary of existing studies [2]. However, these studies are still very preliminary. There is no method of self-tuning in algorithms. Therefore, the main objective of this chapter is to provide a framework for self-tuning algorithms so that an algorithm can be used to tune its own parameters automatically, based on the self-tuning framework developed by Yang et al. [8]. As far as we are concerned, this is the first of its kind in parameter tuning.

12.2 Algorithm Analysis and Parameter Tuning

An optimization algorithm is essentially an iterative procedure, starting with some initial guess point/solution with an aim to reach a better solution or ideally the optimal solution to a problem of interest. This process of searching for optimality is generic, though the details of the process can vary from algorithm to algorithm. Traditional algorithms such as Newton-Raphson methods use a deterministic trajectory-based method,

Nature-Inspired Optimization Algorithms. http://dx.doi.org/10.1016/B978-0-12-416743-8.00012-9

whereas modern nature-inspired algorithms often are population-based algorithms that use multiple agents. In essence, these multiple agents form an iterative, dynamic system that should have some attractors or stable states. On the other hand, the same system can be considered a set of Markov chains so that they will converge toward some stable probability distribution.

12.2.1 A General Formula for Algorithms

Whatever the perspective, the aim of such an iterative process is to let the system evolve and converge into some stable optimality. In this case, it has strong similarity to a self-organizing system. Such an iterative, self-organizing system can evolve according to a set of rules or mathematical equations. As a result, such a complex system can interact and self-organize into certain converged states, showing some emergent characteristics of self-organization. In this sense, the proper design of an efficient optimization algorithm is equivalent to finding efficient ways to mimic the evolution of a self-organizing system [1,3].

From a mathematical point of view, an algorithm A tends to generate a new and better solution $\boldsymbol{x}^{t+1}$ to a given problem from the current solution $\boldsymbol{x}^t$ at iteration or time t. In modern metaheuristic algorithms, randomization is often used in an algorithm, and in many cases randomization appears in the form of a set of m random variables $\boldsymbol{\varepsilon} = (\varepsilon_1, \ldots, \varepsilon_m)$ in an algorithm. For example, in simulated annealing, there is one random variable, whereas in particle swarm optimization, there are two random variables. In addition, there is often a set of k parameters in an algorithm. For example, in particle swarm optimization, there are four parameters (two learning parameters, one inertia weight, and the population size). In general, we can have a vector of parameters $\boldsymbol{p} = (p_1, \ldots, p_k)$. Mathematically speaking, we can write an algorithm with k parameters and m random variables as

$$\boldsymbol{x}^{t+1} = \boldsymbol{A}\left(\boldsymbol{x}^t, \boldsymbol{p}(t), \boldsymbol{\varepsilon}(t)\right), \tag{12.1}$$

where $\boldsymbol{A}$ is a nonlinear mapping from a given solution (a d-dimensional vector $\boldsymbol{x}^t$) to a new solution vector $\boldsymbol{x}^{t+1}$.

12.2.2 Type of Optimality

Representation (12.1) gives rise to two types of optimality: optimality of a problem and optimality of an algorithm. For an optimization problem such as min $f(\boldsymbol{x})$, there is a global optimal solution, whatever the algorithmic tool we may use to find this optimality. This is the optimality for the optimization problem. On the other hand, for a given problem Φ with an objective function $f(\boldsymbol{x})$, there are many algorithms that can solve it. Some algorithms may require less computational effort than others. There may be the best algorithm with the least computing cost, though this may not be unique. However, this is not our concern here. Once we have chosen an algorithm A to solve a problem Φ, there is an optimal parameter setting for this algorithm so that it can achieve the best performance. This optimality depends on both the algorithm itself and the problem it solves. In the rest of this chapter, we focus on this type of optimality.

That is, the optimality to be achieved is

$$\text{Maximize the performance of } \xi = A(\Phi, \boldsymbol{p}, \boldsymbol{\varepsilon}) \tag{12.2}$$

for a given problem Φ and a chosen algorithm $A(., \boldsymbol{p}, \boldsymbol{\varepsilon})$. We denote this optimality as $\xi_* = A_*(\Phi, \boldsymbol{p}_*) = \xi(\Phi, \boldsymbol{p}_*)$, where $\boldsymbol{p}_*$ is the optimal parameter setting for this algorithm so that its performance is the best. Here we have used a fact that $\boldsymbol{\varepsilon}$ is a random vector that can be drawn from some known probability distributions. Thus the randomness vector should not be related to the algorithm optimality.

It is worth pointing out that there is another potential optimality. That is, for a given problem, a chosen algorithm with the best parameter setting $\boldsymbol{p}_*$, we can still use different random numbers drawn from various probability distributions and even chaotic maps so that even better performance may be achieved. Strictly speaking, if an algorithm $A(., ., \boldsymbol{\varepsilon})$ has a random vector $\boldsymbol{\varepsilon}$ that is drawn from a uniform distribution $\boldsymbol{\varepsilon}_1 \sim U(0, 1)$ or from a Gaussian $\boldsymbol{\varepsilon}_2 \sim N(0, 1)$, it becomes two algorithms $A_1 = A(., ., \boldsymbol{\varepsilon}_1)$ and $A_2 = A(., ., \boldsymbol{\varepsilon}_2)$. Technically speaking, we should treat them as different algorithms. Since our emphasis here is about parameter tuning to find the optimal setting of parameters, we omit the effect of randomness vectors and thus focus on

$$\text{Maximize } \xi = A(\Phi, \boldsymbol{p}). \tag{12.3}$$

In essence, tuning an algorithm involves tuning its algorithm-dependent parameters. Therefore, parameter tuning is equivalent to algorithm tuning in the present context.

12.2.3 Parameter Tuning

To tune $A(\Phi, \boldsymbol{p})$ so as to achieve its best performance, a parameter-tuning tool, i.e., a tuner, is needed. As with tuning high-precision machinery, sophisticated tools are required. For tuning parameters in an algorithm, what tool can we use? One way is to use a better, existing tool (say, algorithm B) to tune an algorithm A. Now the question may become: How do you know B is better? Is B well tuned? If yes, how do you tune B in the first place? Naïvely, if we use another tool (say, algorithm C) to tune B. Now again the question becomes, how has algorithm C been tuned? This can go on and on until the end of a long chain, say, algorithm Q. In the end we need some tool/algorithm to tune this Q, which again comes back to the original question: How can we tune an algorithm A so that it can perform best?

It is worth pointing out that even if we have good tools to tune an algorithm, the best parameter setting and thus best performance all depend on the performance measures used in the tuning. Ideally, these parameters should be robust enough for minor parameter changes, random seeds, and even problem instance. However, in practice, they might not be achievable. According to Eiben [2], parameter tuning can be divided into iterative and noniterative tuners, single-stage and multistage tuners. The meanings of these terms are self-explanatory. In terms of the actual tuning, existing methods include sampling methods, screening methods, model-based methods, and metaheuristic methods. Their success and effectiveness can vary, and thus there are no well-established methods for universal parameter tuning.

12.3 Framework for Self-Tuning Algorithms

12.3.1 Hyperoptimization

From our earlier observations and discussions, it is clear that parameter tuning is the process of optimizing the optimization algorithm; therefore, it is a hyperoptimization problem. In essence, a tuner is a meta-optimization tool for tuning algorithms.

For a standard unconstrained optimization problem, the aim is to find the global minimum f_* of a function $f(\boldsymbol{x})$ in a d-dimensional space. That is,

$$\text{Minimize } f(\boldsymbol{x}), \quad \boldsymbol{x} = (x_1, x_2, \ldots, x_d). \tag{12.4}$$

Once we choose an algorithm A to solve this optimization problem, the algorithm will find a minimum solution $f_{\min}$ that may be close to the true global minimum f_*. For a given tolerance δ, this may require t_δ iterations to achieve $|f_{\min} - f_*| \leq \delta$. Obviously, the actual t_δ will largely depend on both the problem objective $f(\boldsymbol{x})$ and the parameters $\boldsymbol{p}$ of the algorithm used.

The main aim of algorithm tuning is to find the best parameter setting $\boldsymbol{p}_*$ so that the computational cost or the number of iterations t_δ is the minimum. Thus, parameter tuning as a hyperoptimization problem can be written as

$$\text{Minimize } t_\delta = A(f(\boldsymbol{x}), \boldsymbol{p}), \tag{12.5}$$

whose optimality is $\boldsymbol{p}_*$.

Ideally, the parameter vector $\boldsymbol{p}_*$ should be sufficiently robust. For different types of problems, any slight variation in $\boldsymbol{p}_*$ should not much affect the performance of A, which means that $\boldsymbol{p}_*$ should lie in a flat range rather than at a sharp peak in the parameter landscape.

12.3.2 A Multi-Objective View

If we look at the algorithm tuning process from a different perspective, it is possible to construct it as a multi-objective optimization problem with two objectives: one objective $f(\boldsymbol{x})$ for the problem Φ and one objective t_δ for the algorithm. That is,

$$\text{Minimize } f(\boldsymbol{x}) \text{ and Minimize } t_\delta = A(f(\boldsymbol{x}), \boldsymbol{p}), \tag{12.6}$$

where t_δ is the (average) number of iterations needed to achieve a given tolerance δ so that the found minimum $f_{\min}$ is close enough to the true global minimum f_*, satisfying $|f_{\min} - f_*| \leq \delta$.

This means that for a given tolerance δ, there will be a set of best-parameter settings with a minimum t_δ. As a result, the bi-objectives will form a Pareto front. In principle, this bi-objective optimization problem (12.6) can be solved by any methods that are suitable for multi-objective optimization. But because δ is usually given, a natural way to solve this problem is to use the so-called ϵ-constraint or δ-constraint methods. The naming may be dependent on the notations; however, we will use δ-constraints.

For a given $\delta \geq 0$, we change one of the objectives (i.e., $f(\boldsymbol{x})$) into a constraint, and thus the problem (12.6) becomes a single-objective optimization problem with a constraint. That is,

$$\text{Minimize } t_\delta = A(f(\boldsymbol{x}), \boldsymbol{p}), \tag{12.7}$$

subject to

$$f(\boldsymbol{x}) \leq \delta. \tag{12.8}$$

In the rest of this chapter, we set $\delta = 10^{-5}$.

The important thing is that we still need an algorithm to solve this optimization problem. However, the main difference from a common single objective problem is that the present problem contains an algorithm A. Ideally, an algorithm should be independent of the problem, which treats the objective to be solved as a black box. Thus we have $A(., \boldsymbol{p}, \boldsymbol{\varepsilon})$. However, in reality, an algorithm will be used to solve a particular problem Φ with an objective $f(\boldsymbol{x})$. Therefore, both notations $A(., \boldsymbol{p})$ and $A(f(\boldsymbol{x}), \boldsymbol{p})$ are used here.

12.3.3 Self-Tuning Framework

This framework was proposed by Yang et al. in 2013 [8]. In principle, we can solve (12.7) by any efficient or well-tuned algorithm. Now a natural question is: Can we solve this algorithm-tuning problem by the algorithm A itself? There is no reason why we cannot. In fact, if we solve (12.7) using A, we have a self-tuning algorithm. That is, the algorithm automatically tunes itself for a given problem objective to be optimized. This essentially provides a framework for a self-tuning algorithm, as shown in Figure 12.1.

This framework is generic in the sense that any algorithm can be tuned this way and any problem can be solved within this framework. This essentially achieves two goals simultaneously: parameter tuning and optimality finding.

In the rest of this chapter, we use the firefly algorithm (FA) as a case study to self-tune FA for a set of function optimization problems.

Implement an algorithm $A(., \boldsymbol{p}, \boldsymbol{\varepsilon})$
  with parameters $\boldsymbol{p} = [p_1, ..., p_K]$ and random vector $\boldsymbol{\varepsilon} = [\varepsilon_1, ..., \varepsilon_m]$;
Define a tolerance (e.g., $\delta = 10^{-5}$);
  Algorithm objective $t_\delta(f(\boldsymbol{x}), \boldsymbol{p}, \boldsymbol{\varepsilon})$;
    Problem objective function $f(\boldsymbol{x})$;
    Find the optimality solution $f_{\min}$ within δ;
    Output the number of iterations t_δ needed to find $f_{\min}$;
  Solve $\min t_\delta(f(\boldsymbol{x}), \boldsymbol{p})$ using $A(., \boldsymbol{p}, \boldsymbol{\varepsilon})$ to get the best parameters;
Output the tuned algorithm with the best parameter setting $\boldsymbol{p}_*$.

Figure 12.1 A framework for a self-tuning algorithm.

12.4 A Self-Tuning Firefly Algorithm

Now let us use the framework outlined earlier to tune the firefly algorithm (FA). As we saw in the chapter on FA, it has the following updating equation:

$$x_i^{t+1} = x_i^t + \beta_0 e^{-\gamma r_{ij}^2}(x_j^t - x_i^t) + \alpha\, \epsilon_i^t, \tag{12.9}$$

which contains four parameters: α, β_0, γ, and the population size n. For simplicity of parameter tuning, we set $\beta_0 = 1$ and $n = 20$, and therefore the two parameters to be tuned are $\gamma > 0$ and $\alpha > 0$. It is worth pointing out that γ controls the scaling, whereas α controls the randomness. For this algorithm to converge properly, randomness should be gradually reduced, and one way to achieve such randomness reduction is to use

$$\alpha = \alpha_0 \theta^t, \quad \theta \in (0, 1), \tag{12.10}$$

where t is the index of iterations/generations. Here α_0 is the initial randomness factor, and we can set $\alpha_0 = 1$ without losing generality. Therefore, the two parameters to be tuned become γ and θ.

Now we can tune FA for a set of five test functions. These functions can be found in the literature (e.g., [4]).

The Ackley function can be written as

$$f_1(x) = -20 \exp\left[-\frac{1}{5}\sqrt{\frac{1}{d}\sum_{i=1}^{d} x_i^2}\right] - \exp\left[\frac{1}{d}\sum_{i=1}^{d}\cos(2\pi x_i)\right] + 20 + e, \tag{12.11}$$

which has a global minimum $f_* = 0$ at $(0, 0, \ldots, 0)$.

The simplest of De Jong's functions is the so-called sphere function

$$f_2(x) = \sum_{i=1}^{d} x_i^2, \quad -5.12 \le x_i \le 5.12, \tag{12.12}$$

whose global minimum is obviously $f_* = 0$ at $(0, 0, \ldots, 0)$. This function is unimodal and convex.

Yang's forest function [4],

$$f_3(x) = \left(\sum_{i=1}^{d} |x_i|\right) \exp\left[-\sum_{i=1}^{d} \sin(x_i^2)\right], \quad -2\pi \le x_i \le 2\pi, \tag{12.13}$$

is highly multimodal and has a global minimum $f_* = 0$ at $(0, 0, \ldots, 0)$.

Rastrigin's function,

$$f_4(x) = 10d + \sum_{i=1}^{d} \left[x_i^2 - 10\cos(2\pi x_i)\right], \quad -5.12 \le x_i \le 5.12, \tag{12.14}$$

has a global minimum of $f_* = 0$ at $(0, 0, \ldots, 0)$. This function is highly multimodal.

Table 12.1 Results of parameter tuning for the firefly algorithm.

Function	Mean $t_\delta \pm \sigma_t$	Mean $\gamma \pm \sigma_\gamma$	Mean $\theta \pm \sigma_\theta$
f_1	589.7 ± 182.1	0.5344 ± 0.2926	0.9561 ± 0.0076
f_2	514.4 ± 178.5	0.5985 ± 0.2554	0.9540 ± 0.0072
f_3	958.1 ± 339.0	1.0229 ± 0.5762	0.9749 ± 0.0047
f_4	724.1 ± 217.6	0.4684 ± 0.3064	0.9652 ± 0.0065
f_5	957.2 ± 563.6	0.8933 ± 0.4251	0.9742 ± 0.0052

Zakharov's function of

$$f_5(\boldsymbol{x}) = \sum_{i=1}^{d} x_i^2 + \left(\frac{1}{2}\sum_{i=1}^{d} i x_i\right)^2 + \left(\frac{1}{2}\sum_{i=1}^{d} i x_i\right)^4 \tag{12.15}$$

has a global minimum $f_* = 0$ at $(0, 0, \ldots, 0)$.

For each objective function, we run the FA to tune itself 50 times so as to calculate meaningful statistics. The population size $n = 20$ is used for all the runs. The means and standard deviations are summarized in Table 12.1, where $d = 8$ is used for all functions.

From this table, we can see that the variations of γ are large, whereas θ has a narrow range. The best settings for parameters are problem dependent. These results imply the following:

- The optimal setting of parameters in an algorithm largely depends on the problem, and there is no unique best setting for all problems.
- The relatively large standard deviation of γ means that the actual setting of γ is not important to a given problem, and therefore there is no need to fine-tune γ. That is to say, a typical value of $\gamma = 1$ should work for most problems.
- Some parameters are more sensitive than others. In the present case, θ needs more fine-tuning due to its smaller standard deviations.

These findings confirm the earlier observations in the literature that $\gamma = O(1)$ can be used for most applications [5–7], whereas α needs to reduce gradually in terms of θ. That is probably why other forms of probability distributions such as Lévy flights may lead to better performance than the random numbers drawn from the Gaussian normal distribution.

12.5 Some Remarks

Parameter tuning is the process of tuning an algorithm to find the best parameter settings so that an algorithm can perform the best for a given set of problems. However, such parameter tuning is a very tough optimization problem. In fact, such hyperoptimization is the optimization of an optimization algorithm, which requires special care because the optimality depends on both the algorithm to be tuned and the problem to be solved. It is possible to view this parameter-tuning process as a bi-objective optimization problem; however, the objectives involve an algorithm, and thus this bi-objective problem is different from the multi-objective problem in the normal sense.

Our framework for self-tuning algorithms is truly self-tuning in the sense that the algorithm to be tuned is used to tune itself. We have used the firefly algorithm and a set of test functions to test the proposed self-tuning algorithm framework. Results have shown that it can indeed work well. We also found that some parameters require fine-tuning, but others do not need to be tuned carefully. This is because different parameters may have different sensitivities and thus may affect the performance of an algorithm in different ways. Only parameters with high sensitivities need careful tuning.

Though successful, the present framework requires further extensive testing with a variety of test functions and many different algorithms. It may also be possible to see how probability distributions can affect the tuned parameters and even the parameter-tuning process. In addition, it can be expected that this present framework is also useful for parameter control, so a more generalized framework for both parameter tuning and control can be used for a wide range of applications. Furthermore, our current framework may be extended to multi-objective problems so that algorithms for multi-objective optimization can be tuned in a similar way.

References

[1] Ashby WR. Principles of the self-organizing system. In: Von Foerster H, Zopf Jr GW, editors. Principles of self-organization: transactions of the University of Illinois symposium. London, UK: Pergamon Press; 1962. p. 255–78.

[2] Eiben AE, Smit SK. Parameter tuning for configuring and analyzing evolutionary algorithms. Swarm Evol Comput 2011;1(1):19–31.

[3] Keller EF. Organisms, machines, and thunderstorms: a history of self-organization, Part II. Complexity, emergence, and stable attractors. Hist Stud Nat Sci 2009;39(1):1–31.

[4] Yang XS. Firefly algorithm, stochastic test functions and design optimisation. Int J Bio-Inspired Comput 2010;2(2):78–84.

[5] Yang XS, Gandomi AH. Bat algorithm: a novel approach for global engineering optimization. Eng Comput 2012;29(5):1–18.

[6] Yang XS, Deb S. Multi-objective cuckoo search for design optimization. Comput Oper Res 2013;40(6):1616–24.

[7] Yang XS. Multiobjective firefly algorithm for continuous optimization. Eng Comput 2013;29(2):175–84.

[8] Yang XS, Deb S, Loomes M, Karamanoglu M. A framework for self-tuning optimization algorithm. Neural Comput Appl; in press. http://dx.doi.org/10.1007/s00521-013-1498-4.

13 How to Deal with Constraints

The optimization we have discussed so far is unconstrained, since we have not considered any constraints. A natural and important question is how to incorporate the constraints (both inequality and equality constraints). There are many ways of dealing with constraints [2,5,3,4]. In fact, such constraint-handling techniques can form important topics of many books and comprehensive review articles [4,6,9,10].

Since the main aim of this book is to introduce nature-inspired algorithms, we now briefly introduce the most widely used constraint-handling techniques in this chapter and provide relevant references.

13.1 Introduction and Overview

Numerous constraint-handling techniques can be classified in a few ways. Loosely speaking, we can divide them into two major categories: classic methods and recent methods. Classic/traditional methods are still widely used in many applications, and new or recent developments have been largely based on the hybrid of evolutionary ideas with these traditional methods. Therefore, the differences between the old and new are relatively arbitrary and purely for the purpose of argument here.

Traditional methods include the penalty methods, transformation methods and special representation, and separation of objectives and constraints.

Penalty methods try to convert a constrained optimization problem into an unconstrained one by incorporating its constraints in the revised objective. However, this introduces more parameters into the problem, but if proper values are used, the converted unconstrained problem can often be solved by many algorithms relatively effectively.

Transformation methods try to map the feasible region into a regular mapped space while preserving the feasibility somehow. For example, the homomorphous map (HM) proposed by Koziel and Michalewicz [7] tries to transform the feasible region into a higher-dimensional cube. Though the method was competitive, it has difficulty in practical implementations because this method involves nontrivial transformations and a very high computational cost. On the other hand, other methods use special representations and operators to construct feasible solutions while preserving their feasibility. But such special operators methods tend to work for linear constraints [7,8]. These transformation methods are also called *decoder* and *special operator* methods in the literature [10].

The separation of objective functions and constraints is another class of methods and has gained attention in recent years. For example, the following approach proposed by Powell and Skolnick [11] uses a fitness function $\rho(x)$:

$$\rho(\boldsymbol{x}) = \begin{cases} f(\boldsymbol{x}) & \text{if feasible} \\ 1 + \mu\big[\sum_{j=1}^{N} \psi_j(\boldsymbol{x}) + \sum_{i=1}^{M} \phi_i(\boldsymbol{x})\big] & \text{otherwise.} \end{cases} \tag{13.1}$$

This definition ensures that a feasible solution should always have a better fitness value than an infeasible solution.

Other methods, or different methods known by other names, can also be put into these categories. For example, direct methods can be classified into the separation of objective function and constraints, whereas the Lagrange multiplier method can be considered the special representation or even penalty methods, depending on our perspective. Direct approaches intend to find the feasible regions enclosed by the constraints. This is often difficult, except for a few special cases. Numerically, we can generate a potential solution and check to see whether all the constraints are satisfied. If all the constraints are met, it is a feasible solution and the evaluation of the objective function can be carried out. If one or more constraints are not satisfied, this potential solution is discarded and a new solution should be generated. We then proceed in a similar manner. As we can expect, this process is slow and inefficient. Better approaches are to incorporate the constraints so as to formulate the problem as an unconstrained one, including the method of Lagrange multipliers and penalty methods.

Recent methods reflect some new trends in constraint-handling techniques, including feasibility methods, stochastic ranking, novel penalty methods and new special operator methods, the ϵ-constrained method, the multi-objective approach, and hybrid or ensemble methods.

13.2 Method of Lagrange Multipliers

The method of Lagrange multipliers has a rigorous mathematical basis, whereas the penalty method is simple to implement in practice. So let us introduce these methods first.

The method of Lagrange multipliers converts a constrained problem to an unconstrained one. For example, if we want to minimize a function

$$\underset{\boldsymbol{x} \in \Re^d}{\text{Minimize}}\, f(\boldsymbol{x}), \qquad \boldsymbol{x} = (x_1, \ldots, x_d)^T \in \Re^n, \tag{13.2}$$

subject to multiple nonlinear equality constraints

$$g_j(\boldsymbol{x}) = 0, \qquad j = 1, 2, \ldots, M, \tag{13.3}$$

we can use M Lagrange multipliers $\lambda_j (j = 1, \ldots, M)$ to reformulate the problem as the minimization of the following function:

$$L(\boldsymbol{x}, \lambda_j) = f(\boldsymbol{x}) + \sum_{j=1}^{M} \lambda_j g_j(\boldsymbol{x}). \tag{13.4}$$

The optimality requires the following stationary conditions:

$$\frac{\partial L}{\partial x_i} = \frac{\partial f}{\partial x_i} + \sum_{j=1}^{M} \lambda_j \frac{\partial g_j}{\partial x_i}, \quad (i = 1, \ldots, d), \tag{13.5}$$

and

$$\frac{\partial L}{\partial \lambda_j} = g_j = 0, \quad (j = 1, \ldots, M). \tag{13.6}$$

These $M + d$ equations will determine the d components of $\boldsymbol{x}$ and M Lagrange multipliers. As $\frac{\partial L}{\partial g_j} = \lambda_j$, we can consider λ_j as the rate of the change of the quantity $L(\boldsymbol{x}, \lambda_j)$ as a functional of g_j.

Now let us look at a simple example:

$$\underset{u,v}{\text{Maximize}}\ f = u^{2/3} v^{1/3},$$

subject to

$$3u + v = 9.$$

First, we write it as an unconstrained problem using a Lagrange multiplier λ, and we have

$$L = u^{2/3} v^{1/3} + \lambda(3u + v - 9).$$

The conditions for optimality are

$$\frac{\partial L}{\partial u} = \frac{2}{3} u^{-1/3} v^{1/3} + 3\lambda = 0, \qquad \frac{\partial L}{\partial v} = \frac{1}{3} u^{2/3} v^{-2/3} + \lambda = 0,$$

and

$$\frac{\partial L}{\partial \lambda} = 3u + v - 9 = 0.$$

The first two conditions give $2v = 3u$, whose combination with the third condition leads to

$$u = 2, \qquad v = 3.$$

Thus, the maximum of f_* is $\sqrt[3]{12}$. In addition, this gives

$$\lambda = -\frac{2}{9} \left(\frac{3}{2}\right)^{1/3}. \tag{13.7}$$

Here we discussed only the equality constraints. For inequality constraints, things become more complicated. We need the so-called Karush-Kuhn-Tucker (KKT) conditions.

13.3 KKT Conditions

Let us consider the following generic, nonlinear optimization problem:

$$\begin{aligned} &\underset{\boldsymbol{x}\in\Re^d}{\text{Minimize}}\ f(\boldsymbol{x}), \\ &\text{subject to } \phi_i(\boldsymbol{x}) = 0,\ (i = 1, \ldots, M), \\ &\qquad \psi_j(\boldsymbol{x}) \le 0,\ (j = 1, \ldots, N). \end{aligned} \tag{13.8}$$

If all the functions are continuously differentiable at a local minimum $\boldsymbol{x}_*$, there exist constants $\lambda_1, \ldots, \lambda_M$ and $\mu_0, \mu_1, \ldots, \mu_N$ such that the following KKT optimality conditions hold:

$$\mu_0 \nabla f(\boldsymbol{x}_*) + \sum_{i=1}^{M} \lambda_i \nabla \phi_i(\boldsymbol{x}_*) + \sum_{j=1}^{N} \mu_j \nabla \psi_j(\boldsymbol{x}_*) = 0 \tag{13.9}$$

and

$$\psi_j(\boldsymbol{x}_*) \le 0, \qquad \mu_j \psi_j(\boldsymbol{x}_*) = 0,\ (j = 1, 2, \ldots, N), \tag{13.10}$$

where

$$\mu_j \ge 0,\ (j = 0, 1, \ldots, N). \tag{13.11}$$

The last nonnegative conditions hold for all μ_j, though there is no constraint on the sign of λ_i.

The constants satisfy the following condition:

$$\sum_{j=0}^{N} \mu_j + \sum_{i=1}^{M} |\lambda_i| \ge 0. \tag{13.12}$$

This is essentially a generalized method of Lagrange multipliers. However, there is a possibility of degeneracy when $\mu_0 = 0$ under certain conditions. There are two possibilities: (1) there exist vectors $\boldsymbol{\lambda}^* = (\lambda_1^*, \ldots, \lambda_M^*)^T$ and $\boldsymbol{\mu}^* = (\mu_1^*, .., \mu_N^*)^T$ such that these equations hold, or (2) all the vectors $\nabla\phi_1(\boldsymbol{x}_*), \nabla\phi_2(\boldsymbol{x}_*), \ldots, \nabla\psi_1(\boldsymbol{x}_*), \ldots, \nabla\psi_N(\boldsymbol{x}_*)$ are linearly independent, and in this case the stationary conditions $\frac{\partial L}{\partial x_i}$ do not necessarily hold. Because the second case is a special one, we will not discuss this further.

The condition $\mu_j \psi_j(\boldsymbol{x}_*) = 0$ in (13.10) is often called the *complementarity* condition or the *complementary slackness* condition. It means either $\mu_j = 0$ or $\psi_j(\boldsymbol{x}_*) = 0$. The latter case $\psi_j(\boldsymbol{x}_*) = 0$ for any particular j means the inequality becomes tight, thus becoming an equality. For the former case $\mu_j = 0$, the inequality for a particular j holds and is not tight; however, $\mu_j = 0$ means that this corresponding inequality can be ignored. Therefore, those inequalities that are not tight are ignored, whereas inequalities that are tight become equalities. Consequently, the constrained problem with equality and inequality constraints now essentially becomes a modified constrained problem with selected equality constraints. This is the beauty of the KKT conditions. The main issue remains to identify which inequality becomes tight, and this depends on the individual optimization problem.

The KKT conditions form the basis for mathematical analysis of nonlinear optimization problems, but the numerical implementation of these conditions is not easy and is often inefficient. From the numerical point of view, the penalty method is more straightforward to implement.

13.4 Penalty Method

For a nonlinear optimization problem with equality and inequality constraints, a common method of incorporating constraints is the penalty method. For the optimization problem

$$\begin{aligned} &\underset{x \in \Re^n}{\text{Minimize}}\ f(\boldsymbol{x}),\ \boldsymbol{x} = (x_1, \ldots, x_d)^T \in \Re^d, \\ &\text{Subject to } \phi_i(\boldsymbol{x}) = 0,\ (i = 1, \ldots, M), \\ &\qquad\qquad \psi_j(\boldsymbol{x}) \le 0,\ (j = 1, \ldots, N), \end{aligned} \tag{13.13}$$

the idea is to define a penalty function so that the constrained problem is transformed into an unconstrained problem. One commonly used penalty formulation is

$$g(\boldsymbol{x}) = f(\boldsymbol{x}) + P(\boldsymbol{x}), \tag{13.14}$$

where $P(\boldsymbol{x})$ is the penalty term defined by

$$P(\boldsymbol{x}) = \sum_{j=1}^{N} \nu_j \ \max\,(0, \psi_j(\boldsymbol{x}))^2 + \sum_{i=1}^{M} \mu_i |\phi_i(\boldsymbol{x})|. \tag{13.15}$$

Here $\mu_i > 0, \mu_j > 0$ are penalty constants or penalty factors. The advantage of this method is to transform the constrained optimization problem into an unconstrained one. That is, all the constraints are incorporated into the new objective function. However, this introduces more free parameters whose values need to be defined so as to solve the problem appropriately.

Obviously, there are other forms of penalty functions that may provide smoother penalty functions. For example, we can define

$$\Pi(\boldsymbol{x}, \mu_i, \nu_j) = f(\boldsymbol{x}) + \sum_{i=1}^{M} \mu_i \phi_i^2(\boldsymbol{x}) + \sum_{j=1}^{N} \nu_j \psi_j^2(\boldsymbol{x}), \tag{13.16}$$

where $\mu_i \gg 1$ and $\nu_j \ge 0$, which should be large enough, depending on the solution quality needed.

As we can see, when an equality constraint it met, its effect or contribution to Π is zero. However, when it is violated, it is penalized heavily as it increases Π significantly. Similarly, it is true when inequality constraints become tight or exact. For the ease of numerical implementation, we should use index functions H to rewrite the preceding penalty function as

$$\Pi = f(\boldsymbol{x}) + \sum_{i=1}^{M} \mu_i H_i[\phi_i(\boldsymbol{x})]\phi_i^2(\boldsymbol{x}) + \sum_{j=1}^{N} \nu_j H_j[\psi_j(\boldsymbol{x})]\psi_j^2(\boldsymbol{x}). \tag{13.17}$$

Here $H_i[\phi_i(\boldsymbol{x})]$ and $H_j[\psi_j(\boldsymbol{x})]$ are index functions.

More specifically, $H_i[\phi_i(\boldsymbol{x})] = 1$ if $\phi_i(\boldsymbol{x}) \neq 0$, and $H_i = 0$ if $\phi_i(\boldsymbol{x}) = 0$. Similarly, $H_j[\psi_j(\boldsymbol{x})] = 0$ if $\psi_j(\boldsymbol{x}) \leq 0$ is true, whereas $H_j = 1$ if $\psi_j(\boldsymbol{x}) > 0$. In principle, the numerical accuracy depends on the values of μ_i and ν_j, which should be reasonably large. But how large is large enough? Since most computers have a machine precision of $\epsilon = 2^{-52} \approx 2.2 \times 10^{-16}$, μ_i and ν_j should be close to the order of 10^{15}. Obviously, it could cause numerical problems if the values are too large.

In addition, for simplicity of implementation, we can use $\mu = \mu_i$ for all i and $\nu = \nu_j$ for all j. That is, we can use a simplified

$$\Pi(\boldsymbol{x}, \mu, \nu) = f(\boldsymbol{x}) + \mu \sum_{i=1}^{M} H_i[\phi_i(\boldsymbol{x})]\phi_i^2(\boldsymbol{x}) + \nu \sum_{j=1}^{N} H_j[\psi_j(\boldsymbol{x})]\psi_j^2(\boldsymbol{x}).$$

It is worth pointing out that the right values of penalty factors can help make the implementation very efficient. However, deciding what values are appropriate may be problem-specific. If the values are too small, it may lead to underpenalty, whereas too-large values may lead to overpenalty. In general, for most applications, μ and ν can be taken as 10^3 to 10^{15}. We will use these values in our implementation.

In addition, there is no need to fix the values of penalty parameters. In fact, the variations with time of penalty parameters may be advantageous. Variations such as the cooling-schedule-like reduction of these parameters have been shown to work in practice. These techniques with time-dependent penalty parameters belong to an active research area of dynamic penalty function methods [10].

Furthermore, many traditional constraint-handling techniques now have been combined with evolutionary algorithms, and these approaches themselves also become evolutionary [15]. This becomes a major trend and constraint handling takes on an evolutionary approach.

13.5 Equality with Tolerance

Sometimes it might be easier to change an equality constraint into two inequality constraints so that we only have to deal with inequalities in the implementation [4,13].

Naïvely, $h(\boldsymbol{x}) = 0$ is always equivalent to $h(\boldsymbol{x}) \leq 0$ and $h(\boldsymbol{x}) \geq 0$ (or $-h(\boldsymbol{x}) \leq 0$), but it will not work in practice. Because the feasibility volume for $h(x) = 0$ is zero, a randomly sampled solution has almost zero probability of satisfying this equality.

One remedy is to use some approximation techniques, and a widely used one is to use a tolerance $\epsilon > 0$:

$$|h(\boldsymbol{x})| - \epsilon \leq 0, \tag{13.18}$$

which is equivalent to two inequalities:

$$h(\boldsymbol{x}) - \epsilon \le 0 \tag{13.19}$$

and

$$-h(\boldsymbol{x}) - \epsilon \le 0. \tag{13.20}$$

Obviously, the accuracy is controlled by ϵ. To get better results, there is no need to fix ϵ. At the begin of the iterations, a large value ϵ can be used, and then as the iterations converge, a smaller ϵ can be used.

13.6 Feasibility Rules and Stochastic Ranking

An effective and yet popular constraint-handling technique in this category was proposed by Deb [4], which is combined with genetic algorithms. In this method, three feasible criteria are used in terms of a binary tournament selection mechanism [4, 10]:

- For one feasible solution and one infeasible solution, the feasible one is chosen first.
- For two feasible solutions, the one with the better objective value is preferred.
- For two infeasible solutions, the one with the lower degree of constraint violation is chosen first.

Within this method, the constraint violation is the penalty term, and that is

$$P(\boldsymbol{x}) = \sum_{j=1}^{N} \max\left(0, \psi_j(x)\right)^2 + \sum_{i=1}^{M} |\phi_i(\boldsymbol{x})|, \tag{13.21}$$

which includes both inequalities and equalities.

Such feasibility-based methods have been extended and applied in many algorithms and applications, often in combination with evolutionary algorithms. In fact, the feasibility rules can be considered some sort of fitness related to the problem, and fitness-based evolutionary methods aim to select solutions that are the fittest in the sense that they are feasible with the lowest objective values (for minimization problems). Feasibility rules can be absolute or relative, and Mezura-Montes and Coello provided a comprehensive review of this constraint-handling topic [10].

Another constraint-handling technique is called *stochastic ranking* (SR), originally developed by Runarsson and Yao in 2000 [13]. One of the advantages of this method is to avoid the under-or overpenalty associated with the penalty methods. In stochastic ranking, a user-defined parameter λ_u is used to control and compare infeasible solutions. The swap conditions between two individuals in the population are based on the sum f constraint violation and their objective function values. Ranking of the solutions is carried out by a bubble-sort-style process. In essence, a uniformly distributed random number u is used to control the switch in the form of $u < \lambda_u$, and therefore, dynamic parameter control methods can be used. Again, SR has been used in combination with evolutionary algorithms such as differential evolution and ant colony optimization in the literature.

A related approach to handling constraints is the so-called ϵ-constrained method, developed by Takahama and Sakai [14]. The ϵ-constrained method essentially uses two parts: the relaxation limits to consider the feasibility of solutions, in terms of the sum of constraint violation and comparison of objective function values, and a lexicographical ordering mechanism such that the objective minimization is preceded by the minimization of constraint violation. Two sets of solutions $\boldsymbol{x}_1$ and $\boldsymbol{x}_2$ can be compared and ranked by objective $f(\boldsymbol{x})$ and constraint violation $P(\boldsymbol{x})$ as follows:

$$\{f(\boldsymbol{x}_1), P(\boldsymbol{x}_1)\} \leq_{\epsilon} \{f(\boldsymbol{x}_2), P(\boldsymbol{x}_2)\}, \tag{13.22}$$

which is equivalent to

$$\begin{cases} f(\boldsymbol{x}_1) \leq f(\boldsymbol{x}_2), & \text{if } P(\boldsymbol{x}_1), P(\boldsymbol{x}_2) \leq \epsilon \\ f(\boldsymbol{x}_1) \leq f(\boldsymbol{x}_2), & \text{if } P(\boldsymbol{x}_1) = P(\boldsymbol{x}_2), \\ P(\boldsymbol{x}_1) \leq P(\boldsymbol{x}_2), & \text{otherwise.} \end{cases} \tag{13.23}$$

Here, $\epsilon \geq 0$ controls the level of comparison. Obviously, we have two special cases: $\epsilon = \infty$ and $\epsilon = 0$. The former is equivalent to the comparison of objective function values only, and the latter $\epsilon = 0$ provides a lexicographical ordering mechanism where the objective minimization is preceded by the minimization of the constraint violation.

It should be noted that this ϵ-constrained method should not be confused with the ϵ-constraint method for multi-objective optimization. They are two different methods and for different purposes.

All these methods, novel/new penalty methods and other evolutionary decoder methods, can be classified into the evolutionary approach of constraint-handling techniques.

13.7 Multi-objective Approach to Constraints

In many cases, multi-objective optimization problems can be converted into single-objective optimization by methods such as weighted sum methods. It seems that the multi-objective approach to constraint handling tends to do the opposite. Naïvely, one may think it might not be a good approach; however, some studies show that such multi-objective approaches can be highly competitive.

For example, one of the multi-objective approaches to constraint handling was the so-called infeasibility-driven evolutionary algorithm (IDEA) proposed by Ray et al.[12], which uses an extra objective in addition to the original objective function. This extra objective measures the constraint violation and the ranking of solutions. If a constraint is satisfied by a solution, a zero rank is assigned to that solution for that constraint, and the total rank of a solution as a measure of the constraint violation is the sum of all the ranks for all the constraints. For evolutionary algorithms, new generations of solutions are sorted into two sets: a feasible set and infeasible set, and nondominated sorting is applied. Results are quite competitive [12].

There are quite a few other multi-objective approaches. Furthermore, constraints can be approximated and even dynamic constraint-handling techniques can be used. A brief survey can be found in [10].

13.8 Spring Design

Tensional and/or compressional springs are used widely in engineering. A standard spring design problem has three design variables: the wire diameter w, the mean coil diameter D, and the length (or number of coils) L.

The objective is to minimize the weight of the spring, subject to various constraints such as maximum shear stress, minimum deflection, and geometrical limits. For detailed description, please refer to earlier studies such as Cagnina et al.[1]. This problem can be written compactly as

$$\text{Minimize } f(\boldsymbol{x}) = (L+2)w^2 D, \tag{13.24}$$

subject to

$$\begin{aligned} g_1(\boldsymbol{x}) &= 1 - \frac{D^3 L}{71785 w^4} \le 0, \\ g_2(\boldsymbol{x}) &= 1 - \frac{140.45 w}{D^2 L} \le 0, \\ g_3(\boldsymbol{x}) &= \frac{2(w+D)}{3} - 1 \le 0, \\ g_4(\boldsymbol{x}) &= \frac{d(4D-w)}{w^3(12566D - w)} + \frac{1}{5108 w^2} - 1 \le 0, \end{aligned} \tag{13.25}$$

with the following limits

$$0.05 \le w \le 2.0, \quad 0.25 \le D \le 1.3, \quad 2.0 \le L \le 15.0. \tag{13.26}$$

Using the cuckoo search, we obtained the same or slightly better solutions than the best solution obtained by Cagnina et al. [1], and we have

$$f_* = 0.012665 \quad \text{at } (0.051690, 0.356750, 11.287126), \tag{13.27}$$

but the cuckoo search uses significantly fewer evaluations than other algorithms.

13.9 Cuckoo Search Implementation

We just formulated the spring design problem using different notations from some literature. Here we try to illustrate a point.

As the input to a function is a vector (either a column vector or, less often, a row vector), we have to write

$$\boldsymbol{x} = \begin{pmatrix} w & D & L \end{pmatrix} = [x(1)\ x(2)\ x(3)]. \tag{13.28}$$

With this vector, the objective becomes

$$\text{Minimize } f(\boldsymbol{x}) = (2 + x(3)) * x(1)^2 * x(2),$$

which can easily be converted to a formula in Matlab.

Similarly, the first inequality constraint can be rewritten as

$$g_1(\boldsymbol{x}) = 1 - \frac{x(2)^3 * x(3)}{71785 * x(1)^4} \le 0. \tag{13.29}$$

Other constraints can be rewritten in a similar way.

Using the pseudo code for the cuckoo search in this book and combining with the penalty method, we can solve the preceding spring design problem using cuckoo search in Matlab as follows:

```
% Cuckoo Search for nonlinear constrained optimization          %
% Programmed by Xin-She Yang @ Cambridge University 2009        %
% Usage: cuckoo_search_spring(25000) or cuckoo_search_spring;   %

function [bestsol,fval]=cuckoo_search_spring(time)
format long;
help cuckoo_search_spring.m
if nargin<1,
    % Number of iteraions
    time=2000;
end

disp('Computing ... it may take a few minutes.');

% Number of nests (or different solutions)
n=25;
% Discovery rate of alien eggs/solutions
pa=0.25;

% Simple bounds of the search domain

% Lower bounds and upper bounds
Lb=[0.05 0.25 2.0];
Ub=[2.0  1.3  15.0];


% Random initial solutions
for i=1:n,
nest(i,:)=Lb+(Ub-Lb).*rand(size(Lb));
end

% Get the current best
fitness=10^10*ones(n,1);
[fmin,bestnest,nest,fitness]=get_best_nest(nest,nest,fitness);

N_iter=0;
%% Starting iterations
for t=1:time,
```

```
    % Generate new solutions (but keep the current best)
     new_nest=get_cuckoos(nest,bestnest,Lb,Ub);
     [fnew,best,nest,fitness]=get_best_nest(nest,new_nest,fitness);
    % Update the counter
      N_iter=N_iter+n;
    % Discovery and randomization
      new_nest=empty_nests(nest,Lb,Ub,pa) ;

    % Evaluate this solution
      [fnew,best,nest,fitness]=get_best_nest(nest,new_nest,fitness);
    % Update the counter again
      N_iter=N_iter+n;
    % Find the best objective so far
    if fnew<fmin,
        fmin=fnew;
        bestnest=best ;
    end
end %% End of iterations

%% Post-optimization processing
%% Display all the nests
disp(strcat('Total number of iterations=',num2str(N_iter)));
fmin
bestnest

%% --------------- All subfunctions are list below -------------
%% Get cuckoos by ramdom walk
function nest=get_cuckoos(nest,best,Lb,Ub)
% Levy flights
n=size(nest,1);
% Levy exponent and coefficient

beta=3/2;
tmpdiv=(gamma((1+beta)/2)*beta*2^((beta-1)/2)))^(1/beta);
sigma=(gamma(1+beta)*sin(pi*beta/2)/tmpdiv;

for j=1:n,
    s=nest(j,:);
    % This is a simple way of implementing Levy flights
    % For standard random walks, use step=1;
    %% Levy flights by Mantegna's algorithm
    u=randn(size(s))*sigma;
    v=randn(size(s));
    step=u./abs(v).^(1/beta);


% In the next equation, the difference factor (s-best) means that
% when the solution is the best solution, it remains unchanged.
stepsize=0.01*step.*(s-best);
```

```
    % The factor 0.01 comes from the fact that L/100 should the typical
    % step size of walks/flights where L is the typical lenghtscale;
    % otherwise, Levy flights may become too aggresive/efficient,
    % which makes new solutions (even) jump out side
    % of the design domain (and thus wasting evaluations).
    % Now the actual random walks or flights
    s=s+stepsize.*randn(size(s));
   % Apply simple bounds/limits
   nest(j,:)=simplebounds(s,Lb,Ub);
end

   %% Find the current best nest
   function [fmin,best,nest,fitness]=get_best_nest(nest,newnest,fitness)
   % Evaluating all new solutions
   for j=1:size(nest,1),
       fnew=fobj(newnest(j,:));
       if fnew<=fitness(j),
          fitness(j)=fnew;
          nest(j,:)=newnest(j,:);
       end
   end
   % Find the current best
   [fmin,K]=min(fitness) ;
   best=nest(K,:);

   %% Replace some nests by constructing new solutions/nests
   function new_nest=empty_nests(nest,Lb,Ub,pa)
   % A fraction of worse nests are discovered with a probability pa
   n=size(nest,1);
   % Discovered or not -- a status vector
   K=rand(size(nest))>pa;

   % In real world, if a cuckoo's egg is very similar to
   % a host's eggs, then this cuckoo's egg is less likely
   % to be discovered, thus the fitness should be related to
   % the difference in solutions.  Therefore, it is a good idea
   % to do a random walk in a biased way with some random step sizes.
   nestn1=nest(randperm(n),:);
   nestn2=nest(randperm(n),:);
   %% New solution by biased/selective random walks
   stepsize=rand*(nestn1-nestn2);
   new_nest=nest+stepsize.*K;
   for j=1:size(new_nest,1)
       s=new_nest(j,:);
     new_nest(j,:)=simplebounds(s,Lb,Ub);
   end

   % Application of simple constraints
   function s=simplebounds(s,Lb,Ub)
```

```
  % Apply the lower bound
  ns_tmp=s;
  I=ns_tmp<Lb;
  ns_tmp(I)=Lb(I);

  % Apply the upper bounds
  J=ns_tmp>Ub;
  ns_tmp(J)=Ub(J);
  % Update this new move
  s=ns_tmp;

%% Spring desgn optimization -- objective function
function z=fobj(u)
% The well-known spring design problem
z=(2+u(3))*u(1)^2*u(2);
z=z+getnonlinear(u);

function Z=getnonlinear(u)
Z=0;
% Penalty constant
lam=10^15;

% Inequality constraints
g(1)=1-u(2)^3*u(3)/(71785*u(1)^4);
gtmp=(4*u(2)^2-u(1)*u(2))/(12566*(u(2)*u(1)^3-u(1)^4));
g(2)=gtmp+1/(5108*u(1)^2)-1;
g(3)=1-140.45*u(1)/(u(2)^2*u(3));
g(4)=(u(1)+u(2))/1.5-1;

% No equality constraint in this problem, so empty;
geq=[];

% Apply inequality constraints
for k=1:length(g),
    Z=Z+ lam*g(k)^2*getH(g(k));
end
% Apply equality constraints
for k=1:length(geq),
   Z=Z+lam*geq(k)^2*getHeq(geq(k));
end

% Test if inequalities hold
% Index function H(g) for inequalities
function H=getH(g)
if g<=0,
    H=0;
else
    H=1;
end
```

```
% Index function for equalities
function H=getHeq(geq)
if geq==0,
   H=0;
else
   H=1;
end
% ---------------- end -------------------------------------
```

References

[1] Cagnina LC, Esquivel SC, Coello CA. Solving engineering optimization problems with the simple constrained particle swarm optimizer. Informatica 2008;32(3):319–26.

[2] Coello CAC. Use of a self-adaptive penalty approach for engineering optimization problems. Comput Industry 2000;41(2):113–27.

[3] Deb K. Optimization for engineering design: algorithms and examples. New Delhi, India: Prentice-Hall; 1995.

[4] Deb K. An efficient constraint handling method for genetic algorithms. Comput Methods Appl Mech Eng 2000;186(2–4):311–38.

[5] Gill PE, Murray W, Wright MH. Practical optimization. Bingley, UK: Emerald Group Publishing Ltd; 1982.

[6] Konak A, Coit DW, Smith AE. Multi-objective optimization using genetic algorithms: a tutorial. Reliab Eng Syst Saf 2006;91(9):992–1007.

[7] Koziel S, Michalewicz Z. Evolutionary algorithms, homomorphous mappings, and constrained parameter optimization. Evol Comput 1999;7(1):19–44.

[8] Michalewicz Z, Fogel DB. How to solve it: modern heuristics. 2nd ed. Berlin, Germany: Springer; 2004.

[9] Mezura-Montes E. Constraint-handling in evolutionary optimization, studies in computational intelligence, vol. 198. Berlin, Germany: Springer; 2009.

[10] Mezura-Montes E, Coello CAC. Constraint-handling in nature-inspired numerical optimization: past, present and future. Swarm Evol Comput 2011;1(4):173–94.

[11] Powell D, Skolnick MM. Using genetic algorithms in engineering design optimization with non-linear constraints. In: Forrest S, editor. Proceedings of the fifth international conference on genetic algorithms, ICGA-93, University of Illinois at Urbana-Champaign. San Mateo, CA, USA: Morgan Kaufmann; 1993. p. 424–31.

[12] Ray T, Singh HK, Isaacs A, Smith W. Infeasibility driven evolutionary algorithm for constrained optimization. In: Mezura-Montes E, editor. Constraint-handling in evolutionary optimization. Studies in computational intelligence series, vol. 198. Berlin, Germany: Springer-Verlag; 2009. p. 145–65.

[13] Runarsson TP, Yao X. Stochastic ranking for constrained evolutionary optimization. IEEE Trans Evol Comput 2000;4(3):284–94.

[14] Takahama T, Sakai S, Iwane N. Constrained optimization by the epsilon constrained hybrid algorithm of particle swarm optimization and genetic algorithm. In: AI 2005: advances in artificial intelligence. Lecture notes in artificial intelligence, vol. 3809. Berlin, Germany: Springer-Verlag; 2005. p. 389–400.

[15] Yeniay O. Penalty function methods for constrained optimization with genetic algorithms. Math Comput Appl 2005;10(1):45–56.

14 Multi-Objective Optimization

All the optimization problems we discussed so far have only a single objective. In reality, we often have to optimize multiple objectives simultaneously. For example, we may want to improve the performance of a product while trying to minimize the cost at the same time. In this case, we are dealing with a multi-objective optimization problem. Many new concepts are required for solving multi-objective optimization. Furthermore, these multi-objectives can be conflicting, and thus some trade-offs are needed. As a result, a set of Pareto-optimal solutions, rather than a single solution, must be found. This often requires multiple runs of solution algorithms.

14.1 Multi-Objective Optimization

The optimization problem with a single objective that we have discussed so far can be considered a scalar optimization problem because the objective function always reaches a single global optimal value or a scalar. For multi-objective optimization, the multiple-objective functions form a vector, and thus it is also called *vector optimization* [3,6,9,10].

Any multi-objective optimization problem can generally be written as

$$\underset{\boldsymbol{x}\in\Re^d}{\text{Minimize}}\ \boldsymbol{f}(\boldsymbol{x}) = [f_1(\boldsymbol{x}), f_2(\boldsymbol{x}), \ldots, f_M(\boldsymbol{x})],$$

$$\text{subject to} \quad g_j(\boldsymbol{x}) \leq 0, \quad j = 1, 2, \ldots, J, \tag{14.1}$$

$$h_k(\boldsymbol{x}) = 0, \quad k = 1, 2, \ldots, K, \tag{14.2}$$

where $\boldsymbol{x} = (x_1, x_2, \ldots, x_d)^T$ is the vector of decision variables. In some formulations used in the optimization literature, inequalities $g_j (j = 1, \ldots, J)$ can also include any equalities, because an equality $\phi(\boldsymbol{x}) = 0$ can be converted into two inequalities $\phi(\boldsymbol{x}) \leq 0$ and $\phi(\boldsymbol{x}) \geq 0$. However, for clarity, here we list the equalities and inequalities separately.

The space $\mathcal{F} = \Re^d$ spanned by the vectors of decision variables $\boldsymbol{x}$ is called the *search space*. The space $\mathcal{S} = \Re^M$ formed by all the possible values of objective functions is called the *solution space* or *objective space*. Comparing with the single-objective function whose solution space is (at most) $\Re$, the solution space for multi-objective optimization is considerably larger. In addition, because we know that we are dealing with multi-objectives $\boldsymbol{f}(\boldsymbol{x}) = [f_i]$, for simplicity we can write f_i as $f(\boldsymbol{x})$ without causing any confusion.

Nature-Inspired Optimization Algorithms. http://dx.doi.org/10.1016/B978-0-12-416743-8.00014-2

A multi-objective optimization problem, unlike a single-objective optimization problem, does not necessarily have an optimal solution that minimizes all the multi-objective functions simultaneously. Often, objectives may conflict with each other, and the optimal parameters of some objectives usually do not lead to the optimality of other objectives (sometimes they even make them worse). For example, we want first-class-quality service on our holidays, but at the same time we want to pay as little as possible. The high-quality service (one objective) will inevitably cost much more, but this is in conflict with the other objective (to minimize cost).

Therefore, among these often conflicting objectives, we have to choose some tradeoff or achieve a certain balance of objectives. If none of these is possible, we must choose a list of preferences as to which objectives should be achieved first. More important, we have to compare different objectives and make a compromise. This usually requires a reformulation, and one of the most popular approaches to reformulation is to find a scalar-valued function that represents a weighted combination or preference order of all objectives. Such a scalar function is often referred to as the *preference function* or *utility function*. A simple way to construct this scalar function is to use the weighted sum

$$\Phi(f_1(\boldsymbol{x}), \ldots, f_M(\boldsymbol{x})) = \sum_{i=1}^{M} w_i f_i(\boldsymbol{x}), \tag{14.3}$$

where w_i are the weighting coefficients.

Naïvely, some may wonder what happens if we try to optimize each objective individually so that each will achieve the best (the minimum for a minimization problem). In this case, we have

$$F^* = (f_1^*, f_2^*, \ldots, f_M^*), \tag{14.4}$$

which is called the *ideal objective* vector. However, there is no solution that corresponds to this ideal vector. That is to say, it is a nonexistent solution. The only exception is when all the objectives correspond to the same solution, and in this case, these multi-objectives are not conflicting, leading to the case when the Pareto front typically collapses into a single point [4].

For multi-objective optimization, we have to introduce some new concepts related to Pareto optimality.

14.2 Pareto Optimality

A vector $\boldsymbol{u} = (u_1, .., u_d)^T \in \mathcal{F}$, is said to dominate another vector $\boldsymbol{v} = (v_1, \ldots, v_d)^T$ if and only if $u_i \leq v_i$ for $\forall i \in \{1, \ldots, d\}$ and $\exists i \in \{1, \ldots, d\} : u_i < v_i$. This "partial-less" or component-wise relationship is denoted by

$$\boldsymbol{u} \prec \boldsymbol{v}, \tag{14.5}$$

which is equivalent to

$$\forall i \in \{1, \ldots, d\} : u_i \leq v_i \wedge \exists i \in \{1, \ldots, d\} : u_i < v_i. \tag{14.6}$$

Here $\wedge$ means the logical *and*. In other words, no component of $\boldsymbol{u}$ is larger than the corresponding component of $\boldsymbol{v}$, and at least one component is smaller. Similarly, we can define another dominance relationship $\preceq$ by

$$\boldsymbol{u} \preceq \boldsymbol{v} \Longleftrightarrow \boldsymbol{u} \prec \boldsymbol{v} \vee \boldsymbol{u} = \boldsymbol{v}. \tag{14.7}$$

Here $\vee$ means *or*. It is worth pointing out that for maximization problems, the dominance can be defined by replacing $\prec$ with $\succ$.

A point or a solution $\boldsymbol{x}_* \in \Re^d$ is called a *Pareto-optimal solution* or non-inferior solution to the optimization problem if there is no $\boldsymbol{x} \in \Re^d$ satisfying $f_i(\boldsymbol{x}) \leq f_i(\boldsymbol{x}_*)$, $(i = 1, 2, \ldots, M)$. In other words, $\boldsymbol{x}_*$ is Pareto-optimal if there exists no feasible vector (of decision variables in the search space) that would decrease some objectives without simultaneously causing an increase in at least one other objective. That is to say, optimal solutions are solutions that are not dominated by any other solutions. When mapping to objective vectors, they represent different trade-offs between multiple objectives.

Furthermore, a point $\boldsymbol{x}_* \in \mathcal{F}$ is called a *nondominated* solution if no solution can be found that dominates it. A vector is called *ideal* if it contains the decision variables that correspond to the optima of objectives when each objective is considered separately.

Unlike the single-objective optimization with often a single optimal solution, multi-objective optimization will lead to a set of solutions, called the Pareto-optimal set $\mathcal{P}^*$, and the decision vectors $\boldsymbol{x}_*$ for this solution set are thus called nondominated. That is to say, the set of optimal solutions in the decision space forms the Pareto (optimal) set. The image of this Pareto set in the objective or response space is called the *Pareto front*. In the literature, the set $\boldsymbol{x}_*$ in the decision space that corresponds to the Pareto-optimal solutions is also called an *efficient set*. The set (or plot) of the objective functions of these nondominated decision vectors in the Pareto-optimal set forms the so-called Pareto front $\mathcal{P}$ or Pareto frontier.

In short, $\boldsymbol{u} \preceq \boldsymbol{v}$ means that $\boldsymbol{u}$ dominates $\boldsymbol{v}$; that is, $\boldsymbol{u}$ is nondominated by $\boldsymbol{v}$, or $\boldsymbol{v}$ is dominated by $\boldsymbol{u}$. This definition may be too theoretical. To put it in practical terms, $\boldsymbol{u}$ is noninferior to $\boldsymbol{v}$ (i.e., $\boldsymbol{u}$ is better or no worse than $\boldsymbol{v}$). Intuitively, when $\boldsymbol{u}$ dominates $\boldsymbol{v}$, we can loosely say that $\boldsymbol{u}$ is better than $\boldsymbol{v}$. The domination concept provides a good way to compare solutions for multi-objective optimization, and the aim of multi-objective optimization is to find such nondominated solutions. For any two solution vectors $\boldsymbol{x}_1$ and $\boldsymbol{x}_2$, there are only three possibilities: $\boldsymbol{x}_1$ dominates $\boldsymbol{x}_2$, or $\boldsymbol{x}_2$ dominates $\boldsymbol{x}_1$, or $\boldsymbol{x}_1$ and $\boldsymbol{x}_2$ do not dominate each other. Among many interesting properties of domination, transitivity still holds. That is, if $\boldsymbol{x}_1$ dominates $\boldsymbol{x}_2$, and $\boldsymbol{x}_2$ dominates $\boldsymbol{x}_3$, then $\boldsymbol{x}_1$ dominates $\boldsymbol{x}_3$.

Using this notation, the Pareto front $\mathcal{P}$ can be defined as the set of nondominated solutions so that

$$\mathcal{P} = \{\boldsymbol{s} \in \mathcal{S} \Big| \nexists \boldsymbol{s}' \in \mathcal{S} : \boldsymbol{s}' \prec \boldsymbol{s}\}, \tag{14.8}$$

or, in terms of the Pareto-optimal set in the search space,

$$\mathcal{P}^* = \{\boldsymbol{x} \in \mathcal{F} \Big| \nexists \boldsymbol{x}' \in \mathcal{F} : \boldsymbol{f}(\boldsymbol{x}') \prec \boldsymbol{f}(x)\}. \tag{14.9}$$

All the nondominated solutions in the whole feasible search space form the so-called globally Pareto-optimal set, which is simply referred to as the Pareto front.

The identification of the Pareto front is not an easy task; it often requires a parametric analysis, say, by treating all but one objective, say, f_i in an M-objective optimization problem, so that f_i is a function of $f_1, \ldots, f_{i-1}, f_{i+1}, \ldots$, and f_M. By maximizing the f_i when varying the values of the other $M - 1$ objectives, there can be enough solution points that will trace out the Pareto front.

Example 14.1. For example, we have four Internet service providers, A, B, C, and D. We have two objectives by which customers choose their service: (1) as cheap as possible, and (2) higher bandwidth. The providers' details are listed here:

IP provider	Cost (£/month)	Bandwidth (Mb)
A	20	80
B	25	112
C	30	56
D	40	112

From the table, we know that option C is dominated by A and B because both objectives are improved (low cost and faster speed). Option D is dominated by B. Thus, solution C is an inferior solution, and so is D. Both solutions A and B are noninferior or nondominated solutions. However, deciding which solution (A or B) to choose is not easy, since provider A outperforms B on the first objective (cheaper) whereas B outperforms A on another objective (faster). In this case, we say these two solutions are *incomparable*. The set of nondominated solutions A and B forms the Pareto front, which is a mutually incomparable set.

For a minimization problem with two objectives, the basic concepts of the nondominated set, Pareto front, and ideal vectors are shown in Figure 14.1. Obviously, if we combine these two into a single composite objective, we can compare, for example, the cost per unit Mb. In this case, we essentially reformulate the problem as a scalar optimization problem. For choice A, each Mb costs £0.25, whereas it costs about £0.22 for choice B. So, we should choose B. However, in reality, we usually have many incomparable solutions, and it is often impossible to compromise in some way. In addition, the real choice depends on our preference and our emphasis on various objectives.

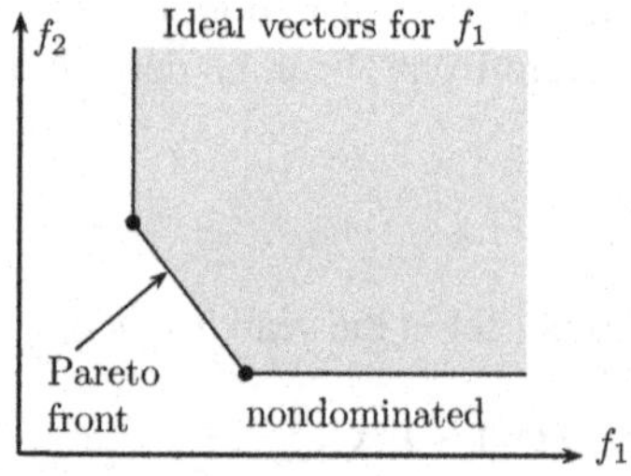

Figure 14.1 The nondominated set, Pareto front, and ideal vectors in a minimization problem with two objectives, f_1 and f_2.

It is worth pointing out that even though we have produced high-quality multiple Pareto-optimal solutions, the final choice of a point on the Pareto front is usually up to the decision makers, who have higher-level information or rules to make the decision. Such higher-level information is typically nontechnical, inaccurate, highly subjective, and often not part of the optimization problem.

Multi-objective optimization is usually difficult to solve, partly due to the lack of efficient tools and partly due to the complexity of this type of problem. Loosely speaking, there are three ways to deal with multi-objective problems: a direct approach, aggregation or transformation, and Pareto-set approximation. However, the current trends tend to be evolutionary approaches to approximating Pareto fronts [4,8].

The direct approach is difficult, especially in the case when multiple objectives seem conflicting. Therefore, we often use aggregation or transformation by combining multiple objectives into a single composite objective so that the standard methods for optimization discussed in this book can be used. We focus on this approach in the rest of this chapter. However, with this approach, the solutions typically depend on the way we combine the objectives. A third way is to try to approximate the Pareto set so as to obtain a set of mutually nondominated solutions.

To transform a multi-objective optimization problem into a single objective, we can often use the method of weighted sum and utility methods. We can also choose the most important objective of our interest as the only objective while rewriting other objectives as constraints with imposed limits.

14.3 Weighted Sum Method

The weighted sum method combines all the multi-objective functions into one scalar, composite objective function using the weighted sum

$$F(\boldsymbol{x}) = w_1 f_1(\boldsymbol{x}) + w_2 f_2(\boldsymbol{x}) + \cdots + w_M\, f_M(\boldsymbol{x}). \tag{14.10}$$

An issue arises in assigning the weighting coefficients $\boldsymbol{w} = (w_1, w_2, \ldots, w_M)$, because the solution strongly depends on the chosen weighting coefficients. Obviously, these weights have be positive, satisfying

$$\sum_{i=1}^{M} w_i = 1, \quad w_i \in (0, 1). \tag{14.11}$$

Let us first look at an example.

Example 14.2. The classical three-objective functions are commonly used for testing multi-objective optimization algorithms. These functions are

$$f_1(x, y) = x^2 + (y - 1)^2, \tag{14.12}$$

$$f_2(x, y) = (x - 1)^2 + y^2 + 2, \tag{14.13}$$

$$f_3(x, y) = x^2 + (y + 1)^2 + 1, \tag{14.14}$$

where $(x, y) \in [-2, 2] \times [-2, 2]$.

If we combine all three functions into a single function $f(x, y)$ using the weighted sum, we have

$$f(x, y) = \alpha f_1 + \beta f_2 + \gamma f_3, \qquad \alpha + \beta + \gamma = 1. \tag{14.15}$$

The stationary point is determined by

$$\frac{\partial f}{\partial x} = 0, \qquad \frac{\partial f}{\partial y} = 0, \tag{14.16}$$

which lead to

$$2\alpha + 2\beta(x - 1) + 2\gamma = 0 \tag{14.17}$$

and

$$2\alpha(y - 1) + 2\beta y + 2\gamma(y + 1) = 0. \tag{14.18}$$

The solutions are

$$x_* = \beta, \qquad y_* = \alpha - \gamma. \tag{14.19}$$

This implies that $x_* \in [0, 1]$ and $y_* \in [-1, 1]$. Consequently, $f_1 \in [0, 5]$, $f_2 \in [2, 4]$ and $f_3 \in [1, 6]$. In addition, the solution or the optimal location varies with the weighting coefficients α, β, and γ. In the simplest case, $\alpha = \beta = \gamma = 1/3$, we have

$$x_* = \frac{1}{3}, \qquad y_* = 0. \tag{14.20}$$

This location is marked with a short, thick line in Figure 14.2.

Now the original multi-objective optimization problem has been transformed into a single-objective optimization problem. Thus, the solution methods for solving single-objective problems are all valid. For example, we can use the particle swarm

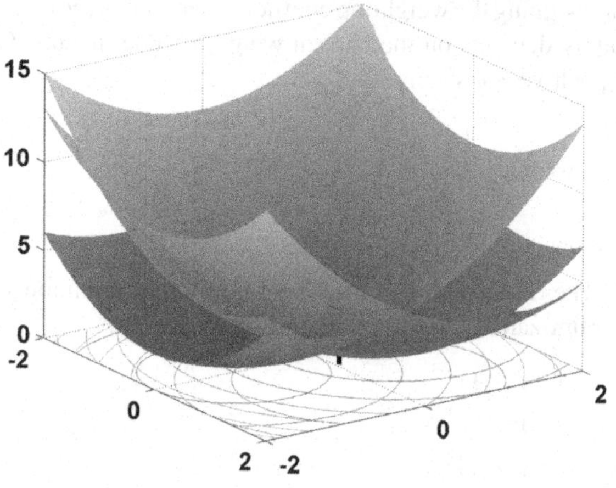

Figure 14.2 Three functions reach the global minimum at $x_* = \beta$, $y_* = \alpha - \gamma$.

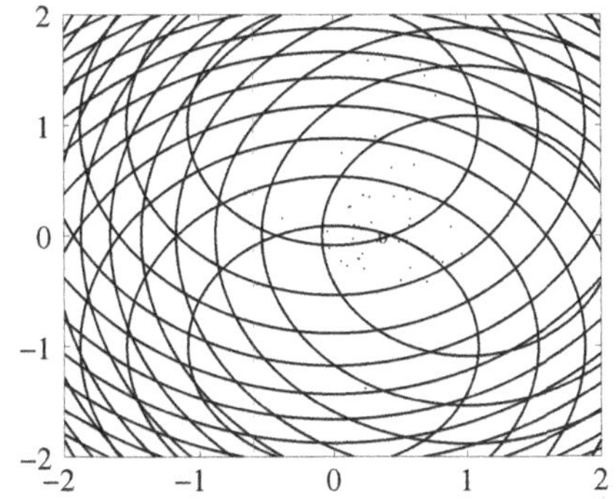

Figure 14.3 Final locations of 40 particles after five iterations. The optimal point is at (1/3, 0), marked with ø.

optimization to find the optimal solution for given parameters α, β, and γ. Figure 14.3 shows the locations of 40 particles at $t = 5$ iterations. We can see that the particles converge toward the true optimal location marked with ø. Obviously, the accuracy will improve if we continue the iterations.

However, there is an important issue here. The combined weighted sum transforms the optimization problem into a single objective, which is not necessarily equivalent to the original multi-objective problem because the extra weighting coefficients could be arbitrary, whereas the final solutions still depend on these coefficients. Furthermore, there are so many ways to construct the weighted sum function, and there is no easy guideline to choose which form is the best for a given problem. When there is no rule to follow, the simplest choice obviously is to use the linear form. But there is no reason that the weighted sum should be linear. In fact, we can use other combinations such as the following quadratic weighted sum:

$$\Pi(\boldsymbol{x}) = \sum_{i=1}^{M} w_i f_i^2(\boldsymbol{x}) = w_1 f_1^2(\boldsymbol{x}) + \cdots + w_M\ f_M^2(\boldsymbol{x}) \tag{14.21}$$

and the others.

Another important issue is that of how to choose the weighting coefficients, since the solutions depend on these coefficients. Choosing weighting coefficients is essentially for decision maker(s) to assign a preference order to the multi-objectives. This leads to a more general concept of the utility function (or preference function) that reflects the preference of the decision maker(s).

Ideally, a different weight vector should result in a different trade-off point on the Pareto front; however, in reality, this is usually not the case. Different combinations of weight coefficients can lead to the same point or points very close to each other, and consequently the points are not uniformly distributed on the Pareto front. In fact, a single trade-off solution on the Pareto front just represents one sampling point, and there is no technique to ensure uniform sampling on the front. All the issues still form an active area of research.

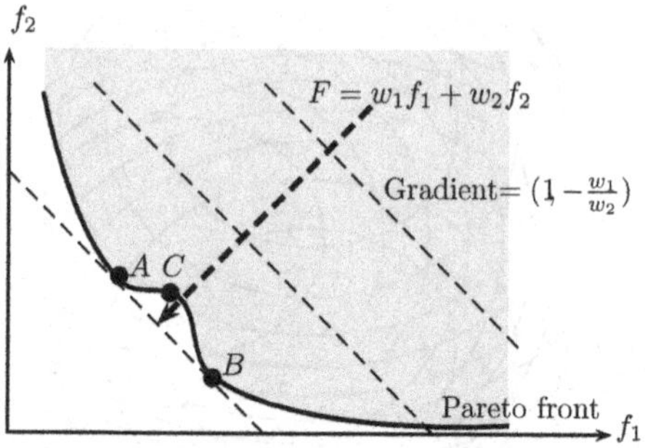

Figure 14.4 Weighted sum method for two objectives f_1 and f_2 and $w_1 + w_2 = 1$.

It is worth pointing out that the linear weighted sum method

$$\Pi(\boldsymbol{x}) = \sum_{i=1}^{M} w_i f_i(\boldsymbol{x}), \quad \sum_{i=1}^{M} w_i = 1, \quad w_i > 0, \tag{14.22}$$

only works for problems with convex Pareto fronts. As we can see from Figure 14.4, where two objectives are combined into one for a given set of $w_1 + w_2 = 1$, the composite function F is minimized. For any given set (w_1, w_2), a (dashed) line has a gradient $(1, -w_1/w_2)$ that will become tangent to the Pareto front when moving downward to the left, and that touching point is the minimum of F. However, at the nonconvex segment, if the aim is point C, the weighted sum method will usually lead to either point A or point B, depending on the values of w_1 (since $w_2 = 1 - w_1$).

The weighted sum method is one of the most widely used due to its simplicity. However, it is usually difficult to generate a good set of points that are uniformly distributed on the Pareto front. In addition, this method only works for convex Pareto fronts. Furthermore, proper scalings or normalization of the objectives are often needed so that the ranges/values of each objective should be comparable; otherwise, the weight coefficients are not well distributed and thus lead to biased sampling on the Pareto front.

For more complex multi-objective optimization problems, another widely used and yet more robust method is the ϵ-constraint method. Before we proceed, let us discuss the utility methods, which can be considered the different ways of forming composite objectives.

14.4 Utility Method

The weighted sum method is essentially a deterministic value method if we consider the weighting coefficients as the ranking coefficients. This implicitly assumes that the consequence of each ranking alternative can be characterized with certainty. This method can be used to explore the implications of alternative value judgment. The utility method, on the other hand, considers uncertainty in the criteria values for each alternative, which is a more realistic method because there is always some degree of uncertainty about the outcome of a particular alternative.

Utility (or preference) functions can be associated with risk attitude or preferences. For example, say that you are offered a choice between a guaranteed £500 and a 50/50 chance of zero or £1000. How much are you willing to pay to take the gamble? The expected payoff of each choice is £500, and thus it is fair to pay $0.5 \times 1000 + (1 - 0.5) \times 0 =$ £500 for such a gamble. A risk-seeking decision maker would risk a lower payoff in order to have a chance to win a higher prize, whereas a risk-averse decision maker would be happy with the safe choice of £500.

For a risk-neutral decision maker, the choice between a guaranteed £500 and the 50/50 gamble is indifferent, since both choices have the same expected value of £500. In reality, the risk preference can vary from person to person and may depend on the type of problem. The utility function can have many forms, and one of the simplest is the exponential utility (of representing preference)

$$u(x) = \frac{1 - e^{-(x-x_a)/\rho}}{1 - e^{-(x_b-x_a)/\rho}}, \tag{14.23}$$

where x_a and x_b are the lowest and highest levels of x, and ρ is called the *risk tolerance* of the decision maker.

The utility function defines combinations of objective values $f_1, \ldots, f_M$ that a decision maker finds equally acceptable or indifferent. So, the contours of the constant utility are referred to as the *indifference curves*. The optimization now becomes the maximization of the utility. For a maximization problem with two objectives f_1 and f_2, the idea of the utility contours (indifference curves), the Pareto front, and the Pareto solution with maximum utility (point A) are shown in Figure 14.5. When the utility function touches the Pareto front in the feasible region, it then provides a maximum utility Pareto solution (marked with A).

For two objectives f_1 and f_2, the utility function can be constructed in different ways. For example, the combined product takes the following form:

$$U(f_1, f_2) = k f_1^{\alpha} f_2^{\beta}, \tag{14.24}$$

where α and β are nonnegative exponents and k a scaling factor. On the other hand, the aggregated utility function for the same two objectives can be defined as

$$U(f_1, f_2) = \alpha f_1 + \beta f_2 + [1 - (\alpha + \beta)] f_1 f_2. \tag{14.25}$$

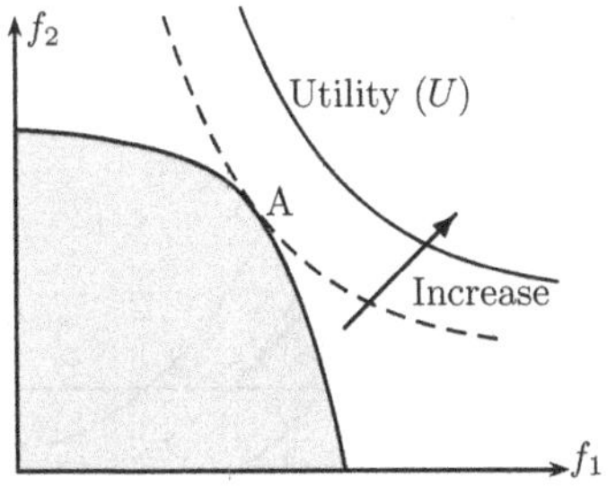

Figure 14.5 Finding the Pareto solution with maximum utility in a maximization problem with two objectives.

There are many other forms. The aim of a decision maker constructing utility functions is to form a mapping $U : \Re^p \mapsto \Re$ so that the total utility function has monotonic and/or convexity properties for easy analysis. It will also improve the quality of the Pareto solution(s) with maximum utility. Let us look at a simple example.

Example 14.3. We now try to solve the simple two-objective optimization problem:

$$\underset{(x,y)\in\Re^2}{\text{Maximize}}\ f_1(x, y) = x + y, \qquad f_2(x, y) = x,$$

subject to

$$x + \alpha y \leq 5, \qquad x \geq 0, \quad y \geq 0,$$

where $0 < \alpha < 1$. Let us use the simple utility function

$$U = f_1 f_2,$$

which combines the two objectives. The line connecting the two corner points $(5, 0)$ and $(0, 5/\alpha)$ forms the Pareto front (see Figure 14.6). It is easy to check that the Pareto solution with the maximum utility is $U = 25$ at $A(5, 0)$ when the utility contours touch the Pareto front with the maximum possible utility.

The complexity of multi-objective optimization makes the construction of utility functions a difficult task because there are many ways to construct such functions.

14.5 The ϵ-Constraint Method

An interesting way of dealing with multi-objective optimization is to write objectives except one as constraints. Let us try to rewrite the following unconstrained optimization as a single-objective constrained optimization problem:

$$\text{Minimize } f_1(\boldsymbol{x}), f_2(\boldsymbol{x}), \ldots, f_M(\boldsymbol{x}).$$

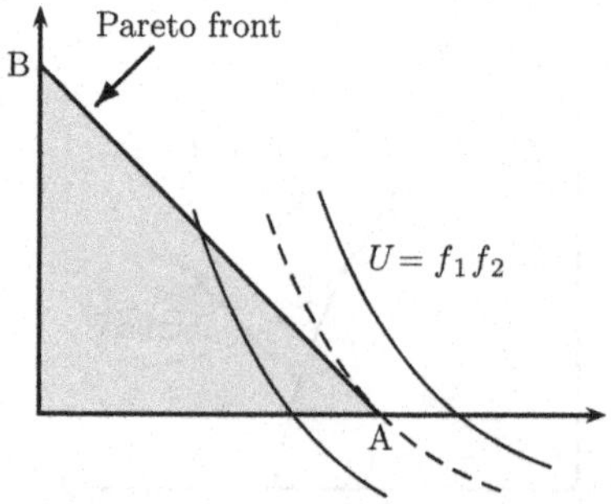

Figure 14.6 The Pareto front is the line connecting A(5, 0) and B(0, $5/\alpha$). The Pareto solution with maximum utility is $U_* = 25$ at point A.

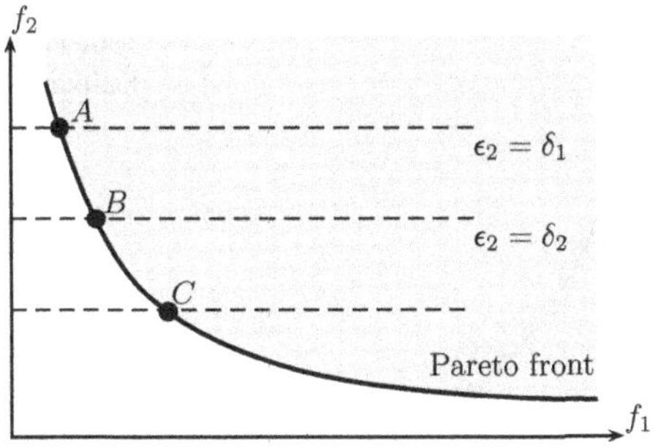

Figure 14.7 Slicing the objective domain in the ϵ-constraint method.

To achieve this goal, we often choose the most important objective of our preference, say, $f_q(\boldsymbol{x})$, as the main objective, while imposing limits on the other objectives. That is,

$$\text{Minimize} \quad f_q(\boldsymbol{x}),$$

$$\text{subject to} \quad f_i \leq \epsilon_i, \quad (i = 1, 2, q-1, q+1, \ldots, M),$$

where the limits ϵ_i are given. In the simplest case, we can choose $q = 1$. Haimes et al. were probably the first to suggest this reformation method [7].

In principle, the problem can be solved using the standard optimization algorithms for single-objective optimization. In essence, this is a slicing method that splits the objective domain into different subdomains. For example, in the case of a bi-objective problem, as shown in Figure 14.7, we take f_2 as the constraint. This problem becomes

$$\text{Minimize } f_1(\boldsymbol{x}), \tag{14.26}$$

subject to

$$f_2(\boldsymbol{x}) \leq \epsilon_2, \tag{14.27}$$

where ϵ_2 is a number, not necessarily small. For any given value of ϵ_2, the objective domain is split into two subdomains: $f_2 \leq \epsilon_2 = \delta_1$ (feasible) and $f_2 > \epsilon_2 = \delta_1$ (infeasible). The minimization of f_1 in the feasible domain leads to the globally optimal point A. Similarly, for a different value of $\epsilon_2 = \delta_2$, the minimum of f_1 gives point B.

Let us look at a bi-objective optimization example, called *Schaffer's min-min function* [11]:

$$\text{Minimize } f_1(x) = x^2, \quad f_2(x) = (x-2)^2, \quad x \in [-10^3, 10^3]. \tag{14.28}$$

If we use f_1 as the objective and $f_2 \leq \epsilon_2$ as the constraint, we can set $\epsilon_2 \in [0, 4]$ with 20 different values. Then we can solve it using a single-objective optimization technique. The 20 points of approximated Pareto-optimal solutions and the true Pareto front are shown in Figure 14.8. However, if we use f_2 as the objective and f_1 as the constraint, we follow exactly the same procedure, with the results shown in Figure 14.9.

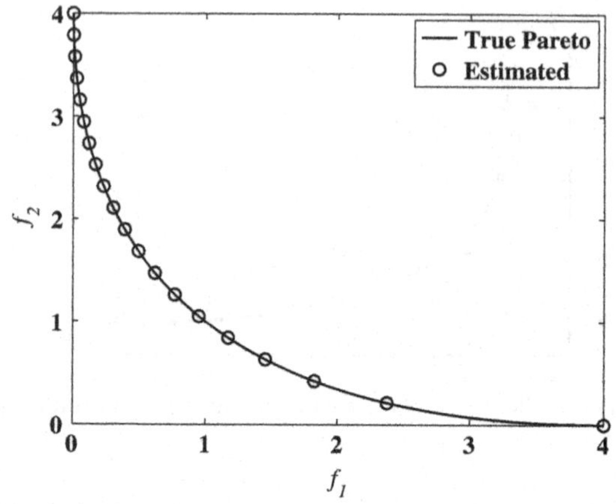

Figure 14.8 A true Pareto front and the estimated front when setting f_1 as the objective and f_2 as the constraint.

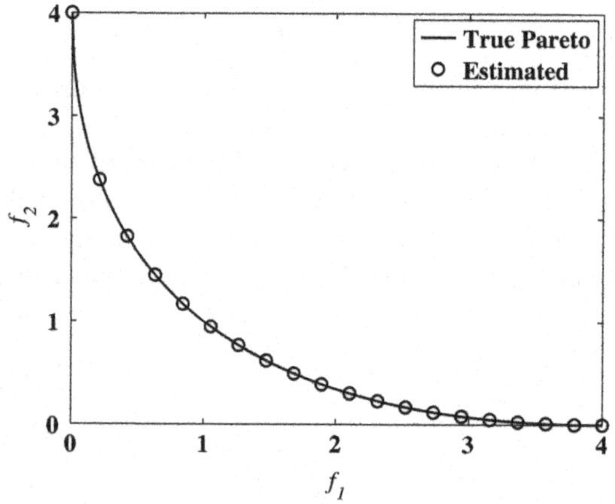

Figure 14.9 The true Pareto front and the estimated front when setting f_2 as the objective and f_1 as the constraint.

As we can see from both figures, the distributions of the approximate Pareto points are different, though they look similar.

As this example has demonstrated, the distributions of the sampling points on the Pareto front may depend on the actual formulation and the order of choosing the main objective.

The advantage of this method is that it works well for complex problems with nonconvex Pareto fronts. However, it does have some disadvantages. There could be many different formulations for choosing the main objectives and the rest of objectives as constraints. Different formulations may lead to different computational efforts. In addition, there is no guarantee that the points generated on the Pareto front are uniformly distributed, as we saw in the previous example.

Furthermore, it is difficult to impose the right range of ϵ_i. In the previous example, if we set ϵ_2 too small, say, $\epsilon_2 \to 0$, there may not be a feasible solution. On the other hand, if we set ϵ too high, it will be difficult to find the minimum of f_1 even if it exists, because the number of evaluations for this single-objective optimization problem may increase. In practice, some prior knowledge is required to impose the correct limits. Otherwise, the solutions obtained may not be the solution to the original problem.

The good news is that recent trends tend to use evolutionary approaches such as genetic algorithms. We briefly introduce some of these metaheuristic methods in the rest of this chapter.

14.6 Metaheuristic Approaches

So far, we have seen that finding solutions to a multi-objective optimization problem is usually difficult, even by the simple weighted sum method and utility function. However, there are other promising methods that work well for multi-objective optimization problems, especially metaheuristic methods such as simulated annealing, particle swarm optimization, cuckoo search, and firefly algorithms [4,14–16,18,19].

There are many potential ways to extend the standard simulated annealing to solve multi-objective optimization problems. A direct and yet simple extension is to modify the acceptance probability as the joint probability

$$p_a = \prod_{j=1}^{m} p_j = \prod_{j=1}^{m} e^{-\Delta f_j / kT_j},$$

where k is Boltzmann constant, which can be taken as $k = 1$, and $\Delta f_j = f_j(\boldsymbol{x}_n) - f_j(\boldsymbol{x}_{n-1})$ is the change of each individual objective. For details, refer to the article by Suppapitnarm et al. [13].

In 1985, Schaffer was probably the first to use vector evaluated genetic algorithms (VEGA) to solve multi-objective optimization, without using any composite aggregation, by combining all objectives into a single objective [11]. Since then, many metaheuristic algorithms such as PSO, SA, and F have been extended to solve multi-objective optimization problems successfully. Interested readers can refer to the list of more advanced literature at the end of this chapter.

The main difficulty in extending any single-objective optimization algorithm to accommodate multiple objectives is that we have to consider the dominance of each candidate solution set. In the standard PSO, we update the velocity

$$\boldsymbol{v}_i^{t+1} = \theta \boldsymbol{v}_i^t + \alpha \epsilon_1 \cdot (\boldsymbol{g}^* - \boldsymbol{x}_i^t) + \beta \epsilon_2 \cdot (\boldsymbol{x}_i^* - \boldsymbol{x}_i^t),$$

where $\boldsymbol{g}^*$ is the current global optimum found so far. A possible extension is to use an external repository or archive to store nondominated solutions at each iteration. Then we select such a solution $\boldsymbol{h}^*$ from this repository to replace $\boldsymbol{g}^*$. This idea was first proposed by Coello et al. [1].

There are many evolutionary approaches to multi-objective optimization, and many variants and new approaches are under active research [12]. For a relative comprehensive review, refer to Deb [4].

Among many widely used methods for multi-objective optimization, we introduce the elitist nondominated *sorting genetic algorithm* (NSGA-II) in the rest of this chapter.

14.7 NSGA-II

The elitist *nondominated sorting genetic algorithm*, or NSGA-II for short, was developed by Deb et al. [5] and has become a popular method for solving multi-objective optimization problems by finding multiple Pareto solutions. Its key features include the use of elitist, diversity-preserving mechanisms and emphasis on nondominated solutions.

The main step in NSGA-II is that the n offsprings S_t are created from the n parents P_t using the standard genetic algorithms. The whole population W_t of size $2n$ is formed by joining S_t and P_t, i.e., $W_t = P_t \cup S_t$. Then the nondominated sorting is applied to W_t. Then the new population is filled, one at a time, by different nondominated solutions. Because the population of W_t is $2n$, only half of it will be put into the new population, selecting the nondominated solutions for the Pareto front with the higher diversity while discarding the rest of the solutions.

The crowding distance D_i used in the NSGA-II is essentially based on the cardinality of the solution sets and their distance to the solution boundaries. The crowded tournament selection is based on ranking and distance. In other words, if a solution $\boldsymbol{x}_i$ has a better rank than $\boldsymbol{x}_j$, we select $\boldsymbol{x}_i$. If the ranks are the same but $D_i > D_j$, we select $\boldsymbol{x}_i$ based on its crowding distance. For details, refer to Deb et al. [5]. The main steps of NSGA-II can be summarized as follows:

1. Create a new population $W_t = P_t \cup S_t$ by combining P_t and apply nondominated sorting.
2. Identify different fronts PF_i $(i = 1, 2, \ldots)$.
3. Generate P_{t+1} from $P_{t+1} = \emptyset$ with $i = 1$ and fill $P_{t+1} = P_{t+1} \cup PF_i$ until size n.
4. Carry out a crowding sort using the crowd distance to sort some PF_i to P_{t+1}.
5. Generate new offspring S_{t+1} from P_{t+1} via crowded tournament-based genetic operators: crossover, mutation, and selection.

There are many other methods for solving multi-objective optimization problems. Some other evolutionary algorithms or approaches include the vector evaluated genetic algorithm (VEGA) [11], differential evolution for multi-objective optimization (DEMO) [2], and the strength pareto evolutionary algorithm (SPEA) [4].

Recent studies show that other methods such as multi-objective cuckoo search (MOCS), multi-objective firefly algorithm (MOFA), and multi-objective flower pollination algorithms (MOFPA) can be equally or even more effective [15–17].

References

[1] Coello CAC, Pulido GT, Lechuga MS. Handling multiple objectives with particle swarm optimization. IEEE Trans Evol Comput 2004;8(3):256–79.

[2] Chakraborty UK. Advances in differential evolution. Studies in computational intelligence, vol. 143. Heidelberg, Germany: Springer; 2008.

[3] Deb K. Optimization for engineering design: algorithms and examples. New Delhi, India: Prentice-Hall; 1995.
[4] Deb K. Multi-objective optimization using evolutionary algorithms. Chichester, UK: Wiley and Sons; 2001.
[5] Deb K, Agrawal S, Pratap A, Meyarivan T. A fast and elitist multi-objective genetic algorithm: NSGA-II. IEEE Trans Evol Comput 2002;6(2):182–97.
[6] Fonseca CM, Fleming PJ. An overview of evolutionary algorithms in multiobjective optimization. Evol Comput 1995;3(1):1–16.
[7] Haimes YY, Lasdon LS, Wismer DA. On a bicriterion formulation of the problems of integrated system identification and system optimization. IEEE Trans Syst Man Cybern 1971;1(4):296–7.
[8] Knowles JD, Corne DW. Approximating the non-dominated front using the Pareto archived evolution strategy. Evol Comput J 2000;8(2):149–72.
[9] Pareto V. Manuale di economica politica. London, UK: Macmillan; 1972.
[10] Sawaragi Y, Nakayama H, Tanino T. Theory of multiobjective optimization. London, UK: Academic Press; 1985.
[11] Schaffer JD. Multiple objective optimization with vector evaluated genetic algorithms. In: Grefenstette J, editor. Proceedings of the International Conference on Genetic Algorithms and their Applications. Hillsdale, NJ, USA: L. Erlbaum Associates; 1985. p. 93–100.
[12] Srinivas N, Deb K. Multiple objective optimization using nondominated sorting in genetic algorithms. Evol Comput 1994;2(3):221–48.
[13] Suppapitnarm A, Seffen KA, Parks GT, Clarkson PJ. A simulated annealing algorithm for multiobjective optimization. Eng Optim 2000;33(1):59–85.
[14] Talbi E-G. Metaheuristics: from design to implementation. Wiley; 2009.
[15] Yang XS, Deb S. Multiobjective cuckoo search for design optimization. Comput Oper Res 2013;40(6):1616–24.
[16] Yang XS. Multi-objective firefly algorithm for continuous optimization. Eng Comput 2013;29(2):175–84.
[17] Yang XS, Karamanoglu M, He X. Multi-objective flower algorithm for optimization. Procedia Comput Sci 2013;18:861–8.
[18] Zitzler E, Deb K, Thiele L. Comparison of multiobjective evoluationary algorithms: Empirical results. Evol Comput 2000;8(2):173–95.
[19] E Zitzler, M Laumanns, S Bleuler. A tutorial on evolutionary multiobjective optimization. In: Gandibleux X, Sevaux M, Sörensen K, T'kindt V, editors. Metaheuristics for multiobjective optimization. Lecture notes in economics and mathematical systems, vol. 535. Berlin, Germany: Springer; 2004. p. 3–37.

15 Other Algorithms and Hybrid Algorithms

There are many other algorithms in the literature, but we have not covered them in detail in this book. One of the reasons is that some of these algorithms, such as ant colony optimization and harmony search, have extensive literature and books devoted to them, so readers can easily find information about them elsewhere. While for some other algorithms, such as some of the hybrid algorithms, their efficiency and performance may be preliminary, and further research is needed to verify these results.

However, for completeness, here we briefly introduce a few other widely used algorithms and briefly touch on some of the hybrid algorithms.

15.1 Ant Algorithms

15.1.1 Ant Behavior

Ants are social insects that live together in organized colonies whose population size can range from about 2 million to 25 million. When foraging, a swarm of ants or mobile agents interact or communicate in their local environment. Each ant can lay scent chemicals or pheromone so as to communicate with others, and each ant is also able to follow the route marked with pheromone laid by other ants. When ants find a food source, they mark it with pheromone as well as marking the trails to and from it. From the initial random foraging route, the pheromone concentration varies. The ants follow the routes with higher pheromone concentrations, and the pheromone is enhanced by the increasing number of ants. As more and more ants follow the same route, it becomes the favored path. Thus, some favorite routes emerge, often the shortest or more efficient. This is actually a positive feedback mechanism.

Emerging behavior exists in an ant colony; such emergence arises from simple interactions among individual ants. Individual ants act according to simple and local information (such as pheromone concentration) to carry out their activities. Although there is no master ant overseeing the entire colony and broadcasting instructions to the individual ants, organized behavior still emerges automatically. Therefore, such emergent behavior can be similar to other self-organized phenomena that occur in many processes in nature, such as the pattern formation in some animal skins (e.g., tiger and zebra skins).

The foraging pattern of some ant species (such as army ants) can show extraordinary regularity. Army ants search for food along some regular routes with an angle of about

Nature-Inspired Optimization Algorithms. http://dx.doi.org/10.1016/B978-0-12-416743-8.00015-4

123° apart. We do not know how they manage to follow such regularity, but studies show that they could move into an area and build a bivouac and start foraging. On the first day, they forage in a random direction, say, the north, and travel a few hundred meters, then branch to cover a large area. The next day they will choose a different direction, which is about 123° from the direction on the previous day, and so cover another large area. On the following day, they again choose a different direction about 123° from the second day's direction. In this way, they cover the whole area over about two weeks and then move out to a different location to build a bivouac and forage in the new region [40].

The interesting thing is that ants do not use the angle of $360°/3 = 120°$ (this would mean that on the fourth day, they will search the empty area already foraged on the first day). The beauty of this 123° angle is that after about three days, it leaves an angle of about 10° from the direction of the first day. This means the ants cover the whole circular region in 14 days without repeating or covering a previously foraged area. This is an amazing phenomenon.

15.1.2 Ant Colony Optimization

Based on these characteristics of ant behavior, scientists have developed a number of powerful ant colony algorithms, with important progress made in recent years. Marco Dorigo pioneered the research in this area in 1992 [6,7]. Many different variants have appeared since then.

If we use only some of the features of ant behavior and add some new characteristics, we can devise a class of new algorithms.

There are two important issues here: the probability of choosing a route and the evaporation rate of pheromone. There are a few ways of solving these problems, although it is still an area of active research. Here we introduce the current best method.

For a network routing problem, the probability of ants at a particular node i to choose the route from node i to node j is given by

$$p_{ij} = \frac{\phi_{ij}^{\alpha} d_{ij}^{\beta}}{\sum_{i,j=1}^{n} \phi_{ij}^{\alpha} d_{ij}^{\beta}}, \tag{15.1}$$

where $\alpha > 0$ and $\beta > 0$ are the influence parameters, and their typical values are $\alpha \approx \beta \approx 2$. ϕ_{ij} is the pheromone concentration on the route between i and j, and d_{ij} is the desirability of the same route. Some *a priori* knowledge about the route, such as the distance s_{ij}, is often used so that $d_{ij} \propto 1/s_{ij}$, which implies that shorter routes will be selected due to their shorter traveling time, and thus the pheromone concentrations on these routes are higher. This is because the traveling time is shorter, and thus less of the pheromone has been evaporated during this period.

This probability formula reflects the fact that ants would normally follow the paths with higher pheromone concentrations. In the simpler case when $\alpha = \beta = 1$, the probability of choosing a path by ants is proportional to the pheromone concentration on the path. The denominator normalizes the probability so that it is in the range between 0 and 1.

The pheromone concentration can change with time due to the evaporation of pheromone. Furthermore, the advantage of pheromone evaporation is that the system could avoid being trapped in local optima. If there is no evaporation, the path randomly chosen by the first ants will become the preferred path due to the attraction of other ants by their pheromone. For a constant rate γ of pheromone decay or evaporation, the pheromone concentration usually varies with time exponentially:

$$\phi(t) = \phi_0 e^{-\gamma t}, \tag{15.2}$$

where ϕ_0 is the initial concentration of pheromone and t is time. If $\gamma t \ll 1$, then we have $\phi(t) \approx (1 - \gamma t)\phi_0$. For the unitary time increment $\Delta t = 1$, the evaporation can be approximated by $\phi^{t+1} \leftarrow (1 - \gamma)\phi^t$. Therefore, we have the simplified pheromone update formula:

$$\phi_{ij}^{t+1} = (1 - \gamma)\phi_{ij}^t + \delta\phi_{ij}^t, \tag{15.3}$$

where $\gamma \in [0, 1]$ is the rate of pheromone evaporation. The increment $\delta\phi_{ij}^t$ is the amount of pheromone deposited at time t along route i to j when an ant travels a distance L. Usually $\delta\phi_{ij}^t \propto 1/L$. If there are no ants on a route, then the pheromone deposit is zero.

There are other variations on this basic procedure. A possible acceleration scheme is to use some bounds of the pheromone concentration, and only the ants with the current global best solution(s) are allowed to deposit pheromone. In addition, some ranking of the solution fitness can also be used. These are still topics of active research.

Because a complex network system is always made of individual nodes, this algorithm can be extended to solve complex routing problems reasonably efficiently. In fact, ant colony optimization and its variants have been successfully applied to the Internet routing problem, the traveling salesman problem, and other combinatorial optimization problems.

15.1.3 Virtual Ant Algorithms

Since we know that ant colony optimization has successfully solved combinatorial problems, it can also be extended to solve the standard optimization problems of multimodal functions. The only problem now is to figure out how the ants will move on a d-dimensional hypersurface. For simplicity, we discuss the 2D case, which can easily be extended to higher dimensions. On a 2D landscape, ants can move in any direction, or $0° \sim 360°$, but this will cause some problems. The question is how to update the pheromone at a particular point, since there are an infinite number of points. One solution is to track the history of each ant's moves and record the locations consecutively, and the other approach is to use a moving neighborhood or window. The ants "smell" the pheromone concentration of their neighborhood at any particular location.

In addition, we can limit the number of directions the ants can move by quantizing the directions. For example, ants are only allowed to move left and right, and up and down (only four directions). We use this quantized approach here, which makes the implementation much simpler. Furthermore, the objective function or landscape can be encoded into virtual food so that ants will move to the best locations where the best food sources are. This will make the search process even more simpler. This simplified algorithm, called the *virtual ant algorithm* (VAA) and developed by Xin-She Yang and his colleagues in 2006 [40], that has been successfully applied to topological optimization problems in engineering.

15.2 Bee-Inspired Algorithms

Bee algorithms form another class of algorithms that are closely related to the ant colony optimization. Bee algorithms are inspired by the foraging behavior of honeybees. Several variants of bee algorithms have been formulated, including the honeybee algorithm (HBA), the virtual bee algorithm (VBA), the artificial bee colony (ABC) optimization, the honeybee-mating algorithm (HBMA), and others [1,19,20,29,41].

15.2.1 Honeybee Behavior

Honeybees live in constructed colonies where and they store honey they have foraged. Honeybees can communicate by pheromone and "waggle dance." For example, an alarming bee may release a chemical messenger (pheromone) to stimulate an attack response in other bees. Furthermore, when bees find a good food source and bring some nectar back to the hive, they communicate the location of the food source by performing the so-called waggle dances as a signal system [26]. Such signaling dances vary from species to species, but they typically attempt to recruit more bees using directional dancing with varying strength so as to communicate the direction and distance of the found food resource.

For multiple food sources such as flower patches, studies show that a bee colony seems to be able to allocate forager bees among different flower patches to maximize their total nectar intake. To survive the winter, a bee colony typically has to collect and store extra nectar, about 15 to 50 kg. The efficiency of nectar collection is consequently very important from an evolutionary point of view. Various algorithms can be designed if we learn from the natural behavior of bee colonies.

15.2.2 Bee Algorithms

Over the last decade or so, nature-inspired bee algorithms have started to emerge as a promising and powerful tool. It is difficult to pinpoint the exact dates when the bee algorithms were first formulated. They were developed independently by several groups of researchers over a few years.

From the literature survey, it seems that the *honeybee algorithm* (HBA) was first formulated around 2004 by Craig A. Tovey at Georgia Tech, in collaboration with Sunil Nakrani, then at Oxford University, to study a method to allocate computers among different clients and Web-hosting servers [29]. Later in 2004 and earlier 2005, Xin-She Yang at Cambridge University developed a virtual bee algorithm (VBA) to solve numerical optimization problems [41], and it can optimize both functions and discrete problems, though only functions with two parameters were given as examples.

Slightly later in 2005, Haddad and Afshar and their colleagues presented a honeybee-mating optimization (HBMO) algorithm that was subsequently applied to reservoir modelling and clustering [11]. Around the same time, D. Karaboga, in Turkey, developed an artificial bee colony (ABC) algorithm for numerical function optimization, and a comparison study was carried out by in the same group later in 2006 and 2008. These bee algorithms and their variants have shown some promising results [2,41].

The essence of bee algorithms is the communication or broadcasting ability of a bee to some neighbourhood bees so that they can "know" and follow a bee to the best source, locations, or routes to complete the optimization task. The detailed implementation will depend on the actual algorithms, and they may differ slightly and vary with different variants.

15.2.3 Honeybee Algorithm

In HBA, forager bees are allocated to different food sources (or flower patches) to maximize the total nectar intake. The colony has to "optimize" the overall efficiency of nectar collection; the allocation of the bees thus depends on many factors, such as the nectar richness and the proximity to the hive. This problem is similar to the allocation of Web-hosting servers on the Internet, which was in fact one of the first problems solved using bee-inspired algorithms by Nakrani and Tovey in 2004 [29].

Let $w_i(j)$ be the strength of the waggle dance of bee i at time step $t = j$. The probability of an observer bee following the dancing bee to forage can be determined in many ways, depending on the actual variant of algorithms. A simple way is given by

$$p_i = \frac{w_i^j}{\sum_{i=1}^{n_f} w_i^j}, \tag{15.4}$$

where n_f is the number of bees in the foraging process and t is the pseudo time or foraging expedition. The number of observer bees is $N - n_f$ when N is the total number of bees. Alternatively, we can define an exploration probability of a Gaussian type $p_e = 1 - p_i = \exp[-w_i^2/2\sigma^2]$, where σ is the volatility of the bee colony, and it controls the exploration and diversity of the foraging sites. If there is no dancing (no food found), then $w_i \to 0$, and $p_e = 1$. So, all the bees explore randomly.

In other variant algorithms, when applying to discrete problems such as job scheduling, a forager bee will perform the waggle dance with a duration $\tau = \gamma f_p$, where f_p is the profitability or the richness of the food site, and γ is a scaling factor. The profitability should be related to the objective function.

In addition, the rating of each route is ranked dynamically, and the path with the highest number of bees becomes the preferred path. For a routing problem, the probability of choosing a route between any two nodes can take the form similar to Eq. (15.1). That is,

$$p_{ij} = \frac{w_{ij}^{\alpha} d_{ij}^{\beta}}{\sum_{i,j=1}^{n} w_{ij}^{\alpha} d_{ij}^{\beta}}, \tag{15.5}$$

where $\alpha > 0$ and $\beta > 0$ are the influence parameters, w_{ij} is the dance strength along route i to j, and d_{ij} is the desirability of the same route.

HBA, similar to the ant colony algorithms, is efficient in dealing with discrete optimization problems such as routing and scheduling. In dealing with continuous optimization problems, it is not straightforward, and some modifications are needed.

15.2.4 Virtual Bee Algorithm

VBA, developed by Xin-She Yang in 2005 [41], is an optimization algorithm specially formulated for solving both discrete and continuous problems. It has some similarity to the particle swarm optimization (PSO) discussed in this book, rather than a bee algorithm. In VBA, the continuous objective function is directly encoded as virtual nectar, and the solutions (or decision variables) are the locations of the nectar. The activities such as the waggle dance strength (similar to the pheromone in the ant algorithms) are combined with the nectar concentration as the "fitness" of the solutions. For a maximization problem, the objective function can be thought of as virtual nectar, whereas for minimization, the nectar is formulated in such a way that the minimal value of the objective function corresponds to the highest nectar concentration.

For discrete problems, the objective functions such as the shorter paths are encoded and linked with the profitability of the nectar explorations, which is in turn linked with the dance strength of forager bees. In this way, VBA is similar to the HBA. However, there is a fundamental difference from other bee algorithms. That is, VBA has a broadcasting ability of the current best. The current best location is "known" to every bee, so this algorithm is more efficient. In this way, forager bees do not have to come back to the hive to tell other onlooker bees via the waggle dance, thus saving time. Similar broadcasting ability is used in PSO, especially in accelerated PSO and other swarm algorithms.

For a mixed type of problem, when the decision variables can take both discrete and continuous values, the encoding of the objective function into nectar should be carefully implemented, so it can represent the objective effectively. This is still an active area of current research.

15.2.5 Artificial Bee Colony Optimization

The ABC optimization algorithm was first developed by D. Karaboga in 2005. Since then, Karaboga and Basturk and their colleagues have systematically studied the performance of the ABC algorithm concerning unstrained optimization problems and its extension [19,20].

In the ABC algorithm, the bees in a colony are divided into three groups: employed bees (forager bees), onlooker bees (observer bees), and scouts. For each food source, there is only one employed bee. That is to say, the number of employed bees is equal to the number of food sources. The employed bee of a discarded food site is forced to become a scout searching randomly for new food sources. Employed bees share information with the onlooker bees in a hive so that onlooker bees can choose a food source to forage. Unlike the honeybee algorithm, which has two groups of bees (forager bees and observer bees), bees in ABC are more specialized.

For a given objective function $f(\boldsymbol{x})$, it can be encoded as $F(\boldsymbol{x})$ to represent the amount of nectar at location $\boldsymbol{x}$. Thus the probability P_i of an onlooker bee choosing to go to the preferred food source at $\boldsymbol{x}_i$ can be defined by $P_i = F(\boldsymbol{x}_i)/\sum_{j=1}^{S} F(\boldsymbol{x}_j)$, where S is the number of food sources.

At a particular food source, the intake efficiency is determined by F/T, where F is the amount of nectar and T is the time spent at the food source. If a food source is tried/foraged at a given number of explorations without improvement, then it is abandoned, and the bee at this location will move on randomly to explore new locations.

Various applications have been carried out in the last few years, including combinatorial optimization, job scheduling, Web-hosting allocation, and engineering design optimization.

15.3 Harmony Search

HS was first developed by Z. W. Geem et al. in 2001 [15,16]. Since then it has been applied to solve many optimization problems, including function optimization, water distribution network, groundwater modeling, energy-saving dispatch, structural design, vehicle routing, and others. The possibility of combining HS with other algorithms such as PSO and GA has also been investigated.

15.3.1 Harmonics and Frequencies

HS is a music-inspired metaheuristic optimization algorithm. It is inspired by the observation that the aim of music is to search for a perfect state of harmony. This harmony in music is analogous to finding the optimality in an optimization process. The search process in optimization can be compared to a musician's improvisation process. This perfectly pleasing harmony is determined by the audio aesthetic standard.

The aesthetic quality of a musical instrument is essentially determined by its pitch (or frequency), timbre (or sound quality), and amplitude (or loudness). Timbre is largely determined by the harmonic content, which is in turn determined by the waveforms or modulations of the sound signal. However, the harmonics it can generate will largely depend on the pitch or frequency range of the particular instrument.

Different notes have different frequencies. For example, the note A above middle C (or standard concert A4) has a fundamental frequency of $f_0 = 440$ Hz. The speed of sound in dry air is about $v = 331 + 0.6T$ m/s, where T is the temperature in degrees Celsius near 0 °C. So, at room temperature $T = 20$ °C, and the A4 note has a wavelength $\lambda = v/f_0 \approx 0.7795$ m . When we adjust the pitch, we are in fact trying to change the frequency. In music theory, pitch p in Musical Instrument Digital Interface (MID) is often represented as a numerical scale (a linear pitch space) using the following formula:

$$p = 69 + 12 \log_2 \left(\frac{f}{440 \text{ Hz}} \right) \tag{15.6}$$

or

$$f = 440 \times 2^{(p-69)/12}, \tag{15.7}$$

Figure 15.1 Harmony of two notes with a frequency ratio of 2:3 and their waveform.

Figure 15.2 Random music notes.

which means that the A4 note has a pitch number 69. On this scale, octaves correspond to size 12 and semitone corresponds to size 1. Furthermore, the ratio of frequencies of two notes that are an octave apart is 2:1. Thus, the frequency of a note is doubled (or halved) when it raised (or lowered) an octave. For example, A2 has a frequency of 110 Hz, whereas A5 has a frequency of 880 Hz.

The measurement of harmony when different pitches occur simultaneously, like any aesthetic quality, is somewhat subjective. However, it is possible to use some standard estimation for harmony. The frequency ratio, pioneered by ancient Greek mathematician Pythagoras, is a good method for such estimations. For example, the octave with a ratio of 1:2 sounds pleasant when played together, and so are the notes with a ratio of 2:3 (see Figure 15.1). However, it is unlikely for any random notes such as those shown in Figure 15.2 to produce a pleasant harmony.

15.3.2 Harmony Search

HS can be explained in more detail with the aid of a discussion of a musician's improvisation process [15]. When a musician is improvising, he or she has three possible choices: (1) play any famous piece of music (a series of pitches in harmony) exactly from memory; (2) play something similar to a known piece (thus adjusting the pitch slightly); or (3) compose new or random notes. If we formalize these three options for optimization, we have three corresponding components: usage of harmony memory, pitch adjusting, and randomization.

The use of harmony memory is important because it is similar to choosing the best-fit individuals in genetic algorithms. This will ensure that the best harmonies will be carried over to the new harmony memory. To use this memory more effectively, we can assign a parameter $r_{\text{accept}} \in [0, 1]$, called harmony memory accepting or considering rate. If this rate is too low, only a few best harmonies are selected, and it may converge too slowly. If this rate is extremely high (near 1), almost all the harmonies are used in the harmony memory, but then other harmonies are not explored well, leading to potentially wrong solutions. Therefore, typically, $r_{\text{accept}} = 0.7 \sim 0.95$.

To adjust the pitch slightly in the second component, we have to use a method such that it can adjust the frequency efficiently. In theory, pitch can be adjusted linearly or nonlinearly, but in practice, linear adjustment is used. If x_{old} is the current solution (or pitch), the new solution (pitch) $\boldsymbol{x}_{\text{new}}$ is generated by

$$\boldsymbol{x}_{\text{new}} = \boldsymbol{x}_{\text{old}} + b_p\,(2\,\texttt{rand} - 1), \tag{15.8}$$

where `rand` is a random number drawn from a uniform distribution [0, 1]. Here b_p is the bandwidth, which controls the local range of pitch adjustment. In fact, we can see that the pitch adjustment (15.8) is a random walk.

Pitch adjustment is similar to the mutation operator in genetic algorithms. We can assign a pitch-adjusting rate (r_{pa}) to control the degree of the adjustment. If r_{pa} is too low, there is rarely any change. If it is too high, the algorithm may not converge at all. Thus, we usually use $r_{pa} = 0.1 \sim 0.5$ in most simulations.

The third component is the randomization, which is to increase the diversity of the solutions. Although adjusting pitch has a similar role, it is limited to certain local pitch adjustment and thus corresponds to a local search. The use of randomization can drive the system further, to explore various regions with a high solution diversity so as to increase the probability of finding the global optimality [42]. So, we have

$$p_a = p_{\text{lowerlimit}} + p_{\text{range}} * \texttt{rand}, \tag{15.9}$$

where $p_{\text{range}} = p_{\text{upperlimit}} - p_{\text{lowerlimit}}$. Here `rand` is a random number generator in the range of 0 and 1.

The three components in HS can be summarized as the pseudo code shown in Figure 15.3, where we can see that the probability of true randomization is

$$P_{\text{random}} = 1 - r_{\text{accept}} \tag{15.10}$$

```
Harmony Search
Objective function f(x),  x = (x_1, ..., x_d)^T
Generate initial harmonics (real number arrays)
Define pitch adjusting rate (r_pa) and pitch limits
Define harmony memory accepting rate (r_accept)
while (t <Max number of iterations)
   Generate new harmonics by accepting best harmonics
   Adjust pitch to get new harmonics (solutions)
   if (rand> r_accept),
      Choose an existing harmonic randomly
   else if (rand> r_pa),
      Adjust the pitch randomly within a bandwidth (15.8)
   else
      Generate new harmonics via randomization (15.9)
   end if
   Accept the new harmonics (solutions) if better
end while
Find the current best estimates
```

Figure 15.3 Pseudo code of a harmony search.

and the actual probability of pitch adjusting is

$$P_{\text{pitch}} = r_{\text{accept}} * r_{\text{pa}}. \tag{15.11}$$

HS has been used in many applications, and a good summary can be found in Geem's book [16].

15.4 Hybrid Algorithms

Hybrid algorithms have been developed by combining two or more algorithms to improve or enhance overall search efficiency. Researchers often try to use the advantages of individual algorithms for the common good; at least that is the intention in principle. In practice, whether a hybrid can really achieve better performance is another matter, and finding ways to combine different algorithms to develop new algorithms is still an open problem.

15.4.1 Other Algorithms

There are more than 40 other algorithms in the literature as reviewed in recent surveys [3,12,13,44], and more algorithms are appearing. Therefore, we do not attempt to provide a full list of algorithms here. Rather, we provide a subset of these algorithms so that readers can see their diversity. Here we put these other algorithms into two broad categories: swarm intelligence (SI)-based and non SI-based.

SI-based algorithms that are not covered in this book:

- Cat swarm (Chu et al. [4])
- Dolphin echolocation (Kaveh and Farhoudi [21])
- Eagle strategy (Yang and Deb [43])
- Egyptian vulture (Sur et al. [36])
- Fish swarm/school (Li et al. [24])
- Great salmon run (Mozaffari [27])
- Group search optimizer (He et al. [18])
- Glowworm swarm optimization (Krishnanand and Ghose [23])
- Krill Herd (Gandomi and Alavi [14])
- Monkey search (Mucherino and Seref [28])
- Shuffled frog-leaping algorithm (Eusuff and Lansey [10])
- Wolf search (Tang et al. [38])

Non-SI-based algorithms and others that are not covered in this book:

- Bacterial foraging algorithm (Passino [31])
- Big bang, big crunch (Erol and Eksin [8])
- Biogeography-based optimization (Simon [35])
- Black-hole algorithm (Hatamlou [17])
- Charged system search (Kaveh and Talatahari [22])
- Differential search algorithm (Civicioglu [5])
- Ecology-inspired evolutionary algorithm (Parpinelli and Lopes [30])

- Galaxy-based search algorithm (Shah-Hosseini [33])
- Gravitational search (Rashedi et al. [32])
- Intelligent water drop (Shah-Hosseini [34])
- Invasive weed optimization (Mehrabian and Lucas [25])
- Self-propelled particles (Vicsek [39])
- Spiral optimization (Tamura and Yasuda [37])
- Water-cycle algorithm (Eskandar et al. [9])

It is worth pointing out that some algorithms may perform well and provide very competitive results, but other algorithms are not so efficient. Overall, mixed results and performance exist in the literature.

It seems that there is a serious problem in the research community in that some research activities have gone astray, to a certain degree. We urge that researchers to place more emphasis on the following important topics and challenging issues:

- Mathematical analyses, such as convergence, stability, and time complexity of metaheursitic algorithms, so as to gain key insight
- Performance comparisons and statistical measures of different algorithms
- Parameter tuning and control of metaheuristic algorithms so as to maximize their performance
- Applicability and scalability of metaheuristic algorithms in large-scale, real-world applications
- Development of truly intelligent, adaptive, and self-evolving optimization algorithms

15.4.2 Ways to Hybridize

By and large, hybrid algorithms are formulated by trial and error. Therefore, hybridization itself is an evolutionary metaheuristic approach. A naïve way of hybridization is to randomly select two algorithms from a list of algorithms (both conventional and new) to form a new one. For example, if there is a list of algorithms such as BA, PSO, DE, ACO, ABC, CS, HS, FA, FPA, SA, and hill climbing, one can formulate hybrid algorithms such as ABC-HS, DE-PSO, SA-PSO, and many others. But the performance of a hybrid can be mixed; some can improve, but some may become worse if such a naïve approach is used.

Developing better hybrids requires insight and understanding of the basic algorithm components. However, this largely relies on the expertise and experience of an algorithm developer. If we can analyze the algorithms as we have done in the first two chapters of this book, we can identify the key algorithm operators such as crossover, mutation, elitism, random walks, Lévy flights, chaos, and gradients. Then it is possible to enhance an algorithm by adding one component or more. So, some researchers produce PSO with chaos, genetic algorithms with chaos, and so on and so forth.

Look at these basic components more closely. We can separate them into four categories:

- *Genetic operators.* Crossover or recombination, mutation, selection, or elitism.
- *Randomization.* Random walks, Lévy flights, probability distributions (such as Gaussian).

- *Chaotic.* Chaos, iterative maps.
- *Attraction and repulsion.* Attraction between agents based on distance or similarity, including light intensity, attractiveness, gravity, electromagnetism, and others. Repulsion based on dissimilarity, predator, opposition, and diversity/variance.

Each category can have a different role in terms of exploration and exploitation capability, and effectiveness also varies greatly among categories. In principle, we can select one component from two or more different categories based on their roles or properties to form a hybrid with combined components. This may be more likely to produce better algorithms than a random or blind combination of any two different algorithms.

15.5 Final Remarks

Nature has provided a vast source of inspiration, especially biological systems. This again can be used for developing new algorithms, as we see from the references listed at the end of each chapter in this book.

Obviously, there are other ways to form and develop new hybrid algorithms. However, it is worth pointing out that we are not encouraging researchers in the optimization community to randomly develop new algorithms. It should not be encouraged to produce any grass algorithm, dolphin algorithm, ocean current algorithm, dove navigation algorithm, human swarm algorithm, or chaotic grass algorithm, chaotic/turbulent flow algorithm, dolphin attraction algorithm, or artificial grass algorithm.

As we have highlighted in this book, truly novel algorithms should provide new ways of thinking, truly efficient new tools, and greater insight into the working mechanisms of efficient optimization methodologies. More important, new algorithms should allow sufficient simplicity, flexibility, and high efficiency so that they can solve a wider range of large-scale, real-world problems in science, engineering, and industry. Important challenges such as theoretical analysis of nature-inspired algorithms, parameter tuning, and parameter control should be addressed. All these should be the main driving force for researchers to develop new techniques and applications in the future in this exciting area.

References

[1] Afshar A, Haddad OB, Marino MA, Adams BJ. Honey-bee mating optimization (HBMO) algorithm for optimal reservoir operation. J Franklin Institute 2007;344(4):452–62.
[2] Bonabeau E, Dorigo M, Theraulaz G. Swarm intelligence: from natural to artificial systems. Oxford, UK: Oxford University Press; 1999.
[3] Binitha S, Sathya SS. A survey of bio-inspired optimization algorithms. Int J Soft Comput Eng 2012;2(2):137–51.
[4] Chu SA, Tsai PW, Pan JS. Cat swarm optimization. Lect Notes Artif Intell (LNAI) 2006;4099(1):854–8.
[5] Civicioglu P. Transforming geocentric cartesian coordinates to geodetic coordinates by using differential search algorithm. Comput Geosci 2012;46(1):229–47.

[6] Dorigo M. Optimization, Learning and Natural Algorithms [Ph.D. thesis]. Italy: Politecnico di Milano; 1992.
[7] Dorigo M, Stützle T. Ant colony optimization. Cambridge, MA, USA: MIT Press; 2004.
[8] Erol OK, Eksin I. A new optimization method: big bang, big crunch. Adv Eng Software 2006;37(2):106–11.
[9] Eskandar H, Sadollah A, Bahreininejad A, Hamdi M. Water cycle algorithm—a novel metaheuristic optimization method for solving constrained engineering optimization problems. Comput Struct 2012;110–111(1):151–66.
[10] Eusuff MM, Lansey KE. Optimization of water distribution network design using the shuffled frog leaping algorithm. J Water Res Planning Manage 2003;129(3):210–25.
[11] Fathian M, Amiri B, Maroosi A. Application of honey-bee mating optimization algorithm on clustering. Appl Math Comput 2007;190(2):1502–13.
[12] Fister Jr I, Fister D, Yang XS. A hybrid bat algorithm. Elektrotehniski Vestnik 2013;80(1–2):1–7.
[13] Fister Jr I, Yang XS, Fister I, Brest J, Fister D. A brief review of nature-inspired algorithms for optimization. Elektrotehniski Vestnik in press; 80(3).
[14] Gandomi AH, Alavi AH. Krill herd: a new bio-inspired optimization algorithm. Commun Nonlinear Sci Numer Simul 2012;17(12):4831–45.
[15] Geem ZW, Kim JH, Loganathan GV. A new heuristic optimization algorithm: harmony search. Simulation 2001;76(1):60–8.
[16] Geem ZW. Music-inspired harmony search algorithm: theory and applications. Berlin, Germany: Springer; 2009.
[17] Hatamlou A. Black hole: a new heuristic optimization approach for data clustering. Inform Sci 2012;222(1):175–84.
[18] He S, Wu QH, Saunders JR. Group search optimizer: an optimization algorithm inspired by animal searching behavior. IEEE Trans Evol Comput 2009;13(5):973–90.
[19] Karaboga D. An idea based on honey bee swarm for numerical optimization technical report TR06. Turkey: Erciyes University; 2005.
[20] Karaboga D, Basturk B. On the performance of artificial bee colony (ABC) algorithm. Appl Soft Comput 2008;8(1):687–97.
[21] Kaveh A, Farhoudi N. A new optimization method: dolphin echolocation. Adv Eng Software 2013;59(1):53–70.
[22] Kaveh A, Talatahari S. A novel heuristic optimization method: charged system search. Acta Mechanica 2010;213(3–4):267–89.
[23] Krishnanand KN, Ghose D. Glowworm swarm optimisation: a new method for optimising multi-modal functions. Int J Comput Intell Stud 2009;1(1):93–119.
[24] Li XL, Shao ZJ, Qian JX. Optimizing method based on autonomous animats: fish-swarm algorithm. Xitong Gongcheng Lilun yu Shijian/Syst Eng Theor Pract 2002;22(11):32–9.
[25] Mehrabian AR, Lucas C. A novel numerical optimization algorithm inspired from weed colonization. Ecol Inform 2006;1(4):355–66.
[26] Moritz RF, Southwick E. Bees as superorganisms. Berlin, Germany: Springer; 1992.
[27] Mozaffari A, Fathi A, Behzadipour S. The great salmon run: a novel bio-inspired algorithm for artificial system design and optimisation. Int J Bio-Inspired Comput 2012;4(5):286–301.
[28] Mucherino A, Onur Seref O. Monkey search: a novel metaheuristic search for global optimization. Data mining, systems analysis and optimization in biomedicine, 953; 2007. p. 162–73.
[29] Nakrani S, Tovey C. On honey bees and dynamic server allocation in Internet hosting centers. Adapt Behav 2004;12(2):223–40.

[30] Parpinelli RS, Lopes HS. An eco-inspired evolutionary algorithm applied to numerical optimization. In: The third world congress on nature and biologically inspired computing (NaBIC 2011); 2011. p. 466–71.
[31] Passino KM. Biomimicry of bacterial foraging for distributed optimization and control. IEEE Contr Syst 2002;22(3):52–67.
[32] Rashedi E, Hossein Nezamabadi-Pour H, Saryazdi S. GSA: a gravitational search algorithm. Inform Sci 2009;179(13):2232–48.
[33] Shah-Hosseini H. Principal components analysis by the galaxy-based search algorithm: a novel metaheuristic for continuous optimisation. Int J Comput Sci Eng 2011;6(1):132–40.
[34] Shah-Hosseini H. Problem solving by intelligent water drops. In: 2007 IEEE congress on evolutionary computation; 2007. p. 3226–31.
[35] Simon D. Biogeography-based optimization. IEEE Trans Evol Comput 2008;12(6):702–13.
[36] Sur C, Sharma S, Shukla A. Egyptian vulture optimization algorithm—a new nature inspired metaheuristics for knapsack problem. In: The ninth international conference on computing and information technology (IC2IT2013). Berlin, Germany: Springer; 2013. p. 227–37.
[37] Tamura K, Yasuda K. Spiral dynamics inspired optimization. J Adv Comput Intell Intell Inform 2011;15(8):1116–22.
[38] Tang R, Fong S, Yang XS, Deb S. Wolf search algorithm with ephemeral memory. In: Seventh international conference on digital information management (ICDIM 2012); 2012. p. 165–72.
[39] Vicsek T, Czirók A, Ben-Jacob E, Cohen I, Shochet O. Novel type of phase transition in a system of self-driven particles. Phys Rev Lett 1995;75(6):1226–9.
[40] Yang XS, Lees JM, Morley CT. Application of virtual ant algorithms in the optimization of CFRP shear strengthened precracked structures. Lect Notes Comput Sci 2006;3991(1):834–7.
[41] Yang XS. Engineering optimization via nature-inspired virtual bee algorithms, IWINAC 2005. Lect Notes Comput Sci 2005;3562(1):317–23.
[42] Yang XS. Harmony search as a metaheuristic algorithm. In: Geem ZW, editor. Music-inspired harmony search: theory and applications. Springer; 2009. p. 1–14.
[43] Yang XS, Deb S. Eagle strategy using Lévy walk and firefly algorithms for stochastic optimization. In: Nature inspired cooperative strategies for optimization (NICSO2010). Berlin, Germany: Springer; 2010. p. 101–11.
[44] Yang XS, Cui ZH, Xiao RB, Gandomi AH, Karamanoglu M. Swarm intelligence and bio-inspired computation: theory and applications. Elsevier: Waltham, MA, USA; 2013.

A Test Function Benchmarks for Global Optimization

Though there are many test functions in the literature, there is no agreed-on list of standard test functions. Various attempts to summarize these functions have been carried out Readers can find more details in [1,3,4,12,6–11], and some online collections also exist and relatively comprehensive [5,2,10]. The current collection in this appendix is largely based on the comprehensive review by Jamil and Yang [12].

The diversity of various functions and their properties can be classified according to their characteristics such as modality, separability, basins and valleys, and dimensionality. For details, refer to Floudas et al. [4] and Jamil and Yang [12]. Here we provide a list of 100 well-selected test functions for unconstrained global optimization.

The parameter D is the dimensionality of the test function under consideration; $f(\boldsymbol{x}^*)$ is the optimal objective value that corresponds to the optimal solution $\boldsymbol{x}^*$.

1. **Ackley's Function**

$$f(\boldsymbol{x}) = -20e^{-0.02\sqrt{\frac{1}{D}\sum_{i=1}^{D} x_i^2}} - e^{\frac{1}{D}\sum_{i=1}^{D}\cos(2\pi x_i)} + 20 + e$$

subject to $-35 \leq x_i \leq 35$. The global minimum is located at origin $\boldsymbol{x}^* = (0, \ldots, 0)$ with $f(\boldsymbol{x}^*) = 0$.

2. **Alpine Function**

$$f(\boldsymbol{x}) = \sum_{i=1}^{D} \left| x_i \sin(x_i) + 0.1 x_i \right|$$

subject to $-10 \leq x_i \leq 10$. The global minimum is located at origin $\boldsymbol{x}^* = (0, \ldots, 0)$ with $f(\boldsymbol{x}^*) = 0$.

3. **Bartels Conn Function**

$$f(\boldsymbol{x}) = \left| x_1^2 + x_2^2 + x_1 x_2 \right| + \left| \sin(x_1) \right| + \left| \cos(x_2) \right|$$

subject to $-500 \leq x_i \leq 500$. The global minimum is located at $\boldsymbol{x}^* = (0, 0)$ with $f(\boldsymbol{x}^*) = 1$.

4. **Beale Function**

$$f(\boldsymbol{x}) = (1.5 - x_1 + x_1 x_2)^2 + \left(2.25 - x_1 + x_1 x_2^2\right)^2 + \left(2.625 - x_1 + x_1 x_2^3\right)^2$$

Nature-Inspired Optimization Algorithms. http://dx.doi.org/10.1016/B978-0-12-416743-8.00021-X

subject to $-4.5 \leq x_i \leq 4.5$. The global minimum is located at $\boldsymbol{x}^* = (3, 0.5)$ with $f(\boldsymbol{x}^*) = 0$.

5. **Bird Function**

$$f(\boldsymbol{x}) = \sin(x_1)e^{(1-\cos(x_2))^2} + \cos(x_2)e^{(1-\sin(x_1))^2} + (x_1 - x_2)^2$$

subject to $-2\pi \leq x_i \leq 2\pi$. Two global minima are located at $\boldsymbol{x}^* = (4.70104, 3.15294)$ and $(-1.58214, -3.13024)$ with $f(\boldsymbol{x}^*) = -106.764537$.

6. **Bohachevsky Function**

$$f(\boldsymbol{x}) = x_1^2 + 2x_2^2 - 0.3\cos(3\pi x_1) - 0.4\cos(4\pi x_2) + 0.7$$

subject to $-100 \leq x_i \leq 100$. The global minimum is located at $\boldsymbol{x}^* = (0, 0)$ with $f(\boldsymbol{x}^*) = 0$.

7. **Booth Function**

$$f(\boldsymbol{x}) = (x_1 + 2x_2 - 7)^2 + (2x_1 + x_2 - 5)^2$$

subject to $-10 \leq x_i \leq 10$. The global minimum is located at $\boldsymbol{x}^* = (1, 3)$ with $f(\boldsymbol{x}^*) = 0$.

8. **Box-Betts Quadratic Sum Function**

$$f(\boldsymbol{x}) = \sum_{i=0}^{D-1} g(x_i)^2,$$

$$g(x) = e^{-0.1(i+1)x_1} - e^{-0.1(i+1)x_2} - e^{[(-0.1(i+1))-e^{-(i+1)}]x_3}$$

subject to $0.9 \leq x_1 \leq 1.2, 9 \leq x_2 \leq 11.2, 0.9 \leq x_2 \leq 1.2$. The global minimum is located at $\boldsymbol{x}^* = (1, 10, 1)$ with $f(\boldsymbol{x}^*) = 0$.

9. **Branin RCOS Function**

$$f(\boldsymbol{x}) = \left(x_2 - \frac{5.1x_1^2}{4\pi^2} + \frac{5x_1}{\pi} - 6\right)^2 + 10\left(1 - \frac{1}{8\pi}\right)\cos(x_1) + 10$$

with domain $-5 \leq x_1 \leq 10, 0 \leq x_1 \leq 15$. It has three global minima at $\boldsymbol{x}^* = (\{-\pi, 12.275\}, \{\pi, 2.275\}, \{3\pi, 2.425\})$ with $f(\boldsymbol{x}^*) = 0.3978873$.

10. **Brent Function**

$$f(\boldsymbol{x}) = (x_1 + 10)^2 + (x_2 + 10)^2 + e^{-x_1^2 - x_2^2} \tag{A.1}$$

with domain $-10 \leq x_i \leq 10$. The global minimum is located at $\boldsymbol{x}^* = (0, 0)$ with $f(\boldsymbol{x}^*) = 0$.

11. **Brown Function**

$$f(\boldsymbol{x}) = \sum_{i=1}^{D-1} \left(x_i^2\right)^{(x_{i+1}^2+1)} + \left(x_{i+1}^2\right)^{(x_i^2+1)}$$

subject to $-1 \le x_i \le 4$. The global minimum is located at $\boldsymbol{x}^* = (0, \ldots, 0)$ with $f(\boldsymbol{x}^*) = 0$.

12. **Bukin Function**

$$f(\boldsymbol{x}) = 100\left(x_2 - 0.01x_1^2 + 1\right) + 0.01(x_1 + 10)^2$$

subject to $-15 \le x_1 \le -5$ and $-3 \le x_2 \le -3$. The global minimum is located at $\boldsymbol{x}^* = (-10, 0)$ with $f(\boldsymbol{x}^*) = 0$.

13. **Camel Function – Three Humps**

$$f(\boldsymbol{x}) = 2x_1^2 - 1.05x_1^4 + x_1^6/6 + x_1x_2 + x_2^2$$

subject to $-5 \le x_i \le 5$. The global minimum is located at $\boldsymbol{x}^* = (0, 0)$ with $f(\boldsymbol{x}^*) = 0$.

14. **Camel Function – Six Humps**

$$f(\boldsymbol{x}) = \left(4 - 2.1x_1^2 + \frac{x_1^4}{3}\right)x_1^2 + x_1x_2 + \left(4x_2^2 - 4\right)x_2^2$$

subject to $-5 \le x_i \le 5$. The two global minima are located at $\boldsymbol{x}^* = f(\{-0.0898, 0.7126\}, \{0.0898, -0.7126, 0\})$ with $f(\boldsymbol{x}^*) = -1.0316$.

15. **Chichinadze Function**

$$f(\boldsymbol{x}) = x_1^2 - 12x_1 + 11 + 10\cos(\pi x_1/2) + 8\sin(5\pi x_1/2) \\ - (1/5)^{0.5}\exp\left(-0.5(x_2 - 0.5)^2\right)$$

subject to $-30 \le x_i \le 30$. The global minimum is located at $\boldsymbol{x}^* = (5.90133, 0.5)$ with $f(\boldsymbol{x}^*) = -43.3159$.

16. **Cola Function**

The 17-dimensional function computes indirectly the formula (D, u) by setting $x_0 = y_0, x_1 = u_0, x_i = u_{2(i-2)}, y_i = u_{2(i-2)+1}$:

$$f(\boldsymbol{x}) = h(x, y) = \sum_{j<i} (r_{i,j} - d_{i,j})^2$$

where $r_{i,j}$ is given by

$$r_{i,j} = [(x_i - x_j)^2 + (y_i - y_j)^2]^{1/2}$$

and d is a symmetric matrix given by

$$\mathbf{d} = [d_{ij}] = \begin{pmatrix} 1.27 \\ 1.69 & 1.43 \\ 2.04 & 2.35 & 2.43 \\ 3.09 & 3.18 & 3.26 & 2.85 \\ 3.20 & 3.22 & 3.27 & 2.88 & 1.55 \\ 2.86 & 2.56 & 2.58 & 2.59 & 3.12 & 3.06 \\ 3.17 & 3.18 & 3.18 & 3.12 & 1.31 & 1.64 & 3.00 \\ 3.21 & 3.18 & 3.18 & 3.17 & 1.70 & 1.36 & 2.95 & 1.32 \\ 2.38 & 2.31 & 2.42 & 1.94 & 2.85 & 2.81 & 2.56 & 2.91 & 2.97 \end{pmatrix}$$

This function has bounds $0 \leq x_0 \leq 4$ and $-4 \leq x_i \leq 4$ for $i = 1 \ldots D-1$. It has a global minimum of $f(\boldsymbol{x}^*) = 11.7464$.

17. **Colville Function**

$$f(\boldsymbol{x}) = 100(x_1 - x_2^2)^2 + (1 - x_1)^2 + 90(x_4 - x_3^2)^2 + (1 - x_3)^2 \\ + 10.1((x_2 - 1)^2 + (x_4 - 1)^2) + 19.8(x_2 - 1)(x_4 - 1)$$

subject to $-10 \leq x_i \leq 10$. The global minimum is located at $\boldsymbol{x}^* = (1, \ldots, 1)$ with $f(\boldsymbol{x}^*) = 0$.

18. **Corana Function**

$$f(\boldsymbol{x}) = \begin{cases} 0.15\left(z_i - 0.05\text{sgn}(z_i)^2\right) d_i & \text{if } |v_i| < A \\ d_i x_i^2 & \text{otherwise} \end{cases}$$

where

$$v_i = |x_i - z_i|, \quad A = 0.05$$
$$z_i = 0.2\left\lfloor \left|\frac{x_i}{0.2}\right| + 0.49999 \right\rfloor \text{sgn}\left(x_i\right)$$
$$d_i = (1, 1000, 10, 100) \tag{A.2}$$

subject to $-500 \leq x_i \leq 500$. The global minimum is located at $\boldsymbol{x}^* = (0, 0, 0, 0)$ with $f(\boldsymbol{x}^*) = 0$.

19. **Cosine Mixture Function**

$$f(\boldsymbol{x}) = -0.1 \sum_{i=1}^{D} \cos(5\pi x_i) - \sum_{i=1}^{D} x_i^2$$

subject to $-1 \leq x_i \leq 1$. The global minimum is located at $\boldsymbol{x}^* = (0, 0)$, $f(\boldsymbol{x}^*) = 0.2$ for $D = 2$.

20. Csendes Function

$$f(\mathbf{x}) = \sum_{i=1}^{D} x_i^6 \left(2 + \sin \frac{1}{x_i}\right)$$

subject to $-1 \le x_i \le 1$. The global minimum is located at $\mathbf{x}^* = (0, \ldots, 0)$ with $f(\mathbf{x}^*) = 0$.

21. Cube Function

$$f(\mathbf{x}) = 100\left(x_2 - x_1^3\right)^2 + (1 - x_1)^2$$

subject to $-10 \le x_i \le 10$. The global minimum is located at $\mathbf{x}^* = (-1, 1)$ with $f(\mathbf{x}^*) = 0$.

22. Damavandi Function

$$f(\mathbf{x}) = \left[1 - \left|\frac{\sin[\pi(x_1 - 2)]\sin[\pi(x_2 - 2)]}{\pi^2(x_1 - 2)(x_2 - 2)}\right|^5\right] \left[2 + (x_1 - 7)^2 + 2(x_2 - 7)^2\right]$$

subject to $0 \le x_i \le 14$. The global minimum is located at $\mathbf{x}^* = (2, 2)$ with $f(\mathbf{x}^*) = 0$.

23. Deb Function

$$f(\mathbf{x}) = -\frac{1}{D}\sum_{i=1}^{D} \sin^6(5\pi x_i)$$

subject to $-1 \le x_i \le 1$. The number of global minima is 5^D that are evenly spaced in the function landscape.

24. Deckkers-Aarts Function

$$f(\mathbf{x}) = 10^5 x_1^2 + x_2^2 - \left(x_1^2 + x_2^2\right)^2 + 10^{-5}\left(x_1^2 + x_2^2\right)^4$$

subject to $-20 \le x_i \le 20$. The two global minima are located at $\mathbf{x}^* = (0, \pm 15)$ with $f(\mathbf{x}^*) = -24777$.

25. Dixon and Price Function

$$f(\mathbf{x}) = (x_1 - 1)^2 + \sum_{i=2}^{D} i\left(2x_i^2 - x_{i-1}\right)^2$$

subject to $-10 \le x_i \le 10$. The global minimum are located at $\mathbf{x}^* = \left[2^{(\frac{2^i - 2}{2^i})}, i = 1, \ldots, D\right]$ with $f(\mathbf{x}^*) = 0$.

26. **Dolan Function**

$$f(\boldsymbol{x}) = (x_1 + 1.7x_2)\sin(x_1) - 1.5x_3 - 0.1x_4\cos(x_4 + x_5 - x_1) + 0.2x_5^2 - x_2 - 1$$

subject to $-100 \leq x_i \leq 100$. The global minimum is $f(\boldsymbol{x}^*) = 0$.

27. **Easom Function**

$$f(\boldsymbol{x}) = -\cos(x_1)\cos(x_2)\exp[-(x_1 - \pi)^2 - (x_2 - \pi)^2]$$

subject to $-100 \leq x_i \leq 100$. The global minimum is located at $\boldsymbol{x}^* = (\pi, \pi)$ with $f(\boldsymbol{x}^*) = -1$.

28. **Egg Crate Function**

$$f(\boldsymbol{x}) = x_1^2 + x_2^2 + 25(\sin^2(x_1) + \sin^2(x_2))$$

subject to $-5 \leq x_i \leq 5$. The global minimum is located at $\boldsymbol{x}^* = (0, 0)$ with $f(\boldsymbol{x}^*) = 0$.

29. **Egg Holder Function**

$$f(\boldsymbol{x}) = \sum_{i=1}^{m-1} \left[-(x_{i+1} + 47)\sin\sqrt{|x_{i+1} + x_i/2 + 47|} - x_i \sin\sqrt{|x_i - (x_{i+1} + 47)|} \right]$$

subject to $-512 \leq x_i \leq 512$. The global minimum is located at $\boldsymbol{x}^* = (512, 404.2319)$ with $f(\boldsymbol{x}^*) \approx 959.64$.

30. **Exponential Function**

$$f(\boldsymbol{x}) = -\exp\left(-0.5 \sum_{i=1}^{D} x_i^2\right)$$

subject to $-1 \leq x_i \leq 1$. The global minimum is located at $\boldsymbol{x} = (0, \ldots, 0)$ with $f(\boldsymbol{x}^*) = 1$.

31. **Goldstein Price Function**

$$f(\boldsymbol{x}) = [1 + (x_1 + x_2 + 1)^2(19 - 14x_1 + 3x_1^2 - 14x_2 + 6x_1x_2 + 3x_2^2)] \times [30 + (2x_1 - 3x_2)^2 (18 - 32x_1 + 12x_1^2 + 48x_2 - 36x_1x_2 + 27x_2^2)]$$

subject to $-2 \leq x_i \leq 2$. The global minimum is located at $\boldsymbol{x}^* = (0, -1)$ with $f(\boldsymbol{x}^*) = 3$.

32. Griewank Function

$$f(\mathbf{x}) = \sum_{i=1}^{D} \frac{x_i^2}{4000} - \prod \cos\left(\frac{x_i}{\sqrt{i}}\right) + 1$$

subject to $-100 \le x_i \le 100$. The global minimum is located at $\mathbf{x}^* = (0, \dots, 0)$ with $f(\mathbf{x}^*) = 0$.

33. Gulf Research Function

$$f(\mathbf{x}) = \sum_{i=1}^{99} \left[\exp\left(- \frac{\left(u_i - x_2\right)^{x_3}}{x_i} \right) - 0.01i \right]^2$$

where $u_i = 25 + [-50 \ln (0.01i)]^{1/1.5}$ subject to $0.1 \le x_1 \le 100$, $0 \le x_2 \le 25.6$ and $0 \le x_1 \le 5$. The global minimum is located at $\mathbf{x}^* = (50, 25, 1.5)$ with $f(\mathbf{x}^*) = 0$.

34. Hansen Function

$$f(\mathbf{x}) = \sum_{i}^{4} (i + 1)\cos(ix_1 + i + 1)$$
$$\sum_{j=0}^{4} (j + 1)\cos((j + 2)x_2 + j + 1)$$

subject to $-10 \le x_i \le 10$. The multiple global minima are located at

$$\begin{aligned} \mathbf{x}^* = (&\{-7.589893, -7.708314\}, \{-7.589893, -1.425128\}, \\ &\{-7.589893, 4.858057\}, \{-1.306708, -7.708314\}, \\ &\{-1.306708, 4.858057\}, \{4.976478, 4.858057\}. \\ &\{4.976478, -1.425128\}, \{4.976478, -7.708314\}), \end{aligned}$$

35. Helical Valley

$$f(\mathbf{x}) = 100 \left[(x_2 - 10\theta)^2 + \left(\sqrt{x_1^2 + x_2^2} - 1 \right) \right] + x_3^2,$$

where

$$\theta = \begin{cases} \frac{1}{2\pi} \tan^{-1}\left(\frac{x_1}{x_2}\right), & \text{if } x_1 \ge 0, \\ \frac{1}{2\pi} \tan^{-1}\left(\frac{x_1}{x_2} + 0.5\right), & \text{if } x_1 < 0, \end{cases}$$

subject to $-10 \le x_i \le 10$. The global minimum is located at $\mathbf{x}^* = (1, 0, 0)$ with $f(\mathbf{x}^*) = 0$.

36. Himmelblau Function

$$f(\boldsymbol{x}) = \left(x_1^2 + x_2 - 11\right)^2 + \left(x_1 + x_2^2 - 7\right)^2$$

subject to $-5 \le x_i \le 5$. The global minimum is located at $\boldsymbol{x}^* = f(3, 2)$ with $f(\boldsymbol{x}^*) = 0$.

37. Hosaki Function

$$f(\boldsymbol{x}) = \left(1 - 8x_1 + 7x_1^2 - 7/3x_1^3 + 1/4x_1^4\right) x_2^2 e^{-x_2}$$

subject to $0 \le x_1 \le 5$ and $0 \le x_2 \le 6$. The global minimum is located at $\boldsymbol{x}^* = (4, 2)$ with $f(\boldsymbol{x}^*) \approx -2.3458$.

38. Jennrich-Sampson Function

$$f(\boldsymbol{x}) = \sum_{i=1}^{10} \left(2 + 2i - \left(\mathrm{e}^{ix_1} + e^{ix_2}\right)\right)^2$$

subject to $-1 \le x_i \le 1$. The global minimum is located at $\boldsymbol{x}^* = (0.257825, 0.257825)$ with $f(\boldsymbol{x}^*) = 124.3612$.

39. Langerman Function

$$f(\boldsymbol{x}) = -\sum_{i=1}^{m} c_i e^{-\frac{1}{\pi}\sum_{j=1}^{D}(x_j - a_{ij})^2} \cos\left(\pi \sum_{j=1}^{D} (x_j - a_{ij})^2\right)$$

subject to $0 \le x_j \le 10$, where $j \in [0, D-1]$ and $m = 5$. It has a global minimum value of $f(\boldsymbol{x}^*) = -1.4$. The matrix $\boldsymbol{A}$ and column vector c are given as

$$\boldsymbol{A} = \begin{bmatrix} 9.681 & 0.667 & 4.783 & 9.095 & 3.517 & 9.325 & 6.544 & 0.211 & 5.122 & 2.020 \\ 9.400 & 2.041 & 3.788 & 7.931 & 2.882 & 2.672 & 3.568 & 1.284 & 7.033 & 7.374 \\ 8.025 & 9.152 & 5.114 & 7.621 & 4.564 & 4.711 & 2.996 & 6.126 & 0.734 & 4.982 \\ 2.196 & 0.415 & 5.649 & 6.979 & 9.510 & 9.166 & 6.304 & 6.054 & 9.377 & 1.426 \\ 8.074 & 8.777 & 3.467 & 1.863 & 6.708 & 6.349 & 4.534 & 0.276 & 7.633 & 1.567 \end{bmatrix}$$

$$\underline{c} = c_i = \begin{bmatrix} 0.806 \\ 0.517 \\ 1.5 \\ 0.908 \\ 0.965 \end{bmatrix}$$

40. Keane Function

$$f(\boldsymbol{x}) = \frac{\sin^2(x_1 - x_2)\sin^2(x_1 + x_2)}{\sqrt{x_1^2 + x_2^2}}$$

subject to $0 \le x_i \le 10$.

The multiple global minima are located at $\boldsymbol{x}^* = (\{0, 1.39325\}, \{1.39325, 0\})$ with $f(\boldsymbol{x}^*) = -0.673668$.

41. Leon Function

$$f(\boldsymbol{x}) = 100\left(x_2 - x_1^2\right)^2 + (1 - x_1)^2$$

subject to $-1.2 \le x_i \le 1.2$. The global minimum is located at $\boldsymbol{x}^* = (1, 1)$ with $f(\boldsymbol{x}^*) = 0$.

42. Matyas Function

$$f(\boldsymbol{x}) = 0.26\left(x_1^2 + x_2^2\right) - 0.48x_1x_2$$

subject to $-10 \le x_i \le 10$. The global minimum is located at $\boldsymbol{x}^* = (0, 0)$ with $f(\boldsymbol{x}^*) = 0$.

43. McCormick Function

$$f(\boldsymbol{x}) = \sin(x_1 + x_2) + (x_1 - x_2)^2 - (3/2)x_1 + (5/2)x_2 + 1$$

subject to $-1.5 \le x_1 \le 4$ and $-3 \le x_2 \le 3$. The global minimum is located at $\boldsymbol{x}^* = (-0.547, -1.547)$ with $f(\boldsymbol{x}^*) \approx -1.9133$.

44. Miele Cantrell Function

$$f(\boldsymbol{x}) = (e^{-x_1} - x_2)^4 + 100(x_2 - x_3)^6 + (\tan(x_3 - x_4))^4 + x_1^8$$

subject to $-1 \le x_i \le 1$. The global minimum is located at $\boldsymbol{x}^* = (0, 1, 1, 1)$ with $f(\boldsymbol{x}^*) = 0$.

45. Mishra Zero-Sum Function

$$f(\boldsymbol{x}) = \left(10000\left|\sum_{i=1}^{D} x_i\right|\right)^{0.5} \tag{A.3}$$

subject to $-10 \le x_i \le 10$. The global minimum is $f(\boldsymbol{x}^*) = 0$.

46. Parsopoulos Function

$$f(\boldsymbol{x}) = \cos(x_1)^2 + \sin(x_2)^2$$

subject to $-5 \le x_i \le 5$, where $(x_1, x_2) \in \Re^2$. This function has a large number of global minima in $\Re^2$, at points $(\kappa\frac{\pi}{2}, \lambda\pi)$, where $\kappa = \pm 1, \pm 3, \ldots$ and $\lambda = 0, \pm 1, \pm 2, \ldots$. In the given domain problem, the function has 12 global minima, all equal to zero.

47. Pen Holder Function

$$f(\boldsymbol{x}) = -\exp[|\cos(x_1)\cos(x_2)e^{|1-[(x_1^2+x_2^2)]^{0.5}/\pi|}|^{-1}]$$

subject to $-11 \le x_i \le 11$. The four global minima are located at $\boldsymbol{x}^* = (\pm 9.646168, \pm 9.646168)$ with $f(\boldsymbol{x}^*) = -0.96354$.

48. Pathological Function

$$f(\boldsymbol{x}) = \sum_{i=1}^{D-1}\left(0.5 + \frac{\sin^2\sqrt{100x_i^2 + x_{i+1}^2} - 0.5}{1 + 0.001(x_i^2 - 2x_i x_{i+1} + x_{i+1}^2)^2}\right)$$

subject to $-100 \le x_i \le 100$. The global minimum is located $\boldsymbol{x}^* = (0, \ldots, 0)$ with $f(\boldsymbol{x}^*) = 0$.

49. Paviani Function

$$f(\boldsymbol{x}) = \sum_{i=1}^{10}\left[(\ln(x_i - 2))^2 + (\ln(10 - x_i))^2\right] - \left(\prod_{i=1}^{10} x_i\right)^{0.2}$$

subject to $2.0001 \le x_i \le 10, i \in 1, 2, \ldots, 10$. The global minimum is located at $\boldsymbol{x}^* \approx (9.351, \ldots, 9.351)$ with $f(\boldsymbol{x}^*) \approx -45.778$.

50. Pintér Function

$$f(\boldsymbol{x}) = \sum_{i=1}^{D} i x_i^2 + \sum_{i=1}^{D} 20 i \sin^2 A + \sum_{i=1}^{D} i \log_{10}\left(1 + i B^2\right)$$

where

$$A = \left(x_{i-1}\sin x_i + \sin x_{i+1}\right)$$
$$B = \left(x_{i-1}^2 - 2x_i + 3x_{i+1} - \cos x_i + 1\right)$$

where $x_0 = x_D$ and $x_{D+1} = x_1$, subject to $-10 \le x_i \le 10$. The global minimum is located at $\boldsymbol{x}^* = (0, \ldots, 0)$ with $f(\boldsymbol{x}^*) = 0$.

51. Periodic Function

$$f(\boldsymbol{x}) = 1 + \sin^2(x_1) + \sin^2(x_2) - 0.1e^{-(x_1^2 + x_2^2)}$$

subject to $-10 \le x_i \le 10$. The global minimum is located at $\boldsymbol{x}^* = (0, 0)$ with $f(\boldsymbol{x}^*) = 0.9$.

52. Powell's First Singular Function

$$f(\boldsymbol{x}) = \sum_{i=1}^{D/4} \left(x_{4i-3} + 10x_{4i-2}\right)^2 + 5\left(x_{4i-1} - x_{4i}\right)^2 + \left(x_{4i-2} - x_{4i-1}\right)^4 + 10\left(x_{4i-3} - x_{4i}\right)^4$$

subject to $-4 \le x_i \le 5$. The global minimum is located at $\boldsymbol{x}^* = (3, -1, 0, 1, \ldots, 3, -1, 0, 1)$ with $f(\boldsymbol{x}^*) = 0$.

53. Powell's Second Singular Function

$$f(\boldsymbol{x}) = \sum_{i=1}^{D-2} \left(x_{i-1} + 10x_i\right)^2 + 5\left(x_{i+1} - x_{i+2}\right)^2 + \left(x_i - 2x_{i+1}\right)^4 + 10\left(x_{i-1} - x_{i+2}\right)^4$$

subject to $-4 \le x_i \le 5$. The global minimum is $f(\boldsymbol{x}^*) = 0$.

54. Powell Sum Function

$$f(\boldsymbol{x}) = \sum_{i=1}^{D} \left|x_i\right|^{i+1}$$

subject to $-1 \le x_i \le 1$. The global minimum is $f(\boldsymbol{x}^*) = 0$.

55. Price Function

$$f(\boldsymbol{x}) = (|x_1| - 5)^2 + (|x_2| - 5)^2$$

subject to $-500 \le x_i \le 500$. The global minima are located at $\boldsymbol{x}^* = (\{-5, -5\}, \{-5, 5\}, \{5, -5\}, \{5, 5\})$ with $f(\boldsymbol{x}^*) = 0$.

56. Quadratic Function

$$f(\boldsymbol{x}) = -3803.84 - 138.08x_1 - 232.92x_2 + 128.08x_1^2 + 203.64x_2^2 + 182.25x_1x_2$$

subject to $-10 \le x_i \le 10$. The global minimum is located at $\boldsymbol{x}^* = (0.19388, 0.48513)$ with $f(\boldsymbol{x}^*) = -3873.7243$.

57. Quartic Function

$$f(\boldsymbol{x}) = \sum_{i=1}^{D} i x_i^4 + \text{random}[0, 1)$$

subject to $-1.28 \le x_i \le 1.28$. The global minimum is located at $\boldsymbol{x}^* = (0, \ldots, 0)$ with $f(\boldsymbol{x}^*) = 0$.

58. Quintic Function

$$f(\boldsymbol{x}) = \sum_{i=1}^{D} |x_i^5 - 3x_i^4 + 4x_i^3 + 2x_i^2 - 10x_i - 4|$$

subject to $-10 \le x_i \le 10$. The global minimum is located at $\boldsymbol{x}^* = (-1 \text{ or } 2)$, $f(\boldsymbol{x}^*) = 0$.

59. Ripple Function

$$f(\boldsymbol{x}) = \sum_{i=1}^{2} -e^{-2\ln 2\left(\frac{x_i - 0.1}{0.8}\right)^2} (\sin^6(5\pi x_i) + 0.1\cos^2(500\pi x_i))$$

subject to $0 \le x_i \le 1$. It has one global minimum and 252,004 local minima. The global form of the function consists of 25 holes, which form a 5×5 regular grid. Additionally, the whole function landscape is full of small ripples caused by a high-frequency cosine function that creates a large number of local minima.

60. **Rosenbrock's Function**

$$f(\boldsymbol{x}) = \sum_{i=1}^{D-1} \left[100 \left(x_{i+1} - x_i^2 \right)^2 + (x_i - 1)^2 \right]$$

subject to $-30 \le x_i \le 30$. The global minimum is located at $\boldsymbol{x}^* = f(1, \ldots, 1)$, $f(\boldsymbol{x}^*) = 0$.

61. **Rosenbrock's Modified Function**

$$f(\boldsymbol{x}) = 74 + 100\left(x_2 - x_1^2 \right)^2 + (1 - x)^2$$
$$-400e^{-\frac{(x_1+1)^2+(x_2+1)^2}{0.1}}$$

subject to $-2 \le x_i \le 2$. In this function, a Gaussian bump at $(-1, 1)$ is added, causing a local minimum at $(1, 1)$, and the global minimum is located at $\boldsymbol{x}^* = f(-1, -1)$, $f(\boldsymbol{x}^*) = 0$. This modification makes it difficult to optimize because the local minimum basin is larger than the global minimum basin.

62. **Rosenbrock and Yang's Function**

$$f(\boldsymbol{x}) = \sum_{i=1}^{D-1} \left[100\epsilon_i \left(x_{i+1} - x_i^2 \right)^2 + (x_i - 1)^2 \right]$$

subject to $-30 \le x_i \le 30$. The random variables ϵ_i are all drawn from a uniform distribution $U(0, 1)$. The global minimum is located at $\boldsymbol{x}^* = (1, \ldots, 1)$, $f(\boldsymbol{x}^*) = 0$.

63. **Rotated Ellipse Function**

$$f(\boldsymbol{x}) = 7x_1^2 - 6\sqrt{3}x_1x_2 + 13x_2^2$$

subject to $-500 \le x_i \le 500$. The global minimum is located at $\boldsymbol{x}^* = (0, 0)$ with $f(\boldsymbol{x}^*) = 0$.

64. **Rump Function**

$$f(\boldsymbol{x}) = \left(333.75 - x_1^2\right) x_2^6 + x_1^2 \left(11x_1^2x_2^2 - 121x_2^4 - 2\right) + 5.5x_2^8 + \frac{x_1}{2x_2}$$

subject to $-500 \le x_i \le 500$. The global minimum is located at $\boldsymbol{x}^* = (0, 0)$ with $f(\boldsymbol{x}^*) = 0$.

65. **Salomon Function**

$$f(\boldsymbol{x}) = 1 - \cos\left(2\pi \sqrt{\sum_{i=1}^{D} x_i^2} \right) + 0.1 \sqrt{\sum_{i=1}^{D} x_i^2}$$

subject to $-100 \leq x_i \leq 100$. The global minimum is located at $\boldsymbol{x}^* = (0, 0)$ with $f(\boldsymbol{x}^*) = 0$.

66. Sargan Function

$$f(\boldsymbol{x}) = \sum_{i=1} D \left(x_i^2 + 0.4 \sum_{j \neq 1} x_i x_j \right)$$

subject to $-100 \leq x_i \leq 100$. The global minimum is located at $\boldsymbol{x}^* = (0, \ldots, 0)$ with $f(\boldsymbol{x}^*) = 0$.

67. Schaffer's First Function

$$f(\boldsymbol{x}) = 0.5 + \frac{\sin^2(x_1^2 + x_2^2)^2 - 0.5}{1 + 0.001(x_1^2 + x_2^2)^2}$$

subject to $-100 \leq x_i \leq 100$. The global minimum is located at $\boldsymbol{x}^* = (0, 0)$ with $f(\boldsymbol{x}^*) = 0$.

68. Schaffer's Second Function

$$f(\boldsymbol{x}) = 0.5 + \frac{\sin^2(x_1^2 - x_2^2)^2 - 0.5}{1 + 0.001(x_1^2 + x_2^2)^2}$$

subject to $-100 \leq x_i \leq 100$. The global minimum is located at $\boldsymbol{x}^* = (0, 0)$ with $f(\boldsymbol{x}^*) = 0$.

69. Schaffer Third Function

$$f(\boldsymbol{x}) = 0.5 + \frac{\sin^2\left(\cos \left| x_1^2 - x_2^2 \right| \right) - 0.5}{1 + 0.001(x_1^2 + x_2^2)^2}$$

subject to $-100 \leq x_i \leq 100$. The global minimum is located at $\boldsymbol{x}^* = (0, 1.253115)$ with $f(\boldsymbol{x}^*) = 0.00156685$.

70. Schmidt Vetters Function

$$f(\boldsymbol{x}) = \frac{1}{1 + (x_1 - x_2)^2} + \sin\left(\frac{\pi x_2 + x_3}{2} \right) + e^{\left(\frac{x_1 + x_2}{x_2} - 2 \right)^2}$$

The global minimum is located at $\boldsymbol{x}^* = (0.78547, 0.78547, 0.78547)$ with $f(\boldsymbol{x}^*) = 3$.

71. Schumer Steiglitz Function

$$f(\boldsymbol{x}) = \sum_{i=1}^{D} x_i^4$$

The global minimum is located at $\boldsymbol{x}^* = (0, \ldots, 0)$ with $f(\boldsymbol{x}^*) = 0$.

72. Schwefel Function

$$f(\boldsymbol{x}) = \left(\sum_{i=1}^{D} x_i^2\right)^{\alpha}$$

where $\alpha \geq 0$, subject to $-100 \leq x_i \leq 100$. The global minimum is located at $\boldsymbol{x}^* = (0, \ldots, 0)$ with $f(\boldsymbol{x}^*) = 0$.

73. Shubert Function

$$f_{133}(\boldsymbol{x}) = \prod_{i=1}^{n}\left(\sum_{j=1}^{5} \cos((j+1)x_i + j)\right)$$

subject to $-10 \leq x_i \leq 10, i \in 1, 2, \ldots, n$. The 18 global minima are located at

$$\begin{aligned}\boldsymbol{x}^* = (&\{-7.0835, \ \ 4.8580\}, \{-7.0835, -7.7083\},\\ &\{-1.4251, -7.0835\}, \{\ \ 5.4828, \ \ 4.8580\},\\ &\{-1.4251, -0.8003\}, \{\ \ 4.8580, \ \ 5.4828\},\\ &\{-7.7083, -7.0835\}, \{-7.0835, -1.4251\},\\ &\{-7.7083, -0.8003\}, \{-7.7083, \ \ 5.4828\},\\ &\{-0.8003, -7.7083\}, \{-0.8003, -1.4251\},\\ &\{-0.8003, \ \ 4.8580\}, \{-1.4251, \ \ 5.4828\},\\ &\{\ \ 5.4828, -7.7083\}, \{\ \ 4.8580, -7.0835\},\\ &\{\ \ 5.4828, -1.4251\}, \{\ \ 4.8580, -0.8003\}),\end{aligned}$$

with $f(\boldsymbol{x}^*) \simeq -186.7309$.

74. Schaffer Function

$$f(\boldsymbol{x}) = \sum_{i=1}^{D} 0.5 + \frac{\sin^2\sqrt{x_i^2 + x_{i+1}^2} - 0.5}{\left[1 + 0.001(x_i^2 + x_{i+1}^2)\right]^2}$$

subject to $-100 \leq x_i \leq 100$. The global minimum is located at $\boldsymbol{x}^* = (0, \ldots, 0)$ with $f(\boldsymbol{x}^*) = 0$.

75. Sphere Function

$$f(\boldsymbol{x}) = \sum_{i=1}^{D} x_i^2$$

subject to $0 \leq x_i \leq 10$. The global minimum is located $\boldsymbol{x}^* = (0, \ldots, 0)$ with $f(\boldsymbol{x}^*) = 0$.

76. Step Function

$$f(\boldsymbol{x}) = \sum_{i=1}^{D} \left(\lfloor |x_i| \rfloor\right)$$

subject to $-100 \leq x_i \leq 100$. The global minimum is located $\boldsymbol{x}^* = (0, \ldots, 0) = 0$ with $f(\boldsymbol{x}^*) = 0$.

77. Stepint Function

$$f(\boldsymbol{x}) = 25 + \sum_{i=1}^{D} \left(\lfloor x_i \rfloor\right)$$

subject to $-5.12 \leq x_i \leq 5.12$. The global minimum is located $\boldsymbol{x}^* = (0, \ldots, 0)$ with $f(\boldsymbol{x}^*) = 0$.

78. Stretched V Sine Wave Function

$$f(\boldsymbol{x}) = \sum_{i=1}^{D-1} \left(x_{i+1}^2 + x_i^2\right)^{0.25} \left[\sin^2\left\{50\left(x_{i+1}^2 + x_i^2\right)^{0.1}\right\} + 0.1\right]$$

subject to $-10 \leq x_i \leq 10$. The global minimum is located $\boldsymbol{x}^* = (0, 0)$ with $f(\boldsymbol{x}^*) = 0$.

79. Sum Squares Function

$$f(\boldsymbol{x}) = \sum_{i=1}^{D} i x_i^2$$

subject to $-10 \leq x_i \leq 10$. The global minimum is located $\boldsymbol{x}^* = (0, \ldots, 0)$ with $f(\boldsymbol{x}^*) = 0$.

80. Styblinski-Tang Function

$$f(\boldsymbol{x}) = \frac{1}{2} \sum_{i=1}^{n} \left(x_i^4 - 16x_i^2 + 5x_i\right)$$

subject to $-5 \leq x_i \leq 5$. The global minimum is located $\boldsymbol{x}^* = (-2.903534, -2.903534)$ with $f(\boldsymbol{x}^*) = -78.332$.

81. First Holder Table Function

$$f(\boldsymbol{x}) = -|\cos(x_1)\cos(x_2)e^{|1-(x_1+x_2)^{0.5}/\pi|}|$$

subject to $-10 \leq x_i \leq 10$. The four global minima are located at $\boldsymbol{x}^* = (\pm 9.646168, \pm 9.646168)$ with $f(\boldsymbol{x}^*) = -26.920336$.

82. Second Holder Table Function

$$f(\boldsymbol{x}) = -|\sin(x_1)\cos(x_2)e^{|1-(x_1+x_2)^{0.5}/\pi|}|$$

subject to $-10 \leq x_i \leq 10$.
The four global minima are located at $\boldsymbol{x}^* = (\pm 8.055023472141116, \pm 9.664590028909654)$ with $f(\boldsymbol{x}^*) = -19.20850$.

83. Carrom Table Function

$$f(\boldsymbol{x}) = -\left[\left(\cos(x_1)\cos(x_2)\right.\right.$$
$$\left.\left.\exp\left|1 - \left[\left(x_1^2 + x_2^2\right)^{0.5}\right] \Big/ \pi\right|\right)^2\right] \Big/ 30$$

subject to $-10 \le x_i \le 10$.
The four global minima are located at $\boldsymbol{x}^* = (\pm 9.646157266348881, \pm 9.646134286497169)$ with $f(\boldsymbol{x}^*) = -24.1568155$.

84. TestTube Holder Function

$$f(\boldsymbol{x}) = -4\left[(\sin(x_1)\cos(x_2)\right.$$
$$\left. e^{|\cos[(x_1^2+x_2^2)/200]|})\right]$$

subject to $-10 \le x_i \le 10$. The two global minima are located at $\boldsymbol{x}^* = (\pm\pi/2, 0)$ with $f(\boldsymbol{x}^*) = -10.872300$.

85. Trecanni Function

$$f(\boldsymbol{x}) = x_1^4 - 4x_1^3 + 4x_1 + x_2^2$$

subject to $-5 \le x_i \le 5$. The two global minima are located at $\boldsymbol{x}^* = (\{0, 0\}, \{-2, 0\})$ with $f(\boldsymbol{x}^*) = 0$.

86. Trid Function

$$f(\boldsymbol{x}) = \sum_{i=1}^{D} (x_i - 1)^2 - \sum_{i=1}^{D} x_i x_{i-1}$$

subject to $-6^2 \le x_i \le 6^2$. The global minimum is located at $f(\boldsymbol{x}^*) = -50$.

87. Trefethen Function

$$f(\boldsymbol{x}) = e^{\sin(50x_1)} + \sin(60e^{x_2})$$
$$+\sin(70\sin(x_1)) + \sin(\sin(80x_2))$$
$$-\sin(10(x_1 + x_2)) + \frac{1}{4}(x_1^2 + x_2^2)$$

subject to $-10 \le x_i \le 10$. The global minimum is located at $\boldsymbol{x}^* = (-0.024403, 0.210612)$ with $f(\boldsymbol{x}^*) = -3.30686865$.

88. Trigonometric Function

$$f(\boldsymbol{x}) = \sum_{i=1}^{D} \left[D - \sum_{j=1}^{D} \cos x_j + i(1 - \cos(x_i) - \sin(x_i)) \right]^2$$

subject to $0 \le x_i \le pi$. The global minimum is located at $\boldsymbol{x}^* = (0, \ldots, 0)$ with $f(\boldsymbol{x}^*) = 0$.

89. Tripod Function

$$f(\boldsymbol{x}) = p(x_2)(1 + p(x_1)) + |x_1 + 50p(x_2)(1 - 2p(x_1))| + |x_2 + 50(1 - 2p(x_2))|$$

subject to $-100 \leq x_i \leq 100$, where $p(x) = 1$ for $x \geq 0$. The global minimum is located at $\boldsymbol{x}^* = f(0, -50)$, $f(\boldsymbol{x}^*) = 0$.

90. Ursem Function

$$f(\boldsymbol{x}) = -\sin(2x_1 - 0.5\pi) - 3\cos(x_2) - 0.5x_1$$

subject to $-2.5 \leq x_1 \leq 3$ and $-2 \leq x_2 \leq 2$ and has a single global optimum.

91. Ursem Waves Function

$$f(\boldsymbol{x}) = -0.9x_1^2 + (x_2^2 - 4.5x_2^2)x_1x_2 + 4.7\cos(3x_1 - x_2^2(2 + x_1))\sin(2.5\pi x_1)$$

subject to $-0.9 \leq x_1 \leq 1.2$ and $-1.2 \leq x_2 \leq 1.2$ and has a single global minimum and nine irregularly spaced local minima in the search space.

92. Watson Function

$$f(\boldsymbol{x}) = \sum_{i=0}^{29} \left\{ \sum_{j=0}^{4} \left((j-1)a_i^j x_{j+1} \right) - \left[\sum_{j=0}^{5} a_i^j x_{j+1} \right]^2 - 1 \right\}^2 + x_1^2$$

subject to $|x_i| \leq 10$, where the coefficient $a_i = i/29.0$. The global minimum is located at $\boldsymbol{x}^* = (-0.0158, 1.012, -0.2329, 1.260, -1.513, 0.9928)$ with $f(\boldsymbol{x}^*) = 0.002288$.

93. Weierstrass Function

$$f(\boldsymbol{x}) = \sum_{i=1}^{D} \left[\sum_{k=0}^{K_{\max}} a^k \cos(2\pi b^k (x_i + 0.5)) - D \sum_{k=0}^{K_{\max}} a^k \cos(\pi b^k) \right]$$

subject to $-0.5 \leq x_i \leq 0.5$. $K_{\max}$ should be large enough and can be set as $K_{\max} = 100$. The global minimum is located at $\boldsymbol{x}^* = (0, \ldots, 0)$ with $f(\boldsymbol{x}^*) = 0$.

94. Whitley Function

$$f(\boldsymbol{x}) = \sum_{i=1}^{D} \sum_{j=1}^{D} \left[\frac{\left(100(x_i^2 - x_j)^2 + (1 - x_j)^2\right)^2}{4000} - \cos\left(100(x_i^2 - x_j)^2 + (1 - x_j)^2 + 1\right) \right]$$

combines a very steep overall slope with a highly multimodal area around the global minimum located at $x_i = 1$ where $i = 1, \dots, D$.

95. **Xin-She Yang First Function** This is a generic stochastic and non-smooth function proposed in [10,11].

$$f(\mathbf{x}) = \sum_{i=1}^{D} \epsilon_i |x_i|^i$$

subject to $-5 \le x_i \le 5$. The variable $\epsilon_i (i = 1, 2, \dots, D)$ is a random variable uniformly distributed in [0, 1]. The global minimum is located at $\mathbf{x}^* = (0, \dots, 0)$ with $f(\mathbf{x}^*) = 0$.

96. **Xin-She Yang Second Function**

$$f(\mathbf{x}) = \left(\sum_{i=1}^{D} |x_i|\right) \exp\left[-\sum_{i=1}^{D} \sin(x_i^2)\right]$$

subject to $-2\pi \le x_i \le 2\pi$. The global minimum is located at $\mathbf{x}^* = (0, \dots, 0)$ with $f(\mathbf{x}^*) = 0$.

97. **Xin-She Yang Third Function**

$$f(\mathbf{x}) = \left[e^{-\sum_{i=1}^{D} (x_i/\beta)^{2m}} - 2e^{-\sum_{i=1}^{D} (x_i)^2} . \prod_{i=1}^{D} \cos^2(x_i)\right]$$

subject to $-20 \le x_i \le 20$. The global minimum for $m = 5$ and $\beta = 15$ is located at $\mathbf{x}^* = (0, \dots, 0)$ with $f(\mathbf{x}^*) = -1$.

98. **Xin-She Yang Fourth Function**

$$f(\mathbf{x}) = \left[\sum_{i=1}^{D} \sin^2(x_i) - e^{-\sum_{i=1}^{D} x_i^2}\right] .e^{-\sum_{i=1}^{D} \sin^2 \sqrt{|x_i|}}$$

subject to $-10 \le x_i \le 10$. The global minimum is located at $\mathbf{x}^* = (0, \dots, 0)$ with $f(\mathbf{x}^*) = -1$.

99. **Xin-She Yang Fifth Function**

$$f(\mathbf{x}) = \left|1 - \exp\left[-\sum_{i=1}^{D} (\epsilon_i x_i^2)\right]\right| + \sum_{i=1}^{D} \epsilon_i \sin^2(2D\pi x_i),$$

subject to $-10\pi \le x_i \le 10\pi$. Here, all the random variables ϵ_i are drawn from a uniform distribution in [0, 1]. The global minimum $f(\mathbf{x}^*) = 0$ is located at $\mathbf{x}^* = (0, \dots, 0)$.

100. **Zakharov Function**

$$f(\mathbf{x}) = \sum_{i=1}^{D} x_i^2 + \left(\frac{1}{2}\sum_{i=1}^{D} ix_i\right)^2 + \left(\frac{1}{2}\sum_{i=1}^{D} ix_i\right)^4$$

subject to $-5 \le x_i \le 10$. The global minimum is located at $\mathbf{x}^* = (0, \dots, 0)$ with $f(\mathbf{x}^*) = 0$.

References

[1] Ali MM, Khompatraporn C, Zabinsky ZB. A numerical evaluation of several stochastic algorithms on selected continuous global optimization test problems. J Global Optim 2005;31(4):635–72.

[2] Andrei N. An unconstrained optimization test functions collection. Adv Model Optim 2008;10(1):147–61.

[3] Averick BM, Carter RG, Moré JJ. The MINIPACK-2 test problem collection, mathematics and computer science division, Agronne National Laboratory, Technical Memorandum No. 150, 1991.

[4] Flouda CA, Pardalos PM, Adjiman CS, Esposito WR, Gümüs ZH, Harding ST. Handbook of test problems in local and global optimization. Boston: Kluwer; 1999.

[5] Hedar AR. Global optimization test problems, <www-optima.amp.i.kyoto-u.ac.jp/member/student/hedar/Hedar_files/TestGO.htm>.

[6] Schwefel HP. Evolution and optimum seeking. New York NY, USA: Wiley; 1995.

[7] Suganthan PN, Hansen N, Liang JJ, Deb, Chen YP, Auger A, Tiwar S. Problem definitions and evaluation criteria for CEC 2005, Special Session on Real-Parameter Optimization, Nanyang Technological University (NTU), Singapore, Tech. Rep., 2005. <www.lri.fr/hansen/Tech-Report-May-30-05.pdf>.

[8] Tang K, Li X., Suganthan PN, Yang Z, Weise T. Benchmark functions for the CEC2010 special session and competition on large-scale global optimization, Tech. Rep., 2010. <http://sci2s.ugr.es/eamhco/cec2010_functions.pdf>.

[9] Whitley D, Mathias K, Rana S, Dzubera J. Evaluating Evolutionary Algorithms. Artif Intell 1996;85(2):245–76.

[10] Yang XS. Test problems in optimization. In: Engineering optimization: an introduction with metaheuristic applications. Hoboken, NJ, USA: Wiley; 2010. Available from: http://arxiv.org/abs/1008.0549 .

[11] Yang XS, Algorithm Firefly. Stochastic test functions and design optimisation. Int J Bio-Inspired Comput 2010;2(2):78–84. Available from: http://arxiv.org/abs/1008.0549 .

[12] Jamil M, Yang XS. A literature survey of benchmark functions for global optimization problems. Int J Math Model Numer Optim 2013;4(2):150–94.

B Matlab Programs

The following codes intend to demonstrate how each algorithm works, so they are relatively simple and we do not intend to optimize them. They are not for general-purpose optimization, because there are much better programs out there, both free and commercial, for that task. These codes should work using Matlab.[1] For Octave,[2] slight modifications may be needed.

B.1 Simulated Annealing

```
% ===================================================================%
% Simulated Annealing (by Xin-She Yang @ 2013)                       %
% Usage: sa_demo                                                     %
% ------------------------------------------------------------------ %
function sa_demo
disp('Simulating ... it will take a minute or so!');
% Lower and upper bounds
Lb=[-2 -2];
Ub=[2 2];
nd=length(Lb);

% Initializing parameters and settings
T_init =1.0;     % Initial temperature
T_min = 1e-10;   % Final stopping temperature
F_min = -1e+100;% Min value of the function
max_rej=250;     % Maximum number of rejections
max_run=150;     % Maximum number of runs
max_accept=15;   % Maximum number of accept
k = 1;           % Boltzmann constant
alpha=0.95;      % Cooling factor
Enorm=1e-2;      % Energy norm (eg, Enorm=le-8)
guess=Lb+(Ub-Lb).*rand(size(Lb));    % Initial guess
% Initializing the counters i,j etc
i= 0; j = 0; accept = 0; totaleval = 0;
% Initializing various values
```

[1]Matlab, www.mathworks.com.

[2]J. W. Eaton, *GNU Octave Manual*. Network Theory Ltd., 2002, www.gnu.org/software/octave.

```
T = T_init;
E_init = fobj(guess);
E_old = E_init; E_new=E_old;
best=guess; % initially guessed values

% Starting the simulated annealling
while ((T > T_min) & (j <= max_rej) & E_new>F_min)
i = i+1;
% Check if max numbers of run/accept are met
if (i >= max_run) | (accept >= max_accept)
% Cooling according to a cooling schedule
T = alpha*T;
totaleval = totaleval + i;
% reset the counters
i = 1; accept = 1;
end
% Function evaluations at new locations
s=0.01*(Ub-Lb);
ns=best+s.*randn(1,nd);
E_new = fobj(ns);
% Decide to accept the new solution
DeltaE=E_new-E_old;
% Accept if improved
if (-DeltaE > Enorm)
best = ns; E_old = E_new;
accept=accept+1; j = 0;
end
% Accept with a small probability if not improved
if (DeltaE<=Enorm & exp(-DeltaE/(k*T))>rand );
best = ns; E_old = E_new;
accept=accept+1;
else
end
% Update the estimated optimal solution
f_opt=E_old;
end
% Display the final results
disp(strcat('Evaluations :', num2str(totaleval)));
disp(strcat('Best solution:', num2str(best)));
disp(strcat('Best objective:', num2str(f_opt)));

function z=fobj(u)
% Rosenbrock's function with f*=0 at (1,1)
z=(u(1)-1)^2+100*(u(2)-u(1)^2)^2;
```

B.2 Particle Swarm Optimization

```
% The Accelerated Particle Swarm Optimization
% (written by X S Yang, Cambridge University)
% Usage: pso(number_of_particles,Num_iterations)
```

```
% eg:   best=pso_demo(20,10);
% where best=[xbest ybest zbest]  %an n by 3 matrix
%   xbest(i)/ybest(i) are the best at ith iteration

function [best]=pso_simpledemo(n,Num_iterations)
% n=number of particles
% Num_iterations=total number of iterations
if nargin<2,   Num_iterations=10;  end
if nargin<1,   n=20;          end
% Michalewicz Function f*=-1.801 at [2.20319,1.57049]
% Splitting two parts to avoid long lines in printing
str1='-sin(x)*(sin(x^2/3.14159))^20';
str2='-sin(y)*(sin(2*y^2/3.14159))^20';
funstr=strcat(str1,str2);
% Converting to an inline function and vectorization
f=vectorize(inline(funstr));
% range=[xmin xmax ymin ymax];
range=[0 4 0 4];
% ----------------------------------------------------
% Setting the parameters: alpha, beta
% Random amplitude of roaming particles alpha=[0,1]
% alpha=gamma^t=0.7^t;
% Speed of convergence (0->1)=(slow->fast)
beta=0.5;
% ----------------------------------------------------
% Grid values of the objective function
% These values are used for visualization only
Ngrid=100;
dx=(range(2)-range(1))/Ngrid;
dy=(range(4)-range(3))/Ngrid;
xgrid=range(1):dx:range(2); ygrid=range(3):dy:range(4);
[x,y]=meshgrid(xgrid,ygrid);
z=f(x,y);
% Display the shape of the function to be optimized
figure(1);
surfc(x,y,z);
% ---------------------------------------------------
best=zeros(Num_iterations,3);   % initialize history
% ----- Start Particle Swarm Optimization -----------
% generating the initial locations of n particles
[xn,yn]=init_pso(n,range);
% Display the paths of particles in a figure
% with a contour of the objective function
 figure(2);
% Start iterations
for i=1:Num_iterations,
% Show the contour of the function
  contour(x,y,z,15); hold on;
% Find the current best location (xo,yo)
```

```
zn=f(xn,yn);
zn=f(xn,yn);
zn_min=min(zn);
xo=min(xn(zn==zn_min));
yo=min(yn(zn==zn_min));
zo=min(zn(zn==zn_min));
% Trace the paths of all roaming particles
% Display these roaming particles
plot(xn,yn,'.',xo,yo,'*'); axis(range);
% The accelerated PSO with alpha=gamma^t
  gamma=0.7; alpha=gamma.^i;
% Move all the particles to new locations
[xn,yn]=pso_move(xn,yn,xo,yo,alpha,beta,range);
drawnow;
% Use "hold on" to display paths of particles
hold off;
% History
best(i,1)=xo; best(i,2)=yo; best(i,3)=zo;
end   %%%%% end of iterations
% ----- All subfunctions are listed here -----
% Intial locations of n particles
function [xn,yn]=init_pso(n,range)
xrange=range(2)-range(1); yrange=range(4)-range(3);
xn=rand(1,n)*xrange+range(1);
yn=rand(1,n)*yrange+range(3);
% Move all the particles toward (xo,yo)
function [xn,yn]=pso_move(xn,yn,xo,yo,a,b,range)
nn=size(yn,2);  %a=alpha, b=beta
xn=xn.*(1-b)+xo.*b+a.*(rand(1,nn)-0.5);
yn=yn.*(1-b)+yo.*b+a.*(rand(1,nn)-0.5);
[xn,yn]=findrange(xn,yn,range);
% Make sure the particles are within the range
function [xn,yn]=findrange(xn,yn,range)
nn=length(yn);
for i=1:nn,
   if xn(i)<=range(1), xn(i)=range(1); end
   if xn(i)>=range(2), xn(i)=range(2); end
   if yn(i)<=range(3), yn(i)=range(3); end
   if yn(i)>=range(4), yn(i)=range(4); end
end
```

B.3 Differential Evolution

```
% Differential Evolution for global optimization
% Programmed by Xin-She Yang @Cambridge University 2008

% The basic version of scheme DE/Rand/1 is implemented
% Usage: de(para) or de;

function [best,fmin,N_iter]=de(para)
```

```
% Default parameters
if nargin<1,
   para=[10 0.7 0.9];
end

n=para(1);        % Population >=4, typically 10 to 25
F=para(2);        % DE parameter - scaling (0.5 to 0.9)
Cr=para(3);       % DE parameter - crossover probability

% Iteration parameters
tol=10^(-5);      % Stop tolerance
N_iter=0;         % Total number of function evaluations

% Simple bounds
Lb=[-1 -1 -1];
Ub=[2 2  2];

% Dimension of the search variables
d=length(Lb);

% Initialize the population/solutions
for i=1:n,
  Sol(i,:)=Lb+(Ub-Lb).*rand(size(Lb));
  Fitness(i)=Fun(Sol(i,:));
end
% Find the current best
[fmin,I]=min(Fitness);
best=Sol(I,:)

% Start the iterations by differential evolution
while (fmin>tol)
    % Obtain donor vectors by permutation
    k1=randperm(n);     k2=randperm(n);
    k1sol=Sol(k1,:);    k2sol=Sol(k2,:);
        % Random crossover index/matrix
        K=rand(n,d)<Cr;
        % DE/RAND/1 scheme
        V=Sol+F*(k1sol-k2sol);
        V=Sol.*(1-K)+V.*K;

        % Evaluate new solutions
        for i=1:n,
           Fnew=Fun(V(i,:));
           % If the solution improves
           if Fnew<=Fitness(i),
                Sol(i,:)=V(i,:);
                Fitness(i)=Fnew;
           end
          % Update the current best
```

```
            if Fnew<=fmin,
                  best=V(i,:);
                  fmin=Fnew;
            end
        end
        N_iter=N_iter+n;
end

% Output/display
disp(['Number of evaluations: ',num2str(N_iter)]);
disp(['Best=',num2str(best),' fmin=',num2str(fmin)]);


% Objective function -- Rosenbrock's 3D function
function z=Fun(u)
z=(1-u(1))^2+100*(u(2)-u(1)^2)^2+100*(u(3)-u(2)^2)^2;
```

B.4 Firefly Algorithm

```
% ------------------------------------------------------------ %
% Firefly Algorithm for constrained optimization               %
% for the design of a spring (benchmark)                       %
% by Xin-She Yang Copyright @2013                              %
% ------------------------------------------------------------ %

function fa_ndim
% parameters [n N_iteration alpha betamin gamma]
para=[20 500 0.5 0.2 1];

help fa_ndim.m

% Simple bounds/limits for d-dimensional problems
d=15;
Lb=zeros(1,d);
Ub=2*ones(1,d);

% Initial random guess
u0=Lb+(Ub-Lb).*rand(1,d);

[u,fval,NumEval]=ffa_mincon(@cost,u0,Lb,Ub,para);

% Display results
bestsolution=u
bestojb=fval
total_number_of_function_evaluations=NumEval

%%% Put your own cost/objective function here --------%%%
%% Cost or Objective function
 function z=cost(x)
% Exact solutions should be (1,1,...,1)
```

```
z=sum((x-1).^2);

%%% End of the part to be modified -------------------%%%

%%% --------------------------------------------------%%%
%%% Do not modify the following codes unless you want %%%
%%% to improve their performance etc                  %%%
% -------------------------------------------------------
% ===Start of the Firefly Algorithm Implementation ======
%          Lb = lower bounds/limits
%          Ub = upper bounds/limits
%   para == optional (to control the Firefly algorithm)
% Outputs: nbest   = the best solution found so far
%          fbest   = the best objective value
%      NumEval = number of evaluations: n*MaxGeneration
% Optional:
% The alpha can be reduced (as to reduce the randomness)
% ---------------------------------------------------------

% Start FA
function [nbest,fbest,NumEval]...
           =ffa_mincon(fhandle,u0, Lb, Ub, para)
% Check input parameters (otherwise set as default values)
if nargin<5, para=[20 500 0.25 0.20 1]; end
if nargin<4, Ub=[]; end
if nargin<3, Lb=[]; end
if nargin<2,
disp('Usuage: FA_mincon(@cost,u0,Lb,Ub,para)');
end

% n=number of fireflies
% MaxGeneration=number of pseudo time steps
% ------------------------------------------------
% alpha=0.25;      % Randomness 0--1 (highly random)
% betamn=0.20;     % minimum value of beta
% gamma=1;         % Absorption coefficient
% ------------------------------------------------
n=para(1);  MaxGeneration=para(2);
alpha=para(3); betamin=para(4); gamma=para(5);

% Total number of function evaluations
NumEval=n*MaxGeneration;

% Check if the upper bound & lower bound are the same size
if length(Lb) ~=length(Ub),
    disp('Simple bounds/limits are improper!');
    return
end

% Calcualte dimension
```

```
d=length(u0);

% Initial values of an array
zn=ones(n,1)*10^100;
% -------------------------------------------------
% generating the initial locations of n fireflies
[ns,Lightn]=init_ffa(n,d,Lb,Ub,u0);

% Iterations or pseudo time marching
for k=1:MaxGeneration,     %%%%% start iterations

% This line of reducing alpha is optional
 alpha=alpha_new(alpha,MaxGeneration);

% Evaluate new solutions (for all n fireflies)
for i=1:n,
   zn(i)=fhandle(ns(i,:));
   Lightn(i)=zn(i);
end

% Ranking fireflies by their light intensity/objectives
[Lightn,Index]=sort(zn);
ns_tmp=ns;
for i=1:n,
 ns(i,:)=ns_tmp(Index(i),:);
end

%% Find the current best
nso=ns; Lighto=Lightn;
nbest=ns(1,:); Lightbest=Lightn(1);

% For output only
fbest=Lightbest;

% Move all fireflies to the better locations
[ns]=ffa_move(n,d,ns,Lightn,nso,Lighto,nbest,...
       Lightbest,alpha,betamin,gamma,Lb,Ub);

end   %%%%% end of iterations

% ---------------------------------------------------------
% ----- All the subfunctions are listed here ------------
% The initial locations of n fireflies
function [ns,Lightn]=init_ffa(n,d,Lb,Ub,u0)
  % if there are bounds/limits,
if length(Lb)>0,
   for i=1:n,
   ns(i,:)=Lb+(Ub-Lb).*rand(1,d);
   end
```

```
else
   % generate solutions around the random guess
   for i=1:n,
   ns(i,:)=u0+randn(1,d);
   end
end

% initial value before function evaluations
Lightn=ones(n,1)*10^100;

% Move all fireflies toward brighter ones
function [ns]=ffa_move(n,d,ns,Lightn,nso,Lighto,...
             nbest,Lightbest,alpha,betamin,gamma,Lb,Ub)
% Scaling of the system
scale=abs(Ub-Lb);

% Updating fireflies
for i=1:n,
% The attractiveness parameter beta=exp(-gamma*r)
   for j=1:n,
      r=sqrt(sum((ns(i,:)-ns(j,:)).^2));
      % Update moves
if Lightn(i)>Lighto(j), % Brighter and more attractive
   beta0=1; beta=(beta0-betamin)*exp(-gamma*r.^2)+betamin;
   tmpf=alpha.*(rand(1,d)-0.5).*scale;
   ns(i,:)=ns(i,:).*(1-beta)+nso(j,:).*beta+tmpf;
      end
   end % end for j

end % end for i

% Check if the updated solutions/locations are within limits
[ns]=findlimits(n,ns,Lb,Ub);

% This function is optional, as it is not in the original FA
% The idea to reduce randomness is to increase the convergence,
% however, if you reduce randomness too quickly, then premature
% convergence can occur. So use with care.
function alpha=alpha_new(alpha,NGen)
% alpha_n=alpha_0(1-delta)^NGen=10^(-4);
% alpha_0=0.9
delta=1-(10^(-4)/0.9)^(1/NGen);
alpha=(1-delta)*alpha;

% Make sure the fireflies are within the bounds/limits
function [ns]=findlimits(n,ns,Lb,Ub)
for i=1:n,
     % Apply the lower bound
  ns_tmp=ns(i,:);
```

```
  I=ns_tmp<Lb;
  ns_tmp(I)=Lb(I);

  % Apply the upper bounds
  J=ns_tmp>Ub;
  ns_tmp(J)=Ub(J);
  % Update this new move
  ns(i,:)=ns_tmp;
end

%% ==== End of Firefly Algorithm implementation ======
```

B.5 Cuckoo Search

```
% -------------------------------------------------------------------
% Cuckoo Search (CS) algorithm by Xin-She Yang and Suash Deb        %
% Programmed by Xin-She Yang at Cambridge University                %
% Programming dates: Nov 2008 to June 2009                          %
% Last revised: Dec  2009   (simplified version for demo only)      %
% -------------------------------------------------------------------

% ================================================================= %
% Notes:                                                            %
% Different implementations may lead to slightly different          %
% behavior and/or results, but there is nothing wrong with that;    %
% this is the nature of random walks and all metaheuristics.        %
% -------------------------------------------------------------------

% Additional Note:This version uses a fixed number of generations %
% (not a given tolerance) because many readers asked me to add     %
%  or implement this option.                                 Thanks.%
function [bestnest,fmin]=cuckoo_search_new(n)
if nargin<1,
% Number of nests (or different solutions)
n=25;
end

% Discovery rate of alien eggs/solutions
pa=0.25;

%% Change this if you want to get better results
N_IterTotal=1000;
%% Simple bounds of the search domain
% Lower bounds
nd=15;
Lb=-5*ones(1,nd);
% Upper bounds
Ub=5*ones(1,nd);

% Random initial solutions
```

```
for i=1:n,
nest(i,:)=Lb+(Ub-Lb).*rand(size(Lb));
end

% Get the current best
fitness=10^10*ones(n,1);
[fmin,bestnest,nest,fitness]=get_best_nest(nest,nest,fitness);

N_iter=0;
%% Starting iterations
for iter=1:N_IterTotal,
    % Generate new solutions (but keep the current best)
     new_nest=get_cuckoos(nest,bestnest,Lb,Ub);
     [fnew,best,nest,fitness]=get_best_nest(nest,new_nest,fitness);
    % Update the counter
      N_iter=N_iter+n;
    % Discovery and randomization
      new_nest=empty_nests(nest,Lb,Ub,pa) ;
    % Evaluate this set of solutions
      [fnew,best,nest,fitness]=get_best_nest(nest,new_nest,fitness);
    % Update the counter again
      N_iter=N_iter+n;
    % Find the best objective so far
    if fnew<fmin,
        fmin=fnew;
        bestnest=best;
    end
end %% End of iterations

%% Post-optimization processing
%% Display all the nests
disp(strcat('Total number of iterations=',num2str(N_iter)));
fmin
bestnest

%% --------------- All subfunctions are list below ------------------
%% Get cuckoos by ramdom walk
function nest=get_cuckoos(nest,best,Lb,Ub)
% Levy flights
n=size(nest,1);
% Levy exponent and coefficient
beta=3/2;
tmpdiv=(gamma((1+beta)/2)*beta*2^((beta-1)/2)))^(1/beta);
sigma=(gamma(1+beta)*sin(pi*beta/2)/tmpdiv;

for j=1:n,
    s=nest(j,:);
    % This is a simple way of implementing Levy flights
    % For standard random walks, use step=1;
```

```
 %% Levy flights by Mantegna's algorithm
 u=randn(size(s))*sigma;
 v=randn(size(s));
 step=u./abs(v).^(1/beta);

 % In the next equation, the difference factor (s-best) means that
 % when the solution is the best solution, it remains unchanged.
 stepsize=0.01*step.*(s-best);
 % Here the factor 0.01 comes from the fact that L/100 should the typical
 % step size of walks/flights where L is the typical lenghtscale;
 % otherwise, Levy flights may become too aggresive/efficient,
 % which makes new solutions (even) jump out side of the design domain
 % (and thus wasting evaluations).
 % Now the actual random walks or flights
 s=s+stepsize.*randn(size(s));
% Apply simple bounds/limits
nest(j,:)=simplebounds(s,Lb,Ub);
end

%% Find the current best nest
function [fmin,best,nest,fitness]=get_best_nest(nest,newnest,fitness)
% Evaluating all new solutions
for j=1:size(nest,1),
    fnew=fobj(newnest(j,:));
    if fnew<=fitness(j),
       fitness(j)=fnew;
       nest(j,:)=newnest(j,:);
    end
end
% Find the current best
[fmin,K]=min(fitness) ;
best=nest(K,:);

%% Replace some nests by constructing new solutions/nests
function new_nest=empty_nests(nest,Lb,Ub,pa)
% A fraction of worse nests are discovered with a probability pa
n=size(nest,1);
% Discovered or not -- a status vector
K=rand(size(nest))>pa;

% In the real world, if a cuckoo's egg is very similar to a
% host's eggs, then this cuckoo's egg is less likely to be discovered,
% thus the fitness should be related to the difference in solutions.
% Therefore, it is a good idea to do a random walk in a biased way
% with some random step sizes.
%% New solution by biased/selective random walks
stepsize=rand*(nest(randperm(n),:)-nest(randperm(n),:));
new_nest=nest+stepsize.*K;
for j=size(new_nest,1)
```

```
    s=new_nest(j,:);
  new_nest(j,:)=simplebounds(s,Lb,Ub);
end

% Application of simple constraints
function s=simplebounds(s,Lb,Ub)
  % Apply the lower bound
  ns_tmp=s;
  I=ns_tmp<Lb;
  ns_tmp(I)=Lb(I);

  % Apply the upper bounds
  J=ns_tmp>Ub;
  ns_tmp(J)=Ub(J);
  % Update this new move
  s=ns_tmp;
%% You can replace the following by your own functions
% A d-dimensional objective function
function z=fobj(u)
%% d-dimensional sphere function sum_j=1^d (u_j-1)^2.
%  with a minimum at (1,1, ...., 1);
z=sum((u-1).^2);
```

B.6 Bat Algorithm

```
% ========================================================= %
% Files of the Matlab programs included in the book:        %
% Xin-She Yang, Nature-Inspired Optimization Algorithms     %
% Elsevier @2013
% ========================================================= %
% --------------------------------------------------------- %
% Bat-inspired algorithm for continuous optimization (demo)%
% --------------------------------------------------------- %
% Usage: bat_algorithm([20 0.25 0.5]);                      %

function [best,fmin,N_iter]=bat_algorithm(para)
% Display help
 help bat_algorithm.m

% Default parameters
if nargin<1,  para=[10 0.25 0.5];  end
n=para(1);      % Population size, typically 10 to 25
A=para(2);      % Loudness  (constant or decreasing)
r=para(3);      % Pulse rate (constant or decreasing)
% This frequency range determines the scalings
Qmin=0;         % Frequency minimum
Qmax=2;         % Frequency maximum
% Iteration parameters
tol=10^(-5);    % Stop tolerance
N_iter=0;       % Total number of function evaluations
```

```
% Dimension of the search variables
d=3;
% Initial arrays
Q=zeros(n,1);   % Frequency
v=zeros(n,d);   % Velocities
% Initialize the population/solutions
for i=1:n,
  Sol(i,:)=randn(1,d);
  Fitness(i)=Fun(Sol(i,:));
end
% Find the current best
[fmin,I]=min(Fitness);
best=Sol(I,:);

% ====================================================== %
% Note:Since this is a demo, here we did not implement the %
% reduction of loudness and increase of emission rates.   %
% Interested readers can do some parametric studies       %
% and,implement various changes of A and r etc.           %
% ====================================================== %

% Start the iterations -- Bat Algorithm
while (fmin>tol)
        % Loop over all bats/solutions
        for i=1:n,
          Q(i)=Qmin+(Qmin-Qmax)*rand;
          v(i,:)=v(i,:)+(Sol(i,:)-best)*Q(i);
          S(i,:)=Sol(i,:)+v(i,:);
          % Pulse rate
          if rand>r
              S(i,:)=best+0.01*randn(1,d);
          end

     % Evaluate new solutions
           Fnew=Fun(S(i,:));
     % If the solution improves or not too loudness
           if (Fnew<=Fitness(i)) & (rand<A) ,
                Sol(i,:)=S(i,:);
                Fitness(i)=Fnew;
           end

          % Update the current best
          if Fnew<=fmin,
                best=S(i,:);
                fmin=Fnew;
          end
        end
        N_iter=N_iter+n;
end
```

```
% Output/display
disp(['Number of evaluations: ',num2str(N_iter)]);
disp(['Best =',num2str(best),' fmin=',num2str(fmin)]);
% Objective function -- Rosenbrock's 3D function
function z=Fun(u)
z=(1-u(1))^2+100*(u(2)-u(1)^2)^2+(1-u(3))^2;
%%%% ============ end ====================================
```

B.7 Flower Pollination Algorithm

```
% ------------------------------------------------------------------%
% Flower pollination algorithm (FPA), or flower algorithm          %
% Programmed by Xin-She Yang @ May 2012                             %
% ------------------------------------------------------------------%

%%%%%%%%%%%%%%%%%%%%%%%%%%%%%%%%%%%%%%%%%%%%%%%%%%%%%%%%%%%%%%%%%%%%%
% Notes: This demo program contains the very basic components of    %
% the flower pollination algorithm (FPA). It usually works well for %
% unconstrained functions only. For functions/problems with         %
% limits/bounds and constraints, constraint-handling techniques     %
% should be implemented to deal with constrained problems properly. %
%%%%%%%%%%%%%%%%%%%%%%%%%%%%%%%%%%%%%%%%%%%%%%%%%%%%%%%%%%%%%%%%%%%%%

function [best,fmin,N_iter]=fpa(para)
% Default parameters
if nargin<1,
   para=[20 0.8];
end

n=para(1);           % Population size, typically 10 to 25
p=para(2);           % probabibility switch

% Iteration parameters
N_iter=2000;            % Total number of iterations

% Dimension of the search variables
d=3;
Lb=-2*ones(1,d);
Ub=2*ones(1,d);

% Initialize the population/solutions
for i=1:n,
  Sol(i,:)=Lb+(Ub-Lb).*rand(1,d);
  Fitness(i)=Fun(Sol(i,:));
end

% Find the current best
[fmin,I]=min(Fitness);
best=Sol(I,:);
S=Sol;
```

```
% Start the iterations -- Flower Algorithm
for t=1:N_iter,
        % Loop over all bats/solutions
        for i=1:n,
          % Pollens are carried by insects and thus can move in
          % large scale, large distance.
          % This L should replace by Levy flights
          % Formula: x_i^{t+1}=x_i^t+ L (x_i^t-gbest)
          if rand>p,
          %% L=rand;
          L=Levy(d);
          dS=L.*(Sol(i,:)-best);
          S(i,:)=Sol(i,:)+dS;

          % Check if the simple limits/bounds are OK
          S(i,:)=simplebounds(S(i,:),Lb,Ub);

          % If not, then local pollenation of neighbor flowers
          else
              epsilon=rand;
              % Find random flowers in the neighbourhood
              JK=randperm(n);
              % As they are random, the first two entries also random
              % If the flower are the same or similar species, then
              % they can be pollenated, otherwise, no action.
              % Formula: x_i^{t+1}+epsilon*(x_j^t-x_k^t)
              S(i,:)=S(i,:)+epsilon*(Sol(JK(1),:)-Sol(JK(2),:));
              % Check if the simple limits/bounds are OK
              S(i,:)=simplebounds(S(i,:),Lb,Ub);
          end

          % Evaluate new solutions
           Fnew=Fun(S(i,:));
          % If fitness improves (better solutions found), update then
            if (Fnew<=Fitness(i)),
                Sol(i,:)=S(i,:);
                Fitness(i)=Fnew;
           end

          % Update the current global best
          if Fnew<=fmin,
                best=S(i,:)   ;
                fmin=Fnew   ;
          end
        end
        % Display results every 100 iterations
        if round(t/100)==t/100,
        best
        fmin
        end
```

```
end

% Output/display
disp(['Total number of evaluations: ',num2str(N_iter*n)]);
disp(['Best solution=',num2str(best),'   fmin=',num2str(fmin)]);


% Application of simple constraints
function s=simplebounds(s,Lb,Ub)
  % Apply the lower bound
  ns_tmp=s;
  I=ns_tmp<Lb;
  ns_tmp(I)=Lb(I);

  % Apply the upper bounds
  J=ns_tmp>Ub;
  ns_tmp(J)=Ub(J);
  % Update this new move
  s=ns_tmp;


% Draw n Levy flight sample
function L=Levy(d)
% Levy exponent and coefficient
% For details, see Chapter 11 of the book
% X. S. Yang, Nature-Inspired Optimization Algorithms, Elsevier, (2014).
beta=3/2;
tmpdiv=(gamma((1+beta)/2)*beta*2^((beta-1)/2)))^(1/beta);
sigma=(gamma(1+beta)*sin(pi*beta/2)/tmpdiv;
    u=randn(1,d)*sigma;
    v=randn(1,d);
    step=u./abs(v).^(1/beta);
L=0.01*step;

% Objective function and here we used Rosenbrock's 3D function
function z=Fun(u)
z=(1-u(1))^2+100*(u(2)-u(1)^2)^2+100*(u(3)-u(2)^2)^2;
```

Printed in the United States
By Bookmasters